D1377139

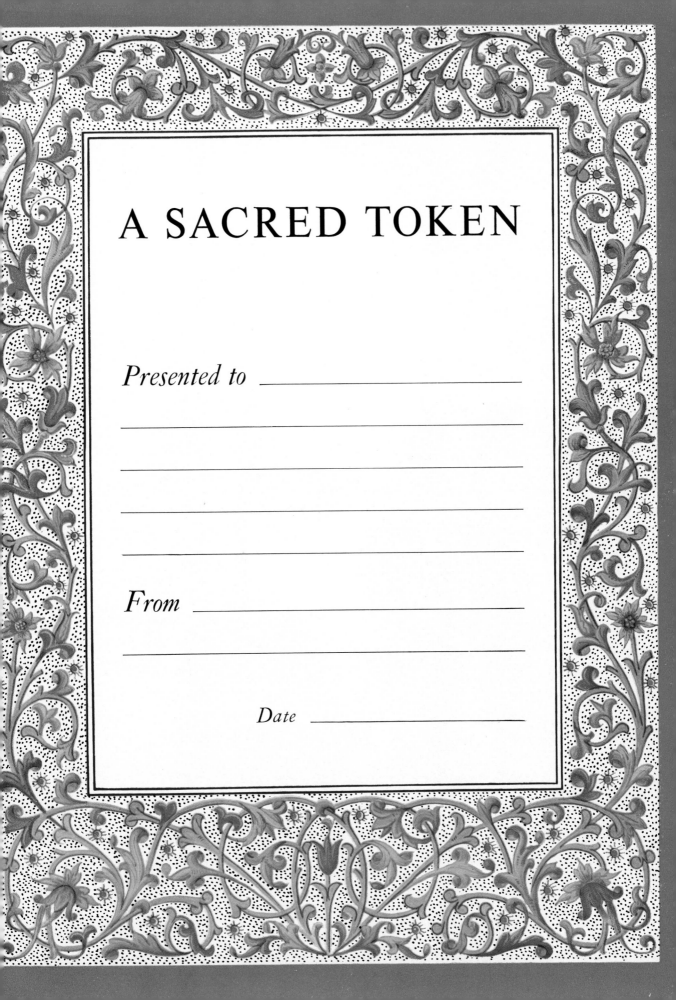

A SACRED TOKEN

Presented to _____

_____

_____

_____

_____

From _____

_____

Date _____

HOPE *of the* NATION

Dedicated to the Restoration
and Expansion of

Our American Heritage

With Illustrations by CELEBRATED ARTISTS

NELSON BEECHER KEYES

EDWARD FELIX GALLAGHER

GOOD WILL PUBLISHERS, GASTONIA, NORTH CAROLINA

Frontispiece

Portrait of George Washington
by Gilbert Stuart
Courtesy of the Yale University
Art Gallery, New Haven

Pen and Ink Sketches

Incidental Illustrations Incorporated
in the Text of This Volume Are by
Bernard Barton

COPYRIGHT, 1952
by Good Will Distributors, Inc.
Gastonia, North Carolina
All Rights Reserved
RRD–1
Distributed Exclusively by: GOOD WILL DISTRIBUTORS, INC.

What Am I Doing
To Help Secure America's Future?

lthough the American people, immersed in materialistic prosperity, might conceivably have some right to smugness and complacency, there is evidence of much soul-searching among them. Many are old enough to remember a devastating depression that brought a killing frost to a period of lush growth after World War I. Still others recall the uneasy peace between the wars, the sickening impact of Pearl Harbor, and their own part in the resulting second global conflict. Even the years since its close, with their demand for guns, as well as for butter, have not been such as to breed too great false confidence.

Many Americans are fully alive to the seriousness of the question posed above. And if they tend to avoid or shun it, they do so too often because they believe the issues involved are far above and beyond influence by any seemingly meager contributions they might make. Such an attitude is most unfortunate.

It is a sobering realization that the future depends largely upon the part our country plays in world affairs; and that its acts, in turn, depend upon what goes on at home within our own nation. Thus each of us has a part to play in the results to be gained; and one which, in these critical times, we must face up to with understanding and resolution. It is frankly the purpose of this volume to aid in discovering wherein our strengths as a nation were born, so we may the better know what direction and form our individual actions should take.

As you read its pages, you must realize that one of the principal sources of America's strength has been its insistence upon a rule of *law,* rather than of men. Let it be ever so; and the responsibility then rests upon each of us to see that all laws enacted are suitable to the needs of the greatest number, and are administered in that same spirit.

Our laws and public documents in the past have come into being out of strong religious and moral backgrounds. Only men roused and guided by a strong moral sense consider others—equally with themselves—when they seek legislation. They know, too, that laws, in the final analysis, are primarily for the control of those whose moral understanding is not sufficient to keep their conduct what it should be.

We will learn also that, while our forefathers came here seeking Liberty, they were shrewd enough not to mistake what they sought for outright license. Circumstances quickly taught them the need to stand staunchly on their own two feet; but at the same time not to trespass upon or actively undermine the rights of others. A reluctant Nature showed them the need for vigorous competition; and at the same time indicated that there were times when she yielded her bounties only to cooperative activity.

Men who seek Freedom, and hope to perpetuate it, soon discover that their lives are a dual affair. In one aspect, they are *private* citizens, in which capacity self-interest is the chief goad to achievement.

In the other, they are caught up in *public* affairs, having a part in larger enterprises by which all may profit, or fail, dependent upon reasoning and attitudes being what they should be.

In both phases of their lives, men and women need suitable guidance; and it is but logical for us to seek the same source which so well served those who have gone before us. And when we do, we find it quickly and surely. The men and women in whose hands our American Heritage was formed and perfected realized that human life is, and always must be centered in God. For us to drift away from this abiding truth would be to court national suicide.

By so centering their lives, those who struggled in the past to build our heritage caught the vision so sorely needed today, that of *Christianity in Action*. They absorbed it in their homes from the *open* Bible, in their churches from the lips of dedicated men of God, in their slowly increasing public schools along with the rudiments of other learning. And at home, at school, at work, and in their public relations and civic polity they put to work that ageless morality that stems only from Above.

What they were able to do in the past, we can and *must* do today. The obligation is ours with the same certainty that it was theirs. Life is no more uncertain, is beset with no greater or more perplexing doubts and problems today than it was in 1607, in 1776, in 1861.

Life has been made better through the ages, and America has gained strength only when men and women have looked critically at the past, found wherein it was wanting, and in the present have set resolutely to work making their own, and their children's future more acceptable and more secure.

Let us then, in the following pages, learn how our forebears met and overcame problems which, in their lifetimes, were as great and seemingly insoluble as our own seem today. Then we, too, may find satisfactory answers to the besetting question, "What am *I* doing to help secure America's future?"

Table of Contents

List of Works of Art

HOPE OF THE NATION — *Our American Heritage*

Foundations of Our American Heritage

UR American Heritage has deep roots indeed. It draws heavily upon our Christian Heritage as it tempers the upward struggle of Western man during the past sixteen hundred and more years. This, however, was but a cycle in its development, for it actually finds its beginnings in a crescent-shaped area, one end of which is lodged in the ribbon of land which parallels the Nile River in Africa and is the storied land of Egypt. From there it swings up over the land bridge on which stand Palestine and Syria, and then bends to the east into the fabulous section that is watered by the twin rivers, the Euphrates and the Tigris.

It was here that light seemingly first came into the affairs of men. Many believe that the Garden of Eden had lain not far from this junction of three continents, and it was in this general area that man seems to have taken his first faltering steps out of savagery and set his feet firmly on the long upward path. Here began the progress from which we benefit and to which it is our duty to contribute. The civilization of which we are a part, and from which our American Heritage is drawn, had its beginnings in that same sec-tion of the world in which the Bible Story is laid.

Civilization is a way of life and can rise to great heights when man properly responds to a challenge placed squarely upon his shoulders by his environment and the circumstances with which he is confronted. He then brings into play his latent, God-given powers, and directs his efforts in a manner so that life finds fuller and better expression.

Surely the first task with which he is confronted is to raise himself above mere subsistence. He has to lay aside mere food gathering and replace its uncertainties with food production. To do this he turns slowly from hunting and fishing to agriculture and a pastoral life; and we find evidence of his having done this at many points scattered across the earth, as we dig up his long-buried tools and find fewer spear and arrow points and increasing numbers of hoes and sickles.

Just where he first tamed the wild grasses that became his wheat, his corn, and his other cereals, we do not know. Where it was that he domesticated the sheep, the cow, the dog, and finally the horse, may never be known exactly. That he did these things at many separate places now seems quite probable. Nonetheless, some of his very earliest

9

successes in this respect came in the lands at the eastern end of the Mediterranean Sea.

Bear in mind, though, that his progress even there was at first faltering and made very slowly. It is said that the wheel, one of man's great achievements, was known first at the eastern end of this crescent that cradled civilization. But it took a full fifteen hundred years before it was understood and put to use in Egypt at the farther tip of the crescent no more than seven or eight hundred miles away. Early man moved but relatively short distances away from the point from which he was born, and then principally in search of better hunting and fishing, and later of more fertile fields and abundant pasturage.

DEMANDS OF CIVILIZATION

One of the principal requirements for solid progress is a stable social order which allows men to live together in considerable numbers in relative peace with those immediately about them. Under such beneficial circumstances, their individual energies can be turned to constructive purposes. Then by exchange of ideas and labor there comes the opportunity to mount up the ladder to a fuller life.

By prudent management, either as individuals or in groups, more is accumulated of some things than can be readily used. Man then begins to look beyond his own needs and to those of others. As he views his own possessions and those of others, and takes into consideration his own needs and those of men about him, he begins to think, "This is mine, and that is thine; and I will exchange a part of what is mine for a part of that which is thine." As he puts this thinking into practice, a huge forward step is taken; for in it lies the impulse to trade and commerce,

without which there can be no great advances in civilization.

Man must first organize his efforts so that he produces a surplus. Then, when he begins to exchange his surplus for that produced by others, he mounts rapidly out of his low estate. This exchange of goods provides a goading incentive to further mastery of the arts and crafts and in the matching of wits and abilities with others. This competitive influence spurs the development of native abilities, and encourages learning from others and the pooling of knowledge.

IMPORTANCE OF WRITING

These things, in turn, point up the need for permanent records, and man learns to write. He can then not only record his achievements, but, better still, has a means of handing on his thinking and his experiences so that still greater accomplishments can be built upon them. His material progress becomes more certain, and life about him takes on more and more meaning. He comes to know that *Knowledge is Power,* and the challenge with which he is confronted becomes even more stimulating.

But as his material progress mounts, and so that it may be better secured, he has still greater need to live in peaceful relations with more and more of his fellows. He is thus forced to develop *rules of conduct* for himself and for those with whom he would associate.

Deep within him is the still, small voice of Conscience, which becomes ever more insistent, demanding to be heard. By its promptings, he evolves *Moral laws,* which at first are the ways of life of the family, or the tribe, of which he is a part. He and those about him determine by trial and error, and by the coaching of the inward voice, what

AN EARLY EGYPTIAN SCRIBE WRITING ON PAPYRUS

their actions must be for what seems the greatest good of the greatest number.

Also man is early impressed by the realization that there is a *Power* abroad in the world, unseen but greater than man himself. In his still imperfect thinking, it seems at first to be lodged all about him in every tree, in every rock, and in sky, water, and air. He has long since bowed down and worshiped this Something and tried to make peace with It, as protection against possible harm. For the religious impulse is latent in man, even as a savage; and as his material progress improves, he does what he can to find better understanding of and access to the Power above and beyond him.

Again let it be emphasized that such upward struggle is world-wide wherever groups of men are found. The results which flow from it depend upon how insistent the challenge and how willing the response to it. In some areas advances may be fairly rapid and considerable in extent. But they can be arrested and go no farther, or even perish and all gains be lost.

In other instances progress made by one group may be absorbed by another group and built upon and greatly expanded. Not only were the civilizations developed about the shores of the Mediterranean vital, continuing, and fairly long-lived, but they were later combined with other vigorous attempts, continued, advanced, and improved upon. During several hundred generations the trend has been upward, albeit there have been many and some costly setbacks.

And it is out of this long climb from crude beginnings that our American Heritage has developed. Our cultural roots go back to Sumeria, long erased from the affairs of men, and to Egypt, where progress has largely slumbered for twenty-five centuries.

11

Whether the earliest start was made in the former land, or in the latter, is of little consequence to us at the moment. We have already found in the Bible Story in Volume One that an advanced civilization was at its height, or was perhaps even beginning to decay, in Ur of the Chaldees, which was in Sumeria, when Abraham played about its narrow, crooked streets as a boy. We have seen, too, that there was an equally advanced civilization in flower in Egypt when he fled there some years later from famine in the land of Canaan.

Then, as the years piled up, we saw another nation of men in the East—the Assyrians—come to power, and lay waste to Israel, and place tiny Judah under tribute. This concentration of naked power added little but misery, and one day it passed to another neighboring group, the Babylonians. They destroyed Jerusalem and led captive the Jews, but their homeland to which the refugees were taken was one of the wonders of the ancient world, and we owe much to what they had been able to accomplish. But their days of greatness were numbered, and their possessions and knowledge were taken over and added to by the Medes and Persians, who set up the first world empire.

GRECIAN CIVILIZATION

While these stirring chapters in man's history were being written in the Near East, a number of small city-states were growing up across an arm of the sea to the west. They were lodged in a rocky peninsula that thrusts down like a gnarled hand from the north shore of the Mediterranean. Sharply stimulated, they had built armies, learned to sail the seas, perfected government and law, and inquired into all phases of life. They were at the height of the *golden age* in Greece about

the time Nehemiah was rebuilding the walls of Jerusalem.

In the period between the Old and New Testaments these Grecians, under the domination of neighboring Macedonia, conquered the East as far as India. Thus they became heirs of the civilization developed in Egypt and Babylon. Although the empire which they built soon broke into several parts, Greek culture laid a firm hand upon the lands that bordered the Mediterranean.

ROMAN CIVILIZATION

To the west of Greece, in a boot-shaped peninsula which we know today as Italy, another people were forging their way toward greatness. A little city had been established on the banks of the Tiber River while Isaiah was prophesying in Judah. As early as 150 years before the birth of Christ, men of this place, now widely known as the city of Rome, were preparing to take over the remains of the Grecian Empire. By 30 B.C. these Romans were masters of the then known world, ruling from Britain to the Persian Gulf, and from the Atlantic Ocean to beyond the Black Sea.

For more than five hundred years Roman might would dominate many lands. This conquest brought peace in greater degree than had ever previously been enjoyed by so huge an area. The result was prosperity, and with it an increase in population, especially in new provinces established in what is now France, Belgium, England, the Rhine Valley, and Spain. Cities of a Greek and Roman pattern were founded in these barbarian lands. What had once been disorderly huddles of hilltop huts or rough forts became well-planned, defensible towns; and by means of them much of Europe was set firmly on its way out of the deep darkness of savagery.

At first the more remote provinces furnished little besides slaves, furs, amber, and timber and raw metals. In return, they acquired pottery, metal- and glasswares, and more important still the rudiments of civilization. Soon they, in turn, became hives of industry and trade. Those that lay inland were connected by excellent military roads.

pire intact were in themselves a great educating force. Soldiers and lesser officers were for the most part recruited in the outlying provinces. Then they were mixed with men from other sections and sent to serve at points far removed from their homelands. In this way widely different cultures were spread throughout all conquered countries. Its emis-

ROMAN POWER LONG STABILIZED THE ANCIENT WORLD

Where they were located by the seaside, they were provided with safe harbors, and the connecting sea lanes were cleared of pirates and marauders. Goods could flow safely and readily from place to place.

Both through trade thus fostered and by other means, the empire ruled from Rome provided a unique means of pooling and distributing the experience which had been acquired through many centuries in the ancient world. While Rome added little to it, still the armies needed to hold the em-

saries pushed out over land routes or along the seaways, to make contacts with remote lands in the interests of peace or trade. It is said that the emperor Marcus Aurelius (A.D. 161–180) even sent an embassy to distant China, another spot at which an early civilization had become far advanced. The world grew measurably smaller while Rome held sway over much of it.

The peculiar contribution of the Romans lay in the field of political and governmental affairs, in which they had superior organ-

13

izing ability. Much of their learning they had borrowed from the conquered Greeks, and they added next to nothing to the original thinking of the long line of illustrious Grecian scholars, artists, writers, and craftsmen.

Similarly, too, they used applied science and techniques which they had inherited from this same people, but without enlarging upon them or perfecting them. Even in so important a field as agriculture, they made no major advances. In a world in which famine was common, they might have contributed much by improving farming in the variety of climates with which people ruled by them had to deal. Lack of progress in this respect was in part the cause of the eventual fall of the Empire.

Religion, however, proved quite a different matter. In the heavy flow of people about the empire in its earlier and middle years, a wide variety of cults were carried from place to place, even to the most remote frontier posts. Altars dedicated to the Egyptian *Isis,* or to the Persian *Mithra,* have been unearthed in recent years in Scotland and in Germany. This latter cult, you may recall, was for a time a strong contender for favor with Christianity.

CHRIST, OR CAESAR?

In Volume One we saw the Church which Christ established come into conflict with Roman emperor-worship. This latter began to build up as government of the Empire came to have more significance than the rights of men which it governed. What had begun as a republic decayed into an autocracy. Early vigor of youth was slowly lost in the political fat of middle age. By the time of Diocletian (A.D. 284–305) all sovereign rights of the Roman people were vested in the emperor. He asserted a *divine right* to rule. Both the person of the monarch and all that pertained to him were said to be "sacred," or "divine." When a ruler becomes a god, rather than the servant, of his people, the end is not far removed.

This new attitude toward imperial power tended to promote a top-heavy civil service. Great numbers of clerks, accountants, messengers, and other employees were added to each bureau, not only in the capital but in the provinces. The resulting *bureaucracy* not only became lazy, corrupt, and opposed to change and reform, but also highly expensive to maintain.

Restrictions which bureaucracy breeds forced agriculture, industry, and trade to decline. In the face of threats which this breakdown cast upon the government, Diocletian and those that followed him as emperors were forced to take drastic action. Either willingly or unwillingly, they were caught in the hampering meshes of a *planned economy.* It seemed prudent to reduce men throughout the Empire to what is termed an *hereditary status.* This means that virtually everyone was forced to remain in the occupation and condition of his father. A man was thus born to be a farmer, a laborer, or to whatever form of livelihood his father had followed. Nothing was left to choice, to preference, or ability. By law imposed from above, men were reduced to a situation little better than that of animals.

Such restrictions were bound to drain away ambition and initiative. Progress was checked, and prosperity rapidly fell away; but taxes continued to mount. Those levied upon land were paid in produce; while those borne by trade had to be met with money. But beyond the staggering taxes, there were assessments of forced labor used to build or maintain public projects, or required in supplying quarters and provisions for armed troops and additional civil servants.

Slowly these burdens crushed the small landholders, the very backbone of the state, out of existence. In the rural districts the lesser farmers lost their lands and became tenants, or serfs, of their larger and more fortunate neighbors. As Rome took away men's freedoms, the Empire became disorganized and headed into decay. The end came in a series of famines.

THE DARK AGES BEGIN

The people of Europe fell heir to what remained of what had once been mighty Rome; but it would take them a thousand years to gain back what had been lost. Then, and only then, could they begin to gain back Freedom, which is man's one certain guarantee to truly great endeavors. Even in their homelands they would not find this Freedom in sufficient measure; but would be forced to set out to unknown lands where they might capture it in sufficient measure.

It will be the chief purpose of this volume to show how men sought Freedom, and finally found and perfected it here in America. We also hope to indicate what has been happening to that Freedom so dearly purchased through the centuries.

We have traced our heritage back to Mediterranean lands, where men perhaps had their start upon earth. We have seen how those who remained in that area lifted themselves out of darkness. But we must realize that others wandered away to populate other portions of the world. We have found some of them in our ancestors in northern Europe. We must not overlook what happened among them during the Middle Ages, which contributed to our American Heritage.

But it can be to our advantage to look in briefly on other of God's children who had wandered halfway round the world, and whose descendants would be on hand when brave souls crossed the forbidding Atlantic for the first time in the fifteenth century. We have spent our time up to this point entirely in the Eastern Hemisphere. Let us turn our attention for just a bit to the other half of the world, and find what lay to the west over uncharted seas.

If we will look at a globe, or a flat map of the world, we will find there is one small point where the land masses in the two hemispheres almost join. What are now called Alaska and Siberia lie but a few miles apart, and are within sight of one another on a clear day across the narrow arm of ocean. It is generally believed that at some time in the far, far distant past men summoned the courage to step across from Asia to North America at this point.

AMERICA'S FIRST INHABITANTS

Who they were, we may never know. They seem to have had dark skins and were perhaps few in number. But as time dragged on they managed to penetrate into all parts of both North and South America. When first seen by Europeans, they were taken to be people of islands in the Far East and wrongly called *Indians*. Although they had perhaps stemmed from a single group, like other peoples in the world, they had come to differ rather widely among themselves. Such differences were in physical appearance and also as measured by their accomplishments.

Before European explorers began to land on American shores, some of the groups, particularly in Central and South America, had developed civilizations that compare favorably in many respects with those in

15

Babylon and Egypt in very early Bible times.

But in North America, where our interests will center, they had for the most part continued as hunters, or were on the lower rungs of the ladder of progress. That they were still very primitive is indicated by the fact they had domesticated none of the animals excepting the dog.

In the far north there were fair-skinned Eskimos. But the remainder were bronze, or copper-colored, which was to win them the name of *redskins*. They were fairly tall, well built, with high, prominent cheekbones, and almost without facial hair, so that the men had no beards.

LIFE AMONG THE INDIANS

They lived principally on a tribal basis, sometimes joining one or more tribes together to form a *nation*. By the early 1600's the number of separate tribes was probably upward of one thousand in North America alone.

Their form of government varied somewhat, but for the most part control lay in the hands of a chief, or a sachem if more than one tribe was involved, together with a council made up of the older men. They were to a large extent communistic; and tribal customs formed very rigid codes of laws under which they lived. There was little freedom, as we like to think of it; and apart from displays of bravery in battle or skill in hunting, there was little chance for a man to be outstanding among the other members of his tribe.

Slavery, however, was little known or practiced. The condition under which the women lived varied widely. In some tribes they had many rights and privileges approaching those of the men. In such cases they enjoyed considerable respect. In other tribes they were treated little better than beasts of burden.

Religious beliefs and practices were also of many kinds. It is true that in some North American tribes there seems to have been a well-founded belief in a *great spirit* and in a future life, at least for the men, in a *happy hunting ground*. But there was universal faith in the powers of magic, particularly as practiced by the medicine men, who were part priest and part doctor.

The more than one thousand tribes that lived in what is today the United States and Canada spoke probably as many as two hundred quite different tongues. This situation seems to have forced the development of a sign language, particularly among the roving buffalo hunters of the great midland plains, by which different tribes could communicate with each other. And among these many, many tribal groups, only two seem to have progressed at all beyond spoken language, whether by hands or lips.

Although the crudest sort of records may have been kept in one form or another by some tribes, chiefly in their ornaments, two tribes separated from each other by but a short distance did achieve writing of sorts. The Delawares, living along the eastern coast, had a fairly expressive picture writing in which were set down tribal history and myths. But the Cherokees, whose homes were in the mountain country reaching down into the high Smokies, had developed a set of script characters, permitting them to write in something of the form known to us. Still the uses of either of these devices were very limited; and tribal history and customs were handed down, as the great bulk of mankind has and still does handle such matters, by word of mouth.

In the area from the Great Lakes to the Atlantic, and from Maine to Virginia, the

MEN HAD LIVED IN AMERICA FOR A VERY LONG TIME WHEN THE FIRST EUROPEANS LANDED HERE

better known groups were the Algonquins, Mohicans, and members of the Iroquois nation. Farther south, and in the country extending west from the Carolinas and Florida into Texas and Arkansas, were the Cherokees, Choctaws, Creeks, and Seminoles. All these eastern tribes lived a more settled life, were in part farmers, and some made pottery, however crude, and wove rude cloth.

By contrast, the buffalo hunters in the great Mississippi Valley plains, and reaching back toward the Rockies, were nomads, following the grazing herds on which they preyed. Among them were the Crees, Chippewas, Ojibwas, Wichitas, Omahas, Dakotas, and especially the Sioux.

Reaching down into our Northwest from British Columbia were such tribes as the Snakes and Flatheads. In the coastal areas these Indians lived in houses built of planks,

and are well known for their carved and painted totem poles, which recorded family history and told who might, or might not, intermarry. They had a well-worked out system of trade and barter, and even business dealings based upon credit.

Very much in contrast in their achievements were the Digger Indians of California, the most primitive and backward of all the groups in North America. They had never been able to raise themselves above subsistence upon berries and roots, and had little indeed in the way of tribal culture and organization.

But in the desert section which we call our Southwest, were some of the most savage fighters and also some of the most advanced tribes north of Mexico. Since they lived almost entirely in communal villages, called in Spanish *pueblos,* this considerable group is known as the Pueblo Indians. Of them, the Apaches and Navajos were particularly warlike.

THE MORE ADVANCED NATIVES

Perhaps the measuring rod most widely used in determining the advances made by ancient people is their ability to mold and bake pottery and also to weave baskets and cloth. The former is the more dependable, since pottery, even in the form of chips, lasts almost indefinitely. Still another measure, although it might at first seem rather trifling, is the production and use of cosmetics. By showings in all these respects, the Pueblos were no doubt the most advanced of all North American groups.

Approaching them were the mound builders, the remains of whose culture is scattered from Wisconsin to the Gulf of Mexico, and from New York State to Georgia. Some of the pottery unearthed from the mounds they erected exceeds in quality that of the Pueblos.

But we must look farther south for anything approaching what may be termed well-rounded civilization. At various points beginning in Mexico, and stretching down through Central into South America, were groups that rose to considerable heights. Living principally by agriculture, they had so organized their common life that they had been able to make great strides in a number of fields. They had developed exceptional ability in engineering and in architecture, and were experienced in the recovery and refining of metals. They set up effective political organizations, had extensive religious systems, and powerful and able priesthoods. Although they did not work in iron, they had become highly skilled in the use of the softer metals, and had amassed huge stores of silver and, particularly, gold implements, utensils, and ornaments. It was this rich plunder that was their undoing, since it brought the Spanish and later the Portuguese in search of this fabulous loot. But since pillage seemed to these two nations a quicker way to wealth than colonization, it also managed to keep them from entering the contest for lands north of the Gulf of Mexico.

The Indian groups living beside the great mountain chain reaching from Mexico down into Peru that had brought their civilizations to very high levels were the Aztecs, Mayas, Toltecs, and Incas. But they were by no means the only native groups, for both Central and South America sheltered many very primitive tribes as well.

NUMBER OF INDIANS HERE

How many Indians lived within the limits of what is now United States and Canada at the time visitors from Europe first began to land on American shores? Estimates vary, but a figure near a million and a quarter seems about right. Some three-quarters of them lived below what has become our Canadian border. Even then, the land was hardly crowded, for the average would be about one Indian man, woman, or child, to each three square miles of countryside. With our present population, we now average about fifty people to each and every square mile. However, the number of Indians then here were probably as many as the land would support at the hunting and primitive agricultural level at which they lived.

Their numbers were rapidly lowered by conquest. But it is probably true that more of them perished by diseases strange to them brought in by the settlers than were slain in combat.

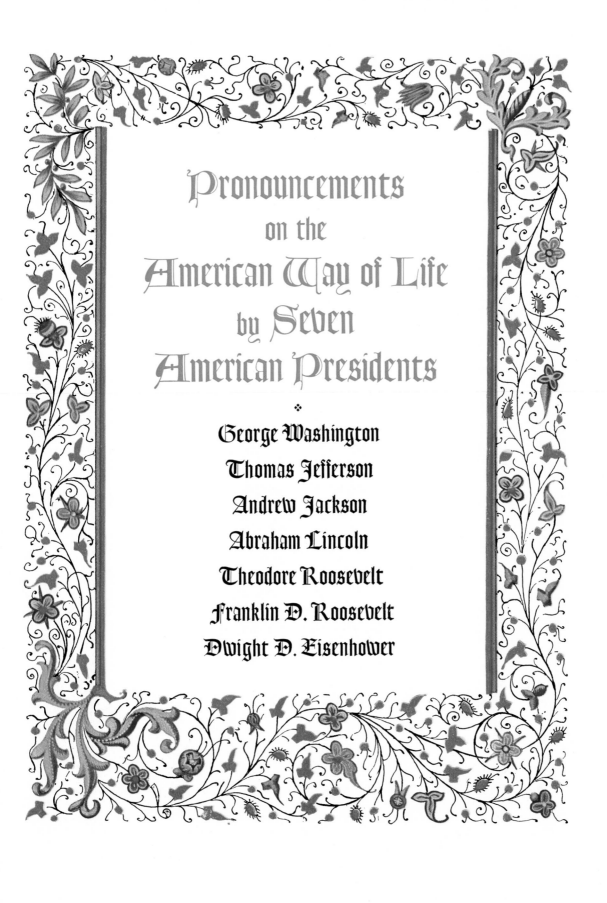

Pronouncements
on the
American Way of Life
by Seven
American Presidents

✦

George Washington

Thomas Jefferson

Andrew Jackson

Abraham Lincoln

Theodore Roosevelt

Franklin D. Roosevelt

Dwight D. Eisenhower

Our Individual Duty

the basis of our political systems is the right of the people to make and to alter their constitutions of government. but the constitution which at any time exists till changed by an explicit and authentic act of the whole people is sacredly obligatory upon all. the very idea of the power and the right of the people to establish government presupposes the duty of every individual to obey the established government.

—GEORGE WASHINGTON
The Farewell Address, 1796

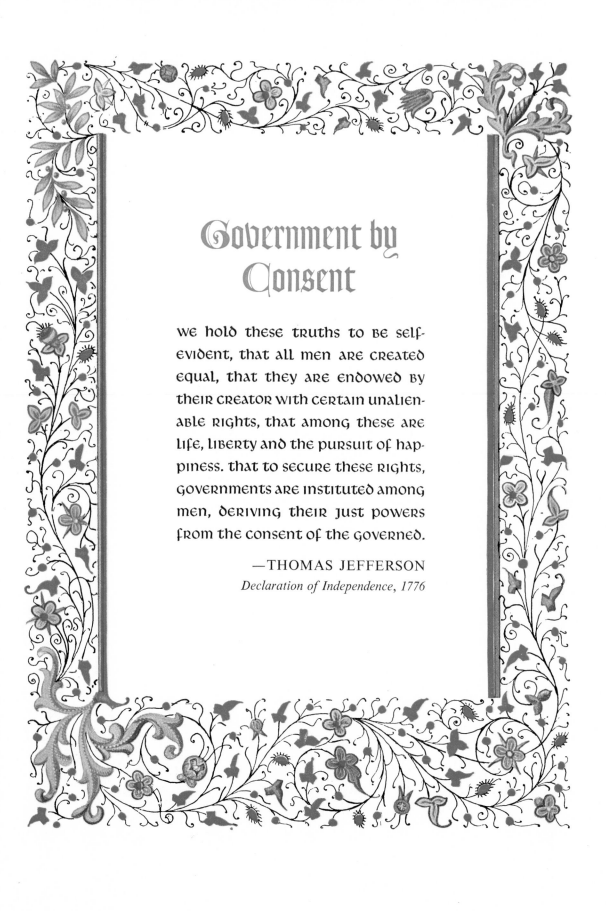

Government by Consent

we hold these truths to be self-evident, that all men are created equal, that they are endowed by their creator with certain unalienable rights, that among these are life, liberty and the pursuit of happiness. that to secure these rights, governments are instituted among men, deriving their just powers from the consent of the governed.

—THOMAS JEFFERSON
Declaration of Independence, 1776

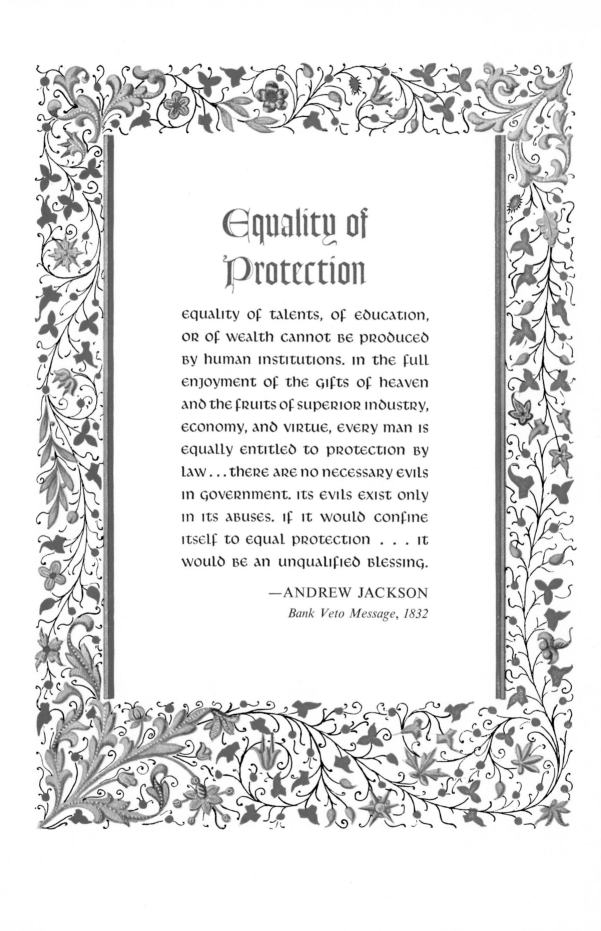

Equality of Protection

equality of talents, of education,
or of wealth cannot be produced
by human institutions. in the full
enjoyment of the gifts of heaven
and the fruits of superior industry,
economy, and virtue, every man is
equally entitled to protection by
law... there are no necessary evils
in government. its evils exist only
in its abuses. if it would confine
itself to equal protection . . . it
would be an unqualified blessing.

—ANDREW JACKSON
Bank Veto Message, 1832

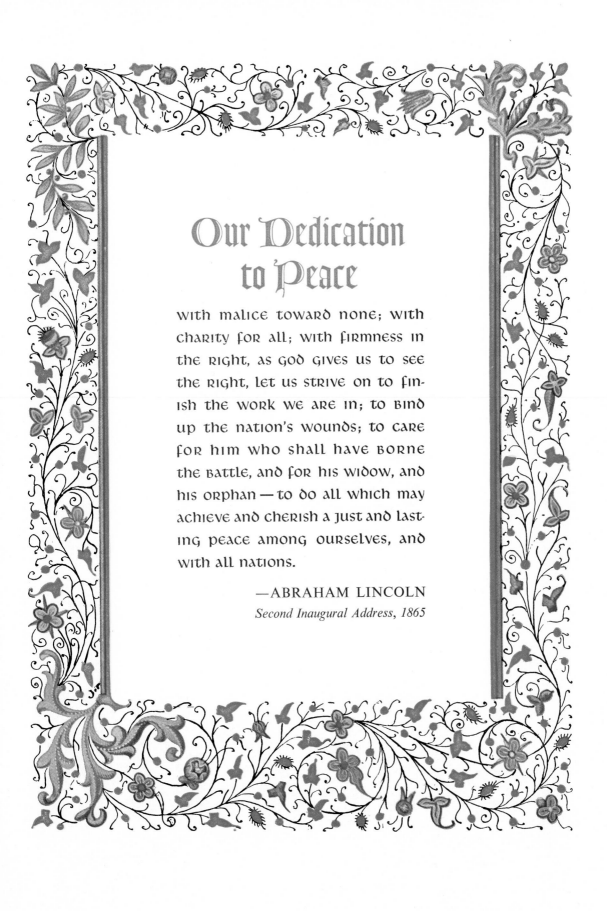

Our Dedication to Peace

with malice toward none; with charity for all; with firmness in the right, as god gives us to see the right, let us strive on to finish the work we are in; to bind up the nation's wounds; to care for him who shall have borne the battle, and for his widow, and his orphan — to do all which may achieve and cherish a just and lasting peace among ourselves, and with all nations.

—ABRAHAM LINCOLN
Second Inaugural Address, 1865

Beneficent Nationalism

I do not ask for overcentralization; but I do ask that we work in a spirit of broad and far-reaching nationalism when we work for what concerns our people as a whole. We are all Americans. Our common interests are as broad as the continent. The national government belongs to the whole American people, and where the whole American people are interested, that interest can be guarded effectively only by the national government.

—THEODORE ROOSEVELT
The New Nationalism, 1910

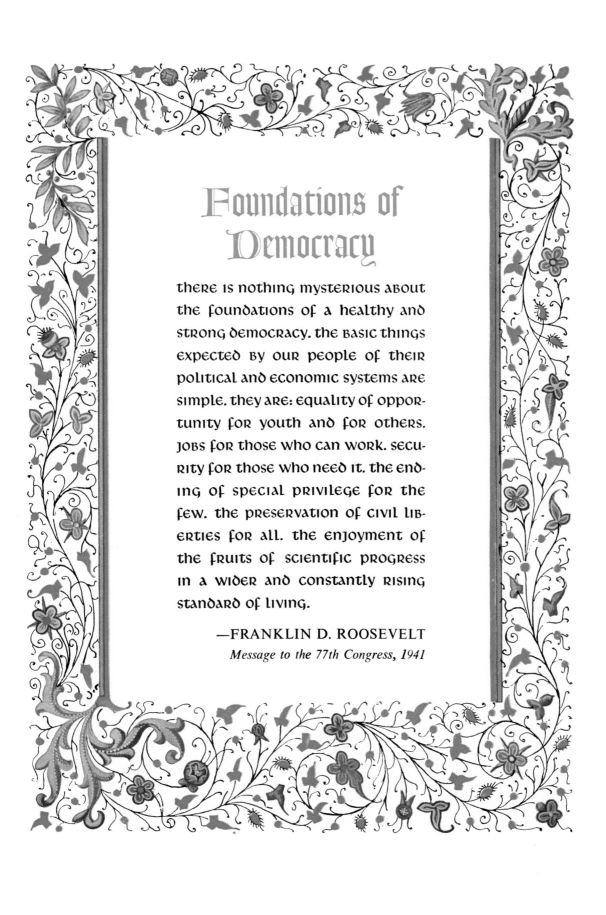

Foundations of Democracy

there is nothing mysterious about the foundations of a healthy and strong democracy. the basic things expected by our people of their political and economic systems are simple. they are: equality of opportunity for youth and for others. jobs for those who can work. security for those who need it. the ending of special privilege for the few. the preservation of civil liberties for all. the enjoyment of the fruits of scientific progress in a wider and constantly rising standard of living.

—FRANKLIN D. ROOSEVELT
Message to the 77th Congress, 1941

Duplication in Government

THERE IS NEED TO REVIEW AND ASSESS, WITH PRUDENCE AND FORESIGHT, THE PROPER ROLES OF THE FEDERAL, STATE, AND LOCAL GOVERNMENTS. IN MANY CASES, ESPECIALLY WITHIN THE PAST TWENTY YEARS, THE FEDERAL GOVERNMENT HAS ENTERED FIELDS WHICH, UNDER OUR CONSTITUTION, ARE THE PRIMARY RESPONSIBILITY OF STATE AND LOCAL GOVERNMENTS. THIS HAS TENDED TO BLUR THE RESPONSIBILITIES OF LOCAL GOVERNMENT. IT HAS LED TO DUPLICATION AND WASTE.

—DWIGHT D. EISENHOWER
Message to the Congress, 1953

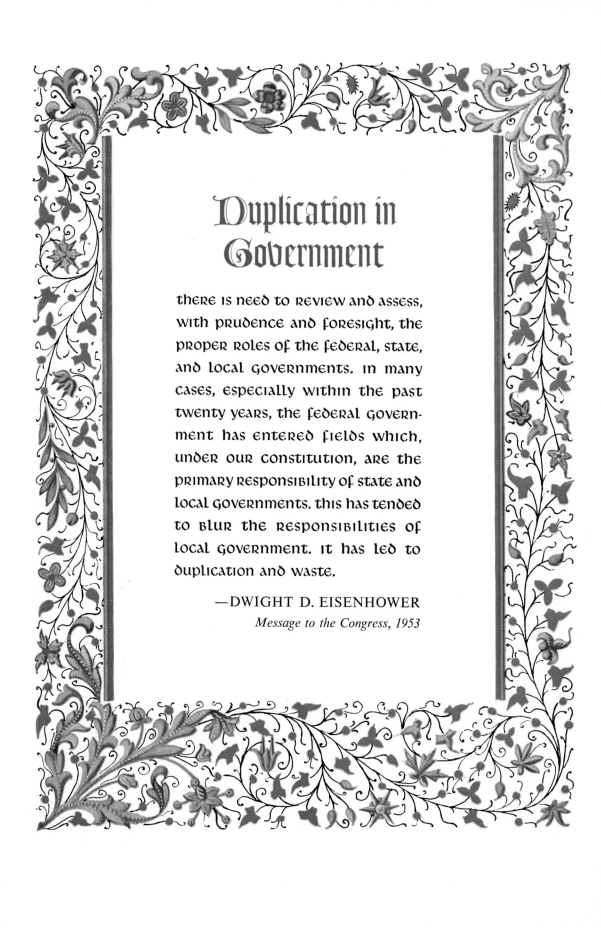

How long had they been here? There is still no exact answer to that question, and we may never know for certain. Surely it had been a very long time. More and more excavations and careful studies of the oldest remains are giving a much fuller picture of their past. Typical among the evidence now being brought to light are the finds recently unearthed at Hells Midden, in the Yampa River country in northwestern Colorado. Here a long-occupied townsite has yielded a continuous record of the slow progress made by the tribe, from early hunting and fishing through to farming and pottery making. By the most conservative estimates, Indians had been living at this same spot as long ago as twenty thousand years before Christ. How much earlier it was when their forebears arrived in America and began to fan out over two continents, we do not have any idea at the present time.

Still more recently, men who search out these ancient records investigated the Tularosa Cave in the White Sands country in southern New Mexico. Its interior is so dry that foglike dust billows up from the floor at every step. Under such conditions things

from the past do not break down readily. In the floor of this unusual storehouse cave were found many thousand intact cobs of corn, some of them very apparently more than four thousand years old. This startling find carried man as a farmer in our Southwest back as much as 3,500 years beyond what previous evidence had shown. Not only was man raising crops at this very early time, but he seems to have been practicing plant breeding to improve his grain in much the same manner progressive farmers do today. And so it is, by such discoveries, that we fill in year by year great gaps in the history of mankind's climb up the ladder of civilization.

Surely men had been in this unknown Western world long enough so that they had the right to be known as *natives,* if not Indians, as they have been mistakenly called.

Now that we know something regarding the inhabitants of this unknown Western world, let us return to the Eastern Hemisphere, and particularly to Europe, and find out what strange urge it was that brought men here to discover them. Actually it was not a *new world* that they sought.

Brighter Days Begin to Dawn

OU WILL perhaps remember that it was pointed out that man first showed great progress and began to build civilizations in the lands that lie at the eastern end of the Mediterranean Sea and in China. Since what happened in faraway China affects our story but indirectly, we will mention that country only as the occasion arises. But some of the other civilizations do have much bearing on what one day will take place in America.

Among the oldest of these were the cultures that grew to greatness in Babylonia to the east of the Holy Land, and in Egypt along the Nile. Here it was that men brought into common use the wheel, the horse, and ships of considerable size. Slowly these great tools of progress filtered into neighboring lands. North along the coast above the land of Israel were two famous cities, Tyre and Sidon, often mentioned in the Bible from the time of David on. Men of these two ports became the great sailors of the ancient world; and their ships are said to have made regular trips out into the Atlantic and up the shore to the south coast of what is now England. Man was beginning to make use of the world's great waterways.

Across the Aegean Sea from these cities a rocky peninsula, looking on the map like a great hand, hung down from Europe into the sea. We know it as Greece; and in cities there another very important civilization was born. It reached its *golden age* at about the time Nehemiah was rebuilding the damaged walls of Jerusalem, or in the fifth century before Christ. We have already seen how, a little later on, under Alexander the Great, a huge empire was conquered toward the east and Grecian culture and learning spread throughout the then known world.

But as this short-lived Grecian Empire began to fall to pieces, a people living in another boot-shaped peninsula, just to the west of Greece, began to rise to greatness. They were the Romans, whom we saw at the time of Christ as the masters of Palestine and other lands reaching from the borders of India to the British Isles.

The Greeks had been great thinkers and had left extensive writings that included their ideas on all phases of human life. From them, the Romans borrowed heavily, since their own strength lay in war and in bringing order to the lands they conquered. Slowly Rome became the capital of the civilized world; and from it ideas on better ways of life crept out into all the countries which it governed.

DARK AGES IN EUROPE

Much of northern Europe in these first Christian centuries was a forest wilderness, in which lived roving tribes whose peoples had raised themselves but little above savagery. But following closely after the Roman armies there were usually Roman traders seeking to do business with all whom the soldiers might conquer. Not only were the northern Europeans impressed by the armed might of Rome, but from the traders they began to get their first taste of some of the things civilization could offer them. Their appetite for the better things of life increased rapidly, and soon they were demanding more than their Roman masters were willing they should have.

This bred trouble, which eventually resulted in the fall of Rome. The Empire was divided in A.D. 476; and while Rome still continued as the capital of the western portion, Constantinople on the shores of the Black Sea became the capital of the lands in the east. Christianity had become the official religion at the time of Constantine. Soon Christian missionaries had begun to follow the Roman troops and convert the heathen. After Roman military power was broken, a period called the *Dark Ages* settled down over Europe. But the missionaries still kept pressing out among the backward peoples to the north and formed a continuing link with civilization.

There was much rivalry between Rome and Constantinople during the next six hundred years. Blows rained down on this divided Christian world from three different sets of opponents. And we must now turn our attention to one of these groups, for some of its members played their part in catching one of the first faint glimpses the peoples of Europe were to have of a strange and quite unknown land that lay far away beyond the western ocean.

In Europe, they were known generally as the *Northmen,* but as the *Danes* by the English. They were a series of Nordic tribes who made their homes about the shores of the Baltic and North seas, and who had accepted Christianity very reluctantly. Their land was cold and forbidding. From what they had heard there were many things in other lands which they could use to advantage. And being brave, bold sailors, filled with energy, they took to the sea and became pirates.

NORSEMEN RAID THE EUROPEAN CONTINENT

They drove their stout ships down the western coast of Europe and raided settlements as far south as Spain. Toward the east, they pushed up the rivers of what is now Russia, dragged their craft overland, or built new ones, and floated down rivers flowing eastward until they came to the Caspian and the Black seas.

About the year 886, they descended in great numbers upon what is now England and conquered half of the kingdom then ruled over by the famous Alfred the Great. A few years later, about 912, they took possession of northern France, which became *Normandy,* by which name a section of this area is still known today.

To the west lay the broad, open ocean. North of the main island which is England and Scotland were groups of small islands. Some of them lay not too far west of the Norwegian coast, and off Denmark, where these Northmen, or Norsemen, made their

21

homes. Such islands were, no doubt, well known to them.

In searching for other lands farther to the north and west, they had come first to Iceland and then to Greenland. The former they seem to have reached at some time between 870 and 930. Then one of their great leaders, Eric the Red, is supposed to have spent three years along the bleak coasts of Greenland during the period 982 to 985. Soon Norway had founded colonies on its bleak coasts, and Christianity seems to have been established there by the year 1000.

BEYOND GREENLAND

It is but a little greater distance westward from the southern tip of Greenland across Davis Strait to Labrador than it is back to Iceland to the east, perhaps a thousand miles. Their ships were small, and these were cold waters and highly dangerous during much of the year because of floating ice. But they were manned by daring, courageous men— the sons of men who had been capable of driving far across Russia and the seas that lay to the east and south.

Surely they found little to plunder and carry home from either Iceland or Greenland. It is only natural, then, that they should push on to the west in search of more promising lands which they might raid. And although some have expressed doubt that they ever did reach the American mainland, there is growing evidence that they were indeed the first Europeans to visit our shores.

Adam Bremensis, a Saxon historian, left perhaps the earliest written record of their visits. In a manuscript work completed about the year 1075, which describes the countries of northern Europe and also Iceland and Greenland, he mentions America as *Vinland*. That would mean that it was a land in which grapevines grew abundantly. He speaks of it as having been discovered by these Norse sea rovers. There are also two ancient sagas, handed along by word of mouth in Iceland for generations, and then written down in the fourteenth century, which tell in some detail of voyages to our shores.

Along much of the western coast line of the Scandinavian peninsula the mountains drop down into the ocean, forming many deep-water inlets, called *vicks*. It was from these rugged harbors that the Norse vessels sailed, and the men who manned them became known as *Vikings*. That term is sometimes confounded with a sea king. But these men were at best no more than sea rovers, and to those in other lands who were often forced to fight them off, they were mere pirates.

VISITS TO AMERICA

Their staunch, high-decked crafts were swift and very seaworthy. They were powered by a sail and also by a single bank of long, sweeping oars. Their oddly formed and carved prows were equal to plowing through the waves of the broad, open ocean. And their determined captains led fearless crews against any and all whom they encountered on their long, perilous journeys.

When their ships were to remain in a harbor for any length of time, they drilled holes about an inch in diameter and a few inches deep in a convenient boulder or ledge beside water deep enough to float them at low tide. Into these they dropped a metal bar, to which they moored their vessels. Such holes, of a size and position which the Norsemen customarily employed, have been found along waterways in America, especially at points on Cape Cod.

LEIF ERICSON PROBABLY VISITED AMERICA ABOUT THE YEAR 1000. IN 1362 THE NORSE MAY HAVE VISITED WHAT IS TODAY MINNESOTA.

Eric the Red, whose picturesque surname presumably indicated the color of his hair, or perhaps that of his wind-lashed face, does not seem to have ventured far beyond Greenland. But his eldest son, Leif Ericson, known as *Leif the Lucky*, apparently had ambitions similar to those of his father. He got possession of a ship, chose thirty lusty, sea-hardened men, and about the year 1000 set sail from Greenland, heading west.

The swirling ocean current that can well have helped his father on the journey from Iceland to Greenland surges about the south cape of this latter land. Then it swings to the north up Davis Strait along Greenland's western shores. There, at a narrow point in this passage that connects the Atlantic and Arctic oceans, it meets and mingles with the cold, southward-flowing waters of the Labrador Current. This icy stream pours on to the

south, bearing huge icebergs and cloaking the shores of Baffin's Land, Labrador, and Newfoundland with dense fogs. Borne by this current, Leif and his men could have quite readily been carried down the coast as far as what is now New England.

They may also well have passed through the narrow Belle Isle Strait, where at one point Newfoundland and the Labrador coast are but fifteen miles apart, and found themselves in the great gulf into which the St. Lawrence River empties. Then skirting the shores about Nova Scotia, they would have come into the slightly warmer waters that reach from the Bay of Fundy to the north shore of Cape Cod. South of this long, crooked, sandy-shored arm of land, they would have found the very much warmer waters they were perhaps seeking. Hugging the Cape's southern coast, they would have

23

passed through Buzzard's Bay and on to the mouth of Narragansett Bay. These would be pleasant shores, alive with game and clothed in many spots by hardwood trees from which dangled grapevines, on which grew in large bunches a black-skinned, very sweet wild grape. They may well have used their juice in place of the mead which they customarily drank, and so named this more hospitable section *Vinland*.

THE NORSE ATTEMPT COLONIES IN THIS COUNTRY

Great, however, must have been their astonishment when they found no cities, no, not even a single snug little town along these fertile, well-wooded shores. Here was indeed a new land, and surely as well favored as the coast of western Europe, which their kinsmen had been plundering for hundreds of years. Could it be there was nothing worth plundering here? There was fish and game in abundance, but where were the people? Not a soul could they seem to find.

There were ashes of campfires, even very rude campsites that had been abandoned. But for the most part it was wild, unspoiled country. It is probable that they fully explored the many bays and inlets in this low-lying and broken coast, easily navigated by their ship. There were a few rivers which would have permitted them to explore the interior for short distances. But to a group who sought pillage and plunder, this was a most unpromising land.

It is thought that Leif wintered in New England, and then, with his ship and crew, found his way back to Greenland. The strange tales he and his men had to tell of a bountiful but unpeopled land may well have made a deep impression upon their hearers.

Supposedly, there were other voyages, one by Thorwald, a younger son of Eric, who may well have worked his way south to what is now New York and New Jersey. He is thought to have spent at least two winters in this queer land, where there were surely people, but whom they somehow failed to find.

Then, during a storm, his ship was driven ashore on Cape Cod. There for the first time the Norse visitors seem to have come upon a number of natives, perhaps no more than eight or ten. Although there was perhaps no show of resistance or even of unfriendliness, the Norsemen fell upon the dark-skinned savages and slaughtered all but one, who fled into the woods.

TROUBLE WITH INDIANS

Summoning aid, there was soon a sufficient number of natives gathered so that they attacked the invaders, drove them back to their ship, and killed their leader. If these vague tales out of Norse legends are indeed true, Thorwald was thus the first European to fall by the weapons of the inhabitants of this new land. Often in the future, these native people—these *Indians*—would be forced to protect their lives, their homes, and hunting areas from men who came in ships over the boundless ocean.

His discouraged followers buried Thorwald, and, with the return of spring, returned to Greenland. Then, so the story goes, a third son of old Eric the Red, together with twenty-five followers and his young, newly wedded wife, also sailed for Vinland. But a storm threw them ashore before they were out of Baffin Bay, and Thorstein, the leader, perished. The survivors turned back to Greenland, but it said that Thorstein's widow remarried, and with her new husband visited Vinland and planted a brief colony there.

Among Eric's children there was at least one daughter, named Freydisa. Tradition has it that she managed to join the colony established during her sister-in-law's visit to our shores. She appears to have been as fierce and untamed as her brothers. Largely because of her acts, the Norse colonists fought among themselves, many of them were killed, and the remnant struggled back to Greenland.

TRACES OF NORSE VISITS

Thus ended the eleventh-century invasions of Vinland by the Norsemen. Developments in Europe diminished their power to ravage lands which they had formerly conquered with great success, and their sea raids came to an end. But whether journeys to this new land then ceased there is possible room for doubt.

Although they are claimed to have attempted colonization in what is now America, their efforts in this respect yielded nothing of lasting benefit. There is an old stone tower supported by seven massive columns which is credited to them, and which stands today at Newport, Rhode Island, as a most interesting and not fully explained relic of very early American times. They were here, if at all, for so short a time that they left little else which might be traced to them, with one important and still somewhat questionable exception.

In 1898 a farmer in western Minnesota dug from among tree roots in a small hill that had been an island in a now dried-up lake a 200-pound slab of stone. It was a rough oblong, and taking up about half of one of its flat faces there were nine lines of strange characters, more than 200 in all.

They proved to be *runes,* an ancient alphabet, and probably the earliest in use among the peoples of northern Europe. For the most part, they were used as inscriptions on crosses, monuments, coins, jewelry, sword hilts and blades, but do not seem to have been generally used as the text of books, or as a customary written language.

They could be translated, however, and the message supposed to have carved on this piece of stone and left behind is thought to read:

> Eight Goths and twenty-two Norwegians on an exploration journey from Vinland westward. We had camped by two islands one day's journey north of this stone. We fished one day. When we came home ten men were red with blood, and dead. A.V.M. [Ave Virgo Maria—Hail Virgin Mary] save [us] from evil. We have left ten men by the sea to look after our ship 14 days' journey from this island. Year 1362.

This curiosity, now called the *Kensington Stone,* was at the time of its discovery branded a forgery and explained away as a trick played upon the farmer who unearthed it. As a consequence, little expert attention was given it for more than fifty years. Recently one of the leading Danish authorities on runic inscriptions who examined it believes it may be entirely genuine.

Who were the Goths? They could have been either a Germanic people so-called, or more probably men of the Swedish island of Gotland in the Baltic Sea. The latter were dauntless sailors at this time.

Fourteen days' journey overland from the spot where this disputed stone was found could take one to the western tip of Lake Superior, near the present city of Duluth. Does this mean that in 1362 the Norsemen were using the St. Lawrence River and the Great Lakes as a waterway across America, as their kindred—particularly the Swedes— had used the rivers of Russia five hundred years before?

We may perhaps never have final and certain answers to this and other similar questions. But such scraps of evidence, however faint, lead one to believe that Europeans of several nations visited and came to know something of this New World long before Columbus visited it. At least there is a map drawn in 1367 showing a great island lying in the north Atlantic west of Ireland and south of Greenland. Why was it set down

as being there unless someone had sighted land of considerable extent in that area? There is every reason to believe that the map maker was working by something more than mere guesswork.

Thus we can perhaps say that the chief contribution of the Norsemen was their adventure stories, which probably came to be well known among all European sailors during many generations. These stimulated belief that there *could* be a New Land beyond the ocean to the west, which some day might be visited.

The World Grows Larger, and Is Found to Be Round

ET US GO back for a moment to the latter half of the eighth century. Europe was then emerging from the three hundred years of the *Dark Ages* which had followed the fall of the Roman Empire in 476. As we look back at this period it seems to have been well named. It is true that there was less real savagery than at the time these lands had been conquered by the Romans just before the birth of Christ. Yet life there was still primitive indeed, and improvement would come at a snail's pace.

In 771 a German, or Frankish, prince had taken the throne of his father, and become king of all the Franks. His name was *Charlemagne*—or, Charles the Great. He was an energetic, intelligent man and founded an empire which brought order and reasonably stable conditions from the borders of Spain eastward to the Oder and the Danube rivers, and from the North Sea down to Italy below Rome. His burning ambition was to weld Europe together into one great Christian empire.

The century previous to his taking the throne is regarded as the most ignorant, dark, and barbarous period in the *Middle Ages*. But under Charlemagne learning, which had long been preserved entirely by the Church, was much broadened and strengthened. Education of all classes was encouraged, even of the lowly serfs. Although this hopeful beginning during his reign was quickly checked after his death in 814, a pattern had been set, and ignorance and disorder were never quite so bad again as in the years just before his coronation.

As his empire fell apart, an age of disorder and of stagnation set in. It is known as the *Feudal Period,* and during it several important happenings took place which have a bearing on the later discovery and development of America. We need not go into them in great detail, but they do deserve brief description.

The first has to do with the Crusades, which perhaps did more to open the eyes of the people of Europe to progress and to the world beyond their own lands than any other happening. But there is a second that is closely linked with it. While there was the welter of war and pillage at home, beyond the Mediterranean Sea to the east and south an Arab, or Saracen, Empire had developed that was so far more civilized than was

27

Europe in the Middle Ages, that there was no room for comparison.

Here literature and learning were prized and sought for in a series of universities that stretched from Spain to India. Science was very much alive. The arts flourished, and men, having thrown off the yoke of fear and superstition, were making life a great adventure, and living had become a profitable, stimulating business.

RISE OF THE
MOHAMMEDAN CULTURE

It had all started in a little city about halfway down the eastern shore of the Red Sea, about a thousand miles south and a little east of Jerusalem. It was called *Mecca,* and had long been an important shrine of widely known pagan gods. Pilgrims came from far and wide to worship a huge black stone thought to have descended from heaven.

A poor boy who had made himself into a very successful businessman lived in this small city of Mecca. He had traveled into many neighboring lands with the caravans as he amassed his wealth. Now toward middle age, he and his able wife kept a fine home, where they entertained important people who visited this holy city. But this man, whose name was *Mohammed,* began to say rather startling things to his friends and visitors.

Over a period of two or three years his remarks began to grow even more pointed. He bluntly told all who would listen to him that pagan gods do not exist. There was but one God, the God of Abraham, of Moses, and of Christ. He was a God of Truth, or Rightness—a Creator and Judge.

Not only did these blunt words shock his hearers, but Mohammed went even farther. He protested that every man and woman is responsible directly to himself for his thinking, his words, and his acts. Still God will judge him in respect to what he thinks, what he says, and what he does.

These were revolutionary ideas indeed. And they could, in fact, be very dangerous ideas, for Mecca depended largely upon the tourist traffic of pilgrims to its pagan shrine. If these ideas got abroad and people began to believe in them, Mecca and its inhabitants would suffer. Thus it was not long before Mohammed was in trouble.

He was forced to flee to nearby Medina and fight off the enemies that had pursued him. There he remained for six years. At the end of that time, with thirty thousand loyal followers, he returned to Mecca in the guise of a pilgrim.

But no fighting ensued. He was met outside the city by a group of its leading men. They had been doing a little sober thinking. They had decided to accept Mohammed's ideas and remove the pagan idols. This happened in the year A.D. 630. A new faith, known to us today as *Mohammedanism,* had arisen. With that of the Christians and the Jews, it became the third religion to worship the One True God.

In the short space of two years (A.D. 632) Mohammed was dead. But like fire in dry grass, the teachings of this able prophet swept over a huge area and became a force for progress and advancement through the next eight hundred years.

Since his teachings emphasized freedom and the responsibility of the individual, his millions of followers never established a single political government that embraced all or even a large portion of them. But their beliefs, which became a way of life, gave them much unity and common purpose. And while Mecca was the holy city to which pilgrims still turn their steps, their secular

SARACEN CULTURE WAS THE ENVY OF THE CRUSADERS

The followers of Mohammed were the truly civilized people of the centuries following
the fall of the Roman Empire. It was such contacts during the Crusades that started
Northern Europeans to begin the long climb out of the Dark Ages.

center was first at Damascus and later at Bagdad on the Tigris River, about fifty miles north of the site of ancient Babylon.

In this fabulous city ruled the Caliphs, which means the successors [of Mohammed]. And about them equally fabulous stories are told. One of the most famous among them—the Caliph Harun-al-Rashid of the *Arabian Nights*—exchanged letters with Charlemagne in faraway and still backward Europe. It was he, too, who sent sumptuous presents to the ruler of the Greek or Eastern Christian Empire at Constantinople. Among these gifts were the keys to the Holy Sepulcher at Jerusalem. This act

quickly brought great strife between the Greek and the Roman empires as to which was the proper protector of the Christians in the Holy City. The Caliph's gesture was turned into a firebrand and used to set ablaze Christian faith throughout Europe, thus launching a great holy war that lasted for nearly two hundred years—the *Crusades*.

Shortly after the death of Mohammed, the Arabs had overrun Syria, and Jerusalem had thus fallen into infidel, or non-Christian, hands. However, the conquerors venerated the places associated with Christ and, for the most part, allowed Christians to visit and worship in them without harm or disturb-

29

ance. This lack of friction continued during four hundred years, and until well into the eleventh century, at the beginning of which, you will remember, the Norsemen came to America.

By then Turkish tribes, which had embraced Mohammed's teachings, proved quite different from earlier converts. They were a much ruder, more warlike people, and took their new faith very simply and fiercely. After Asia Minor and the Holy Land fell into their hands in 1071, pilgrims to Jerusalem began to bring home tales of great hardships. Not only were its new Turkish masters a threat to Christians visiting the Holy City, but they offered a great threat to Constantinople, and thus to eastern Europe. So great was this menace that the eastern emperor made an appeal for help to the head of Christendom in Rome, Pope Urban II.

THE CRUSADES

In the year 1095 a great church council was held at Clermont in south central France. It was still the age of disorder in Europe, with a host of barons and knights at almost constant war with one another. The prevailing feeling was that the world had been created completely and finally. Everything was fixed as to quantity and extent. One man could gain only by taking something away from his neighbors, who were thus looked upon largely as enemies. Christ's teachings had, during the first thousand years, not made much of an impression.

The Pope arose to address this conclave. In what he said, he amply proved that ideas have consequences. Perhaps no speech ever made had more immediate and remarkable results. He exhorted knights and soldiers to put away the petty wars between Christian brothers. In place of strife at home, they

were to join hands and rescue their fellow Christians in the East. These savage Turks had Christ's grave in their foul hands. No pilgrim's life was safe. They would, if unchecked, conquer more and more of Christendom. "Besides," urged the Pope, "France is too poor a land to care for all its people. But the Holy Land flows with milk and honey . . . Enter upon the road to the Holy Sepulcher; wrest that land from this wicked race, and make it subject to yourselves."

BEGINNINGS OF FREEDOM AND DEMOCRACY

The effect was well-nigh electric. By the spring of the following year (1096), a great army had collected through France and along the Rhine intent upon freeing and taking possession of the place where they had laid the Saviour. The fact that it was more than two thousand miles away did not deter them in the least. Adventure was in the air, fired by great purposes. Within a year their numbers had swelled to three hundred thousand soldiers, drawn from all stations of life from highest to lowest.

We cannot follow here the great adventures and for the most part, the unhappy consequences of this first crusade. We can only mention that four more were to follow during the 132 years until Frederick II embarked upon the sixth and last in 1228, and acquired temporary possession of Jerusalem.

The impact of this great movement, however, was immense. Following the address of Urban at Clermont, the first task was to preach the Crusade far and wide. Among the many who undertook this task, perhaps the best known name is that of Peter the Hermit. His and his associates' fiery words in the preaching of the First Crusade brought about the initial stirring of the common peo-

PETER THE HERMIT LAUNCHES THE FIRST CRUSADE

ple of Europe. If it was not actually the birth of modern democracy, it was surely its conception and beginning.

Again and again, it would stir and gather strength and raise disturbing questions which were ultimately to find most nearly complete answers in the establishment of our own Constitution, twenty or more generations later.

Not only did the Crusades start men to thinking and acting for themselves, and also as great groups welded together in some common purpose, but those who journeyed to the East and came into contact with the Moslem, or Saracen, civilization, brought back ideas and objects that opened up and revolutionized life in Europe. They discovered that the world in which we live is by no means fixed and unchanging. Their eyes were opened wide to the need for progress.

And they set about clearing out old, restrictive, and repressive ways of thinking, so that progress might come.

But another of the influences that had its full effect upon the colonization of America came from more than halfway round the world. For that story we must go briefly to China, where in the thirteenth century we find that land sorely divided. Taking advantage of its weakness, a young Mongol emperor, Genghis Khan, and his horde of hard-riding tribesmen, attacked and conquered the northern Chinese empire in 1214. He then turned westward, and by a series of rapid invasions had before his death made himself master of Turkestan, Persia, Armenia, northern India, and southern Russia.

His son, Ogdai Khan, pushed on farther west, his well-organized and -equipped armies humbling opposition almost at will.

31

One of his most effective and surely a very terrifying weapon was a small field piece that hurled destruction great distances. These early cannons were fired with a recent Chinese discovery, gunpowder.

OUTSIDE INFLUENCES STIMULATE PROGRESS

Even though all Europe could not hear the Khan's barking cannon, the people there soon began to feel the effect of its explosive qualities. Just as the English longbowmen changed the pattern of warfare when they repulsed the French knights in full armor at Crécy [KRAY-see]; so would men armed with bows and arrows one day give way to more effectively equipped men bearing blunderbusses and muskets. It was the hard-hitting, longer-ranged firearms soon to come that would give decided advantage over the American Indians in the days ahead.

The Crusades had indeed opened men's eyes by taking them far from their homes and showing them new and better ways of life. Europe was shaken to its foundations by the ideas and experiences brought back from a more enlightened and civilized East. The darkness which had hung like a pall over much of that continent began to gray, and then yielded to a new light during the 1100's. Private and petty wars that had bred turmoil were suppressed. There was a demand for more comfort and for more security. With large areas that had known little but war and strife now at peace much of the time, trade began to spring up. Common men gained a little more freedom. Education spread out from the Church and was made available to laymen. And in this more favorable social climate, great advances were made in the thirteenth and fourteenth centuries.

Towns grew, and the larger of them became cities of rapidly increasing importance. The more important among those in Christian Europe were: Venice, Florence, and Genoa in Italy; Lisbon in Portugal; Paris in France; Bruges and Antwerp in Belgium; Hamburg and Nuremberg in Germany; Novgorod in Russia; Visby on the Swedish island of Gotland; and Bergen in Norway.

Universities sprang up at Bologna, Paris, Oxford, and other centers. The Schoolmen clarified language, more carefully defined the meaning of words, and so arranged for easier exchange of thought. Scholars began to commit their thoughts to writing, and some of them began to delve into original and independent research. Head and shoulders above the rest in this latter respect was the Franciscan monk Roger Bacon. Working at Oxford, where he was the most celebrated teacher of his day (1214–94), he became the father of modern experimental science.

From out of that part of the world dominated by the followers of Mohammed (the Saracens), which stretched south of the Mediterranean Sea and up into Spain, there slowly seeped many discoveries which aided learning to increase and spread. One of the most helpful of these was paper, first made in China and brought into Europe even before gunpowder. With the invention of printing from movable type in the mid 1400's, men at last had a means of multiplying thought through books, and light then began to displace darkness with startling rapidity.

But if men ashore were beginning to make progress, so, too, were those who sailed upon the seas. And what was this strange idea that was being whispered about among them, that the world was round? How could they seriously believe it to be anything but flat, as it surely must be? They were liable

AN UNSOLVED MYSTERY

There is reason to believe that European fishermen were landing on the eastern shores of North America during the century before Columbus arrived

to find themselves in trouble for believing such heathen ideas.

With the exception of the intrepid Norsemen, the sailors of the coastal countries of Europe had hugged the shore line rather closely in traveling from place to place. Either that, or they had ventured chiefly only across seas that were known to be landlocked. The men of Tyre and Sidon had been sailing the Mediterranean in the time of David and Solomon, and even as far as Britain, so it was said. When Christ was upon earth, this great sea was a Roman lake over which St. Paul sailed, to be shipwrecked on the island of Malta, but to land finally at Puteoli in Italy. Beyond the Mediterranean, ships had been sailing out through the Red Sea to India and Ceylon, and also south

along the east coast of Africa as long ago as when Solomon built his shipyard close by his copper smelter at Ezion-geber. Trade with the East had been an extensive and lively enterprise from early times. But it declined to a mere dribble, as far as most of Europe was concerned, following the fall of the Roman Empire.

But it never quite disappeared, since it continued active among the Saracen peoples. Then, as interest in the East and its marvelous products was renewed by the Crusades, it began to spring to life again. Also as the Mongol horsemen with their barking cannon began to range toward the West, the Pope began to dispatch missionaries into the land of the Great Khan far beyond the Black Sea, the last body of water directly connected to the Mediterranean toward the East. Travel is one of the great

(Continued on page 40)

LANDING OF LEIF ERICSSON

Edward Moran

UNITED STATES NAVAL ACADEMY, ANNAPOLIS

Lack of details regarding Norse explorations in the New World helps to make the Vikings most romantic figures; and our artist has captured this feeling in his picture, which may well be laid on a south-shore beach on Cape Cod. Recent discoveries seem to indicate that these voyagers spent some time there near Bass River and Follins Pond about the year 1003. There seems to be other evidence that in 1362 they had made a brief visit to western Minnesota. Moran is particularly well known for his marine scenes.

COLUMBUS LANDS IN AMERICA

John Vanderlyn

ROTUNDA, UNITED STATES CAPITOL, WASHINGTON

This artist, born in Kingston, N.Y. in 1775, studied with the famous Gilbert Stuart, and spent much time in Europe. Largely because of the popularity of his historical work, the *Massacre of Miss McCrea,* he was allotted one of the panels in the Rotunda of the national capitol, then under construction. To fill it, he chose the landing of Columbus on San Salvador in the Bahamas. Could it be that tales of lands beyond the ocean, which Columbus may well have heard in Iceland on a voyage there in 1477, helped to strengthen his resolve?

SIGNING OF THE MAYFLOWER COMPACT

Percy Moran

PILGRIM SOCIETY, PLYMOUTH, MASS.

This artist was a son of the Edward Moran who painted our picture of the landing of the Norsemen. After studying with his father, and in London and Paris, he returned to this country to win fame with his chosen specialty, colonial subjects. In a spread on following pages is one of his better-known works, the signing of the compact drawn up by the resolute Plymouth colonists. This simple, straightforward document combines the best features of both our Christian and our American Heritages.

The scene is laid in the main cabin of the *Mayflower.* Before the great pine chest being used as a desk sits William Brewster, the *elder* of the brethren, emphasizing the merits of their compact. The young man who listens so intently may well be John Alden. The officer in helmet and great cloak, guiding the signature of the younger man wearing a sword, is no doubt Miles Standish, the brave, blustery but able military leader among them. Arms have been gathered for the exploring party that will go ashore to seek out a suitable site for their village.

The women relax in the sunlight streaming in through the cabin window after the tedious two-months voyage over the stormy Atlantic. While the young mother fondles her baby son being played with by his older sister, the older woman at her right reads comforting passages to them from the Bible. The ocean has been crossed; but the wilderness they must now conquer will try both their faith and their courage in the months ahead.

THE FIRST THANKSGIVING

Frederick A. McNeal
ANCIENT & HONORABLE ARTILLERY CO., BOSTON

During the first few months at Plymouth after the landing on December 11, 1620, nearly half of the one hundred brave souls perished. Indeed at one time during that first severe winter there were only seven well persons in the colony. Governor Carver's son was among the first victims, and the governor himself died in April, his wife following him to the grave shortly afterward.

In the spring, however, peace was made with the Indians, who aided the colonists in planting crops. It was found that the forests abounded with game, and the streams and the ocean at their very doors with fish. With more and better food and the coming of warmer weather, their health improved. The land yielded to cultivation, houses and barns were erected, and life became more endurable. Those who had any special talents among them were called upon for pottery and utensils. Then, as the harvest was gathered, there was new assurance, and a harvest festival planned. But rather than a time of revelry, it would be one of *Thanksgiving* for the bounties the earth had yielded them, and for the care God had shown to those willing to exert themselves in caring for themselves. In the picture we see their pastor, John Robinson, invoking the Lord as they sit at the feast. Although three of the Indian guests seem to be partaking of the food with much gusto and relish, there is a distinct note of hesitancy in the facial expression and attitude of the fourth. It could be that the *New England Boiled Pudding* proved too rich for him.

THE FAMILY DINNER

Matthieu LeNain
TOLEDO MUSEUM OF ART

This French artist, born in Laon in 1607, and who died in Paris in 1677, here gives us a picture of a typical family of the early colonial period. Many such families were among the French Protestants, called the *Huguenots,* who sought refuge in America. By the *Edict of Nantes* in 1598, they had received a measure of religious freedom. When this law was revoked in 1685, and their civil and religious liberties were withdrawn, no less than 400,000 fled the homeland, and migrated to other countries. Many settled in South Carolina, and the name of New Rochelle, one of the leading New York suburbs, was chosen by its early Huguenot settlers.

LeNain, an excellent portraitist, provides an excellent impression of costuming in Colonial times. In the group are a father and mother, and their two daughters and three sons, together with the serving maid. The male hair was worn long, and the adult male felt some sense of security in the wearing of a beard. The elder son has achieved a mustache, and probably often stroked his chin hopefully. The mother, quite characteristically, has an admonition for her youngest son; while the small daughters were well protected from becoming "tomboys" by their heavy garments, and their long petticoats and draped velour dresses.

stimulants to an inquiring mind. Europeans were laying the foundation of a world outlook.

However, it seems to be the businessman and trader who are able to bring peoples closer together. It was the caravan men of early Bible days, rather than soldiers, who made the fortunate contacts between nations in the little area which, in those faraway times, was separated by what seemed great distances. Roman traders had done their full share in bringing some rays of light to the far reaches of the Empire before the Dark Ages.

Now once again it was the merchants who were helping to bring the peoples of Europe closer together, and who encouraged them to think out ways of finding access to far-off lands which could supply luxuries and greatly wanted goods. It was easier and less expensive to move such goods by ship; and thus ships and the handling of ships began to receive especial attention. Sailing in those days was a craft and, like many another early craft, badly burdened by tradition and strange beliefs.

Then certain individuals and groups began talking among themselves about the world being round. It is true that the Ionians and the Greeks had debated such a matter nearly two thousand years before, and had accepted the fact that we do live on a great sphere or ball.

Then another discovery credited to the Chinese fortunately found its way to Europe. It had long been known that pieces of magnetized iron (lodestone) attracted other bits of iron. Then it was found that if a small, thin piece of such iron ore was so arranged that it could freely swing about, it came to rest along a line close to true north and south. When it had been proved that this always happened, the sailors of the world received one of their most important tools —the magnetic compass.

No longer were known shore lines or the stars overhead the navigator's chief means of finding his way. With an almost magic needle that could be depended upon to point in a given direction, man had a means of finding his way from place to place with much greater certainty. Clouds could mask out the night sky or the sun by day. Thick fog could lay over the waters, or along the shores. But the compass continued to point in a known direction, and it could be relied upon with assurance.

The astrolabe, a device for measuring the position of the stars or the sun, had perhaps been known in principle by the priests of ancient Egypt. It now came into wider use, and was slowly improved to become the modern sextant. With the aid of these better navigating instruments, the more hardy sailor began to venture farther out into the open sea. Frenchmen had discovered the Canary Islands off the coast of Africa by 1334. The Portuguese had landed on Madeira in 1419; and had reached the Azores, twelve hundred miles to the west, by 1432.

Increased travel, both over land and by water routes, developed another need which began to be filled. Maps and charts were worked up by *cartographers*. Borrowing from old Greek and Roman maps hidden away through the years in the libraries of monasteries and universities, there were new corrections to be made and new lands to be added. Returning travelers and missionaries contributed such knowledge as they had acquired. While the results were sometimes far from accurate, these early charts were remarkably good, considering the data on which they were necessarily based.

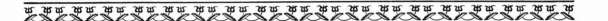

Wanted, a Water Route to India

OR many hundreds of years, and particularly since the beginning of the Crusades, goods from the Far East had been coming into Europe. The more important among them were tea, silks, perfumes, and particularly spices. Some of these came from China, but spices came directly from the East Indian Islands.

There were no refrigerators in those days, and foodstuffs, especially meat, were hard to keep. In fact, much tainted meat was probably eaten through necessity. If it could be spiced, some of its strong flavor could be covered up. An herb garden beside one's house was a necessity. But eastern spices were even more flavorful. In Bible times, spices had been much in demand. They add savor to many foods; and if they were taken away from us today, we would surely miss such staple items as pepper, cinnamon, cloves, and nutmeg.

It would hardly be true to say that the demand for spices alone led to the discovery of America. But we may be certain, nonetheless, that it played a most important part. Here is how it influenced later events.

The trade with the East India Islands—which were also called the Moluccas, or Spice Islands—was in the hands of Mohammedan, or Saracen, spice merchants. Sea lanes to the East by way of the Red Sea were closely guarded. If another way could be found, say, around Africa, this monopoly could be broken and spices brought to European ports by an all-water route.

The west coast of Africa had been explored but for a short distance below where the Canary Islands lie just offshore. The great desert across the northern third of this continent reaches to the western ocean; and early explorers felt that all they would find on down this coast was a similar sandy, torrid, uninhabited land.

Then, about 1445, a hardy group pushing on south, came to a great headland clothed with tropical trees, which they named Cape Verde, or *green cape*. How much farther they ventured is not known. But in 1459 a Venetian geographer produced a map showing Africa ending in a point, and with a possible water route around it to the East Indies.

At last in 1486 Bartholomeu Diaz [DEE-as], navigator of the king of Portugal, set out to check discoveries along the African west coast. Caught by a raging storm, his ships were carried around the Cape of Good Hope, although he did not clearly realize

41 ❧

what a momentous happening had taken place. His badly frightened sailors prevented him from continuing; and thus the waterway on to India and the East still remained to be discovered.

But the urge to reach the spices and other products there continued to mount. Also belief in the fact that the earth is round was becoming more widely accepted, particularly by those skilled in mathematics. Based upon this being true, an astronomer at Florence, in Italy, named Toscanelli, came forward with a rather startling theory. He claimed that if a ship sailed due west, it would be bound to reach the Indies. He not only wrote out his reasoning for this bold plan, but he also sketched a map to show how it could be carried out. This theory must have been much discussed by shipowners and ship captains of Italy's two great seaports, Venice, and Genoa.

CHRISTOPHER COLUMBUS IS BORN IN ITALY

This latter city, which lies on the beautiful curving shore near where Italy and France meet, was a bustling trading center at the middle of the fifteenth century. And either here, or possibly in Milan, seventy-five miles to the north, a boy was born in 1451 whose memory we venerate in this country each October 12. His name was Christopher Columbus.

Except that his father was a weaver, we know very little of his early life. There is evidence, however, that he had some formal education. If he was not a native of Genoa, he found his way there and became a sailor. In 1474 he made a voyage to Chios, one of the islands off the coast of Asia Minor. Two years later he sailed to England. On the return, his ship was attacked and forced to take refuge for a time in the harbor at Lisbon.

Liking the city, he returned there the following year; and in 1479 married the daughter of a noted Italian navigator then serving the king of Portugal. Through his influential father-in-law, Columbus was given access to the finest charts and to a large store of knowledge about newly explored areas. This material, plus his own practical experience, induced him to give his life and efforts to geographical discovery.

He began to correspond with those who might help him increase this knowledge. And there are letters still preserved which were exchanged with the famous Toscanelli of Florence in 1481, in which Columbus sought to gather more data regarding a western route to the East Indies.

Although details are lacking, it is supposed that he made one or more voyages down the west coast of Africa in 1482. He was by then well versed in the theory that the world is round. The equator crossed the Gulf of Guinea [GIHN-eh] into which he sailed; and he claims to have measured the length of a degree of longitude at that point, where the length would be greatest, or about sixty-nine miles.

Returning from these voyages, Columbus felt that the field of discovery promised great rewards. There were wealth and fame on the one hand; yet perhaps as great an incentive lay in the hope of carrying Christianity to heathen peoples. But he needed backers, and ships, and men, and money in abundance.

First he sought such aid in Genoa. When it was not to be had there, he turned to King John II of Portugal. But a westward voyage to the Spice Islands still seemed fantastic and impossible. The world could be flat, despite what some might believe. But the big stumbling block was the fact that men had al-

IN 1486 DIAZ OF PORTUGAL SAILED AROUND THE CAPE OF GOOD HOPE

ways reached the coveted goal by sailing to the east. A voyage in the opposite direction looked too much like sheer folly.

In the year 1485 the still hopeful man made his way to the south of Spain to solicit the assistance of the dukes of Medina. Although they turned a deaf ear to his project, they did one encouraging thing for this earnest and determined man. They gave him a letter to Queen Isabella of Castile.

In 1469 she had married Ferdinand of Aragon. And with this union began the period of Spain's great importance in European affairs. During the next hundred years that country enjoyed greater military power than any of the other European states. But at that very moment the king and queen were heavily involved in completing the conquest of the Spanish peninsula. They were attempting to drive out the *Moors,* as the Mohammedans, or Saracens, were called in that country. These able, enterprising, freedom-loving people had for more than two hundred years held the mountainous kingdom of Granada along Spain's southern coast.

Thus it was two years before Columbus could approach them with his scheme. Their efforts and funds were well taken up with their own enterprises, and they gave this voyage of discovery but halfhearted interest through three more long years. Then in 1490, his patience sorely tried after five unfruitful years, Columbus demanded a final decision. So insistent was he that a conference was arranged at Salamanca; but it resulted in refusal of support.

Deciding that he must exert influence through important members of the Spanish court, his next appeal was through the queen's former confessor. With his aid, Columbus at long last persuaded Pinzón, the head of a family of navigators living at Palos, of the soundness of his plans. Through his interest further interviews were had with the queen.

Finally, Ferdinand and Isabella signed an agreement, known as the *capitulations,* which gave the hopeful explorer the authority he sought. This document was signed at Santa Fe, and dated April 14, 1492. By it the navigator was to search for and take pos-

43 ᘓ

session of certain islands. A few days later, in Granada, he received his commission as admiral and viceroy of such lands as he discovered.

COLUMBUS SAILS

Once the monarchs' consent was granted, preparations for the voyage were hurried along. There were to be three ships. The two smaller, the *Pinta* and the *Niña,* were commanded by two brothers of the Pinzón family. The *Santa María* was the flagship and under Columbus' personal command. In four months all was ready; and the expedition sailed from Palos on the morning of August 3. All told, there were 120 persons aboard the three little vessels.

Laying their course south southwest, they came to the Canary Islands on the sixth day. The tiny *Pinta* had broken a rudder, which was repaired, and fresh water and provisions were being taken aboard, when disturbing news arrived. Three Portuguese ships were cruising offshore, intending to destroy the expedition.

The die was cast. Feeling that he would not be pursued into unknown waters to the west, Columbus stole out into the open sea and headed into the setting sun. At once fear gripped the crew. Nor were their shaken minds eased as they soon ran past the volcanic island of Teneriffe [ten-er-IF], largest in the Canary group and whose blazing mountain was then in eruption.

Now they were in unfamiliar seas, and even the staunch captain may have had moments of grave doubt. His compass, which in all his previous sailing pointed directly at the North Star, began to move slightly to one side. Day by day it pointed more and more away from its customary direction. It was not long before the crew noticed and fran-

tically demanded to know why. Almost as though he had been inspired, Columbus gave them the correct answer, one, however, which would not be proven correct for hundreds of years. He explained that the needle did not actually point at the star, but to a point nearly beneath it. It would vary even more as they moved on. Their admiral's greater learning and superb faith in himself relieved the disquieted crew's fears for the time being.

But doubt again took hold of them, and they began to grow sullen. Trouble was surely brewing. Day after day with nothing but water about them was more than these simple men could stand. Mutiny was not far off. And to replace their fears with hope, Columbus began to paint rosy pictures for them of the lands which lay ahead. There would be wealth and glory for all. Once again the tension lessened.

LAND IS SIGHTED

Then there were more trying days as the ships struggled through the Sargasso Sea, slowed down by a deep, seemingly endless mat of seaweed. It was just about as they were breaking out of the clutches of this evil area, avoided even today by ships, that a heartening thing happened. A land bird circled above them, and, perhaps startled by the strange sight of a winged ship, turned and sped away toward the *west.* Here was a good omen indeed.

In addition, before leaving Spain, the king and queen had promised a pension to the first man to sight new land. The speeding bird gave promise that land must be near, perhaps not too far to the west. How the eyes of every man aboard the three ships must have now been fastened on the horizon. The tiny vessels always hugged closely together when night fell. The sea and sky had

COLUMBUS' MEN WERE TERRIFIED BY AN ERUPTING
VOLCANO ON THE ISLAND OF TENERIFFE

already begun to darken, when a cry suddenly rang out. It was the voice of Martin Pinzón, master of the *Pinta,* shouting with all his might, "Land! Land dead ahead! I make claim to the king's pension!"

Was it indeed true? It must be! For there on the skyline, in the half light, lay what seemed to be a long, low island. How 120 hearts must have thrilled at the sight. The ships hove to and waited out a night that was long indeed.

But as morning light crept over the sea from the east at dawn, their hopes turned to bitter recrimination. Apparently a low-lying evening cloud had deceived them. Disappointment seized hold of them. Patience was at an end. And the angry crew demanded that their leader turn about and head for home. When he refused, they threatened to hurl him over the side into the greedy waves. It was only by putting up a fearless front that Columbus withstood them. The outcome

hung in the balance for another day or two. Then more good omens brought renewed cheer.

It was now October 11, and the afternoon was slowly slipping by. First one of the ships sighted the branch of a bush with green leaves and fresh berries on it. Then but a little later they passed a paddle, surely the work of human hands, floating by. Mutinous voices fell silent as word was handed along from the master that land must indeed be close at hand. Once more every eye turned to the west, as the promise of a fine doublet was added to that of the king's pension.

But night fell with tropic suddenness, and all was swallowed up in darkness. The air was warm and pleasant, and Columbus remained on deck. The sky was dotted with stars even well down toward the horizon. How fascinating they were, he thought to himself. And then one of them surely began to move strangely. The master jumped to his

45 ॐ

feet to have a closer look and pressed against the ship's rail.

Doubting his own eyes, he called first one, and then another of those with him aboard the *Santa María*. Yes, they, too, saw the moving light, saw it go out, then reappear, and finally disappear altogether. It could mean but one thing; but after the recent disappointment it might be well to wait for morning to be fully certain.

Then, before the sun had risen, a shot rang out. One of the small deck pieces on the *Pinta* had been fired, for one of its seamen on watch had spied the outline of land nearly a league away. It was an island in a group of several hundred, stretching offshore from the tip of Florida to Haiti and now known as the Bahamas. The first seen was probably Watlings Island, called *San Salvador* by Columbus as he landed upon it, on October 12, 1492.

AMERICA, NOT INDIA

As he planted the cross and the banner of Ferdinand and Isabella on its sandy beach, Columbus had no doubt in his mind but that he had found a new route to the East Indies. This belief, in fact, he carried to his dying day. And as one evidence of how intense was his belief, and that of the explorers who soon followed after him, the natives of the New World he had chanced upon are still known as *Indians*.

There was some exploration of other islands in the group, and the party landed on Cuba and on Haiti before returning to Spain. There they were received most royally. But although Columbus did not realize it at the time, his greatest triumph had already been achieved in plowing a new path across an uncharted ocean. His later exploits were much less glorious, and intrigue and jealousy and heartache darkened his later life.

DISAPPOINTMENTS OF COLUMBUS' LATER LIFE

He made a second voyage in 1493, this time with seventeen ships, and discovered Jamaica and other islands in the Caribbean Sea. In a third westward journey in 1498, he touched at Trinidad and landed on the South American continent just below the mouth of the Orinoco River, in what is now Venezuela. Unfortunately, the facts of this trip were long kept a state secret, and perhaps deprived Columbus of the honor of having the two continents in the Western Hemisphere bear his name.

From this trip, too, he was returned to Spain a prisoner in chains. In dishonor and without royal patronage, it was not until 1502 that he was able to undertake a fourth voyage. From this he returned in 1504, to die in poverty two years later. The queen, his true patron, had died before him. Ferdinand, cold and austere, had withheld promised honors from the great sailor and explorer. Now that he was dead, the king sought to make amends by a huge funeral. The weary bones of the great man rested in two places in Spain and were then taken to Santo Domingo, in the island of Haiti. Finally, in 1795, they were removed to the cathedral in Havana, Cuba.

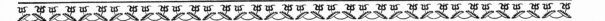

A New World to Conquer

E must keep in mind that Columbus died firm in the belief that he had penetrated to the long-sought East. He knew that he had not reached the fabulous Spice Islands. He had not encountered people capable of producing any of the wonderful products which had made men wealthy through trade. But he, and those who immediately survived him, were certain they were near the goal they all sought.

This much, however, he did achieve. His six weeks' voyage over open water and out of sight of land had given courage to others. It had been a tremendous forward step in navigation. Had not the Spanish authorities kept secret as far as possible the results of at least one voyage, hoping to shut out others from the knowledge that had been gained? But many of the details were carried from port to port, wherever ships sailed.

Then, in 1497, a Genoese navigator in the employ of Henry VIII of England struck off to the west in northern latitudes, and reached the shores of North America. Whether this man, John Cabot, was the first white man to visit this new northern continent in the five hundred years since the Norsemen had re-putedly been here is open to question. There were stories that hardy fishermen from the coast of Europe had already found their way here and gone ashore long enough to fill their casks with fresh water. Nonetheless, it was Cabot's early voyage which gave England a lively interest in this strange new land, and on which it pinned its later claims to prior rights of ownership.

AMERICA IS NAMED

In this same year of 1497, another Italian, in the employ of commercial interests in Spain, is supposed to have accompanied an expedition which cruised for hundreds of miles along the coast of South America. On his return he published a report, known today only in a shortened version in which scholars find many statements hard to adjust to known facts. If he did actually complete this trip and really landed upon the South American mainland, it was after Columbus had already been there. But since Columbus' accomplishments on this third voyage had been kept a close secret, while this other man's rather profuse account had been spread abroad, our continent, as well as that to the south of it, took their names from this

47

much less important person. The navigator whose exploits are subject to doubt was called Amerigo Vespucci [ves-POOT-chee], and hence the new lands in the west about which he wrote came to be known as *America*.

AROUND THE WORLD

At the time Columbus, and perhaps Vespucci, were on voyages to the west (1498), a Portuguese, Vasco da Gama, succeeded in rounding Africa. After visiting India, he returned home with glowing reports of that land and the opportunity for trade.

Then in 1519, and lest there be any further doubt that the world was round, another daring Portuguese, named Magellan, started on what is perhaps the most remarkable voyage ever undertaken. In the employ of Charles V of Spain, he took the course first charted by Columbus. This led to the Canary Islands, from which he struck southwest and reached South America near the great bulge of Brazil.

By the next year, he had worked his way south to the mouth of the Río de la Plata. Edging his way along, now in colder waters, he finally passed through the treacherous strait which has come to bear his name, at the southern tip of South America. After pressing up the forbidding coast of what today is lower Chile, he swung to the northwest across the broad Pacific, which he so named because it seemed less storm-tossed and more peaceful than the Atlantic.

He finally reached the Philippine Islands, where he was killed in a fight with its natives in 1521. The following year his men, after visiting Borneo and the Moluccas, crossed the Indian Ocean, rounded the Cape of Good Hope, and returned home in the fall of 1522. Not only had the world been proven

to be round, but this great voyage helped to fix many new coast lines with greater accuracy on maps, charts, and globes.

Water routes had now been opened around both South America and Africa. One had been discovered by men under the patronage of the king of Spain, the second by the Portuguese. This caused other monarchs to liven their interest in a passage to India; and the king of France was the next to try his hand. Choosing an Italian navigator, named Verazzano, he instructed him to attempt a water crossing north of the Americas. Striking west from Madeira in 1524, he presumably came to land about where the Carolinas lie today. Moving up the coast, he failed to find a northwest passage; but he did give the throne of France what it considered valid rights in its later attempts at settlement in this new world.

Both of the Americas had now definitely been visited. But they had to be more thoroughly explored, and, if possible, possessed. The contest for footholds in a huge wilderness was about to begin. What, beside discovery, would encourage the Spanish to lead in conquest in the New World?

For our answer, let us return to the city of Granada in southern Spain, just previous to Columbus' first visit to Ferdinand and Isabella, and see what was taking place there.

We have repeatedly mentioned the followers of Mohammed, and spoken of them as Mohammedans, or Saracens. Permitted a freedom unknown to Europeans during the Dark Ages, they had achieved a remarkable civilization. It had flowed to the west across the northern rim of Africa, leaped the narrow straits at the western end of the Mediterranean Sea, and taken possession of southern Spain. There it came into full flower under followers of Mohammed known as the *Moors*. Through wealth based upon trade, they had built a progressive, enlightened, and thriving community at one edge of backward, stagnant Europe.

THE MOORS
ARE DRIVEN FROM SPAIN

They knew that the earth was round, and it was through their hands that the compass had passed from China into use in the West. Sailors of other Saracen groups had control of the seaways to India and had them highly organized for trade, and in this profitable commerce the Moors took an active part. They were wealthy and they were able. But they found themselves living beside a world in which pagan beliefs still held sway. Chief among them was the feeling that any gains were possible only at the expense of one's neighbors. Some day the study of the Saracen culture will have a deserved place in our schools, at least equal in importance to that given the rather sorry history of Europe to the beginning of the sixteenth century. These people through the Middle Ages were more like Americans of today than any peoples from whom most of us are directly descended. But in Spain their destiny was to be brutally murdered or driven out.

And driven out they were—murdered and deported by the hundreds of thousands. But the idea of full employment of human energy, which they had put to use to their own great benefit, remained, and at first gave a tremendous impulse to the new Spanish nation. This burst of zeal lasted for about one hundred years, then burned out suddenly during the days of the evil Inquisition and left a devastated land, still sick and ailing today.

During that virile sixteenth century the military power of Spain not only laid a heavy hand on much of the rest of Europe, but also sent many of its bravest young men to the New World, bent upon conquest.

Leaving the route around Africa to the Portuguese, the Spaniards focused on the areas first visited by Columbus. One of his early companions, Pinzón, pushed through the Caribbean in 1508 and explored the shores of Central America. In 1513 Balboa revisited this same section, pressed inland, crossed the Isthmus at Panama, and looked out over the ocean which Magellan was to cross and name a few years later.

SPANISH EXPLORATION

In this same year of 1513 Ponce de León [PON-thuh—day-LEE-un] skirted what is now Florida and took possession of it for the Spanish crown. Ocean crossings were by now frequent, and Spain was laying firm claim to all lands visited. But up to this time all that had been encountered were rude natives living under very primitive conditions. The returns from all the effort and money expended had not paid off. There may have been hope of extending Christianity, but the real object turned out to be trade and particularly wealth. Colonization was one thing; but piracy always had, by European standards, brought more certain results. There were priests and clerics in the parties sent out, it is true. But they were made up principally of armed men intent upon trade if it could be had in that fashion, or plunder if that method yielded better returns. Seeking booty, these Spaniards were not long to be denied.

As a young man, Hernando Cortes [kor-TAZE] had taken up law, only to later become a soldier in an expedition to Cuba. At thirty-four, he was put in command of seven hundred men and sent against Mexico. Landing on its east coast, he founded the present city of Vera Cruz in 1519 and

49

promptly burned his ships so that his men would have no means of avoiding the task ahead of them. Then he moved his small army up over the two hundred-odd miles of mountain trails to the plateau on which stands Mexico City.

IN SEARCH OF PLUNDER

He met with no resistance, and, in fact, was received in a most friendly reception by Montezuma, ruler of an empire far, far finer than any other yet encountered in this western New World. In the exhilarating atmosphere of the highlands, they had built a beautiful capital city, connected with other fine cities by excellent highways. Irrigated fields produced bumper crops. There were skilled artisans at work. But, above all, there were great stores of gold, silver, and jewels —enough to set fire to men already hot with greed.

After the seizure of Montezuma, the emperor and his peace-loving native subjects turned on the invaders. Although loss of life was great, Cortes finally succeeded in overcoming all opposition. He annexed Mexico to Spain. But in a costly battle at the pass of Tlacopon, much of the rich booty which they had stolen was sunk in a nearby lake and never recovered.

Here was proof, however, that there was rich plunder to be had. Then, as the Catholic missionaries took over and began their fine, peaceful task of restoring order, and laying the basis for Spanish colonists soon to follow, the blood-stained explorers turned elsewhere in search of further treasure.

On the strength of mouth-watering rumors heard in Mexico, Pizarro [peh-THAR-roh], a Spanish adventurer, took it upon himself to sail down the west coast of South America to investigate whether or not there was any

truth in them. Curving back from the western bulge of this little-known continent was the mountainous land of Peru. It was 1524 when he landed on its coast at Gallo. What he saw induced him to make the trip to far-off Spain, to obtain proper authority there to conquer this isolated country.

Royal sanction was given in 1529, and two years later the doughty captain sailed south again from Panama. He had three ships, but less than two hundred men. Fortune was kind to him, however, for when he arrived on this second visit, civil war was in progress between two sons of the late emperor.

THE INCAS CONQUERED

Biding his time until one of them, Atahualpa [aw-taw-WAHL-puh], gained a signal victory and became the reigning Inca, Pizarro hastily made peace with him. He then secured the right to visit the interior of the land. At a great banquet given by the invader in his honor, the new ruler, or Inca, was taken prisoner. Then began a horrible slaughter of his subjects. By torture, the seized monarch was forced to disclose where the treasures of his realm were hidden. Then he was treacherously slain.

The easily portable wealth for which the bloodthirsty Spaniards had been seeking was found in great abundance. Soon great fleets of galleons were shuttling back and forth, heavy-laden with golden cargoes. Temples, palaces, tombs, homes were all ransacked. Greed had found food sweet to its taste. The New World, to which Christianity was to be transplanted, must first be opened up by merciless pillage. What a pitiable travesty on the teachings of the Master. Human energy set in motion by Saracen ways of life had most unfortunately com-

BALBOA DISCOVERS THE PACIFIC OCEAN

bined with pagan methods. And the Spanish conquest, fortunately experienced principally in Central and South America, added many dark and bloody pages to the history of man's struggle to achieve likeness to his Creator.

Some attempts were made to find suitable booty in the area to the north of Mexico and along the waters of the great gulf which took its name. Ponce de León landed for a second time in Florida. He was this time in search of a magical spring—the *Fountain of Youth* —capable of restoring the powers of younger years to the aged. He was seeking treasure, too; and both had eluded him on the first visit. But the Indians had not forgotten his bloody touch. This time a rain of arrows welcomed him as he came ashore. One of them found a weak spot in his armor, and he was hurried off to Cuba, there to die of his wound.

In 1520 a party from Haiti headed by D'Allyon [dal-YONE] landed on the coast of the Carolinas. Disgusted with the poor condition of the natives from whom there was nothing to steal, its members finally enticed a group of them aboard ship and sold them as slaves on their return to their island base. On a second trip, a temporary colony was established at what is now Beaufort, South Carolina. But neither had the Indians there forgotten the Spaniard's former visit. While D'Allyon and a few others escaped, he, too, had a mortal wound which soon removed him from the ranks of these cruel *conquistadores*.

Then came Hernando de Soto, one of Pizarro's former soldier companions, and now governor of Cuba. Not deterred by de León's disappointments, he also chose Florida. He and his men were nearly lost in its treacherous swamps; but they pressed on over a course lined with the greatest of hardships, and totally without reward. They circled through parts of what are now several of our southern states, under frequent attack by savage red men who were fast learning that these white men were surely not brothers. At last they came to the broad waters of the Mississippi. And here de Soto died. To save his body from desecration at the hands of the ever-lurking savages, his companions were forced to drop it at night into the river-bottom mud. With empty pockets and minus a leader, they had to make their way by stealth back to the island fastness of Cuba, secure in Spanish hands.

EXPLORATION INTO KANSAS

There is but one more of this cruel and bloody band who has any claim on our attention. His name was Coronado, and details in regard to him are lacking. In Mexico he had heard of seven fabulous golden cities which lay to the northeast. Off he went in vain search of them, covering much of the territory as far as the present state of Kansas. But there were no glittering cities. Neither were there any such stores of wealth among any of the settled or roving tribes north of Mexico as had been found and plundered in lands to the south of the Rio Grande.

All explored territory was annexed to the Spanish crown. This embraced many of the islands of the West Indies, and also much of the mainland bordering the Caribbean Sea. So substantial, in fact, seemed his rights, that the king of Spain claimed the whole of North and South America. This somewhat amused Francis I, the French king, who demanded to see Adam's will that he might learn from it if the Spanish Charles was indeed heir to any such huge portion of the earth.

Spain, however, was now importing treasure by the shipload from her new domains. Its total value must have been staggering. This wealth helped maintain her military power, a tremendous threat to all of Europe. And so that she would be unmolested in enjoying returns from these lands beyond the seas, she prohibited other Europeans from entering this whole area. To other European rulers, this came as sort of a taunt; and was soon taken up as a challenge by the French and by the English, both willing and anxious to contest such excessive Spanish claims.

Europe's Rivalries Reach to America

ow much traceable benefit Verazzano's voyage in 1524 had netted the French monarch is an open question. Perhaps his Breton and Norman sailors and fishermen had learned as much about the North American coast, for many of them apparently had visited it during the past fifty years. There was a trace of a claim here, however; and perhaps the time had come to follow it up.

Francis I was in keen competition at home with Charles V of Spain. Also the plunder from Mexico and South America was something to envy. Access to such wealth, or to the East Indies and China trade, would be of distinct advantage to the French. So the king selected Jacques Cartier [KAR-tyā], one of his own subjects from Brittany, and commissioned him to further explore the North American coast.

Between 1534 and 1543 he completed three fairly successful voyages. Although he was disappointed in finding that the St. Lawrence River did not afford a water route to the north into the Pacific, he did provide France with a first-class claim to the basin of that fine waterway. A few others followed Cartier; but the French were heavily in-volved at home, and little real progress was made by them in America during the next two generations. These were critical years, and had they pressed exploration during them, American history might have been quite different.

With the ending of civil war and the restoration of the broken power of France under Henry IV, the time had come to consider a *New France,* to be developed in the lands across the ocean. This new king dispatched one of his naval officers, Samuel de Champlain [sham-PLAIN], to follow through on the work begun by Cartier, now long neglected.

Sailing up the broad St. Lawrence, he established a military post at Quebec in 1607–8, and a second at Montreal in 1611. He explored the upper river and the lakes as far as Huron, and also discovered the lake between New York State and Vermont which bears his name. He made treaties with the Indians and supported the Hurons in a war against the Iroquois and their English allies.

As governor of *New France,* he was taken prisoner to England when English forces overran and captured that province in 1629. Four years later, when peace restored her colonies to France, Champlain returned and was again made governor. He died at Quebec in 1635.

Mention has just been made of English activities in the New World. And since that country was destined to play a dominant part in the colonization of North America, it will be well to go back at this point and set the stage for her entrance into the competition about to ensue.

Following its conquest in 1066 by the Normans, descendants of the Norsemen, England benefited greatly by being an island. Close to Europe, but not quite a part of that continent, the English Channel formed a barrier behind which this nation was able to develop to its decided advantage. While the seeds of democracy and of individual freedom were first sowed during the Crusades, it was in England that the rights of men, in contrast to the rights of kings, were first separated, written down, and enlarged upon as they became law.

Upon ascending the throne in 1100, Henry I, younger son of William, the Norman Conqueror, had given his people a charter, promising to redress their wrongs. Then a *Magna Charta*—or Great Charter—was forced from his grandson, John, at Runnymede in 1215. It is perhaps the most famous document in all the history of government. And perhaps its most potent section is that providing no free man is to be arrested, imprisoned, or deprived of his property, unless he be immediately sent before a court made up of his peers, or equals. No such rights as these were to be known in France, just across the narrow channel, for nearly six hundred years.

Another provision which has an important bearing on our story is that in respect to trade. Under the *Charter,* the king was forced to permit merchants to move about freely from place to place. And the king's officers were no longer allowed to exercise arbitrary and despotic powers.

LIBERTIES WON IN ENGLAND

Under John's son, Henry III, a Parliament was assembled. While at first it contained only the nobles and church authorities, beginning in 1265 a new class of members, the commons, made up of commen men, were included. While there was still a long way to go to the liberties which we know and enjoy in this country today, Englishmen in these early times obtained and profited by a greater amount of individual freedom than any of their near neighbors on the European continent.

By the end of the 1200's England was already a trading nation. Coal fields were being extensively worked, and a considerable volume was being exported to the Low Countries, or what is now Holland, and to Belgium, Luxemburg, and Germany. There was a flourishing iron industry in Sussex and Kent, and English metalworkers were important artisans. Even the goldsmiths of London had formed themselves into a powerful guild.

There was considerable shipping in and out of England at the time of Columbus' voyage. But, while John Cabot had been sent on an exploration of the western ocean in 1497, Henry VIII had his hands full with affairs at home during the first half of the following century. Also Englishmen had need to keep a wary eye on their freedom.

When Henry's daughter, Elizabeth, finally came to the throne, Englishmen again relaxed, and began to look out over the ocean and to stir abroad. The Spanish had built considerable seapower, and to offset it the English began to develop a navy of their own. However, this was accomplished through individual initiative, which took the form of *privateering*. A privateer is a privately owned vessel, armed with cannon and permitted to cruise against the commerce or war vessels of other nations. Thus it was a sort of refined piracy with government blessing. But such were the relations of most of Britain's early *sea dogs* to their government. The ships were their own, and so was whatever booty they captured. Lessons learned the hard way by their ancestors at the hands of the Norsemen, or Danes, some seven hundred years before could have been their pattern. But, it was a well-known, widely used pagan pattern; and it served England well, and would one day serve her colonies quite as satisfactorily.

ENGLISH ACTIVE AT SEA

The exploits of such swashbuckling admirals as John Hawkins, or Francis Drake, make exciting reading. Not to be outdone by Magellan, the doughty Drake sailed around the world in the years 1577 to 1580. He financed this trip principally by preying on Spanish vessels and their trading ports. His course lay down the east coast of South America, then through the straits, and up its west coast, plundering as he went.

He remained in Puget Sound long enough to refit his ships and take possession of that area for England under the name *New Albion*. This action provoked a border question to be settled nearly three hundred years later. Then, striking off across the Pacific, he touched at the Spice Islands, rounded the Cape of Good Hope, and after three years dropped anchor again in the Thames. The good Queen Bess was pleased to take dinner with this dauntless man aboard his flagship. But she was more pleased, no doubt, with

the treasure with which it was burdened, and in which she shared liberally. That same year he received knighthood. Stout ships and men able and fearless in fighting with them were to be the foundation of English might in the centuries just ahead.

But the Spaniards, smarting at the hands of these fast-sailing, hard-fighting buccaneers, took quite a different view of the matter when Drake and other English captains began to play havoc with Spanish shipping. In 1585–86 Sir Francis successfully raided their harbors in the West Indies. And then, as though to humiliate them even more, he sailed into their great home port of Cadiz and sank many ships the following year.

It was 1588 before Spain was fully prepared to wipe out these English insults. Also Philip II, then Spanish ruler, had two other purposes beside protecting his shipping and his colonies. He wished to overthrow Protestantism in England, and also to prevent that country from giving aid to the Netherlands. So he assembled the greatest fleet Christendom had yet seen and headed it for the English Channel. The 130 huge vessels which comprised it moved that far with safety.

THE SPANISH ARMADA

But the English had been able to gather 197 smaller vessels, and with them they harried and sank many of the Spanish ships. The remainder of this *Spanish Armada* was forced to head out into the North Sea and flee around Scotland. Here furious gales drove some of them ashore, and less than half of all that had left Spain returned safely. Although this English victory was not exactly the turning point in history sometimes claimed for it, English hopes in foreign lands were greatly encouraged. Spain grew more and more feeble. The legacies of free and determined action left them by the Moors had been squandered. And by the time the war which had been raging was over in 1604, England was ready seriously to consider colonies in North America.

It was felt that there was no huge store of precious metals or other easily taken loot in the land to the north. But there was excellent fishing where the waters of two great ocean currents met and mingled under a blanket of fog on the Grand Banks south of Newfoundland. The mainland promised a lucrative fur trade. And one other factor entered heavily into English interest in America. The last traces of serfdom—the status in which a peasant is bound to the soil on which he is born—had disappeared in England during Elizabeth's reign. Many of these freed men, now able to take up and cultivate land in their own right, were ready for immigration to colonies where such land could be found. Also there were other situations in that tight little island that made many of its people cast eager glances at a new land across the western ocean, as we shall see.

ENGLISH EFFORTS, AND THE STIMULUS OF TRADE

In addition to the dauntless sea captains who with their proud crews were giving the English control of the waves, this country had developed an able merchant class as well. Although looked down upon as a "nation of shopkeepers" by some of its neighbors on the Continent, English trade was destined to make her a first-class world power. Beyond an active trade at home, these merchants were already dealing with Russia, the Baltic and Mediterranean ports, and even the far-off Malay, or Spice Islands. As this trade fell off, they turned their attention to the west.

While such trading activities were carried on under rights granted by, and sometimes with the patronage of, the government, they were primarily private affairs. Merchants formed *companies,* made up of groups wishing to invest their money and efforts in a business undertaking. Here was democracy at work, for these companies made their own bylaws, or rules, to govern their activities. Then they elected officers to carry out these common purposes.

TYPE OF COLONIZATION

The documents granting the rights under which they operated were called *charters.* The chartered company could do, with governmental sanction, whatever was set forth in this formal document. It was thus like the charter of a corporation today. With the charters of the companies formed to colonize America went a grant of land. This the company might hold and operate, or it could be sold in large or small tracts to private persons. Also the company had exclusive right to trade in the area covered by its charter. The Dutch also used this method of fostering colonies and overseas activities, as we shall see. And you will find that English companies accounted for the founding of four colonies—Virginia, Massachusetts Bay, the Dutch New Netherlands (after that colony was taken over and renamed New York), and later Georgia. Under this arrangement there was greater opportunity for eventual self-government.

But the kings of England still retained considerable personal power. Also they had friends who had to be repaid for favors done for the Crown or for the nation. To such, either as individuals or to small groups of two or more, the king would grant land, the use of which was to be under the direction and control of a *proprietor,* or several *proprietors.* Since they were either wealthy men or had access to money which they could borrow, they financed their own way, as did the privateers their own ships. If they wished, they could govern in their own right under their *patent* from the king. Or, they could allow the colonists under them such self-government as the proprietors were willing to permit. Such was the arrangement under which the colonies of Maryland, Delaware, Pennsylvania, New Jersey, and the Carolinas were established.

INDIVIDUAL EFFORT

In either event, the colonies were founded through individual enterprise, rather than as strictly governmental projects. Men were thus forced to think and act for themselves, and not by some planned arrangement which tended to cut down their willingness to exert their human energies, to make progress, and to build greater security through their own efforts.

Although Thorstein brought his new bride to Vinland in the early eleventh century, the period of conquest brought only men to the New World. This was especially true of the Spanish, who readily intermarried with the natives. By the beginning of the seventeenth century, this situation was changing. Permanent, progressive colonies must be established upon homes, and homes demanded women capable of founding and maintaining them.

To the conditions favoring colonization by the English already mentioned, there was still another which would prove equal to, if not actually greater in importance than the

others combined. The 1500's had been a century of religious turmoil in that country. The break with the Catholic Church had been a decisive move, which not only encouraged greater exercise of choice in religious matters, but also a burning desire for greater civil liberty as well.

RELIGIOUS CONSIDERATIONS

Although the Anglican Communion had become the Church of England, many men and women demanded the right to separate from it and to worship according to the dictates of their own consciences. Thus there were soon a number of Christian denominations struggling to form and maintain churches that would be separate from the *established* church. Such *dissenters* were subjected to many restrictions and to no small amount of outright persecution.

Also there were considerable numbers who staunchly refused to forsake and abandon loyalty and obedience to the Roman Catholic faith, which had been largely supplanted.

As a consequence, there were, between the growing Calvinist groups and the large Catholic remnant, a host of men and women quite willing to risk life in a New World where hoped-for freedom might extend to public worship.

Out of these and kindred situations, much of Colonial America came into being. And, spurred by the desire for individual freedom and relief from the rivalries which were transplanted in some measure from Europe to this country, the colonies would, almost from their founding, begin to reach out for means of self-government.

England's First Attempts at Settlement

HE first attempt at colonization by the English was made by Sir Walter Ralegh—or, as he sometimes spelled his name, Raleigh. After being educated at Oxford, he served with great distinction in wars in the Netherlands and in Ireland. In 1579 he financed a voyage of exploration in America which was under the command of his half brother, Sir Humphrey Gilbert. But storms forced a return without any accomplishments.

In 1583 another venture was made, this time with a fleet of five small ships sailing from Plymouth. After an early mishap to one of them, the party finally arrived two months later in the harbor at St. John's, Newfoundland. Gilbert promptly took possession of that island in the name of the queen. Trouble fell upon them at that point. Mutiny took part of the ships' crews and one of the ships. Illness forced the return of a second ship bearing those who were sick and the remainder of the rebellious sailors. As the survivors swung to the south, a tempest sank a third ship, together with one hundred men. In a storm shortly afterward Sir Humphrey perished with a fourth vessel.

Although this disaster weighed heavily upon Ralegh, a new and more liberal patent from the queen gave him courage to equip a third party with two vessels in 1584. Taking a more southerly course, the ships arrived in Pamlico Sound off the coast of North Carolina. There they found friendly Indians, two of whom were persuaded to go to England when the vessels returned.

Having made contact with the coast, in what seemed a most favorable locality, the party was warmly received at home by Ralegh and also by the queen. Enthusiasm ran high again, and preparations were at once begun to send a group of colonists the following year. A start was made in April, 1585, with the hope that a longer period would be available before the ships would be forced to return. But much valuable time was lost on the way, while Grenville, who was in command, succeeded in plundering several Spanish ships. This was perhaps not the most fortunate prelude to what was hoped might be a peaceful colony.

In July they debarked on Roanoke Island, and began to explore the neighboring country. Grenville, through bad judgment, antagonized the Indians by burning one of their

JOHN WHITE RETURNS TO FIND THE FIRST VIRGINIA COLONY HE HELPED TO PLANT HAS UTTERLY DISAPPEARED

villages. Shortly afterward, he sailed home again, little realizing how disastrous his act could be. One Ralph Lane, left in charge, made matters worse by his continued brutal treatment of the natives. When provisions ran scarce, the Indians quite naturally refused to sell any food to the hungry settlers. They might all have died of starvation, had not Sir Francis Drake appeared with his fleet of ships and taken the thoroughly homesick and discouraged colonists back to England.

There was one fortunate happening in this return, however. With them they carried the potato, which became a staple vegetable in the homeland. Also they took tobacco,

which soon became so great a fad, and then a habit, throughout Europe that its culture was an important source of income to later colonists.

One misadventure after another had dogged Ralegh's attempts. But in April, 1587 another expedition of three ships and about 150 men and women set sail for the land of promise. John White, their leader, sought to emphasize peaceful pursuits among them, but apparently to little avail. They could not come to a satisfactory understanding with the Indians or among themselves.

White returned to England with the ships, hoping that he might soon rejoin them with more colonists and supplies. But the Spanish Armada described above was just then threatening the British Isles, and the homeland was in turmoil. It was not until three years had passed that Ralegh was able to send White back, with two shiploads of supplies. How, as he approached the new land, he must have wondered about those he had left behind him. Especially there was his daughter, Mrs. Eleanor Dare. She had given birth to a daughter soon after landing, the first white child of record born in North America. The proud grandfather had named her *Virginia Dare*. She would be a fast-growing girl by now.

A HEART-RENDING MOMENT

When the ships dropped anchor offshore, a boat was put down and headed for the beach. Caught in the breaking waves at the shore line, six sailors were drowned. It was not until the following afternoon that another group could be persuaded to attempt to land. By the time they came to the beach it was nearly dark. And as Mr. White walked up the sand, he could see lights moving among the trees. Hurrying forward to meet his family and friends, a rude awakening was in store for the anxious man. No one appeared to welcome him. Then suddenly the lights disappeared, and unbroken darkness settled down.

Although he and his companions shouted and even sang hymns and songs, there was no response. Stumbling about in the darkness, it was not until daylight returned that they found the spot where the leader had parted with the handful of colonists three years before. There were moccasin prints in the softer ground, but none of English boots. Finally upon a beech tree they found carved the letters C R O.

Then White remembered that before he left there was some talk among them of shifting over to the mainland. Farther on was a stockade, and here the full word CROATON. In a log dwelling, now in ruins, there were a few scattered bits of tools and rags,

pieces of metal, and lockers which had been buried, then dug up, and their contents scattered about. But not a single human being appeared.

White, finally convinced they had all been slaughtered, led this final attempt at settlement back to England. Still there was no definite evidence that such a fate had overtaken them. But what had become of the eighty-odd people left behind? That question has never been satisfactorily answered. There have been many attempts at explanation, but none have been verified. But even today you will find people in the southern mountain country, and in the Ozarks and Osage hills, who believe their ancestors came from Ralegh's *Lost Colony*.

Ralegh's funds, however, were at last exhausted. His rights in the coastal area, which had been named Virginia, were assigned to a group of London merchants. While they seem to have done a small amount of trading with the Indians there, no further attempts were made at colonization for nearly a generation.

AN OVERSEAS EMPIRE BEGINS TO TAKE SHAPE

But under Elizabeth, England had forged to the front. It was not so much the acts of the queen herself as the fact that she had done nothing to curb the enterprise of able men who were willing and anxious to act for themselves. Natural ambition, when allowed full play, can achieve much progress and enviable results. Englishmen were finding their small homeland too restricted, and were anxious to move out into the larger world. Soon pressures building up at home would encourage more and more to look hopefully toward other lands in which they might carve out new homes.

Elizabeth died in 1603, and James, king of Scotland, took the throne as James I of England. Feeling that he was born to reign, the new monarch did his best to recapture power which the good Queen Bess had treated with indifference. In attempting to bring some semblance of order out of religious chaos, he did succeed in giving his name to the King James Version of the Bible. But he also added much fuel to the fires of religious intolerance. This sore point, and that of heavy taxation, finally flamed up as civil war under his son and successor, Charles I.

Between these growing burdens at home, and, no doubt, in some measure because James would willingly have ruled an empire made up of colonies in the New World, a lively desire to colonize America again developed. But the attempts this time would be by groups and favorites of the king, rather than by leaders acting on their own.

TWO COLONIZATION COMPANIES ARE SET UP

Two companies were set up, the London Company to operate in the area which had interested Ralegh, and the Plymouth Company, with a patent covering lands farther to the north. The grant of the former reached from Cape Fear to the Rappahannock River, and was known as *South Virginia*. That of the Plymouth group reached from near the mouth of the Hudson River to the easterly point of Maine, and was called *North Virginia*. A space of about three degrees of latitude separated the two, and would be covered by later grants.

The London Company acted first, and in 1606 dispatched three ships and 143 settlers to their grant. The king, anxious to have a hand in the enterprise, had put them in charge of one of the six masters of his navy, Captain Christopher Newport. It was May, 1607, before they found anchorage in a tidewater stream, promptly named the James in honor of the monarch. It flowed out through a broad, promising valley, so a fort was erected, rude log houses laid up, and the little settlement became Jamestown.

EARLY DAYS AT JAMESTOWN

But although it was destined to be the first permanent colony, its early years were not too fortunate. Dissatisfaction with conditions at home was by no means all that was necessary to making a thoroughgoing colonist. Also, even though these people sought greater freedom, they had to gain experience in using it. They had to learn that with the right to enjoy it there are certain definite responsibilities which must be assumed to gain its fullest benefits.

Perhaps, too, there was a little too much planning on the part of the managers of the company back home. There was too much hope of establishing a Utopia—a place of complete perfection—on the one hand, plus a greedy emphasis on quick profits on the other. These conditions appear to be the basis of much of their difficulties. Many English grains and other plants brought over did not thrive in this new land. Neither did the attempted cultivation of tropical fruits, and other ill-advised schemes. Also the settlers could not seem to realize that the Indians were human enough to resent being deprived of their lands, or being shot at on every small provocation.

But more than these, or the mosquitoes that swarmed over the settlement in the warmer months and sapped strength by the malaria they carried, there was yet another

61

cause. Basically this community was at first *communistic*. By that it is meant that what each raised or produced was turned into a common, or community, storehouse. Then his needs were supplied from the common store.

In practice, such a scheme is always a snare and a delusion. It sounds very noble

They began to acquire an immunity to malaria—or *summer sickness,* as they called it. But it was not until each freeman among them was allowed to own property in his *own* name, and to profit by the fruits of his *own* labors, that any real progress was made.

Then inventiveness began to show forth, as in the case of John Rolfe. Ralegh's curi-

COLONISTS LANDING AT JAMESTOWN

and fine to say, "Let everyone produce as he is able, and share as he has need." It was far from a new idea in 1607, and had been disproved many, many times in man's already long experience upon this earth. It makes life a bed of roses for the lazy—at least for a time. And it puts a heavy penalty on those willing and anxious to work. Then, after such a scheme has been carried on for but a short time, the willing grow discouraged at carrying the lazy upon their shoulders. They begin to lay down their double burdens, and soon all come to hard times and much grief.

These first Virginians quickly learned to deal more successfully with the red men.

osity, tobacco, had by this time grown so popular in Europe as to be in great demand. The colonists tried raising it, only to have it spoil during the long voyage home. Rolfe, sensing the profits that could be made, set to work and discovered a means of properly drying and curing the leaves. With a cash crop which could be safely delivered to expanding markets, greater prosperity was at once assured.

This same John Rolfe did his colony another lasting good by marrying the daughter of the chief of the local tribe. Her name was Pocahontas. She may have saved the life of Captain John Smith, but it was to the enterprising Rolfe that she was wed. She was converted to Christianity, baptized, and later went to England to live, where she was accepted as a great lady. The better relations between the colonists and their Indian neighbors provided the period of peace needed to let the colony get a firm start and begin to expand.

THE NEED FOR HOMEMAKERS

Another grave fault in the earliest days of this colony was the absence of the feminine touch. This the London Company soon remedied by sending over a shipload of marriageable women. Their passage was paid for by the settlers whom they married, and the homes they were able to found made for permanence.

In the year 1619 there occurred an incident that was to develop a condition which, more than two hundred years later, threatened to cast the United States of America onto the rocks of disaster. There had been Negro slaves in the party organized by Cortes to plunder Mexico in 1518–19. Ten years later the Portuguese were doing a thriving business kidnaping natives along the coast of Africa and shipping them to be sold as slaves in the Islands and South American ports. Either one of their ships dropped at Jamestown, or some of the English privateers were not above trading in human beings, for twenty were set down in the twelve-year-old colony. And while it is believed that these Negroes were later freed, the pattern of slavery had been established in this country. It fell to the lot of the British Navy, founded by these early privateers, to stamp out slave trading over the ocean two hundred years later. In this country this same issue was a principal cause of one of the bloodiest civil wars the world has ever known.

Another weakness from which this colony and others which would follow it suffered stemmed from the organization which fostered it. The London Company was made up of men of wealth, who purchased shares in it, and thus must accept the risk as well as any profit which the venture might make. While it is true that the shareholders did form a self-governing body under the Crown, this privilege did *not* extend to the colonists themselves. They had no voice in their own affairs; but were at the disposition for good, or for ill, of the owners of stock, far away over thousands of miles of ocean in the homeland.

At first, perhaps, they were too busy in the unequal struggle to raise sufficient food to care very much. Then, after the first few years of living out of a common storehouse, when their individual efforts came to count for more, their interest began to liven. Finally, with the right to own property and to profit by its use and improvement, the need was forced upon them for governing themselves.

GOVERNORS CREATE FRICTION

Some of the governors sent to administer colonies in this country proved to be most unfortunate choices. Incapable of being *leaders,* they covered their lack of ability by attempting to be petty rulers. The result was a bad clash between men seeking security under freedom, and despots who fear progress and change. The American Revolution which dates from the early 1770's actually had its beginnings in this very first colony.

Slowly the needs of its inhabitants were made sufficiently clear back in the homeland so that the London Company revised its charter to include self-government. Patterned somewhat after the early House of

63

Commons, two freemen from each locality were chosen to sit with the governor and his council. They were the representatives of their neighbors, were to be consulted about, and to express the common will in regard to the affairs of the colony. Thus in 1619 the first popular assembly was set up in America —the *House of Burgesses,* in the colony of Virginia.

Conditions in England were then very unsettled. The Thirty Years' War raging on the Continent tempered the relations between king and Parliament. The roundly hated James, wedded to complete belief in the divine right of kings, did his best to limit the power of the people. He repeatedly said, "The king is from God, and law is from the king." And in attempting to live up to this attitude, he envied the rights given the settlers in Virginia.

THRONE ATTEMPTS TO RESTRICT COLONIAL RIGHTS

In a move in 1623 to prevent their gaining further liberties, he withdrew the charter and abolished the London Company. Virginia was henceforth to be a *royal province.* It would be ruled by royal governors, together with a small council chosen by the throne.

The House of Burgesses stoutly resisted this new arrangement. James died in 1625, and to pacify them his son, Charles I, restored their favorite governor, Sir George Yardley. Although he died two years later, succeeding governors were reasonable men, and for some years the colony prospered.

Despite its faltering steps at the beginning, the colony had enjoyed a vigorous growth. By 1644, twenty-seven years after settlement, its numbers had risen to more than twenty thousand. Using Jamestown as

the base, plantations had been pushed out over the James peninsula itself and across the bordering streams into other tidewater sections. There had been trouble at the outset with the Indians, followed by a long period of freedom from serious threats from the natives.

TROUBLE WITH THE INDIANS

Then, as more and more of their land was taken over, the neighboring tribes joined hands and fell upon the outlying settlements, and three hundred colonists were slain. The reaction was swift and decisive. The savages were badly beaten, and in making peace were forced to give up large tracts of land and withdrawn from all neighborhoods opened up by the colonists.

However, conditions in England were .equally alarming. A civil war, long brewing, had broken out. In this *Puritan Revolution,* Charles would eventually be dethroned, and the government taken over as a Commonwealth and Protectorate by Oliver Cromwell. But the Virginians, by and large, continued loyal to the throne and the royal house, rather than to Cromwell and his followers. When the king was deposed and beheaded, they recognized his son as the lawful sovereign, and were probably the last English group to submit to the new Puritan authority.

This attitude so displeased Cromwell when he became *Lord Protector* that he sent a fleet of warships in 1652 to persuade the colony. Allegiance was reluctantly accorded him; but eight years later the Commonwealth ceased, and Charles II ascended the throne of the restored monarchy. In remembrance of the loyalty shown him and his father, he established the province as an independent member of the empire. Virginia thus assumed the status of a dominion, and is still spoken of as the *Old Dominion State*.

Sir William Berkeley, whom Charles II appointed royal governor, proved to be reactionary, bigoted and tyrannical. Restrictions imposed upon trade by the British government and increased taxation bore down heavily upon the people. Still the province continued to grow. By 1670 there were forty thousand inhabitants, including about two thousand slaves, and some eighty ships were required to handle its profitable tobacco trade.

Representative government, however, was being repressed. And in 1673 the king turned over the province to the Earl of Arlington and to Lord Culpeper. The colonists, fearing for such rights as were still left to them, protested violently. But their protest was ignored. The immediate effect was the formation of two strongly opposed groups.

One, loyal to the king—the royalist faction —joined with the governor. The other consisted of those who felt their freedom being torn from them, or who saw the possibility of civil strife ruining the prosperity which was widely enjoyed.

Tension mounted over a period of two years in which there were times when revolt against the despotic government seemed certain. Then the Indians struck again from the north. A force of five hundred armed men quickly gathered and were ready to march, when the governor ordered them to disband. The cry at once went up that this unscrupulous man was more interested in the profitable trade in beaver hides with the savages than in the lives and safety of the settlers. Naturally this imprudent act of Berkeley's made the red men that much bolder.

When Nathaniel Bacon, a leading planter, and some of his friends asked permission to

POCAHONTAS SAVES THE LIFE OF CAPTAIN SMITH

65

arm for their protection, they were promptly and curtly refused. In this act they found a definite challenge. If men were to have and enjoy freedom, they must when necessary be prepared to fight for it. Bacon stepped to the front and assured his neighbors that he was willing to lead them against the savages whether the governor consented or not. When one of his own plantations was raided and he called for volunteers, the response was overwhelming. The aroused colonists formally chose him as their leader, and he paid the governor the compliment of asking that he be properly commissioned.

THE BACON REVOLUTION

When this was refused, Bacon waited no longer, but set out in pursuit of the Indians. Berkeley again showed poor judgment. At the head of a troop of cavalry, he started after what he considered to be a band of rebels. But his rash act touched off sufficient hatred so that the lower portion of the province flared into revolt also. By the time he had returned to Jamestown, the insurgents were organized and ready for him with many demands. The situation was so critical that he had no choice but to grant their requests.

Bacon attacked the Indians with such vigor that further threats from them seemed remote. Returning home with his volunteer troops, he promptly disbanded them. When shortly afterward he was elected to the House of Burgesses, he was named commander-in-chief of the colonial militia. But once again Berkeley refused to sign the necessary commission. It took an armed body of the enraged colonists to persuade the obstinate man to change his mind and also to redress other wrongs.

When the Indian outrages unexpectedly sprang up anew, Bacon called the militia to duty and marched against them a second time. The governor then completely lost his head. He proclaimed Bacon a traitor, tried to rally a number of the royalists to his support, even promising their slaves freedom and plunder for aid in stamping out what he termed a rebel uprising. To make himself secure until he could build up strength, Berkeley had fled Jamestown and took refuge across the York River in Gloucester County to the north.

When word reached Bacon, he knew that this intemperate act of the governor had actually brought about an unwanted revolution. Thoroughly peaceable and with no thought of seeking power or advantage for himself, the leader called other important men to meet with him to decide what was best for their common good. In this he set the pattern for what must ever be the *American Way* of meeting crises.

BURNING OF JAMESTOWN

They came together at the Middle Plantations, now Williamsburg. Willingly they pledged support to Bacon in his efforts to subdue the Indians and also in preventing, if possible, the threatened civil war. Among this group was a man named John Washington, whose great-grandson would one day make the family name illustrious in another period of revolution. Or, was this later struggle to come just a continuation of the rebellion now being joined?

Another who took part was William Drummond, first governor of North Carolina. He proposed that the flight of Berkeley from Jamestown was an abdication, a surrender of the government. When this was agreed to, a call was sent out to elect an assembly which would provide a new government. These were indeed revolutionary acts.

FOLLOWERS OF NATHANIEL BACON PROTEST TO LORD BERKELEY

Whether a peaceful settlement might have been possible, we cannot tell. For shortly after this critical moment a fleet of fifteen armed ships arrived and removed the governor and his followers to Jamestown. Once again Bacon was proclaimed a traitor. He was then just returning from a third sally against the Indians. Between these latter and the perfidy of the king's governor, there was no security. A time for settlement had arrived; and Bacon and his followers marched upon Jamestown.

As these forces approached, Berkeley took refuge on the anchored men-of-war. Knowing that the original settlement could continue to afford a place of refuge and a base of operations for the royalists, the so-called rebels decided to burn the town. It had many fine homes; but Drummond, who owned one of the finest, set it afire with his own hand. Such determination, such willingness to make great sacrifices in behalf of

freedom, deserves to be remembered always. Jamestown was burned to the ground. Other towns, in other colonies, would suffer a similar fate one hundred years later.

Berkeley's followers then began to desert him in great numbers. Rallying to Bacon's leadership, the united colonists set up an insistent demand to drive the governor from the province. Most unfortunately, at this decisive moment the able Bacon was struck down by a violent fever, of which he quickly died, in October, 1676. With victory apparently within their grasp, the colonists' cause soon fell to ashes, as had their first settlement. There seems to have been no one capable of taking this able man's place. Twenty-two of the ring leaders, including Drummond, were hanged. Others who were condemned either died in prison or were fortunate enough to escape.

But it was no triumph for Berkeley, who was censured by the king and removed from

67

his post. Neither did this provoked insurrection, which took place in the years 1675 and 1676, make the full impression which it should have upon the British government. That body continued through another century to fail to measure the full determination of those who had chosen America so they might achieve the freedom which is man's God-given right. Although the American Revolution was three generations in getting into full swing, it had a definite beginning as the torches set fire to Jamestown, the first permanent English settlement on this continent. Virginia had great vitality and appeal, nonetheless. When it joined the other colonies in 1788 "to form a more perfect union," it had more than three-quarters of a million people, and was thus the most populous among the original thirteen.

But let us turn back now and review other early English attempts at colonization to the north along the Atlantic coast.

The Settlement of New England

AMES I not only fell heir to a century of religious chaos in England, but he managed to greatly intensify the bitterness between the three major factions in this huge controversy. Henry VIII had broken relations with the Pope and established the Church of England, but marked differences of opinion had developed among its followers. Many felt that ceremonies and practices which had been taken over in but slightly altered form from Roman Catholic belief and ritual should be modified further, or completely removed. Ministers and their congregations who did not wish to conform to the newly established service were spoken of as *Nonconformists*. And since they took the attitude that they were purifying church services, they were scornfully termed *Puritans*. Although this group wished to remain within the Church of England and change its form, it eventually did break away.

Others were so heartily dissatisfied that they parted entirely, and were thus called *Independents,* or *Separatists*. They set up their own church groups and worshiped apart. At least they did so far as possible, for they were bitterly persecuted, even during the reign of Elizabeth. When there seemed hope of little relief under Elizabeth's successor, James, at least one group fled to Holland, where religious liberty was extended to all. They later became known as the *Pilgrims,* and after the first party left in 1608, others continued to follow them, until there was a considerable number gathered at Leyden, under the direction of their chief elder, William Brewster. Sober, industrious, upright, and godly, they quickly won the admiration of their Dutch neighbors.

While there was welcome relief from persecution, they were among people who had different customs and who spoke a different language. What they hoped for was a *New England*, and quite naturally they began to think of founding one in the lands across the Atlantic. During twelve years the subject was discussed, weighed, and prayed over. Finally it appeared to be the will of God that they form a colony on these faraway shores.

The charter of the Plymouth Company had never been put to use, and in 1620 it was reorganized as the Council of Plymouth. It was to be the vehicle under which a colony in *North Virginia* would be attempted. The joint-stock company set up involved both

(*Continued on page 76*)

69

FOUNDING OF THE MARYLAND COLONY
Emanuel Leutze
MARYLAND HISTORICAL SOCIETY, BALTIMORE

Cecil Calvert, Lord Baltimore, dispatched about three hundred servants and laborers, together with twenty *gentlemen,* to found his colony in the New World. After three months on the wintry Atlantic, they sighted Point Comfort on February 24, 1634. Continuing up the James River, they called first at Jamestown, where they received but an indifferent welcome. After a brief stay, they explored the western coast of Chesapeake Bay, and on March 25 went ashore on an island some thirty miles above the mouth of the Potomac. Here a mass was said at an altar set beneath a huge cross, and the *Litanies of the Sacred Cross* were repeated. The Indians looked on during this service with awe and wonderment.

Leonard Calvert, who was in command, took the wise course and made a treaty of peace with the natives. Here we see it being solemnized before the altar and the cross, a most fitting spot. It was nine years before the Indians gave trouble, and it was then outlying tribes, stirred up by unprincipled adventurers who wished to see the Maryland colony obliterated.

THE BAPTISM OF POCAHONTAS
John Gadsby Chapman
THE UNITED STATES CAPITOL, WASHINGTON

This artist was a Virginian, born at Alexandria in 1808. Little is known of his early life except that he studied in Italy. He worked for a time in New York in the 1830's, lived again in Italy, and then had a studio in the nation's capital where the painting *Marriage of Pocahontas,* now in the Rotunda of the Capitol, was done.

This handsome, intelligent Indian princess, daughter of the powerful Powhatan, was born in 1595. When she was seventeen, she was kidnapped, and held as a hostage for the return of Jamestown settlers taken prisoner by her father's braves. It was perhaps then that she fell in love with John Rolfe, one of the ablest men of the colony. By his persuasion, she accepted Christianity, and was baptized in 1613. The following year they were married.

The artist, true to the classic spirit still prevailing in his time, makes the church a well appointed and commodious structure. By early records, the columns seen would have been unpeeled pine log posts, the pews of fragrant, but very rough-hewn cedar, the pulpit and communion table more carefully made of black walnut, and the dusky convert would have stood before a font "hewn hollow like a canoe." At the ceremony she was given the name of *Rebecca.*

In the year 1616 she and her husband sailed for England, where she was feted by royalty as the daughter of an American *king.* She died at Gravesend, England, in 1617, leaving a son, named Thomas. In later years he, too, settled in Virginia, where several prominent families proudly trace their ancestry to this union.

ABOVE, **THE PILGRIMS GOING TO CHURC**

PAGE ONE, TOP

FOUNDING OF THE MARYLAND COLONY

Maryland Historical Society

PAGE ONE, BELOW

THE BAPTISM OF POCAHONTAS

J. G. Chapman, Capitol, Washington

G. H. Boughton, New York Historical Society

NEXT PAGE, TOP
DE SOTO DISCOVERS THE MISSISSIPPI
W. H. Powell, U.S. Capitol, Washington

NEXT PAGE, BELOW
LANDING OF ROGER WILLIAMS
Alonzo Chappel, R. I. School of Design

PILGRIMS GOING TO CHURCH

George H. Boughton

NEW YORK HISTORICAL SOCIETY

This popular picture has been an aid to several generations of children and adults in visualizing the early days in America. Its artist was English born, but was brought to this country when but three years old, and thus grew up in its traditions. His specialty was landscapes, and the Plymouth colony called forth several of his better known works, such as, *The Return of the Mayflower, On the March with Miles Standish, Pilgrim Exiles*, and another laid in the Bay Colony, *Puritan Thanksgiving*.

The party goes to worship under armed escort. The minister, in the skull cap and robe, carrying his Bible, is John Robinson, and with him his good wife. Tradition would have it that the serene maid in white hood and yellow cloak is none other than Priscilla, while the apprehensive but good looking young man at the very rear is John Alden. Miles Standish could at this moment have been on an expedition.

DISCOVERY OF THE MISSISSIPPI BY DE SOTO

William Henry Powell

THE UNITED STATES CAPITOL, WASHINGTON

This artist, born in Ohio in 1824, has two of his major works in the national capitol, the other being his conception of the *Battle of Lake Erie*. He is also well known for his *Landing of the Pilgrims*. It is interesting to know that in this scene of De Soto's party at the banks of the Mississippi, Powell drafted people working about the capitol to pose for the different characters.

THE LANDING OF ROGER WILLIAMS

Alonzo Chappel

MUSEUM OF ART, RHODE ISLAND SCHOOL OF DESIGN, PROVIDENCE

But little is known of this artist, who seems to have been born in this country about 1820. The scene which he portrays, however, lives today in a phrase used in the name of many places and firms in and about Providence.

Roger Williams, banished from the Bay Colony because of religious beliefs, settled first in what is now East Providence. Much to his discomfort, he found the land there belonged to Plymouth. Moving on down the Seekonk River, he sought a favorable spot beyond the jurisdiction of Massachusetts authorities. On the west shore was a rock on which stood an Indian who called out, "What cheer, Netop (friend)?" Tradition has it that Williams landed at this spot, the first place in which he set foot in the new colony, later called *Rhode Island and Providence Plantations*. Finding the natives friendly, he then moved on around the point, where he found a fine spring, and established a settlement soon to be sought out by many who wished to be free of the religious bigotry in the colonies to the north.

75

THE PILGRIMS GOING TO CHURCH

the Pilgrims and certain London merchants. As many of the former as were able put up varying sums of money. The remainder bound themselves to work out the cost of their passage. Any profits realized were to accumulate for a period of seven years, when a proportionate settlement was to be made.

From the congregation at Leyden, two men were chosen to wait upon King James, to obtain a guarantee of full religious liberty. While the sovereign very suavely refused any written agreement, he did promise that they would not be molested as long as there was no breach of the peace upon their part in their new homes. Feeling that any such assurance coming from James was largely

worthless, they nevertheless had to be content and take the risk of its being kept.

At last the long negotiations were completed, and the younger and more able were chosen to go as colonists. Two ships had been purchased to transport them. But the smaller was so unseaworthy that it could not sail. Finally more than one hundred hopeful settlers were crowded onto the tiny *Mayflower,* and it set out from Plymouth, England, in September, 1620, which was rather late in the year for sailings to found colonies in those days.

There were two terrifying and uncomfortable months at sea, during which many of the settlers and most of the mutinous crew

wished to turn back. But at long last, on November 9, they came in sight of a low, curving, sandy arm of the mainland, known even then as Cape Cod. European fishermen during perhaps as much as two hundred years had most likely been drawing their nets along its beaches.

These Pilgrims had suffered much for many years and had learned that each must not only do his best individually, but also work for the common good. And so that, with God's aid, they might each acquit themselves as men and women, and still live together peaceably and effectively as children of the Heavenly Father, they drew up the historic compact whose text is given on the following page, and which we would do well to read carefully.

By this instrument these hardy souls de-termined to make their own rules for living together. They would stand upon their own two feet first, and then join hands for the good of all. They did not look to the king or to a royal charter for rights, but to God, whom they felt intended every man to be free to choose and act in his own behalf. Thus in compacting as they did, they helped pave the sure path to the *American Way of Life*.

John Carver was chosen to be their first governor; and Miles Standish, having had some military experience, was selected as captain. Although small in stature, he was large in courage and good sense. At the head of an armed party, he went ashore to explore the bleak coast. It was a full month before a suitable location for a settlement was found back on the mainland. There, on what was then December 11, but which to-

77 ક્રે

day would be December 21, Standish and some of the men went ashore and began the construction of rude cabins and a common storehouse. It was two weeks later before there was sufficient shelter so the balance of the settlers could leave the ship.

Previous visitors to these shores had tried to kidnap some of the Indians, so at first the natives carefully avoided the white men. And distrust was great enough in the other direction to warrant a high palisade about the tiny group of houses. The weather was already bitter cold, and the first winter proved a most wretched period.

THE MAYFLOWER COMPACT

In the name of God, Amen. We whose names are here underwritten, the loyal subjects of our dread sovereign, King James, by the grace of God, of Great Britain, France, and Ireland, King, Defender of the Faith, etc., having undertaken, for the glory of God, and advancement of the Christian faith, and honour of our king and country, a voyage to plant the first colony in the northern parts of Virginia, do, by these presents, solemnly and mutually, in the presence of God and of one another, covenant and combine ourselves together into a civil body politic for our better ordering and preservation, and in furtherance of the ends aforesaid; and by virtue hereof to enact, constitute, and frame just and equal laws, ordinances, acts, constitutions, and offices, from time to time as shall be thought most meet and convenient for the general good of the colony; unto which we promise all due submission and obedience. In witness whereof we have hereunto subscribed our names at Cape Cod, the 11th of November, in the year of the reign of our sovereign lord, King James, of England, France, and Ireland, the eighteenth, and of Scotland the fifty-fourth, Anno Domini 1620.

By the time spring returned, at least half of the colonists were dead. But those who remained were still fully determined to carry on. The Indians, now less distrustful, showed them how to plant corn, where and how to fish and hunt. By the fall of that year, 1621, conditions had improved sufficiently to warrant a festival in which to give thanks to God

READING THE FIRST THANKSGIVING PROCLAMATION

for His providence and care. Thus, after the crops and winter stores had been gathered, our first Thanksgiving Day was held. The governor issued a proclamation, read aloud by the town crier, or bellman, and setting the pattern for the annual proclamations issued today by the President and the governors of the states.

The Council back in England, anxious for profits on its venture, was not quite so careful in its choice of colonists sent during the next few years. Soon a group of sixty men arrived and planted a settlement at Weymouth, on the lower shore of Massachusetts Bay, about twenty-five miles to the north and west. Less industrious than the Pilgrims, they attempted to plunder the Indians and thus opened up hostilities which lasted over many years and cost many lives.

While some trade in lumber and in furs developed, the Plymouth colony cannot be said to have thrived, as did Jamestown with its tobacco culture. Neither did it grow rapidly; for after its first seventy years it embraced only about seven thousand people. Being a strict religious brotherhood, it did not appeal to the highly adventurous and had neither time for nor patience with the lazy or the vicious.

James, as we have already seen, was succeeded by his son Charles I in 1625, and mounting tensions in England were coming to a crisis. In 1629 he chartered the Massachusetts Bay Company. Unlike the London Company which had settled Jamestown with men loyal to the Crown and to the Church of England, this new company was made up principally of nonconformists, or *Puritans*. And it was also somewhat unlike the Plymouth group, which was made up of Independents, or Separatists. The London Company, too, remained in England and governed the Virginia colony from the mother country. This new company was quite in contrast, for its members came to America and operated there. The king had presumed this newest enterprise to be largely a trading venture, and had thus yielded all jurisdiction to the company.

Authority was vested in a governor, a deputy, and eighteen assistants called *magistrates,* elected each year by the members of the company. All freemen were to meet no less than four times annually to pass any acts needed to govern the colony.

BAY COLONY SETTLEMENTS

There had been some casual attempts made in this area at other settlements, such as a fishing colony that failed to materialize on Cape Ann, at the present site of Gloucester. And probably there were others at points beside Weymouth. But it was in 1630 that the Bay Company sent over more than one thousand men, women, and children. They embraced some three hundred families and were under the leadership of the courtly lawyer, John Winthrop, who had given up much to take part in this pioneering venture.

Here was a colony launched with bright prospects and the hope of permanence. The colonists arrived first at Salem. But a small settlement already there was not sufficient to their needs, and soon they spread down into what became Charlestown, Roxbury, Cambridge, Watertown, and Dorchester. Late in 1630 a few removed to what the Indians called *Shawmut,* or place of many springs. From the three hills on the small peninsula, it was first called *Trimountain.* But since many of these colonists had come from a certain market town in Lincolnshire, the settlement was promptly renamed *Boston* in its honor. To a considerable degree the history of this city is the history of New England.

Despite a slow beginning at Plymouth and meager achievements at some other points, the Bay Colonies seemed destined to prosper. Close to fine fishing grounds, with excellent highly needed timber in the back country and with access to fine furs, there was the basis of ample trade. Glowing letters from the first settlers encouraged many to follow after them. These newcomers were land-hungry, and the country back from tidewater began to fill in with settlements. There was prosperity to be won, work and thrift were strongly encouraged, and great accomplishments, although hard-won, were achieved.

Separation of the colonial government from England had decided advantages. But at the outset it led to excesses. While most of these people had come here to purify the forms of the Church of England, they rapidly lost touch with worship there and in its place formed self-governing *Congregational* churches in each community. The right to vote was restricted to membership in this church. Church and state were again tied together, and this situation was filled with explosive forces, soon to be touched off.

MOVEMENT TO THE INTERIOR

In a comparatively short time settlements had thrust well back into the interior toward the hill country. Distances which take but an hour or two over today's roads then consumed two or three days, sometimes even more, over the rugged early trails. Thus the gathering of all colonists at one place to enact common laws, as called for in the Charter, became too great a burden. The result was an assembly, to which the various communities sent selected men to act in the interest of all. These delegates provided, with the Burgesses of Virginia, our pattern of representative government.

For the most part the administration of the Bay Colony was a remarkable success. By the time of the death of its first governor, John Winthrop, in 1649, it was to all purposes an independent commonwealth. But in the matter of religious liberties which its settlers had sought in America, the administration at the outset was not such as to promote harmony. A Puritan pattern of form and belief of the most rigid type was soon established. Any who differed with it were subjected to persecutions similar to those that had brought them to these shores. Religious fanaticism had actually been transported, rather than left behind. While the results might have been most unfortunate, there was room in which to expand and re-

lieve the resulting pressures, and the results were quite the contrary.

This is typified in the experience of the very devout clergyman, Roger Williams. He staunchly believed that neither the government in England nor that set up by the Bay Colony had the right to tell him what he should believe, or how he should worship. And when colonial authorities attempted to restrain him, he became very outspoken. The result was a warning of banishment from the colony, a sobering threat in those days.

However, Williams soon found he was by no means alone in his feelings. Moving first from Boston to Salem, he here touched upon the point where man is most vulnerable—his pocketbook. He claimed that no one had a right to acquire land for his use until after it had been purchased from its original own-

NOTICE OF BANISHMENT READ TO ROGER WILLIAMS

81

ers, in this case the Indians. When this reasoning was put in writing in the form of a pamphlet, the authorities soon lost patience and the order of banishment was issued in 1635.

At first refusing to obey, friends finally prevailed upon him to seek out the Indians in the Narragansett Bay country, about forty miles southwest of the Plymouth colony. Making his way overland alone and on foot, he found the lodge of the powerful chief Massasoit. Here he was welcomed, and a considerable tract of land was given him. Joined by a few others in 1636, he founded a settlement at the head of the long bay, which he named *Providence,* as a token of God's goodness.

Two years later Ann Hutchinson, banished under similar circumstances from Boston, founded another settlement at the mouth of the bay, on Rhode Island. Thus began the colony of Rhode Island, and Providence Plantations, chartered by Charles II in 1663. Just as Massachusetts had become the stronghold of the Puritan Congregationalists, Rhode Island became a refuge for Baptist colonists. By 1790 68,000 people had crowded into our smallest state so far as area is concerned.

Many of the Puritan colonists came from rural England. They had been either *yeomen,* or small farmers highly skilled in tilling the soil, or they were *freemen,* who had not long since been serfs and had had no opportunity to acquire land of their own. Both groups were thus land-hungry; but they found the soil along the seaboard for the most part thin and very stony. In hope of finding better, deeper soil for gardens and fields, they pressed to the west in search of bottom land to open up and cultivate.

Vigilance in religious matters eased very slowly, and another preacher, Thomas Hooker, who had headed a church at Cambridge, led a dissatisfied band of followers to the broad Connecticut Valley and then down that stream to found Hartford, and nearby Windsor and Wethersfield in 1636. This was the beginning of the Connecticut colony.

Two years later a group direct from England established a settlement at the mouth of a small river flowing into Long Island Sound, which was soon named New Haven. Milford, Saybrook, and other towns quickly sprang up along the nearby shore.

Other restless groups from the Bay Colony moved up into the Merrimac Valley, and on north into the wilderness rich in timber and furs, topped by the snow-clad White Mountains. There was a sufficient inducement to settlement in this area so that another royal province, New Hampshire, was chartered in 1679.

Even the recently settled town of Hartford began within three years to move the local court for "enlargement of their accommodations." A committee was appointed to survey and report on what was considered a suitable area in a valley over the hills some nine miles to the west. The section was first known as Tunxis Sepus, which meant the bend of the little river. And upon the committee's favorable recommendation, a *plantation* appears to have been established there about the year 1640. A few years later its name was changed to *Farmington.*

While it would be difficult to choose any early town and call it typical of the many that found their start from Massachusetts to Georgia in the first half of the seventeenth century, Farmington might be a most interesting place in which to sample the manner of life in Colonial times. It was a small village and thus closer to what the greater portion of our ancestors first knew as a home in America.

Life in Colonial America

NE of the first considerations facing any new settlement was relations with the Indians. The tribes varied in numbers, in power, and also in their attitude toward these white men who pushed in among them. A pattern of peaceable arrangements had already been made in the founding of the three towns in the Connecticut Valley. The Tunxis Indians, inhabiting the area in which Farmington was to grow, were a small tribe, and a treaty, probably verbal at first, was entered into with them.

By it, the nearby lands were divided between the red men and the first settlers. It was ten years later before a written document was drawn up, in the nature of a deed, and described as: "A discovery in writing of such agreements as were made by the magistrates with the Indians of Tunxis Sepus concerning the lands and such things in reference thereto as tend to settle peace in a way to truth and righteousness betwixt the English and them."

Interesting indeed is the provision which it made that the settlers were to plow up certain land for the Indians, who were also allowed to cut wood upon it. This was a distinct attempt at co-operation and mutual well-being. Fishing, fowling, and hunting were to be enjoyed by English and Indians alike. The rights of the Indians were to be fully protected, and provision was made for them to profit by a lucrative trade in corn and furs. This deed remained in force for twenty-three years; and was then altered to the satisfaction of the Indians and renewed in 1673. This second writing was signed by twenty-one of the native males and by five of their squaws. It appears that, in at least some of the tribes, rights of inheritance passed through the mother, rather than down the father's side of the family.

As a consequence, peaceful relations continued as long as any members of the Tunxis tribe remained in the area. Those unfortunate incidents which did occur seem to have been at the hands of Indians not native to that locality. A considerable number accepted Christianity, and provision was made for a gallery over the entrance of an early meetinghouse to accommodate them at services. The remnants of the tribe left to join the Stockbridge Indians in Massachusetts at about the time of the Revolutionary War. They later joined with the Oneidas in New York State, with whom they were removed to Wisconsin in 1831.

83 &

A number of them were educated at the expense of the Colony during the early 1700's; and in 1733 the Rev. Samuel Whitman reported to the governor of the province as follows: "I have leisure only to inform your Honour that of the nine Indian lads that were kept at school last winter, three can read well in a testament, three currently in the psalter, and three are in their primers. Testaments and psalters are provided for those that read in them. Three of ye Indian lads are entered in writing, and one begins to write a legible hand."

At another time those being schooled were taught by a member of their own race. He had attended Wheelock's Indian Charity School in the eastern part of the province, and was later ordained a minister at the famous Indian Mission School at Hanover, New Hampshire, which later became Dartmouth College.

Thus relations with the Indians in this community were more than satisfactory, as they were in almost all other localities where these native peoples were justly treated.

The first white men in the town came via Hartford from Boston, Newton, and Roxbury in Massachusetts Bay colony. In the original plot, fifteen miles square, there was much meadowland as well as timbered hillsides to be divided among the eighty-four "proprietors." But the principal settlement was made on gently rolling land that rose from the east bank of the small river.

The Indians willingly helped these first-comers plant their corn. At about the time the land was ready, the shad, seeking spawning grounds, swarmed up the nearby river in great quantities. There the savages gathered by a gentle rapids with openwork wicker baskets and scooped out quantities of the struggling fish. The largest and best were cleaned, baked, and eaten. Certain others were dropped into holes in the fields, to fertilize the hills of corn planted above them. The remainder were left to decompose and made a compost to further stimulate the growing crops.

In laying out the town, a main street was run parallel with the river and back a considerable distance from it. To each settler was allotted a strip of land about two hundred feet wide, and in this instance running from the river at the west up to the foot of the mountain behind the town at the east. This was at first sufficient. But as numbers and flocks increased, the meadowland beyond the river was put to use. This latter was fenced in part, but for several miles was protected by a deep ditch, traces of which can be found even today. Its purpose was to keep the cattle from wandering into the forested areas; and it was also apparently intended as a barrier against wolves, who do not climb any obstruction readily.

ALL WERE FARMERS

At first all were farmers, and their minister was the biggest farmer of them all, for he was allotted a double portion of land. Records of the estate of the second pastor of this flock, who died in 1697, show him to have been well off by the standards of that day. His farm was valued at the goodly sum of £440, or about $2,200. He had many horses, cattle, and sheep, wheat, rye, barley, and corn in granaries, and an abundance of farm equipment. Only one other man of the town of that time had amassed a greater inventory of this world's goods.

The farm work was done principally by oxen, each farmer having at least one yoke, and some two. Horses, although about twice as numerous as the oxen, were used principally for riding, but also to some degree in

WHEN TREATIES WITH THE INDIANS WERE FRANK, OPEN AND KEPT LITTLE TROUBLE ENSUED

land cultivation, for many items of harness are listed, in addition to saddles.

There was a cow or two to each homestead, but herds of as many as six were rare. Sheep in quantities were pastured, for their wool was the chief item in the warm clothing needed for the long, cold New England winters. Fifteen seems to have been about the average per family. There were many pigs, and always a few hives of bees. Chickens, ducks, geese, or turkeys are seldom mentioned.

Carts and plows were at first homemade, although wheels and iron parts were probably brought in from the outside for some years. And the number and assortment of needed tools was large. Even those required to raise, break, and process flax into fibers

to be spun into linen thread were in themselves considerable.

And flax was the principal crop, or at least the one most commonly planted, for it provided the bulk of the lighter clothing worn in the warmer months. Next in importance was wheat, extensively raised at first. But since it soon exhausted the land, rye came to take its place. Whenever there was doubt, a mixture of the two, known as *mislen,* was sown in the hope one or the other would grow. The other chief grain crop was corn, although much barley was at first planted and also some oats. Both were malted for use in making beer. The early colonists, unused in England to springs and other natural water supply free from contamination, consumed much beer. But as apple trees came into

85 ৡৡ

bearing, this brewed drink gave place to cider. Ten barrels of the latter were valued in 1680 at four pounds, or about two dollars per barrel.

LIFE IN THOSE DAYS

The potato seems to have been unknown, or at least very little used in the early years in the northern colonies, although peas and beans were common. But the sowing of seed, and especially corn, was attended by one great inconvenience—the birds. The Indians met this threat by camping their older children in the midst of a patch and having them scare away the preying birds in the early morning.

There were blackbirds, perhaps known to us today as grackles, and also the crow. They were so much of a menace that the town set a bounty on them in 1694 of twopence for crows, and a shilling a dozen for the smaller blackbirds. Thirteen years later Hartford ordained that each citizen should either kill a dozen blackbirds each year or pay a fine of a shilling. But if he did kill more than the dozen quota, he was entitled to a penny each for the extra birds.

Some wolves did get beyond the ditch calculated to turn them back; and wolf pits, properly baited, were dug in which to capture them to obtain a sizable bounty posted for their destruction. There were a few bears, but they seem to have made little trouble. But the creature that struck real terror into the hearts of lonely travelers was the so-called *lion,* whose "roar," often referred to fearfully in early records, seems to indicate the catamount. There were also wildcats, and some of them were large enough to be recorded in bounty records as panthers.

Slowly, as must have happened in scores of other towns, there was something in the nature of division of labor. Spinning and weaving were common home industries. But those that either had previous training, or were particularly deft with the loom, began to appear as *weavers.* Several such suddenly find mention in old records. Then came a *tailor.* And in connection with this latter hangs a tale.

Wardrobes began to blossom out, and homespuns gave place to clothes of finer texture and greater variety. In the effects of one respectable farmer toward the end of the 1600's are listed four coats, one of kersey, one of serge, and a lined cape-coat, together with an *old* coat, probably homespun. To go with them were breeches of drugget, serge, and leather, with waistcoats of blue, and of serge.

He had a hat of castor beaver, several fringed muslin neckcloths, two pair of gloves, and two "speckled" shirts. But others in the community wore broadcloth, with silver buttons to match silver buckles on shoes, and even damask vests. The age of luxury was setting in, and was generally deplored.

LUXURY FROWNED UPON

In fact, one young gentleman of Farmington who removed to a neighboring town, together with his luxurious wardrobe, was "presented by the grand jury to the court at Northampton, March 26, 1676, for wearing of silk, and that in a flaunting manner, and others for long hair and other extravagances contrary to honest and sober order and demeanor, not becoming a wilderness state, at least the profession of Christianity and religion." There seem to have been *fast* dressers in those days, but whether this should all be laid to the charge of the first lowly tailor is debatable.

Then there were *cordwainers,* or shoe-makers, tanners, and coopers. It was fairly well on in the century before there is mention of a mason and bricklayer. Although they were not specifically so mentioned, some of the tool inventories would make it appear that certain men, perhaps primarily farmers, did specialize in woodworking and carpentry. Finally there was a blacksmith, one Samuel Gridley, who also became one of the first local shopkeepers and merchants. The progress of his business venture is perhaps typical of many such enterprises.

The first inventory taken at the time he set up his store consisted of some thirty-eight animal skins from a variety of creatures, together with certain iron implements of his own forging. But bulking large in this meager assortment was a supply of some 2,300 four-penny nails, 2,350 six-penny, 1,900 eight-penny, and 200 hob nails. These were precious enough in those days to be sold by the piece, and not by the pound. Larger timbering was joined by wooden pegs, so that no spikes were then forged by hand.

MONEY WAS VERY SCARCE

Cash was scarce, and much trade was carried on by exchange of goods, or barter, and even Indian bead wampum passed as a sort of money. Both at the forge and by dealing with others, his stock slowly grew until in time it embraced virtually everything a farmer needed, including even his powder, flints, and lead balls. But the farmer's wife could also find calicos, crepes, laces, ribbons, combs, fans, pins, knitting needles, pewter spoons and dishes for the table, and pots for the pantry.

Several such general stores grew up, some of them running more to hardware and tools,

and others to soft goods. One might look in vain for any who handled, say, musical instruments, for but three types were permitted under the Blue Laws—the drum, bell, and jew's-harp.

A DRUMMER SUMMONED PEOPLE TO GATHERINGS

The first two were used to summon gatherings, and the town employed a regular drummer for this purpose, paying him in one year 13 shillings 4 pence for drumming. These two devices, and also the conch shell, were used to call people to the meeting-house.

Although there were frequent intensive searches made for metals, the particular area in which the town was located was not productive. Copper-bearing veins were discovered short distances west and north, and both these deposits were worked, the latter by prisoners during the Revolutionary War. Much of the iron was at first bog iron, dredged from the bottoms of ponds which, in a strip across the northern portion of our country, were long ago carved out by the glaciers.

Houses in all New England were for the most part of wood, for at first there was a fine stand of virgin pine over much of this whole section. There were no log cabins in any of these first settlements, nor were there any in the early settlements from Virginia south. The settlers there were from England, and began to build with types of construction with which they had been familiar at home. The log house appears to have been brought into the Delaware River country by the Swedes and Finns, who adapted the log wall construction common in their countries to conditions in this new land. It proved ideal for pioneering and spread from that section into other areas as the press toward western lands began in the 1700's.

There may have been temporary shelters of branches while timbers, planking, and sheathing boards were whipsawed from felled logs. Shingles and shakes were readily split from the straight-grained wood. And some bricks were brought over from England as ship ballast, but local red clay was soon put to use, both for bricks, and for rough pottery. Along the coast, lime produced from seashells was used for mortar, and, stone being plentiful, many masonry homes and barns were built, especially in the Pennsylvania colony. Earliest roofs may have been thatched, but wooden shingles, and then slate, which occurred in many places, became the common roofing material. But the log cabin, with its bark roof, developed later.

Grist mills seem to have been fairly late in arriving in Farmington; and even after the Revolutionary War, the town found it necessary to encourage the erection of a second mill, so that the people need not be "obliged to carry their grain five or six miles to get it ground."

A TYPICAL WELL-TO-DO HOME AND ITS EQUIPMENT

Unfortunately, there is little recorded that gives a detailed picture of life within one of the town's many fine homes during the first sixty or seventy years. But we can visit that of Mr. Gridley, the first merchant of consequence there, who was mentioned above. It will be on that day in 1712 when three appraisers went, following his death, to list his estate. The family now consisted of his widow, and three daughters, aged eighteen, four, and four months. A man in those days surely had use for several *sons*.

The house was entered from the front through a porch and into a main hall, on one side of which was the kitchen, then an all-purpose room, and on the other what was then termed the *parlor*. But let us pause a moment on the porch, which is hardly what we would expect it to be.

There, not necessarily in disorder but consuming much space, were harnesses, saddles, and the pillion and pillion cloth on which the good wife rode behind her husband to church and elsewhere. There was a chest and tools, cart ropes, a steel trap, and various and sundry other things. The porch was thus more a storehouse than an outdoor sitting room.

Placed about the center hall was a group of furniture, including a wainscot, or fine oaken chest; a table; one great and four smaller chairs; three cushions, and a pillow. Here, too, was a rack to hold the necessary arms without which no household was in those days complete. These involved a gun, pike, bayonet, rapier, two-edged sword, and a cutlass.

No doubt the hall abutted the central chimney, and thus had a substantial fireplace, for much fireplace gear is listed. There were two *heaters,* which very likely may have been foot-warmers into which live coals could be put for use in the unheated meetinghouse. There were two smoothing irons, probably *tailors' gooses,* used in pressing clothes or in blocking newly woven cloth. By the side of the fireplace was a spit for revolving roasting meat, a pair of bellows to puff up a lazy fire, and two trammel hooks, by which kettles could be hung at different heights above the hot coals.

Here also was a large supply of pots and kettles of various sizes, and of both brass and iron. There was a large array of pewter tankards, plates, basins, beakers, porringers, cups, measurers, and even bottles. Other utensils were of wood, of earthenware, and a few pieces of china.

These halls customarily had a shallow cupboard, called the rum closet, let into one wall. This spiritous liquor was the polite beverage of the day, and even the minister making his pastoral calls would have been served a glass before departing. It was perhaps in this cupboard that the supply of medicines listed was stored, such, in this case, as Matthew's pills, blistering salve, and a number of drugs considered household necessities nearly three hundred years ago.

It was in this common room that the master of the house kept his balance scales, equal to weighing even the few coins which passed through his hands. Convenient perhaps to the great chair where he could sit holding a burning taper in a light candlestick in one hand, and his book in the other, were his spectacles. Close by would be such volumes as he chose to delve into. A list of those found in this home include some of the best sellers of that day.

MR. GRIDLEY'S LIBRARY

There was an old Bible, a psalmbook, and one bearing the main title KOMETOPPAH, and explained as "a Discourse Concerning Comets; wherein the Nature of Blazing Stars is Enquired into: With an Historical Account of all the Comets which have appeared from the Beginning of the World unto the present Year, 1683," . . . By Increase Mather. There was also: *Time and the End of Time,* being two discourses by the Rev. John Fox of Woburn, Mass., 1701; *Zion in Distress, or the Groans of the Protestant Church,* printed in 1683; *Spiritual Almanack, The Unpardonable Sin, Divine Providence Opened, Man's Chief End to Glorifie God,*

or Some Brief Sermon-Notes on 1 Cor. 10:31—By the Rev. Mr. John Bailey, Sometime Preacher and Prisoner of Christ at Limerick in Ireland, and now Pastor to the Church of Christ in Watertown, New England, 1689. Three other texts were *Commentary on Faith, How to Walk With God,* and *The Wonders of the Invisible World.* This latter was a remarkable book on witchcraft in Salem and elsewhere and the ordinary devices of the devil, by the doughty Puritan cleric, the Rev. Cotton Mather. There was also an answer to it, titled *More Wonders of the Invisible World* by Robert Calef, which was publicly burned by order of Dr. Increase Mather, early president of Harvard College, in the college yard. Mr. Gridley was evidently broad-minded enough to pursue both sides of a controversial subject.

We find also *A Warning to Prepare for Death,* a New Testament, and *A Book of Numbers,* which may have been either an arithmetic, or possibly a commentary on the Old Testament book of that name. And the list closes with "a law book," and "several pieces of books." This last entry would seem to indicate that the library had been much read and used, and that even the fragments of books that had broken down in their bindings had been carefully preserved. A book was still something of a rarity, and very much a heritage, in those days.

THE HOME'S KITCHEN

In the kitchen, most likely on the sunny side of the house, we would, of course, find another very large fireplace, with firedogs and other fittings, for here many of the enterprises of living in the home centered. There would also be a great table, a master's and several smaller chairs, and a sizable storage chest. There would, of course, be an assortment of tubs, pails, kettles, and baskets. But on the unusual side, as far as we are concerned today, would be the loom, the great spinning wheel, and the two smaller flax wheels, the yarn reel, and the stores of yarn, and unspun wool linters, tow, and flax.

SPINNING AND WEAVING

The eighteen-year-old daughter might even now be busy spinning, weaving, and storing up supplies of linen in anticipation of a hoped-for wedding day. Spinning bees, at which a group of ladies gathered for common employment and much conversation, were not infrequent. And there were occasional spinning matches, which might last from sunup until late evening, by which time one or more of the contestants would drop over exhausted.

Together with food preparation, and such a seasonal task as we today call "canning," or the necessary soap making, syrup boiling, and a score of endeavors no longer household duties, the kitchen was a hive of activity from the crack of dawn until well toward bedtime.

Some activities extended to the lean-to which set against the width of the back of the house. It was really the dairy, and would have in a prominent place the churn, the butter tubs, and the cheese press, together with pans, paddles, and the other tools and implements needed to process milk. But of especial interest would be the hour-glass, by the sand of which the affairs of the household were timed. In many yards there would be a sundial; but in this town down to the year 1700 there is record of but one watch and one clock, both in the possession of the minister.

Let us now move into the room at the other side of the front of the house, called the parlor. A surprise may be in store for us here, for it contained a fine bedstead, with a feather bed and a large supply of linens and coverlets. This central piece of furniture was a high poster, had a tenter cover at the post tops, and a muslin curtain with ruffled valance above about the three sides. One bedded in strict privacy in those days, and fresh air was less a consideration than warmth.

To defrost sheets on a crisp winter's night, there was a long-handled brass warming pan. Hot coals from the fire on the hearth were dropped into it, the cover closed down, and then it was passed between the sheets to take away the chill.

The bed often stood well above the floor and had to be mounted into by a portable step. This was so that a truckle, or trundle, bed for the small children could be stored beneath it. On the day of the appraisers' visit, this latter stood in the kitchen. Possibly the good widow now shared the space lately occupied by her husband with the two younger daughters, and the low children's bed was not in nightly use.

There were also three chests for the bedding and for clothing, a trunk, a round table, a great and three small chairs, a jointed stool, and five cushions. There was a standing cupboard, with a *carpet,* or embroidered cloth, to cover it; while a rug, perhaps woven from strips of rag, covered the floor. On a wall peg, convenient to the bed, hung a holster and the owner's pair of pistols, loaded and ready to prime, cock, and fire. No doubt the holster had a small horn of powder and pouch of wadding attached. The parlor was actually the master bedroom.

On the second floor, above the chief rooms below, were three bedrooms. One of these, the *parlor chamber,* was probably better furnished than the other two. In it was

THE VILLAGE BLACKSMITH WAS AN IMPORTANT MAN, AND HIS SHOP NOT INFREQUENTLY A GATHERING PLACE

a bed, with silk grass pillow and two leather pillows weighing ten pounds each. In one of these upper rooms there were storage chests for yarn and other household effects. But space had also been found for the storage of no less than fifty bushels of wheat and eighty of rye, kept within the house itself and under the guardianship of the cat, as in the nursery rhyme which goes:

> This is the cat
> That killed the rat
> That ate the malt
> That lay in the house that Jack built.

And so that the cat might earn its keep, we find in other chambers and in the third-floor attic further stores of wheat, barley, corn, and peas in baskets, bags, and barrels. It might seem like Joseph making provision for the seven years' famine in Egypt; but it was common practice in prudent, practical, thrifty New England of another day.

Yes, there was a cellar under the entire house. And in it you would have found bar-rels, casks, tubs, and jars filled with salted pork, beer, hops, cider, oatmeal, boiled cider applesauce, and other food supplies. There would no doubt have been salted fish, and on the floor in a cool, dampish corner, under a mat of salt and hay, there might, of all things, have been a small supply of oysters still in the shells, brought up from the Sound to Hartford.

This home of Mr. Gridley, the blacksmith, merchant, and farmer, was somewhat better than average, and in a town in which staid ways, hard work, and peaceful arrangements with the original inhabitants had brought a large measure of prosperity, even from its very early days.

91

The scope of the gentleman's library, with its strong emphasis upon religious matters, indicates that the day-to-day interests bore heavily in the direction of salvation. Each New England town was held in restraint by its secular laws and also by its Ecclesiastical Society. Where the province of one left off and the other began was often hard to determine.

There was freedom, more of it in many, many respects than we know today. This is usually true in sparsely settled communities. It is only as men press together tightly in great numbers that freedoms tend to melt away. But there were restrictions as well, as in that case of the young man who wore silk garments "in a flaunting manner," and paid a substantial fine for his independence. It might seem that being one's *brother's keeper* was in some cases overdone.

Life was real and life was earnest, but despite the Blue Laws it was by no means sterile or too narrowly restrained. The home was an active place, and the center of one's life. Here there were tasks enough to go around, and from six or seven years onward there was work parceled out to each member. One came to know not only one's own duties but those of every other member of the family as well. The home was thus the great schooling ground.

But in such a community, where everyone was known, and known rather intimately, there was need for a considerable measure of co-operation and neighborly understanding. It was necessary to place a certain amount of *authority* in others' hands for the common good. But wherever there were common problems, whether it was a new barn or house being raised or a barn or a house afire, the townspeople attacked it as a group.

Men and women, for the most part, were capable of standing solidly on their own two feet and took great pride in being able to do so. But they were ever ready and willing to extend a helping hand when one was needed, and the pride in their community closely paralleled that which they took in their own homes and possessions.

Such attitudes of mind extended up and down the Atlantic coast, settled in such considerable numbers by people out of very similar backgrounds, who had come here for like purposes. And having looked briefly at a typical example of the circumstances under which they lived in pre-Revolutionary days, let us leave New England and see what was taking place elsewhere.

Attempts to Find Religious Freedom

E MAY RECALL that the religious ferment in England resulted in three principal groups. There were the loyal followers of the newly established Church of England, members of whom had taken part in settling Virginia. Then there were the nonconformists and independent groups which broke away, many of them taking refuge in New England, including Rhode Island, New Hampshire, and Connecticut. The third was the Roman Catholics, who also had suffered grievous persecution and even banishment, and who had been in and out of favor depending on who was at the moment occupying the throne.

Charles I, although nominally a Protestant, had married a French Catholic princess, and both he and his father, James I, had shown their willingness to enter into agreements with both France and Spain to protect Catholic subjects in England. One of the leaders among them was the very fine Catholic gentleman, Sir George Calvert. He had entered Parliament in 1609, was knighted in 1617, and two years later King James appointed him Secretary of State.

In 1625, however, he declared himself a Catholic, resigned from his high office, was created Baron of Baltimore in the Irish peerage and retired to his estates in Ireland. As early as 1621 he had helped plant a small colony in Newfoundland as a place of refuge for those of his faith. This he visited in person in 1627, and again in 1629. Disappointed in the climate of that bleak island, he attempted to settle in Virginia. But this move was so strongly disputed by that colony that he returned to England.

He stood high in the new king's favor, and Charles granted him a charter. But since it conflicted with that of the Virginians, a second was drawn covering an area just to the north. This Lord Baltimore named *Maryland* in honor of Charles's wife Henrietta Maria. But before this document was signed, the *proprietor* died.

His son Cecelius (Cecil) Calvert succeeded to his father's title and to the proprietary patent. It was a most liberal grant, in that it left the Lords Baltimore free to govern the great tract and its colonists, quite as they chose, and without having to account to the throne. Not only were political rights secured to all settlers, but there could be no discrimination for or against any religious sect or belief. In this respect, this newest colony was the most liberal in both political and religious views; and many Virginians and New Englanders migrated there soon after the colony was established early in 1634.

TOLERATION IN MARYLAND

Although the original purpose had been to prepare a refuge for persecuted Catholics, the practice of extreme tolerance, plus an invitation to persecuted Protestants, soon filled the colony with the latter. Then one of the struggles which was filling the mother country with hatred and civil war was translated to this enlightened settlement on Chesapeake Bay.

In 1649 the fanatical Puritan element had grown strong enough to pass an act which put distinct limitations upon the completely free spirit of toleration in which the settlement had been undertaken fifteen years before. Freedom of worship was now limited to those who professed belief in Jesus Christ. This, of course, denied rights to the Jews, who had suffered persecution for centuries in Europe; and also to a new faith developing on this continent, the Unitarians. Both groups were distinct minorities; and men had not learned, as they had need to before the United States could become a reality, that the rights of minority groups must be recognized and preserved.

However, the original intents of the Lords Baltimore to give men greater freedom were remembered and had their full impact upon the development of the American Constitution 150 years later. But other men, in other areas open to settlement, were also seeking freedom from restraint by narrow-minded neighbors.

Since Ralegh's several unfortunate attempts to plant a colony in the Pamlico Sound area in the previous century, the Carolinas had seen little activity. The London Company's charter had embraced the land as far south as Cape Fear. And while some of the more adventurous Virginians had tried to establish homes in the country to the south of the James River in the early part of the 1600's, for the most part what is now North Carolina had remained virgin wilderness.

In 1630 Charles I granted a huge strip, six degrees in width and lying below Virginia, to his attorney-general, Sir Robert Heath. But since this gentleman failed to fulfil some of its conditions, this grant was recalled. Certain Presbyterians wishing to get out of Jamestown moved down to the Chowan River section about 1653. A group wishing to be done with both the rigorous climate and religious intolerance of New England soon followed them.

Then in 1663 Charles II granted a group of eight noblemen a proprietary patent to this same six-degree strip. Like other grants, it reached from the Atlantic through to the Pacific Ocean. The name chosen for it was Carolina, a Latin form of the king's name.

At once the Virginia settlement near what is now Edenton on Albemarle Sound became important in the eyes of that colony. Governor Berkeley quickly extended his jurisdiction over it. The northern boundary of this new patent had been set on the 36th parallel, which ran through the center of the Sound. Hastily he set up a separate government, called the Albemarle County colony, and appointed the ill-fated William Drummond as its governor. He, with six associates and an assembly chosen from among the settlers, administered its affairs, subject, of course, to the approval of the proprietors in England.

**SLASH-TAPPING PINE TREES
IN THE EARLY DAYS IN CAROLINA**

New Englanders had tried to plant a colony to the south at the mouth of Cape Fear River, only to fail in the attempt. Then, in 1663, a group from the West Indies Islands took up a considerable tract in this same area and founded a settlement. They were joined the following year by several hundred from Europe. This new domain, known as the Clarendon County colony, doubtfully claimed jurisdiction from Cape Fear south to the Spanish lands on the St. Johns River in Florida.

The Society of Friends—or Quakers—were being sorely pressed in England and began migrating in considerable numbers. Many of them found their way into the Albemarle colony back from the upper coast and claimed by Virginia. To clear up this situation, the Carolina charter was amended in 1665 to take in another half degree to the north, or to the present bound-

ary of North Carolina. Thus Drummond, to die ten years later for his part in the Bacon Rebellion, is credited as the first governor of that colony.

The land along the coast tended to be poor, but lumber was plentiful and in great demand in the West Indies. Turpentine, too, found ready sale there and in Europe. Individuals began to open up this trade; but it was not until 1670 that the proprietors sent settlers direct from England. Three shiploads landed in that year on Beaufort Island. This first site proved impractical, and a move up the coast was made in 1680 to the present site of Charleston.

The proprietors had the most extravagant ambitions for their colony. One was to develop it into an American empire. The scheme was set forth in a plan known as the *Grand Model.* One of the proprietors, Sir Ashley Cooper, with the aid of the famous philosopher, John Locke, worked out the details. Today it seems quite absurd, especially since it was designed to extend titles and aristocratic distinction and control to America. When finally submitted to the settlers, they had the good sense to reject it almost to a man.

However unfitted this scheme was to the free society taking shape in no uncertain manner in this New World, we should not allow his part in it to cloud our opinions of John Locke. Perhaps no other man so dominated the thinking of those leaders who, a century later, were to found our country. He and the great English scientist, Sir Isaac Newton, in a large sense, established the groundwork on which our Constitution was built.

Although their grand model of an American empire came to nothing, the proprietors did their best to fill their Carolina colony with people. To help sell off land rapidly, they followed the lead of the Lords Baltimore and saw to it that Carolina enjoyed religious tolerance. This brought additional settlers from New England and from Virginia. It also attracted the thrifty, freedom-loving Dutch and the Protestant Huguenots from France. There were willing Presbyterians from Scotland and from Ireland, and Germans and Swiss as well. Probably the early influx of peoples into the Carolinas drew from a greater number of countries than any of the other early colonies.

But they were freedom-loving and made many difficulties for the proprietors when the latter attempted to levy burdensome taxes. Distances were still great, and to exercise better control the great Carolina grant was divided into North and South Carolina. Still there was friction between the proprietors and their colonists during much of the sixty-six years in which they held their

patent. The original group and their heirs had been cheated out of an American empire. Also their profits from the venture had been most unsatisfactory. By 1729 they were quite willing to turn the colonies over to George II, to remain a royal province until independence was declared.

But if the early settlers in Carolina had the good sense to discard ill-considered plans made at a distance for them, there was still another colony in which the proprietor's solid thinking, much of it done in the colony itself, gave it a substantial foundation on which to grow to greatness. He filled it with simple people dedicated to profound belief in freedom, but in freedom governed by constant application of the golden rule.

THE FRIENDS, OR QUAKERS

Religious dissention in England reached into all classes, from the highest to the lowest. William Brewster, leader of the Pilgrims, came from the landed gentry. John Winthrop of the Puritans was a wealthy lawyer of highest social rank. Lord Baltimore had been a favorite of James I, and then of his son, Charles I.

Now we meet another patrician, William Penn, son of one of England's famous admirals. While a scholar at Oxford, he joined the Society of Friends, founded by George Fox. His zeal in furthering this new religious movement resulted in his expulsion from the university. His father had no patience with such views and disowned him. There was fortunately a reconciliation before the father died, thus giving young Penn possession of a sizable fortune.

One item in his inheritance was a claim for some eighty thousand dollars due the admiral from the British government for services rendered. In lieu of payment in

AN EARLY QUAKER MEETING HOUSE

The term *meeting house* was used rather extensively in the other colonies as well. In early colonial times all gatherings were held in the places of worship, and public and religious affairs intermingled.

money, young Penn was given the grant of an extensive tract lying north of Maryland and west of the Delaware River. The area was at first named *New Wales*. But this did not seem appropriate, and Penn suggested *Sylvania*. The king, to honor his faithful admiral, insisted it be *Pennsylvania* or Penn's Woodland, and so it became. Penn's Quaker modesty was deeply shocked, for to one of Quaker views this name would smack of arch vanity. He did his best to have the *Penn* portion removed, but to no avail.

The charter was granted in March, 1681; and in May the proprietor sent his cousin, William Markham, to the colony as deputy governor. A *Company of Free Traders* had bought lands of Penn and, through their efforts, a considerable number of colonists

accompanied Markham. The great Quaker proprietor was thoroughly trusted in England and also on the Continent. He promised that it would be a place of refuge from religious intolerance, and thousands throughout Europe began to make preparations to go there.

With due deference to the fine spirit of the Calverts in settling Maryland, probably no colony launched in America had a more humane and Christian background than Penn's. He had faith in his fellow man rare in his own day. He did his best to do away with capital punishment, only to be overruled in the cases of murder and treason. Justice with him extended to all men, and especially the despised Indians. Whenever an Indian was to be tried in Penn's colony,

97

at least half the jurors must be Indians. But perhaps his chief contribution in civil matters was expressed in the colony's *law of arbitration,* by which all disputes—even those between nations—were to be decided by peaceful means and in a *meeting of minds.*

In 1682 Penn came himself on a visit, bringing about one hundred Quaker acquaintances. But an epidemic of smallpox struck down thirty of them while at sea. His ship touched first at New Castle, where a settlement of several thousand had already taken firm root, and was then within the bounds of his grant. The Swedes, whose early numbers in America were not very great, had been active in this area. They had a stone fort at Claymont, a mill at what later became Darby, and many trading cabins scattered along the Delaware River and the creeks emptying into it.

Penn's next stop was at Upland, now Chester. Here he was met by Markham; and in a Friends' meetinghouse already erected there a general assembly was held, and additional lands were allotted. Certain parcels were sold at fourpence (about eight cents) an acre, and were made subject to a yearly quit-rent of about twenty-five cents per hundred acres.

Then Penn continued upstream to Shackamaxon, now a part of Philadelphia, where he made a treaty with the Indians. He paid them their agreed price, plus many rich presents. He had already paid for this land by releasing the British government from the claims which he held against it. But the double price when considered in the light of the lasting peace which ensued in this colony, was indeed cheap. Great treasures in money and in human life might have been saved in other colonies by similarly fair treatment of the red men.

Penn had brought with him a surveyor named Thomas Holme. They skirted the western shore of the Delaware and finally selected a townsite at a narrow point between that larger stream and the Schuylkill [SKUL-kil] River. Here Holme proceeded to lay out Penn's *greene country towne*. For it, the proprietor chose the name *Philadelphia,* meaning brotherly love. By the middle of the next century it was the largest, finest, and most important city in America.

To the scattered Swedes and Dutch whom Penn found upon his land and the Quakers whom he induced to come here, there was added a steady stream of immigrants, notably German Protestants. Some of these latter remained in Philadelphia; but more of them pushed to the west and north and opened up the storied area known as the *Pennsylvania Dutch Country*.

Thrift was a key word; the colony rapidly filled with people, trade and crafts flourished, and it became a keystone community in the ever-increasing chain of colonies forming along the Atlantic seaboard.

The Delaware area separating Penn's grant from that of the Calverts in Maryland was made a separate colony in 1702. But both it and Pennsylvania remained under some control from the Penn family until independence was declared.

There are two stretches of the American coast for which we have not yet accounted. One lies between the Connecticut colonies about New Haven and runs south through what is now New York and New Jersey to Pennsylvania. The other is the Georgia area, for a time claimed by the Clarendon County colony, but in which little had taken place. Let us leave English activities in America for the moment and look over the efforts made by another European nation, a close neighbor of the English across the Channel.

Colonization of the Atlantic Seaboard
Is Completed

MPORTANT as were the efforts of England in colonizing North America, we must not overlook those of the Dutch. While they were not as fruitful in results, they did help keep the Spanish out of the northern continent during the 1500's when the English were heavily involved at home, and also during the early years of settlement.

By the beginning of the seventeenth century, Holland was the greatest maritime nation in the world. The brooms lashed to the mastheads of her many vessels were no idle boast. Her ships indeed *swept* the oceans of all the world. The men who owned and operated them cared little for glory, but much for profits. Trade was their very lifeblood. They sensed that it could be developed in America and they prepared to go after it there.

The Dutch East India Company was formed to exploit spice and other commercial products of the Far East. And although the English captain, Henry Hudson, had made at least two unsuccessful attempts to find a passage north of America for London merchants, the Dutch were willing to send him once again. Sailing in 1608 in the tiny

Half Moon, but with an excellent Dutch-English crew, he was once again turned back by polar ice. But swinging southward, he sighted the Maine coast the following July, touched at Cape Cod, went as far down as the mouth of the Chesapeake, and perhaps to the James River.

Learning of the settlement of Virginia, he moved north and into what is now New York habor. The broad waterway leading between a long, narrow island on the east and steep palisades to the west looked very much like an arm of the sea. Perhaps it led to the western ocean. He moved upstream, carefully testing the water for saltiness. Slowly the river began to narrow, and the water to freshen. But to be certain, he continued until he came to near where Albany now stands. Disappointed in his chief project, he still appreciated that he had pierced far into virgin country. So he at once took possession of it for the States-General of Holland.

In 1610 he made still a fourth attempt at a polar passage, and sailed into the great bay north of Canada which bears his name. Here a mutinous crew set him, his son, and seven others adrift in a small boat, and he and his companions perished. His ship, however, returned home. The Dutch felt that the country into which Hudson had penetrated deserved their attention, and in 1613 they built the first few rude structures on Manhattan Island at the mouth of the great river which was to be named for its discoverer. From this base, they began explorations along Long Island Sound and up the coast beyond Boston. The following year a charter was granted to a group of Amsterdam merchants giving them exclusive rights of trade in the area from 40° to 45° north, or from central New Jersey to the eastern point of Maine.

THE HUDSON RIVER VALLEY

Since this embraced all of New England, it was certain to bring trouble when the English were to move in this direction seven years later. But the Dutch pressed up the Hudson Valley and established another base, called Fort Orange, a short way below the present site of Albany. Then they turned west out through the Mohawk Valley, made a treaty with the Iroquois Indians, and opened up a rich trade in furs.

In the same year in which the Pilgrims were getting established in Plymouth, the Dutch West India Company was organized. It had powerful financial backing and received valuable aid from the Dutch government. During the next twelve years it scoured the Atlantic, and from bases in the West Indies Islands captured or sunk more than six hundred Spanish vessels. From these prizes, cargoes worth $150,000,000 today were seized. And again it should be pointed out that this activity largely prevented Spain from settling or molesting settlements in North America.

It was this new company that truly settled Manhattan Island in 1624 and purchased it from the Indians two years later. The first shipload of settlers, some thirty families, rapidly spread out. Some went into Connecticut, others onto Long Island, some down the Delaware to encounter the Swedes at points below where Philadelphia was to rise, and the remainder up the Hudson. The ship which had brought them took back a huge cargo of furs. This so pleased the directors of the Company that colonization was begun in real earnest.

The town on Manhattan Island, named New Amsterdam, grew slowly. To hold possession of the large area, it was necessary to move people out into the back country, for a firm grip on the Hudson Valley meant ready access to the interior. To encourage settlements there, large tracts were granted to wealthy men—called *patroons*—who agreed to pay the transportation of those willing to emigrate. They also had to provide seeds, tools, and assistance to such people so they might get a proper start in their new homes.

This development continued at a good pace through some forty years. The New Netherlands colony thrived, but it lay between growing English colonies and in the midst of what England now considered her *empire* on this new continent. The British claimed the entire Atlantic coast line, basing their claim upon Cabot's voyage in 1497. Also their Navy was increasing in size and power to the point where it was now in a position to threaten the Dutch. The latter, with long sea lanes to the other side of the world to safeguard, found it increasingly difficult to give the required protection to their colony in North America.

Finally, in 1664, war broke out between Holland and England. An English fleet seized some of the Dutch West Indies Islands. Another sailed into New Amster-

THE DUTCH PURCHASE MANHATTAN ISLAND

dam habor and demanded its surrender. Peter Stuyvesant, its governor, had no choice but to comply; and the Dutch attempt to open up a valuable trading area on the North American continent came to an end.

The Hudson was then called the *North River;* while the Delaware was the *South River.* The English King Charles had granted the territory lying between these streams to his brother, the Duke of York. And being anxious to increase both colonies and commerce, English emigration into the colony, promptly renamed *New York,* was heavily stimulated. The Dutch settlers, however, were not driven out, but became English subjects.

The Act of Uniformity, passed in England in 1662, had forced the clergy to conform to the Book of Common Prayer. Two thousand of them immediately resigned their position in protest. Then an even harsher act in 1664 made all who attended any religious meeting not held in accordance with the practices of the Church of England subject to deportation to some distant colony.

Such measures materially helped emigration to New York from the British Isles; and there were also many French Protestants—or Huguenots—soon to join them. Religious frictions perhaps more than any other one cause were responsible for peopling America in early Colonial times. Most of those who came here were seeking Freedom. And in finding and perfecting it, they provided us with our greatest heritage.

Most of the land taken from the Dutch, and granted by Charles to his royal brother, today lies within the state of New Jersey. There seems to have been little activity in any of this area before 1623, when a French sea captain sailed up the Delaware River and sought to claim territory in the name of his monarch. To counter this, the governor of the Dutch West India Company, then in possession, planted temporary settlements near the present site of Westville and nearby at Gloucester. But no permanent settlements were made at any point in this area for another forty years.

THE DUTCH SETTLEMENTS ARE CEDED TO THE ENGLISH

After the transfer to Britain took place, the southern portion of his grant was promptly turned over by the Duke of York to Lord Berkeley and Sir George Carteret, proprietors of North Carolina. And to honor the latter's brave defense of the Isle of Jersey some years before, it was called *New Jersey*. A liberal form of government was drawn up, with a governor and council and an assembly to be made up of elected representatives. To encourage immigration, every able-bodied man who accompanied the newly appointed governor to the province was to receive 150 acres of land, plus six months' provisions.

But only thirty persons were with Captain Philip Carteret, cousin of Sir George, when he arrived in 1664. In August of that year he made a picturesque entrance upon his domain at what is now Elizabeth, with a hoe thrown over his shoulder. He, too, aspired to be a planter among the settlers.

Two years later, in 1666, a group from Milford, in the Connecticut colony, purchased the present site of Newark and established a town. They were soon followed by others from New Haven, who settled in the bottom lands along the Passaic River. Because of the liberal attitude that prevailed, the colony had much to offer at the beginning and soon began to fill up.

But in 1670 a rent war broke out, which eventually ousted Philip Carteret as gov-

ernor. Then, in August, 1673, the sturdy Dutch recaptured New Netherlands and held it for more than a year, after which it again passed into English possession. Although the quit-rent question was solved, and the colonists enjoyed some measure of prosperity, Lord Berkeley, in disappointment at its progress, made over his interest to two English Quakers, thus dividing the province in 1676 into East and West Jersey. From then until it became a royal province in 1702, there was much involvement over ownership and authority. For a time it was attached to New York; but finally, in 1728, it was separated again and given its own government.

For the most part its government was very liberal. Consequently it attracted extensive immigration of Quakers and Puritans from England and from the other colonies and also considerable numbers of Scotch and Irish Presbyterians. Still it did not grow with near the rapidity that did Penn's colony to the south and west.

GEORGIA IS ESTABLISHED AS THE LAST COLONY

This leaves but one other primary colony to consider, that established under rather unusual conditions in what is now Georgia.

Below South Carolina there was a stretch of coast line running down to the Spanish settlements at St. Augustine which had seen little activity. The Spaniards had explored it during their first visits to the North American continent, but after several unfortunate expeditions they seem to have preferred to leave it in possession of the Indians. With continuing pressure to escape religious persecutions on the Continent, as well as in the British Isles, and considering its milder climate, it seems strange that it had been neglected by other Europeans. But there it

IN PRISON FOR DEBT

Debtors' prisons were not entirely limited to England. There were quite a few built in the colonies in the early days; and in a few of the states they have withstood the ravages of time, and are pointed out today as mementoes of another and more exacting age.

remained during the active seventeenth century, a wilderness buffer between English and Spanish colonies.

Although England probably granted a larger measure of freedom to its citizens in these times than any other of the major European powers, one can well question a form of government which managed to drive Protestants and Catholics alike out of the country in search of peace of mind and soul and even safety for one's very life. Also much doubt would center about such a law as that permitting one man to put another in prison,

and to keep him there until a debt was paid.

Thousands suffered confinement on this score. So great was their number that they had to be crowded into overflowing jails, there to live sometimes for years under the most horrible conditions. By the early 1700's, the situation had grown so bad that Parliament was forced to take action. Prime mover in the committee of investigation was Colonel James Edward Oglethorpe, a prominent British soldier and a volunteer in the war between Austria and the Turks.

After much thought upon his part, he worked out a plan to give many of these poor wretches an opportunity to make a new start in a New World. The government would like to colonize this buffer zone below South Carolina. And with this as a lever, he sought and obtained a grant of land stretch-

103 ଛଚ

ing south from the Savannah to the Alta-maha [AWL-tuh-muh-HAW] River in 1732. The proposed colony was named *Georgia* in honor of the current ruler, George I.

Naming a board of prominent noblemen and gentry as trustees, an appeal was made for financial aid. The response, tempered in part by charity, but perhaps no little by hope of quick profits, was tremendous. In fact, the scheme seems to have suffered largely because of its huge popularity. Because the area lay in about the latitude of the Mediterranean Sea, there was great hope of building up large trade in wine, olives, and raw silk. In the interest of freedom for all, slavery was forbidden. And to maintain sobriety, the sale of rum was prohibited, after its first unfortunate use to persuade the local Indians.

The first settlement was made at Savannah, the immigrants landing there, after a stop at Beaufort, on the first day of February in 1733. Later that same year Augusta was founded. Some who had financed their own passage did well enough; but the transported debtors were very much a disappointment. Other more effective colonists were then sought out, not only in the British Isles but from Europe, and sent over. Among those who came to the colony with Oglethorpe on his second trip in 1736, were the famous brothers, John and Charles Wesley, founders of Methodism, but then still attached to the Church of England. Charles was the governor's secretary; and John a missionary to the Indians.

Both the sale of rum and the ownership of slaves flourished in the neighboring South Carolina colony, and slave labor was well adapted to use on the plantations which now sprung up in Georgia. There was bootleg traffic in both for a time, and as the colony grew it became so thoroughly established that Parliament was finally compelled to rescind the acts of prohibition. Negroes were then openly brought in and put to work. Some silkworm cultivation thrived for a time; but the most profitable of early ventures was the growing of indigo, a shrub of the pea family from which a blue dye was prepared.

Islands along the coast were fortified, which activity brought on trouble with the Spanish. Backed up by military aid from England, and from the Indians with whom he had made strong ties, Oglethorpe invaded Florida in 1740. He reached the stout fortress at St. Augustine, but did not, even with troops from Virginia and the Carolinas, have sufficient men or artillery to take it.

Two years later, the Spanish came into Georgia in force. The province might have suffered heavily had not an English fleet appeared off St. Augustine, forcing the Spaniards to hurry back and aid in its defense. After this threat had been quelled, Georgia had a period of peace but hardly of prosperity. Too much planning, and perhaps too great an expenditure of funds from home, failed to stimulate effort and thrift. Twenty years after it was first settled there was not a single place large enough to be called a town, and at most but three small villages. The white population was then no more than two thousand.

In 1752 the original patent was surrendered by the defeated proprietors to the Crown. It continued as a royal province until the outbreak of the Revolution, now but a few years away. This shift of control seems to have given a new lease on life to the struggling colony, for by the time it was admitted into the Union in 1788 its population had swelled to more than eighty thousand.

Finding a Place in the Sun

E HAVE been watching the unfolding of a great drama—the peoples of Europe seeking refuge from oppression and for a better opportunity and greater freedom in a promising New World. During a period which lasted for more than one hundred years, we have seen the coastal area along the Atlantic seaboard fill in with people. Growing out of five or six major and many smaller efforts, thirteen separate colonies have been taking shape.

The greater part of this effort seems to have been expended by the English, and so it proved to be. The first careful numbering of people on this continent was not completed until the year 1790. But studies made of those living here about the time independence was gained show that fully six out of each ten residents were originally of English origin. The next largest group came from German stock, followed closely by the Scotch, and then by the Scotch-Irish. The Dutch, French, and Swedes combined represented only about five out of each one hundred. While there were a few from the south of Ireland, it was not until the next century that people from that section came in such great numbers.

Perhaps more varied than this classification by nationalities was that of customs and religious beliefs. In the 1600's there were several fairly clear-cut dialects spoken within England itself, not considering local tongues used in Scotland, Ireland, and Wales. There were similar situations on the Continent; and beyond speech, they embraced dress, skills, and other local characteristics. Many who made the long and perilous journey to America had perhaps never before been twenty-five miles from the place of their birth in their homeland.

Thus America could quite readily have been a replica of Europe, divided by nationality, customs, and beliefs. In a few sections national characteristics did predominate and continued to prevail. But this was a new land, and old ways—some of them centuries old—quickly began to break down and became *American Ways*. From the outset, America was a *melting pot*. People soon learned to be individuals. There was elbow-room over here. A new type of life demanded a new outlook. Intermarriage was much easier. The English language did become the one great common denominator. But other social ways were borrowed and

(*Continued on page 112*)

105

ACCUSED OF WITCHCRAFT

Douglas Volk

ROBERT SIMON COLLECTION, NEW YORK

Volk was born in Pittsfield, Mass., in 1856, and studied in Italy and France before becoming an instructor at the famous Cooper Institute in New York. Among well-known items from his brush is the *With Malice Toward None* portrait of Lincoln. While primarily a figure and portrait artist, he has dramatically captured the spirit of the times in Salem. In 1692 there was a violent outbreak of the medieval witchcraft superstition, during the summer of which year no less than nineteen persons were convicted and executed, charged with exercising witchcraft. This emotional eruption seems to have stemmed from the ardent preaching of the Mathers and other clergy. For a time no one was safe from accusation, even parents and their children charging one another.

TRIAL OF GEORGE JACOBS FOR WITCHCRAFT

Tompkins Harrison Matteson

ESSEX INSTITUTE, SALEM, MASSACHUSETTS

The witchcraft excesses began in the village of Danvers. Here several girls who had read and talked the subject at length started the avalanche by accusing certain friendless elderly people with bewitching them. From then on the mischief spread rapidly until prominent people, even including the wife of the governor, were the objects of totally unfounded charges. In this picture of one of the colony's prominent men on trial for his very life we catch the frenzied spirit into which Salem was drawn in that terrible summer of 1692. Witnesses and courtroom spectators often went into convulsions and allowed pent-up emotions to run riot.

But so intemperate did the whole business become that the people rebelled, and public sanity was restored. Matteson, who painted this graphic scene, was born in New York State in 1813, and is probably best known for his ever popular work, the *Spirit of '76*.

PURCHASE OF MANHATTAN ISLAND

Joseph Boggs Beale

IN THE COLLECTION OF MODERN ENTERPRISES

This Philadelphia artist was born in that city in 1841, and received his training there. By the time that he died at the age of 85, he had completed some 1700 paintings, many of them historical and religious. Since he averaged more than two paintings a month through his active years, they lack much in finish and technique; but are often direct and factual. In this scene he portrays the Dutch negotiating the purchase of Manhattan Island for a few gaudy trinkets. Beale here shows by the houses in the background that this transaction did not take place until the settlement was well under way. The traditional value of the merchandise traded to the Indians was 60 guilders, or about $24.12 for the 22-square-mile island. Three hundred years later the assessed value of this same real estate was in excess of seven billion dollars.

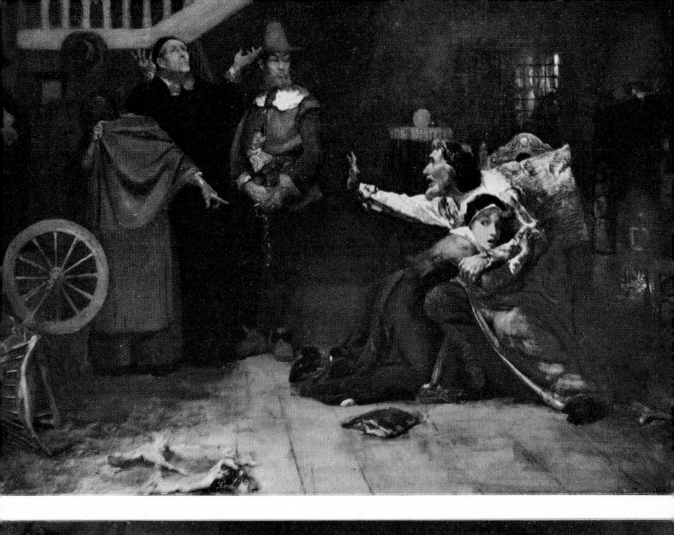

ABOVE, **PURCHASE OF MANHATTAN ISLAND**   Joseph Boggs Beale, Modern Enterprises

PENN'S TREATY WITH THE INDIANS
Benjamin West
PENNSYLVANIA ACADEMY OF FINE ARTS, PHILADELPHIA

Penn's "greene country towne" was in course of construction when he first arrived in the colony in 1682. The following year he entered into an enduring treaty of friendship with the local Indians. This was made under the branches of a spreading elm on the bank of the Delaware at Shackmaxon, a spot long famous as a meeting place for Indian councils.

This historic scene was done by one of the great masters of American painting, Benjamin West. Born in a house on what is now the campus of Swarthmore College, twenty miles west of the site of this picture, he was destined to spend much of his life in England. His great masterpiece depicting the death of Wolfe at Quebec revolutionized historical painting, for he was among the first to insist on clothing his subjects with the actual dress of their times.

THE CHARTER OAK
Charles DeWolf Brownell
CONNECTICUT HISTORICAL SOCIETY, HARTFORD

This artist, famous for his paintings of the beautiful Connecticut Valley, was born at Providence, R.I., in 1822. Beginning his studies in Hartford, he did not feel that they had been properly completed, but it was not until middle age that he went for a time to work in Europe. In this picture he sketches the historic *Charter Oak* which was standing in his student days, and is still recalled with affection in the *Nutmeg State*.

In 1686 James II of England appointed Sir Edmund Andros governor of all New England, with instruction to consolidate it into a single dominion. This required the recall of the separate charters, and threatened a distinct restriction of their liberties. In trying to seize that of Connecticut, he was kept waiting until after dark before it was produced and shown him by candlelight. Suddenly the candles were extinguished, and when relit, the charter had disappeared, to be hidden in a hollow in this oak until after Andros departed empty-handed for England.

THE *CONSTITUTION* AND THE *JAVA*
Carlton Theodore Chapman
NEW YORK HISTORICAL SOCIETY

This scene at sunset actually took place in December of 1812, when *Old Ironsides* roundly thrashed the *Java*. Chapman, a great painter of marines, historicals, and landscapes, has here shown the havoc which could be administered by accurate gunfire and superior navigation.

THE FIRST PRAYER IN CONGRESS
T H. Matteson
GOOD WILL DISTRIBUTORS, GASTONIA, N.C.

The original painting of this momentous incident although actively sought seems to have been destroyed, and has lived on as a now rather scarce engraving made from it. So pertinent was the subject portrayed to the spirit of this volume that an artist was specially commissioned to repaint the historic scene in full color. The identity of many of the characters in it can be readily recognized, and especially Washington with folded hands at the lower left.

adapted from the whole European background. This was America. It was different —and it was distinctly better in many ways. Early travelers, when they returned to their native lands, had to admit the fact, even if some of them did so reluctantly.

As we have seen, the various national groups were fairly well scattered through all of the colonies. While there were, as an example, a large percentage of Germans in Pennsylvania, they were not unknown elsewhere. The settlers migrated, too, within the colonies, even in early days. America by then was on the move and Americans are still a restless people.

COLONISTS' BACKGROUNDS

We had best be frank about it, however, and face the fact that not all colonists arriving here during the Colonial period came on anything like an equal basis. It has already been indicated that some were able to furnish their own passage money, and had perhaps enough in addition to buy land or set themselves up in trade. They were the more fortunate.

There were many who wished to come but who had to be financed. They borrowed for their needs, if they were lucky; but more often they indentured themselves to work out the cost of their transportation as bond servants. Upon arrival, they were *bought* from the bondholders, and might have to work as long as seven years to liquidate the obligation. To them, the price of freedom came somewhat higher.

But there were not a few who were forced to emigrate quite against their will. Yes, they were white people, some of them convicts who had run afoul of the law. Others were banished for political purposes, or family convenience. And there were many instances of men, women, and not infrequently children, being kidnaped and forced aboard ship, to be sold as bond servants upon arrival. This portion of the colonization picture is not at all attractive, but, nevertheless, we must remember that there was this seamy side.

THE SLAVE TRADE

Lower still in the scale was the kidnaping of defenseless Negroes in Africa. No, the Dutch did not start it. Slavery was as old, or older, than written history. But the Hollanders were doing a thriving business in this human traffic in early Colonial times; and the English, and then the Americans, began to find it lucrative. By 1790 there were seven hundred thousand Negro slaves, or about one to each four white people in the country. For most of them, eventual freedom was doubtful, for their servitude was almost without exception for life.

Here were the raw materials out of which colonies were to develop and a new nation was one day to be built.

Man started life upon this earth as a hunter. And that was the means of livelihood of the very first colonists. The woods, the streams, and the ocean had to yield much of their food in the earliest years people were here. But as quickly as possible they took the next step, to agriculture, and it remained the chief occupation until long after independence had been gained. Land could be purchased cheaply, or had for the taking. Thus fully nine out of every ten families farmed, either their own plots or as tenants of the wealthy landholders, such as the *patroons* in the Hudson Valley, or on the large plantations owned in Virginia and the South. Early settlements were for the most part near tidewater. But as families grew and multiplied, the tendency was to push back into the hill country and take up small holdings. Through all of the Colonial period the very great majority were either closely tied to or received their living or income directly from the soil.

TRADE DEVELOPS FURTHER

We have already visited in a typical village during this Colonial period. We have seen that trade developed slowly, and that earliest manufacturing centered in the home and expanded only as men began to specialize. The farmer convenient to a dependable water power set up a grist mill to grind grain, a whipsaw to cut timber, or a cider press. Or the shallow lake bottom on his place yielded bog iron, which he could hook up, smelt over a charcoal fire, and cast or forge into usable items. Mr. Gridley's father, Thomas, one of Farmington's early settlers, may have so started the "smithy" which the son built into a mercantile enterprise.

Freed to use their own energies to the fullest, and with wind, water, and other sources of power to be harnessed, the settlers set to work with such vengeance in the production of things to fill their own needs that it was not too long before they had items for export. Then British merchants at home became thoroughly alarmed. These enterprising colonists were ruining their trade.

While Ralegh's first colonists either perished or tossed in their lot with the Indians when supplies failed to arrive from England during three long years, men and women in the other colonies were soon virtually self-supporting as respects their necessities, and many of them included some of the amenities of life. Men put on their own and blessed with freedom, soon found their way toward greater abundance. At least, and for the first

time in some six thousand years of recorded history, there was never to be a major famine and widespread hunger in this new land. This in itself is one of mankind's greatest accomplishments.

There are few places in the eastern part of our country where anything faintly resembling the virgin stands of timber found by the early settlers can still be seen today. Fine, tall, straight-grained pines which then grew here made excellent timbers and planking. Bent-rooted tamaracks made stout, easily formed ship's bows. There were turpentine and pitch, hemp for cordage and caulking; and shipbuilding soon dotted the coast from Maine to the Virginia Capes. Not content to employ their boats merely in fishing or in intercolony trading, the more venturesome began to open up markets in the West Indies, and then in the ports of Europe. This developed not only a merchant class, but artisans trained in ship construction, and above all provided ships and sailors one day needed for an American Navy.

AMERICAN SHIPPING

The following is a summary of a report on ship clearances for the year 1730, from Franklin's *Gazette*. Some 161 vessels entered the Philadelphia port, mostly from the West Indies; while 171 cleared, chiefly for the West Indies and Madeira Island. New York did somewhat better, with 211 entering and 222 leaving that port. These, too, were largely in the West Indies trade. But Boston was indeed busy. No less than 533 ships entered that harbor, and 628 cleared for a far greater number of destinations than those of either Philadelphia or New York.

These were the three largest cities, Philadelphia having the greatest population. And after Boston, slightly ahead of New York, fourth place in general importance went to Charleston, South Carolina, while the fifth port was, surprisingly enough, Newport, Rhode Island. Norfolk, near the mouth of Chesapeake Bay, was of fair size and quite active, as was Baltimore, farther up the same bay. The smaller towns were, for the most part, very small and rather primitive. But many were on their way to becoming small but thriving centers before the Revolutionary War began.

In the smaller communities the magnet that drew and held the people together was above all else the local church. This, of course, tended to make the minister a powerful figure. Most of them were first of all farmers, and the maintenance of a farm was demanding enough in itself. But beyond that there would be two sermons, not of the shortest, to write each week. There would also be an address to be delivered on "lecture day," with an occasional election sermon. And there was much public work which fell to a minister's lot because of the position which he held. He was indeed a busy man.

TOLERATION INCREASES

For a time in the Bay Colony it seemed that the clergy might completely dominate colonial life. But religious toleration became sufficiently widespread by the early 1700's so that their control over daily affairs began to wane.

It was the clergy, however, that established the first schools and in some instances taught the gathered children. Massachusetts was hardly twenty years old when laws were passed making it compulsory for children and servants to learn to read the Bible. While similar stress was not put upon education outside of New England, schools for boys— and in some places these admitted girls—did

begin to appear elsewhere. Illiteracy, which was widespread even in Europe at the beginning of this century, began to decrease in the colonies. And the ability to read was a decided advantage when the time for decision came in the third quarter of the following century.

THE EARLIEST COLLEGES

The first colleges were established largely to train young men for the ministry. Such was the purpose of Harvard, founded as early as 1636, and of William and Mary, opened in 1693. Yale followed in 1718, and Princeton in 1746. Dartmouth, which had its beginning in 1769, was at first a mission to the Indians. Of the colleges and universities in existence today, at least twelve were under way before the colonies became an independent nation; and some thirteen more were formed by the end of the 1700's. For the most part they were organized by and long remained under firm control of certain religious faiths. The first exception to this strict religious background was probably the Philadelphia Academy launched in 1740, ultimately to become the University of Pennsylvania. This school, and Brown in Rhode Island, under way in 1764, did not require religious adherence among their trustees. In the belief that higher education was definitely needed in professions other than the ministry, in trade and civic affairs, the aim of these two schools was largely secular from the outset.

Harvard College had the distinction, too, of fostering the first printing establishment north of the Rio Grande River. A small press was set up in Cambridge in the year 1638, and it is said that the first item to issue from it was *The Freeman's Oath*. During the first twenty-five years, however, its output was

A COLONIAL PRINTING ESTABLISHMENT

Printing equipment, particularly type, came first from England. When the Revolution cut off the supply, enterprising men here began to produce for the expanding needs in this country. Printing volume is an important gauge of a country's progress.

largely religious material, including among other items three editions of the famous Bay Psalm Book, in which the Psalms from the Bible were arranged for singing by early Puritan congregations. There was also a rendering of the whole Bible in the tongue of the local Massachusetts Indians.

Those of the earlier settlers who had some formal education purchased books published in England; and from publishers there a wide variety of literature flowed into all colonies throughout Colonial times. As more and more learned to read, the number of local printers increased. At first they were largely public printers, subsidized by local governments, since laws, proclamations, and proceedings were given permanent form in type. Slowly the need for handbills, advertise-

ments, and then books and newspapers assured the print shops a more independent status.

True to its fanatical Puritan background, the output of literature in the Massachusetts Bay colony in the middle part of the 1600's revolved entirely about sermons and pious works, based upon the approved but rather savage Calvinistic dogma in vogue there. Literature of this type did produce a *best seller* as early as 1662, a long, dreary poem by the Rev. Mr. Wigglesworth, entitled *The Day of Doom*. It is said that some 1,800 copies were sold within a year. For a book to do equally well in America today, it would need to sell the unheard-of number of four and a half million. In fact, there were eight separate works issued before the year 1700 which, by their sales, could have been classed as best sellers. Seven of these were religious, an indication of the interests in those days. We have already seen that such texts made up the great bulk of Mr. Gridley's library. Of the six best sellers between 1701 and 1725, five were distinctly religious; while the sixth was the ever-popular *Mother Goose,* first made into a book in the colonies in 1719.

SECULAR READING INCREASES

From then on, however, to the time of the Revolution, the more popular sellers among locally printed books were chiefly those on secular subjects.

Type was produced in England and imported into this country. Thus it was expensive and also relatively scarce. It was not until restrictions laid upon the colonies in the years ahead of the Revolution forced native ingenuity to step into this situation that any American type was cast. The first to attempt it was Abel Buell, a jeweler and gem-setter, in tiny Killingworth, Connecticut, who developed a small font of letters in 1769.

But since the printers were usually booksellers as well, they managed, by ordering titles from Europe, to give their readers what they wanted. As newspapers began to spring up, the book lists advertised indicate that by the early 1700's reading tastes had grown fairly broad. While illiteracy still continued high by today's standards, there are ample indications that books were much sought after. Their price? About two shillings (fifty cents) for the small, pocket-sized volumes, very popular in that day, and up to as much as eight shillings (two dollars) for the larger tomes. That would make them equal in price in that time to about one and four bushels of

wheat respectively. No, they were far from cheap, were prized possessions, in fact; and read and reread until their contents in many instances were known almost by heart.

Printing being an effective means of conveying thought to the masses, books grew in importance, as did newspapers. Among the latter, the first to appear, very briefly, was *Public Occurrences* at Boston in 1690. It was soon suppressed for printing an article on politics. The authorities in those days, too, could not tolerate criticism. In 1704 the *Boston News Letter* was first issued, followed in 1719 by the *Boston Gazette*.

A TEST IS MADE OF
THE FREEDOM OF THE PRESS

This latter was for a time printed by James Franklin, Benjamin's older brother by nine years. Having lost his printing contract, he decided in the summer of 1721 to establish a sheet of his own, which he named the *New England Courant*. Using it to speak his mind and vigorously attack wrongs as he saw them, he was soon sentenced to a month's imprisonment by the authorities for his *insolence*. As soon as he was free, he again used its columns to flay those whom he felt were persecuting him. The reaction was more violent this time, and he was promptly prohibited from printing or publishing his newspaper, or any pamphlet or paper of similar nature unless he henceforth received permission in each instance from the secretary of the province.

Thus was the power of the press demonstrated and also restricted when it ran counter to those in power. There were other occasions when groups in authority attempted to throttle it; and one day soon its freedom would need to be defended and guaranteed.

In 1719 Andrew Bradford began to issue the *American Weekly Mercury* in Philadelphia; while William Bradford established the *New York Weekly Gazette* in that city in 1725. This latter was quite frankly an organ of the local authorities.

But Bradford had an apprentice, who later became a business partner, named John Peter Zenger, who was induced to start an opposition paper. This new sheet made its first appearance in November of 1733. At once it began to publish biting criticisms of the royal governor and his associates. These attacks had even greater sting since they were based solely upon fact. Once again the power of this new instrument—the newspaper—was being demonstrated, this time in the New York colony. After a few issues there was a violent reaction. By order of the governor and his council, copies having what were deemed offensive items in them were gathered up, and publicly burned by "the common hangman, or whipper, near the pillory."

THE DAYSTAR OF THE AMERICAN REVOLUTION

On Sunday the 17th of November, 1734, Zenger was arrested and cast into jail. After the Grand Jury failed to find ground for an indictment, another charge was trumped up on which to hold him prisoner. When the matter finally came to trial in April of 1735, the two defense lawyers retained by Mr. Zenger were debarred by the Chief Justice, and the matter put over until August. This postponement had its advantages, since the case began to be much talked about throughout other colonies as well.

Without doubt the ablest lawyer in America at this time was Mr. Andrew Hamilton. He had held every important post in Penn-

sylvania and had been Speaker of the Assembly of Delaware as well. In legal and political matters there was probably no more influential figure in any of the colonies. And what he was about to do won him the title of *Daystar of the American Revolution.*

He volunteered his services and without hope of a fee went to New York to defend the hard-pressed Zenger. This he did in so masterly a fashion that his client was not only set free, but he is credited with establishing freedom of speech and of the press in this country. Equally important, his efforts in this celebrated case also established freedom of the jury from pressure from any source.

THE NEED FOR FREE ACCESS TO INFORMATION

The times were on trial in this instance quite as much as Zenger. And Hamilton was indeed a *daystar,* in that he was one of the first to arise and fight ably and valiantly in the cause of freedom. Men can be free only when they have free access to information and to its unhampered exchange. In this test, Americans had won the right to freedom of speech and of the press. There would soon be further tests in other phases of daily life, and, fortunately, there would be similarly able men to meet and win them.

Where there is a thirst for freedom, there is a thirst, too, for information. The number of printers capable of supplying printed information continued to increase. By 1775 and the beginning of hostilities, there were no less than twenty-five newspapers being regularly printed throughout the colonies. They were weeklies, it is true, for the first daily paper in this country did not appear until 1784. But their effectiveness in forming public opinion was very great.

What the Thirteen Colonies Had in Common

PAIN, too, had been planting colonies in this New World, although none of them had thrived in eastern North America. We can perhaps better understand why the English colonies had grown and prospered there if we contrast the spirit in which the settlements made by each country were launched and administered.

The earliest Spanish attempts were frankly based upon plunder. Since this could not last, a colonization bureau was finally set up in the home government to guide these attempts more carefully. It was established in the belief that most men are pretty ineffectual and need to have their thinking done for them. Bureaucrats are always like that. They feel that the more men are controlled, the greater the ultimate common good. So they planned to do the thinking for men and women who would live and operate more than three thousand miles away, where they would encounter conditions and problems far different from those that obtained in Europe. How ridiculous!

Spanish settlers were carefully selected. And, since the government would finance them, the communities set up would be in the nature of collectivist farms. Instructions for just what was to be done in clearing and opening up new lands were all set down. What crops, how they were to be planted, harvested, and divided, was all settled in advance. Conditions as they obtained in Spain were to be transplanted overseas. The people would live elbow to elbow in tight little villages, with a body of soldiers to protect them or to keep them in line with the authorities if need be. There was a commandant to tell them what to do, and when, and how to do it. He was the father, they the children.

Yes, they led sheltered, orderly lives, and perhaps better lives by far than they would have experienced by remaining at home in Spain. But they did not lay the foundation for a new type of nation, they did not make progress and build a greater future for those who were to follow. They did little or nothing to throw off the heavy yoke of authority which had held men back for thousands of years from their rightful destiny.

And neither to any marked degree had the French, who had established a long chain of similarly snug little outposts up the St. Lawrence Valley, about the Great Lakes, along the Ohio, and down the Mississippi toward the Gulf. Europe had tried to spread its own outworn pattern to America in the planned settlements of those two nations.

FREEDOM OF ACTION IN THE ENGLISH COLONIES

The English, by contrast, had tended to dump discouraged and disgruntled people on these shores and leave them in large measure to their own devices. The results had been electrifying. Men thrown on their own had employed their God-given efforts for their own great good, and, through necessity, for the common good as well. They had, perhaps without fully realizing it, started a great revolutionary change in man's affairs. Under a large measure of individual freedom, they had conquered a firm foothold and established a sound base on which to build what was to be in the fullest sense of the term a *New World.*

The thirteen original colonies underwent this common experience. They had been thrown very much upon their own resources. And they were rapidly working out a joint destiny in which they must be free if they were to carry the noble experiment to its final conclusion.

Let us review briefly how these thirteen colonies had their various origins. They were established by *companies*, or under the direction of *proprietors*. In either instance, the hope was for profits; and when these were not promptly forthcoming, either the companies disappeared or the proprietors withdrew; and control passed for the most part to the British crown. It is hardly necessary to cover the details involved. It should suffice to say that by the time independence was declared, eight of the thirteen colonies were royal provinces, while three remained under proprietory setups and only two, Connecticut and Rhode Island, could choose their own governors and pretty much order their own affairs.

The exercise, or threat, of British control in one form or another gave them all something very immediate and disturbing with which to deal. And as their total population mounted until it began to approach the number of people in England, exclusive of Scotland and Wales, they began to feel sufficient strength to warrant something more than colonial status. The tail was getting big enough to threaten some day to wag the dog.

Slowly, too, the forces developing in what had once been only struggling outposts of empire began to be realized in England. This power, at first political and later economic, held definite threats. The first reaction was to curb it, to hold it firmly in check. We have already seen something of how this control, either by the Crown or by Parliament, was extended bit by bit in various of the colonies.

ENGLAND'S CHOICE OF ADMINISTRATORS WAS POOR

The chief bone of contention was usually the royal governors. These men, chosen by the Crown and too seldom experienced in American conditions, customs, and thought, had extensive powers. Their chief responsibility was to their king. He made the appointments and controlled their individual futures. Thus they used their power, or grasped for greater powers, rather arbitrarily, and too seldom in the best interests of the colonists.

Although they governed with the consent of a council in many instances, they had many privileges of appointment and otherwise, with which they could bargain or threaten. In this way they were able to surround themselves with hangers-on, to whom and for whom they were forced to grant

favors and concessions, often at the expense of the people as a whole.

The common man's rights, in an atmosphere which encouraged him to seek more and more liberty, were still somewhat limited. He could hope to counter or block the power of royal governors principally through popular assemblies. But to elect his chosen representative to an assembly, he must, of course, be a voter. And to qualify as a voter,

he must be a property owner, or a taxpayer, and of no nominal amount either. This pretty well limited the franchise to the larger landholders and merchants, leaving a fair share of artisans and laborers without too much say in how they should be governed.

Political concern during the early part of the 1700's centered largely in contests for power between royal governors and colonial assemblies. Wherever the assemblies voted the funds for the salaries of these governors, there was bound to be some measure of control over their acts. As this situation came to be realized in England, it aroused fears in

THE COLONISTS' BEST TREES WERE APPROPRIATED BY THE CROWN FOR THE USE OF THE BRITISH NAVY

Select trees were blazed under a law passed during Anne's reign, and the owner was not permitted to use them. This was but one of many ill-advised statutes that began to bind the colonists together in common cause against Britain early in the 1700's. Put yourself in the place of this farmer and his sons.

Parliament. These colonies were British *possessions*, and laws to govern them could and should be made just as certainly as for any other British subjects. And the laws must be enforced without let or hindrance.

Actually, however, what was happening was a translation of tensions at home to the affairs of the colonies. Through the seventeenth century there had been a lively contest between Crown and Parliament. James I had begun the struggle; there had been civil

war under Charles I, followed by the Puritan Commonwealth.

When the monarchy was restored under Charles II, that ruler tended to leave the colonies to their own ways. His brother, James II, had ambitions to weld them together and might have done so, had not a second revolution forced him to flee to France in 1688. But he did set a despotic governor, Sir Edmond Andrus, to rule over New England, New York, and New Jersey.

121

Although this satrap lasted but a few months, he gave that section a bitter taste of what its sons and grandsons might expect in the years ahead. Berkeley had done much the same for Virginia, except that he succeeded in bringing on Bacon's Rebellion.

William and Mary, brought over from the Netherlands to rule England, ushered in a better era. The Stuart kings, who had claimed their rule was by divine right, were out and done with. Parliament's power was now dominant, and, by the Bill of Toleration, religious liberties were pretty well secured throughout the empire. In the colonies, too, there was a return to other liberties at first enjoyed.

William was succeeded by Anne in 1702, and she, in turn, by the first of the Georges in 1714. These latter were Germans, and the first two were so little interested in America that until the passing of George II in 1760 there was no personal interference by the ruling monarch in American affairs. That does not mean, however, that control was not exercised during this time by the government at home.

While a royal committee made up of the king's officers had kept a constant eye on matters on this side of the Atlantic since 1660, this scrutiny was made more exacting in 1696. A group bearing the title *Lords of Trade and Plantations* was then established to make recommendations to colonial governments. This body was also to check all bills passed by colonial assemblies, and to hear and deal with agents sent to plead colonial causes in England. This royal board, reporting to the king, had most extensive powers—for good or for evil. And since the interests of its members were British, and not Colonial American, it managed much irritation and some mischief from time to time. Also it was the chief instrument by which the colonies were slowly but certainly saddled with imperial dominion.

With the hand of Parliament much strengthened, two things began to bring colonial affairs into stronger focus. One was trade with and by the colonies. The other was the reflection on America of wars taking place in Europe, or in which European powers were involved.

ENGLAND FEELS COLONIAL COMPETITION

England had long been engaged in extensive foreign trade and had become a great mercantile power. Actually she was largely dependent upon such commerce for her well-being. Raw material from abroad was manufactured and processed at home, and reshipped as finished products to possessions and backward areas. Profits came in two ways, by manufacture and through shipping. The carriage of goods by ship was of primary importance as a source of English income. To keep this exclusively in English vessels, a series of laws, termed the Navigation Acts, were passed, beginning about the mid-1600's. At first these gave an impulse to shipbuilding in the colonies.

Then, as the colonies began to manufacture and process their own raw materials and exchange them in world markets, English manufacturers and traders felt the pinch of this competition. The merchant class in the home island enjoyed extensive power in Parliament. For their protection, new legislation was passed restricting such trade, even between the colonies themselves. And, as though this were not sufficient, other laws were enacted which attempted to force the colonies to ship certain commodities to Great Britain or her possessions, and not elsewhere

These Navigation Acts became progressively more restrictive during the 1700's. Trouble was definitely in the making and would have come sooner if these laws had been strictly enforced. The determined colonial merchants and shipowners, recalling the privateers that had made England great upon the seas a hundred odd years before, merely took the long chance and kept on building up American commerce. Quite naturally there were contests over this supposedly *illegitimate* trade. But the net result was to bind all colonies closer together in opposition to the imperial will set against their progress and best interests.

COLONIAL EXPANSION ANTAGONIZES THE INDIANS

As population increased and thrust back away from the coast, the Indians began to grow fearful. They were rapidly being driven from their homes and hunting areas and into conflict with other tribes farther inland. In some cases their lands had been purchased, but far more often merely wrested from them by force. The red man was now disposed to contest further encroachments.

Spain, still rankling over being swept from control of the sea, still held firmly to settlements in Florida and the Far Southwest. She bided her time, hoping there might come a day when these English colonies could be taken over.

But a greater threat lay to the north and west. The French entrance to North America had been slow. There had been trading posts in the St. Lawrence basin, then out along the Great Lakes, and now they were marching down into the valleys of the Ohio and the upper Mississippi. By and large, the French authorities had succeeded in forming strong alliances with the Indians.

England, Spain, and France had been and still continued to be serious rivals in Europe; and it was quite natural that tensions there should reach to and tend to embroil their subjects in the New World. America had need to free itself from old enmities.

There seems no purpose in detailing here these European struggles based in intrigue and the ambitions of decadent ruling houses. Ill will between the crowns of England and France did play its part in the American contest over French claims on this continent, but conditions here were perhaps sufficient to have brought on conflict. While royal governors pulled the strings and made the first moves, the colonists themselves cannot but have been deeply concerned.

Grants of colonial lands had usually ceded areas reaching through from the Atlantic to the still little known Pacific coast. Thus when the French turned south from Canada, they began to gain footholds first in territory claimed by the New England colonies, then by New York, and finally by Virginia. When, in 1718, Frenchmen settled New Orleans and promptly claimed the Mississippi Valley, they offered a challenge to most all of the thirteen colonies.

CONTEST WITH FRANCE

You may recall the story of how the young surveyor, George Washington, was sent by Governor Dinwiddie of Virginia to warn the French to cease operations and get out of the area in the vicinity of what is now Pittsburgh. But the French had no intention of leaving, and the shots exchanged there were felt around the world. They were the opening guns in what was known in Europe as the *Seven Years War,* which shook the European continent and reached even into the faraway subcontinent which is India.

123

As a contest strictly between English and French colonists, it would have been a most uneven one. The former outnumbered the latter by ten to one, perhaps even more. But the French enlisted the aid of great numbers of Indians, and thus the struggle was here called the *French and Indian War.*

It began in 1754, when the ill-fated General Braddock was dispatched to drive out the French at Fort du Quesne [doo-KANE], only to be killed himself, and his troops sadly routed. This was the twenty-two-year-old Washington's baptism of fire in real warfare.

Greater success attended the taking of French forts at Ticonderoga, at the south end of Lake Champlain and at Niagara, between Lakes Ontario and Erie. Quebec was won in Wolfe's heroic attack in 1759; and the following year control of all Canada and French territory east of the Mississippi passed into British hands.

BRITISH ARE VICTORIOUS

The French then ceased to be contenders for a place in the New World. The Spanish might remain on the fringes of the continent, but not as a particular threat from here on.

The chief results on the British colonies following these six years of war were twofold. They had been forced to arm, train, and maintain a considerable number of troops. This burden had been spread among them and had tended to bring them closer together. True, the British government had been to a large extent the go-between, for there had been need of liberal assistance from the home government while hostilities lasted. But now that the French and their Indian allies had been removed as a threat and an enemy, it was increasingly easy for

the colonies to substitute British imperialism as the common foe.

The Indian threat of a hundred years before had forced the calling of a New England Confederation. As common problems multiplied, the urge to extend mutual aid reached down as far as Virginia. Thus as early as 1684 the principal colonies had sent representatives to an assembly called at Albany to talk over those things which were of general interest.

PLAN OF COLONIAL UNION

To better prepare the colonies for war, the British government had suggested another general conference, which was finally held at Albany in 1754. Seven colonies were represented; and Ben Franklin had one of his first opportunities to demonstrate his abilities as a thinker, planner, and diplomat. At this meeting he drew up a plan of colonial union so effective that it frightened the British crown into stern disapproval. And so it was that steps were being taken, falteringly and slowly perhaps, yet steadily leading in the direction of eventual federation.

But the incident which clearly showed the need for common action occurred when Britain presented the bill for the war just won. When she demanded and began to exact payment, the revolution can be said to have been under way.

It was perhaps during this French and Indian War that the British government first awoke to the realization that the American colonies were not exactly "poor relations." They were at times very annoying, but actually they were fairly wealthy and had a potential that promised far greater wealth. Certainly they had cost the home government a pretty penny during the recent struggle. So, since they were able, why shouldn't they bear their fair share of this growing expense? Also, why shouldn't they continue to maintain a, well let's say, *reasonably small* standing army of British troops, which would be for their protection, of course?

The next problem was how to go about collecting the revenue demanded by these

ernors from such control as colonial assemblies had managed to gain over them. Since the colonies, as pointed out above, had paid the salaries of both governors and judges, it was now thought better to tax the colonies and make these payments from Britain. This would free these agents of the British government from colonial pressure.

WASHINGTON RECEIVES HIS BAPTISM OF FIRE

While many of the colonists had had experience in fighting Indians, it took the French and Indian War to provide the training for many of the men who covered themselves with glory a few years later during the Revolution. Above Washington takes part in the sorry defeat of General Braddock.

plans. The new monarch who had ascended the throne in 1760 was to be a great aid. He was George III, and the first among the three that had borne that name in succession to take up ruling vigorously. His ambitious mother is said to have brought him up on the phrase, "George, be king!" And he tried resolutely to live up to her hopes. Between the Crown and Parliament, things began to happen in earnest in 1763.

The first step was to free the royal gov-

The next revolved about another pained cry from the great merchants in the homeland. It is said they had been drawing *hard* money from the colonists at such great rates that local governments in America had had to meet their expanding needs through printed paper currency, backed principally by mortgages and notes. Now, burdened with war debts, the colonial printing presses were speeded up. But worse still, the colonists were trying to force their English creditors to accept payment of debts in this *cheap* money. Consequently, an act was rushed through in 1764 prohibiting the printing of paper money in the colonies. Also there could be no forced extension of the time in which debts were to be paid. Hardly had the blow of this thunderbolt been absorbed when another was readied.

The Sugar Act, also of 1764, laid a heavy duty on sugar, textiles, and many other essential commodities brought into the colonies in great quantities. There had been mild attempts at such restriction before, but now the government in England meant business.

Shipowners on this side of the ocean, who had previously been pretty much privateers, were now promptly registered and forced to post bonds. Also—and this hurt—British revenue cutters began patrolling the coast, with the right of boarding and searching every passing vessel. To make more certain that these laws were carried out to the letter, prizes were awarded to Crown officers in all cases where fraud was successfully uncovered and prosecuted.

Then, as though to add insult to injury, a *Stamp Act* was proposed and quickly passed in 1765. It required the colonists to purchase and affix revenue stamps to every sort of legal document, and to other items as well. The amount may not have been great, but the annoyance was. No matter what their color may be, such tax stamps always tend to make those who must use them see red.

On legal documents, they provoked chiefly the lawyers; but when constantly seen on pamphlets, newspapers, handbills, and even calendars and almanacs, they soon infuriated the colonists almost to the last man.

The British government had been amply warned of the resentment its callous acts were surely building up; but it was determined to show its authority. And to make that authority emphatic, it almost immediately passed another act which required the colonists to house and feed soldiers being sent over to guarantee enforcement of these roundly hated laws.

This threat to quarter soldiers among them, perhaps even in some cases in their own dwellings, brought home one truth to even the rank and file of these *Americans*. They learned what government, in the final analysis, really is, the legal monopoly of the use of physical force—by persons, upon persons.

This Parliament, which had bared its teeth and claws in the form of red-coated regulars carrying loaded guns, held its sessions some three thousand-odd miles away. The colonists had no voice, no not even a whisper, in its actions. Still their freedom, their destiny, their very lives, were in its hands and subject to its whims. How long were they prepared to dance to its piping? The answer was not long in coming, and was distinct enough so that it was clearly heard across the broad ocean.

Revolution in the Making

HATEVER Parliament's *rights* may have been, the methods of this august body were surely open to considerable questioning. The colonists had every right to be highly indignant. Many of the most influential among them were affected directly, and all to varying degrees. But feeling was not of one accord, and the lines of cleavage were soon drawn. Those whose stake was deeply driven in this new land, and to whom it had been home for perhaps several generations, were naturally drawn together as *Patriots*. In opposition to them was another group, including many of the "best" people in the several colonies, who preferred to remain loyal to the Crown. They were called *Tories*. The term is a corruption of an old Irish word that once meant an armed robber.

While the wealthier Patriots tried to keep their heads, and to register their protests in a manner, and at times and places where they might be most effective, the great body of the people felt no such restraint. They began to organize, the men as *Sons of Liberty*, the women as *Daughters of Liberty*. The former of the two groupings was not above riot or arson in making its views known and in carrying its points. The women's groups were content either to boycott the use of British goods, or they strove hard to produce such goods at home. Surely and rapidly the great bulk of the colonists was being welded together, and around certain of their basic liberties and rights. They had not been unwilling to aid the mother country, if and as the need was there. But they were determined that a Parliament in which they were not represented had no right to tax them, or to infringe the liberties they and their fathers had gained by honest effort.

As a consequence, in this same fateful year of 1765 representatives of nine colonies met in New York and denounced the Stamp Act as evidence of "a manifest tendency to subvert the rights and liberties of the colonies." This action, plus many idle ships lying at British docks, convinced Parliament at last that America was thoroughly aroused.

Reluctantly, the following year, the hated Stamp Act was repealed. But lest this action be misunderstood, the Lords and Commons immediately passed an act of declaration affirming that the colonies were subject to control by the king and Parliament. Then, as if given renewed courage by this assertion, a new tax measure was pushed through in

127 ❧

FLAG OF TRUCE FIRED UPON AT ALAMANCE CREEK

Where did the Revolution truly begin? There had been the *Boston Massacre* in 1770, and then this clash in North Carolina the following year. These recurring incidents seemed to lead in but one direction—full-scale warfare. In but a few years it came.

1767 laying a tax upon lead, glass, paper, paint, tea, and other items. This act had teeth in it, since it provided collectors to be quartered in the colonies, but to be totally free of colonial control. To this was added a Tea Act which so favored the East India Company as to make competition with that concern next to impossible.

Sand, so liberally sprinkled, was now being rubbed in through the right of collectors to search American homes and places of business. Patience was wearing thin; and the idea began to take firm hold in this country that liberties won here by blood, sweat, and tears were well worth dying for, if that were to become necessary.

But at first the colonists were willing to fight back through votes. The assembly of New York colony showed the temper of its feelings by refusing to vote money to sustain the British troops quartered there. Promptly Parliament closed out that body. Finally its members yielded to the pressure from overseas, and it was reopened. But not before all thirteen colonies were made to see how easily they could be deprived of the last threads of self-government. The moment was at hand for far-reaching decisions.

Two million-odd people were not prepared to see what their ancestors had fought valiantly for snuffed out without resistance. It was a time to stand up and be counted, to raise one's voice and register protests that carried weight. Massachusetts decided to cast the die, and under the direction of Samuel Adams the assembly in that colony issued a *circular letter,* addressed to like bodies in all the others. It was a frank, stinging statement of what had become a one-sided, muddled British imperial policy. It said simply, but firmly, that without representation there was no right to tax, and added that representation in Parliament was impractical because of distance. It cited abuses already existing; and then, without resort to passion or sign of rebellious spirit,

asked that opinions be formed about the problems which confronted them all.

The result was curt but widespread disbanding of assemblies by royal governors in the several colonies. These representatives of the Crown felt the ground swell beneath their feet, and thought perhaps that one more show of force would quell it. But the reaction was quite contrary. Feeling welled up and got out of hand in Boston. There was a brush between the *Patriots* and British regulars. Shots were fired, and five men fell, never to rise again.

Word of this *Boston Massacre,* backed by a sketch made by Paul Revere, swept the length of the Atlantic coast line and back into the interior regions like wildfire. Were these shots fired on the night of March 5,

1770, the opening volley of the Revolution? If not, they were straws in a wind soon to be full of such flying fragments. And unrest began to rumble and spread.

BATTLE OF THE ALAMANCE

Governor Tryon, an arch royalist and Tory, ruled North Carolina with so vengeful a hand that bands of *Regulators* were formed in that colony. A man thrown into prison at New Berne was released by them. The governor's wrath flared up, and, with some three hundred militiamen and several pieces of artillery, he set out to punish these rebels. Ammunition and powder being sent him were intercepted by the Regulators, who were later discovered along the Alamance Creek.

There was an attempt to parley, but Tryon, provoked at an old man who had come under cover of a flag of truce to bring a message, shot him dead. The second Regulator who had borne the white flag ran for his own lines under a hail of shots. Although he reached them safely, twenty of his companions perished in the fighting that followed. Nine of the militia also lost their lives. The time was May, 1771, and this was in many respects the first true battle of the War for Independence.

The next incident took place in New England, in the Rhode Island colony. It was in the summer of the following year that a British armed revenue schooner sailed into Narragansett Bay to enforce the laws. When the lieutenant in command was asked by the sheriff acting upon orders of the governor to show his commission, he curtly refused. And, angered by this act, he ordered all vessels passing his ship, the *Gaspé* [GAS-pay], to lower their colors in salute on penalty of being fired upon.

A few days later, and perhaps to further vex the insolent officer, a small packet sailed blithely by without paying homage. At once the *Gaspé* unfurled sail and put after the offender, but soon ran fast aground. Before the tide could free her, a party in eight boats under cover of night succeeded in boarding the offensive craft. The crew and her wounded commander were sent ashore, the vessel was set afire, and her magazine finally blew up. Although liberal rewards were offered for the capture of those who had taken part in this raid, they were never betrayed. A royal commission was hurriedly appointed and sent into the state to force convictions, but not a single informer could be found. There were perhaps fewer Tories here than in other centers, notably Boston.

Even the action of appointing this commission antagonized the various colonies, but it brought a particularly strong reaction in Virginia. In March of 1773 its House of Burgesses set up a committee of correspondence to contact the other colonies in their common defense. Conditions between the mother country and her *possessions* were worsening rapidly; and another minor incident seemed all that was needed to bring an open break.

THE BOSTON TEA PARTY

Parliament considered that it was being very fair when it removed all but the nominal tax of threepence a pound on tea, which was in those days something of a luxury. But the colonists insisted it was a matter of principle. As long as there was no representation, there should be no taxation whatsoever. And when they learned that several shiploads of tea sent by the East India Company were on the way to various American points, it was decided the cargoes should not be

THE BOSTON TEA PARTY, DECEMBER 16, 1773

landed. Groups called *Mohawks* were to take care of this matter.

Three of the vessels arrived in Boston harbor in December, 1773. An assemblage was called at the Old South Meeting House on the evening of the 16th; and so great was the response that the church was more than filled, and a crowd surged about outside as addresses were being made by Josiah Quincy and Samuel Adams. The governor had been petitioned to have the ships return to England; and, while Adams was still speaking, word was brought of his refusal.

There was a tense moment of excitement. Then every eye was focused upon the great Patriot. If he spoke certain words, an agreed-upon action would immediately be carried out. Briefly he reviewed the governor's refusal. Then, with special emphasis, he added, "This meeting can do no more than save the country!"

Ah, that was the *trigger* phrase. In the gallery at the back, what appeared to be an Indian bounded to his feet, and let out a piercing war cry. This was promptly answered by the cries of others similarly dressed. At once the crowd hurried out and down the dark streets in the direction of the wharves. As it surged along, more and more *Indians* joined it, seemingly out of nowhere.

When it reached the waterside, there were the three tea ships, made fast to a single quay. As many as sixty of the *savages* divided them between them, and within three hours they had carried from the holds and dumped over the rails into the harbor water the contents of no less than 342 chests of tea. The *Boston Tea Party* thus completed, those who had taken part disappeared into the night.

The ship destined to land at New York did not make port until April, 1774. Threats to its captain were sufficient to send the cargo back to England. Similar action occurred in Philadelphia. But in Charleston, South Carolina, the chests were allowed to be put ashore; but they were stored in a damp cellar, where the tea soon spoiled. In October of that same year the tea ship which appeared at Annapolis was set afire and totally destroyed.

PORT OF BOSTON CLOSED

Word of the Boston affair reached London soon after the turn of the year, and an angry Parliament jammed through an act which closed that port and decreed it was to remain so until the destroyed tea was paid for.

Then, to show that its authority was above question, Parliament passed four additional acts aimed at bringing these treasonable colonists into line. One of these took away Massachusetts' charter, and made the holding of town meetings possible only with consent of the royal governor, who was also to appoint councilors and judges. Another arranged for transportation of certain offenders to other provinces, or to Great Britain, for trial. The next fully legalized the quartering of troops at any point in Massachusetts. The last annexed territory east of the Mississippi and north of the Ohio River to Quebec, and placed them under governance of a viceroy.

Although there was some opposition, these *Intolerable Acts* were pressed through quickly. But neither their speed nor their harshness developed the spirit of meekness upon the part of the colonists which George III had expected them to. Instead Patriots saw in these acts only a concerted further threat to their liberties. In the Quebec Act they felt a thinly veiled attempt to turn French Canada against the colonies to the south. And with the arrival of more and more soldiers to enforce these harsh acts, war appeared to be inevitable. Preparations for it began to be made.

It was May of 1774 when the Port Bill reached Boston. General Gage had been appointed British military governor just previously. Its contents had been known even earlier in New York, and the Patriots there prepared to assist Massachusetts in any way possible in what was now frankly a common cause. They sent out a call for a congress of all the colonies to assemble at a convenient central point.

The port of Boston was closed on June 1, and in most large communities throughout the other colonies the day was one of fasting and prayer. There was soon hardship in the Boston area, despite assistance from other centers, even to a gift of three-quarters of a million dollars from the city of London.

TRAINING FOR WAR

But in place of the expected meekness, *training days* were appointed, and veterans of the French and Indian struggle began to teach a younger generation the arts of war. The song "Yankee Doodle" probably had its origin in these activities. Blacksmiths laid aside work to forge muskets, bayonets, and swords. Charcoal, sulphur, and saltpeter were gathered and mixed into gunpowder. Shot towers were set up for casting lead-ball shot. And such preparations showed unmistakably the trend of thinking.

Surely the purposes behind marching soldiers could not be mistaken by English visitors to these shores. They marked well the spirit of the people here, and reported these facts on their return. There were still a few sober thinkers at home to listen and to de-

TRAINING DAY ON THE VILLAGE GREEN

Many of the colonists used guns frequently either in hunting game or in fending off Indians. To stimulate competition, so-called *Rifle Frolics* were often held. These now became *Training Days*, and were carried on in real earnest to prepare for the uncertain days ahead.

fend the colonists. Outstanding among them was Edmund Burke, whose speech on conciliation is still read and studied in many high schools. But the Court and Parliament were well along on a program calculated to stamp out the *rebels*.

On September 5, 1774, the first *Continental Congress* met in Carpenter's Hall in Philadelphia. To it came the leaders from all colonies except Georgia. These outstanding Patriots, by this bold act of asserting their right to assemble, made themselves targets for wrath from the forces arrayed against them in England, and also from Tory sympathizers on this side of the water. Still they valued their freedom and their rights sufficiently to risk all in thus opposing the imperial will.

Their deliberations were temperate, and the feeling was general that the moment for separation was not yet at hand. Rather there was still hope that the king and Parliament would reconsider and modify their stubborn stand. However, they did resolve to support Massachusetts in its opposition to the restrictive acts passed by Parliament. And General Gage was warned that fortifications he was erecting in the Boston area were very liable to involve the colonies in civil war.

There was also a *Declaration of Colonial Rights,* which claimed the recent restrictive acts of Parliament to be an infringement on the just claims of the colonies. The *American Association* was set up to boycott goods from Great Britain, Ireland, the West Indies, and Madeira. There was a *Memorial* to the

British people, and a *Petition* to the king. And before adjournment, it was arranged that if grievances were not adjusted during the recess, another session would be called on May 10 of the following year, 1775.

But the king was adamant, and Gage was ordered to crack down vigorously in Massachusetts. However, Patriots in that colony managed to hold a Provincial Congress at which they voted to enrol 12,000 *Minutemen,* and equip them as volunteers to be ready for call on a minute's notice. Connecticut, Rhode Island, and Virginia set up similar contingents in their several militias.

By the spring of 1775 all that was needed was another tiny spark to explode the powder keg of pent-up feelings on both sides. Wendell Phillips, in a speech three quarters of a century later, made the often-quoted remark that, "Revolutions are not made; they come." Here surely was one that seemed to have been made out of distance, muddled greed for power, and a complete lack of the meeting of minds. And, worst of all, it was irresistibly on its way, and both sides seemed unable to prevent its outbreak.

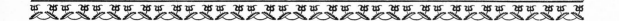

Trial by Battle; and Independence

HERE had been bloodshed in the *Boston Massacre* in 1770, and again at *Alamance Creek* the following year. Now, almost three years later, another incident was shaping up. The Provincial Congress was again secretly meeting, this time at Lexington, ten miles northwest of Boston. Samuel Adams and John Hancock, two especially sharp thorns in the side of the military governor, were attending.

Six miles beyond, at Concord, colonial military stores were quietly being assembled. When word of these matters reached General Gage, he decided to kill two birds with a single stone. He would not only capture the stores, but if he could seize and muzzle these two ardent Patriot leaders, he was certain the situation in the Massachusetts colony would cool down quickly. A sortie made at night would raise less disturbance in Boston. Also he could pick up his prisoners while they slept and be in Concord to complete the mission by sunup.

But his plans leaked out, and the Patriots were alerted. As his soldiers set out by boat about ten o'clock in the evening of April 18 headed across the Charles River for Cambridge, several horsemen raced away toward Lexington, spreading the alarm as they rode. Paul Revere arrived first to warn Adams and Hancock. Then, as he pushed on toward Concord, he was suddenly seized by advance guards posted by Gage's force.

LEXINGTON AND CONCORD

Before daybreak, a sizable number of minutemen had gathered on Lexington Common before the meetinghouse. Since it was a chilly morning, the men took refuge in nearby houses. As it began to grow light, the church bells started to ring wildly, a sign the British were approaching. Seventy of the militia were soon lined up again, their muskets loaded and cocked.

Up the street marched the British regulars in their brilliant red coats. They turned in onto the common, halted, and loaded. Then they stood eying the determined Patriots before them. Each side preferred the other to fire first. The returned shots would then be in the nature of self-defense. There was a long, uneasy pause, which threatened to become a stalemate.

Finally Major Pitcairn, commander of the British detachment, began to lose patience. Spurring his horse, he whipped out his sword and rode toward the Americans, shouting, "Disperse, you scoundrels!"

Since his officers and troops had followed him at the double, thinking he intended to charge, there was a moment of confusion and an exchange of shots. But which side fired first will never be known. Several more volleys were fired, and then the minutemen, heavily outnumbered and about to be surrounded, quickly scattered behind neighboring buildings and walls. Eight of them had been killed, and ten wounded. From such vantage points, they soon made it hot enough for the redcoats that Pitcairn withdrew his troops and started his men in the direction of Concord.

This longer pause at Lexington had given sufficient added time to remove the stores to a place of safety. And so it was that Concord, too, was to prove a disappointment. Armed men were now behind every stone wall and tree. And as the surprised and hard-pressed British retreated in haste from Concord toward Boston, they were subjected to an almost continuous deadly fire.

In the annals of British warfare the shots fired that morning of April 19, 1775, on the green in Lexington might be recorded as but a small skirmish. But they proved enough to fan the flames of suspicion and smoldering hatred into a full-scale war. It was no longer to be a contest of words and legislation, but seemingly of arms. It had passed beyond the question of the rights of these colonists *as Englishmen*. They had engaged in a struggle to determine their natural, God-given right to Freedom. But even then the majority of them were still not fully convinced that there was no other alternative but war.

Within a month of this skirmish, the delegates assembled again in Philadelphia for the second *Continental Congress*. Its sessions started on a peaceful, conciliatory tone, but resolutely refused such offers in this direction as were proposed by the British government. Yet it carefully left the way open for further negotiations.

But suddenly, as though he recalled his mother's frequent caution as a boy, King George decided to "be king." Toward the end of August he issued a proclamation declaring the colonies to be in open rebellion. This was followed in a short time by an act of Parliament, the purpose of which was to stop trade with all the American colonies. This being a certain attempt to starve them into submission, there was no longer much uncertainty as to what their course must now be.

CONTINENTAL CONGRESS

Late arrivals had swelled the numbers hurrying to attend the Congress, and forced the moving of the sessions from Carpenter's Hall to the larger rooms in Province House, a short distance up Chestnut Street. This building, designed by Andrew Hamilton, who had so successfully defended Zenger, was one day soon to have a new name— *Independence Hall*. But at the moment the Congress meeting there found itself without power to enforce a single act, since no authority had been delegated to it by the colonial assemblies. But the needs pressing down upon it were real and earnest. Britain had already sent over three of her top-flight commanders, Generals Howe, Clinton, and Burgoyne. War was imminent; and so these dedicated men forged ahead, trusting in God and the good intents of the several colonies.

They set about recruiting a Continental Army of twenty thousand men. They authorized the issuance of three million dollars in paper money to equip it. And then they

THE COSTLY RETREAT FROM LEXINGTON AND CONCORD

nominated George Washington to be its commander-in-chief.

To offset these moves by the assembled Patriots and bring the rebellion to a speedy ending, the British began a feverish campaign of recruiting in their home islands. But the results were highly disappointing; and, troops being urgently needed, there was but one thing to do, hire them. A deal was thus made with the German prince of Hesse for sixteen thousand of his men, conveniently located at the time in Holland. Shipped over here for duty, they became the much hated *Hessians*.

It is well to re-emphasize the lack of authority of the Congress. What had opened up was actually a civil war, the brunt of which was first borne by Massachusetts. We may term it a *Revolutionary War,* but at the outset it was hardly a united struggle.

Distances were great, communications were slow, and people were scattered in small communities. Also, of the total population approaching, or perhaps just above two million, a full third were outright Tories, loyal to the homeland. Not all of the remainder were, by any stretch of the imagination, virile Patriots. Their support was halfhearted and often doubtful. Even as Paul Revere's cry sounded out that night along the Medford road, there were perhaps not a few who preferred to remain in bed. But those astute enough to realize what was actually at stake were sufficient in number and force to carry through. A double armful of great names have come down to us as heroes; and so they were. Still the revolution that did get under way was fought and won principally by the thousands of nameless heroes, each willing to do his bit.

137

About two months following the brush with the British at Lexington, Massachusetts forces, acting without any authorization from the recently assembled Congress, laid siege to Boston. By the middle of June they were preparing to intrench themselves on some of the hills that overlooked the city. A force stole across Charlestown Neck on the night of the 16th, headed for Bunker Hill. But since Breed's Hill was closer in, fortifications were worked on there during the hours of darkness.

BATTLE OF BUNKER HILL

English men-of-war lying close by spied the earthworks at dawn and opened fire. By noon Gage had a stout force with several cannon close at hand, but by evening, the Americans' ammunition long since having run out, the hill was firmly in British hands. This battle has always been known as *Bunker Hill*. And although misnamed, and a defeat by the enemy, the militia that fought there had learned that they could confront trained troops, even in conventional warfare, and inflict severe losses.

A little over two weeks later, on July 3, Washington arrived and took command of American forces on Cambridge Common. General Gage seemed to prefer to keep his forces in the safety of Boston, and they remained penned up there during the remainder of the year 1775.

About two weeks previous to the battle just mentioned, it was the last day in May of 1775, there had been a training day, or military muster, at Charlotte, North Carolina. Word had been received there of the clash at Lexington and the punishment given the British on the way from Concord back to Boston. In view of these happenings, a very vigorous set of resolutions was adopted. All civil and military commissions were voided, and a local administration was established to govern until laws were provided by the Continental Congress.

A copy of this document, known as the *Mecklenburg Resolves,* was sent to England, where it is still preserved. The draft retained in this country was apparently lost, and a copy is thought to have been reproduced from memory some years later. A difference in the reckoning of time also gives a difference in date, along with certain of the wording, between the original, and what came to be known as the Mecklenburg *Declaration.* But this was surely one of the first formal expressions in favor of independence; and sprung from the thinking of the people themselves, rather than out of the deliberations of the Congress.

"COMMON SENSE"

Earlier still in this same year, Ben Franklin had given a letter of introduction to a rugged, middle-aged Englishman, suggesting that he present it to another of the Philadelphia printers. The latter at once hired the man to launch a new magazine, *The Pennsylvanian.* To help spice up its first issue, he printed an item giving detailed instructions for preparing homemade gunpowder. This receipt went far toward guaranteeing success for the venture.

Its editor—his name was Thomas Paine —managed to save enough money from his salary of five dollars per month, so that about the beginning of 1776 he was able to print and distribute a small pamphlet, which he gave the salty title *Common Sense.* Waving aside the customary grandiose style of the day, he had written it so simply that all who could spell out the words could get the liberal dose of common sense which it contained. Almost overnight it had reached the best-seller class; and nothing in the five hundred years of printing, save only the Scriptures, has ever achieved so phenomenal a sale. It was scattered far and wide and reprinted many, many times. Boiled down to the smallest compass, it told people to cut loose from England and establish a sound

him, and he began to show it to his acquaintances, nine-tenths of whom favored casting adrift from England. As he went on to Philadelphia to the Congress, he found there a letter from a friend of college days, John Page, in which he urged "For God's sake declare the colonies independent, and save us from ruin." Sentiment sufficient to sustain

JEFFERSON DRAFTING THE DECLARATION

government, "for we have it in our power to build a New World." What a prophetic and timely document!

Independence was in the air. The Congress had even been giving some consideration to Franklin's proposal for a federal constitution. What a singular impact this statement of *Common Sense* must have had upon the delegates in session at the Province House.

Jefferson received copies while still at home at Monticello. The pamphlet pleased

such an action seemed to be embedded in the minds of the people.

A resolution passed by the Congress was sent to each of the colonies suggesting that they form new governments. It is interesting to see what happened in this connection in Virginia. Williamsburg had long since succeeded Jamestown as the provincial capital. A convention in session there instructed the delegates in Philadelphia to introduce a resolution declaring the colonies to be *free and independent* states. It was twelve days later

139

before these instructions were received, and not until June 7 that Richard Henry Lee could so move the earnest men meeting at the Province House. Then it was, of course, necessary for a suitable document to be drawn up. A committee consisting of Benjamin Franklin, Thomas Jefferson, Roger Sherman, John Adams, and Robert Livingston were appointed to draft it. While they were at work on this task, the resolution lay tabled.

VIRGINIA LEADS THE WAY

However, the people in Virginia were so certain that it had already been passed and the Old Dominion was now independent that a new flag, the *Continental Union,* was hoisted over their Capitol. By June 28, a new constitution was adopted, and the Virginians were convinced that they were indeed a free and independent commonwealth. Thus the first, the largest, and probably the strongest of the original colonies demonstrated in no uncertain manner what its attitude was.

While Philadelphia seemed to lag behind, it was largely because it was necessary to sound out the feelings in the other colonies. Also among the many pressing matters in the Congress, the document declaring independence did not seem of the importance which we of today might attach to it. Although the five-man committee met several times to consider its contents, the actual writing was thrust upon Jefferson, already burdened with affairs of the Congress and deeply concerned as to what his countrymen at Williamsburg were doing. It is quite certain that neither he, his associates on the committee, nor even the fifty-six men who would soon sign what he wrote, felt that it was destined to become immortal.

Jefferson's contribution to the task was scattered through some seventeen days. His good friend, George Mason, had drawn a Bill of Rights which his compatriots in the Virginia Convention of Delegates had willingly adopted on June 12. Now he must produce a similar document which would meet the approval of the Congress of all thirteen colonies. While a few of its phrases have been credited to Franklin and to Adams, and others are doubtfully assigned to the remaining members of the committee, the bulk of the credit must go to the lawyer and planter from Albemarle County, then thirty-three years old.

His draft was reported to the Congress on June 28; but several days would elapse while that body debated the subject of independence itself, and a favorable decision would not be reached until July 2. At once the Declaration as drawn was brought up and its consideration begun. For three tedious days Jefferson, pledged to silence, sat and listened while it was subjected to criticism word by word. Still this detailed examination resulted in changes at but two points; and these, impartial judges believe, tended to strengthen it.

THE DECLARATION SIGNED

Then—on July 4—twelve of the *states* agreed to accept it as a Declaration of their intents and purposes. The single exception was New York, from whose local legislature resolutions giving approval did not reach Philadelphia until the 15th of the month. Before these arrived, John Hancock had signed a copy in a bold hand as president of the Congress; and printed copies were prepared and dispatched to the state legislatures, and to any and all who exercised

(*Continued on page 161*)

ATTACK ON THE *GASPÉ*

Charles DeWolf Brownell, RHODE ISLAND HISTORICAL SOCIETY

Brown University in Providence, one of the first *liberal* colleges in the country, takes its name from the city's most illustrious family. In Revolutionary times there were four brothers, of whom John was the most adventurous. It was he who met with the group of plotters in the old Sabin Tavern, and became their leader in the capture and burning of the British revenue cutter *Gaspé* off Bristol. This was probably the first instance of armed resistance by the colonists.

THE BOSTON TEA PARTY

Darius Cobb, ANCIENT & HONORABLE ARTILLERY COMPANY, BOSTON

This Boston painter of the middle 19th century here pictures the episode in 1773 in which local citizens disguised as Indians dumped 342 chests of tea from the East India ships into the harbor. This protest against the duty on tea destroyed property valued at about £18,000, and was a forerunner of the Revolution.

THE BLOODY MASSACRE

Paul Revere, GARDINER GREEN HUBBARD COLLECTION

Revere was as thorough a craftsman as he was an ardent patriot. Primarily a silver-smith, he seized upon this most unfortunate *incident* to engrave a melodramatic picture of it calculated to stiffen resistance to British treatment of the colonists. The stilted verses beneath the gory scene are in the same spirit as the picture itself.

STUMP SPEAKING

George Caleb Bingham, BOATMEN'S NATIONAL BANK OF ST. LOUIS

Political persuasion is by no means a modern *art*. Here we see it portrayed in action in the early days of our country, and by an artist noted for his historical and folk scenes and his portraits. In his later years he was professor of art at the University of Missouri; and his picture is of the early 19th century. The political technique portrayed was very much in use, however, a generation earlier.

INSPECTING THE FIRST COINED MONEY

John Ward Dunsmore, OSBORNE COMPANY, CLIFTON, NEW JERSEY

This handsome picture shows Washington and his wife and a party of friends viewing the first minted coins. Dunsmore was very meticulous about the details of his works, and thus the costumes, furniture and machinery are exact for the period in which it was laid, the early 1790's.

THE BATTLE OF LEXINGTON

Alonzo Chappel, OSCAR T. BARCK COLLECTION

One wonders whether this little-known artist ever saw the site of this first formal battle of the Revolution, which took place on a not too large triangular *common* surrounded by rather sedate homes. The action, however, is vigorous, and the presence of the drum is highly authentic. By it, rather than a bugle, orders were given in the height of battle. There was even a drum call to a *parley,* when one side was prepared to yield to the other.

THE VIRGINIA CONSTITUTIONAL CONVENTION

George Catlin, NEW YORK HISTORICAL SOCIETY

Virginia adopted its state constitution in June 1776, the first portion of which was a *bill of rights,* the earliest document of its kind drawn up in America. This scene presumably shows the able George Mason, who framed the historic document, defending his glorious handiwork. The artist became our foremost painter of the American Indian.

PATRICK HENRY ADDRESSING THE HOUSE OF BURGESSES

Peter Frederick Rothermel, PENNSYLVANIA ACADEMY OF FINE ARTS, PHILADELPHIA

Although this Pennsylvanian artist's treatment is classic, he catches the spirit and power of the fiery Virginian's oratory. This was the speech of 1765 in which the speaker had cried out, "Treason!" And Henry had replied, "If *this* be treason, make the most of it." The "give me liberty, or give me death" passage occurred in a speech at Richmond some ten years later. The gauntlet in the foreground is the symbol of defiance and challenge.

READING OF THE DECLARATION

Peter Frederick Rothermel, UNION LEAGUE, PHILADELPHIA

On August 2, 1776 the official copy of the Declaration was signed by the members then present. It was quickly set in type, printed, and distributed throughout the colonies, where it was read in various localities to highly interested listeners. This document brought an immediate need for each colony to set up its own state government, which was rapidly done.

TESTING THE LIBERTY BELL

Jean Leon Gerome Ferris, SMITHSONIAN INSTITUTE, WASHINGTON, D.C.

This famous bell was originally cast in England in 1752, but was damaged in transport to the extent that its tone was ruined. Here we see it being tested after it was recast in Philadelphia in 1753. It was at that time that the words "Proclaim Liberty throughout the land unto all the inhabitants thereof" were prophetically inscribed upon it.

THE DECLARATION OF INDEPENDENCE

John Trumbull, YALE UNIVERSITY ART GALLERY

The artist of this memorable scene was an aide to Gen. Washington, and wrote his letters and orders. Although a capable draughtsman, he had had no formal training in art and painting. In 1780 he went to London to study with Benjamin West, where he was arrested for treason, jailed for eight months, and then ordered to leave England. But he was able to return there in 1784, and renew his studies with West.

BETSY ROSS AND OUR FIRST FLAG

Jean Leon Gerome Ferris, SMITHSONIAN INSTITUTE, WASHINGTON, D.C.

Mrs. John Ross, wife of a signer of the Declaration, was chosen in 1777 to develop a flag from the design decided upon by the Congress. On its adoption, she was awarded a contract from then on to make all government flags. Following her death in 1836, this business was continued by her daughter, a Mrs. Wilson, until 1857.

ABOVE
REVERE ENGRAVING

PAGE ONE, TOP
ATTACK ON THE GASPÉ

PAGE ONE, BELOW
THE BOSTON TEA PARTY

ABOVE, **STUMP SPEAKING**   BELOW, **COINING THE FIRST MONEY**

ABOVE
BATTLE OF LEXINGTON

BELOW
VIRGINIA CONVENTION

RIGHT
PATRICK HENRY'S ADDRESS

PREVIOUS SPREAD
BATTLE OF BUNKER HILL
John Trumbull, Yale University

AT THE LEFT
WASHINGTON AT YORKTOW
Jas. Peale, Maryland Hist. Soc.

ABOVE

CORNWALLIS' SURRENDER

John Trumbull, Yale University

AT THE RIGHT

CAPTURED BATTLE FLAGS

J. W. Dunsmore, Fraunces Tavern

ABOVE

JOHN PAUL JONES

Cecilia Beaux, U.S. Naval Academy

AT THE LEFT

BONHOMME RICHARD AND THE SERAPIS

Richard Patten, U.S. Naval Academy

THOMAS JEFFERSON Gilbert Stuart, Williamsburg

BENJAMIN FRANKLIN J. S. Duplessis, N.Y. Public Library

AT THE RIGHT
SIGNING THE CONSTITUTION
H. C. Christy, U.S. Capitol, Washington

BATTLE OF BUNKER HILL

John Trumbull, YALE UNIVERSITY ART GALLERY

As an aide to Washington, Trumbull's Revolutionary experiences ideally fitted him to portray its battles and other incidents. This picture at Bunker Hill is one of his most noted canvases, and his superb draughtsmanship gives to it superior sweep and action. This sharp conflict, although not decisive in itself, paved the way to the evacuation of Boston by the British. It showed that the colonial militia, held in contempt by the British regulars, was fully competent to inflict most severe losses.

THE SURRENDER OF CORNWALLIS

John Trumbull, YALE UNIVERSITY ART GALLERY

Trumbull, the artist, was in jail in England as a traitor at about the time this scene took place. Although the British were finished, and America was free, peace terms dragged on for many months. The question is often asked what happened to Lord Cornwallis following his surrender. He was held in this country as a hostage, and later exchanged for our own Henry Laurens of South Carolina, who had been seized by the British while en route to Holland in 1780.

WASHINGTON AND HIS GENERALS AT YORKTOWN

James Peale, MARYLAND HISTORICAL SOCIETY

This artist also served as an officer in the Revolution, and was a younger brother of the even more noted Charles Wilson Peale. A miniature painter, he did two portraits of Washington.

CAPTURED FLAGS LAID AT FEET OF CONGRESS

John Ward Dunsmore, FRAUNCES TAVERN, NEW YORK

This was both a dramatic and a fully satisfying moment. The captured colors of the British forces taken at Yorktown were hurried to Philadelphia, where they were laid at the feet of the Congress, and thus symbolically at the feet of the American people who had at last conquered after years of grueling struggle.

THE *BONHOMME RICHARD* AND THE *SERAPIS*

Richard Patten, U. S. NAVAL ACADEMY MUSEUM, ANNAPOLIS

The *Bonhomme Richard,* or "good man Richard," was the name given the 40-gun ship *Duras* by Paul Jones to honor Benjamin Franklin, who had long used the title "Poor Richard" for his famous almanac. Perhaps the outstanding among its many encounters under command of its sterling captain was that with the *Serapis* in which the *Richard* sank, but not until after the enemy vessel had surrendered to him.

JOHN PAUL JONES

Cecilia Beaux, U. S. NAVAL ACADEMY MUSEUM, ANNAPOLIS

This gallant sailor was born in Scotland and bore the name John Paul until after he settled in Virginia, when he assumed the name of Jones. He ardently embraced the American cause, offered his services, and rose to be the best known of the resolute group of officers who during the Revolution built so proud a heritage for the United States Navy.

159

THOMAS JEFFERSON

Gilbert Stuart, COLONIAL WILLIAMSBURG, VIRGINIA

Although Stuart was American born, he spent much of his life in England, sailing to that country on the last ship to slip out of Boston at the outset of the Revolution to study with Benjamin West. He did more than one thousand portraits, of which 124 alone were of Washington.

BENJAMIN FRANKLIN AT THE AGE OF 77

Joseph Silfrede Duplessis, NEW YORK PUBLIC LIBRARY

This portrait was painted in France at the time Franklin was completing the treaty of peace between England and her former colonies, and nine years before his death. He was then the best known man in America, a distinction which he had won by the earnest application of a remarkable native intelligence. His genius was above all that of a practical man, goaded on throughout his long, useful life by a compelling passion for human betterment.

SIGNING OF THE CONSTITUTION

Howard Chandler Christy, UNITED STATES CAPITOL, WASHINGTON

This scene was the culmination of long weeks of secret conferences which had stretched through the humid summer of 1787. The day of the signing was September 17, and as the signatures are added, Washington, watch in hand, stands to say a few words of encouragement. Behind him is the famous *speaker's chair,* still to be seen in Independence Hall. Hamilton, Patterson, Wilson, Jay, and Madison can readily be recognized.

At the lower left, in blue satin, is Dr. Franklin. As Washington finished and resumed his seat, the old gentleman rose to reply. Calling attention to the carving at the top of the back of the speaker's chair, he said that during their often stormy deliberations he had wondered whether it represented a *rising* or a *setting* sun. Now that this mighty document about which a great nation would be built had been agreed upon, he was fully convinced that it was indeed a *rising* sun. How truly prophetic were his words.

RESIGNATION OF GENERAL WASHINGTON

John Trumbull, YALE UNIVERSITY ART GALLERY

The American people are naturally peace-loving. War is not an ambition with them. This fact was well symbolized by the promptness with which Washington resigned his commission on December 23, 1783, so he might retire to Mount Vernon and peaceful pursuits.

WASHINGTON RECEIVING NOTICE OF HIS ELECTION

John Ward Dunsmore, FRAUNCES TAVERN, NEW YORK

Able though he undeniably was, Washington was less distinguished by his brilliancy than by his towering moral strength, sound judgment, and ready, impartial understanding. These were the very characteristics needed in the first president of the new, and untried republic. It was but natural then that the electors should have decided unanimously upon him. Here at Mount Vernon he receives a committee sent to announce his election, booted and spurred after their eight-day ride on horseback from New York.

authority in what was now a community of independent, sovereign states. It was not until August 2 that an official copy received the signatures of the fifty-six delegates who happened to be present at the session held on that particular day.

THE CRADLE OF LIBERTY

But it was on July 8 that it was first proclaimed publicly. On that day a member of the Philadelphia Committee of Safety read it to a great gathering of people at the south entrance of the Province House. From that moment this building was to take on new stature, and as *Independence Hall* would come to be probably the best known and loved structure in these United States.

The document that was read there that July morning was also destined to become immortal and known and prized throughout the whole world wherever men value Liberty. It met with fervent acclaim from those who first heard it read, and this public reading touched off a celebration which lasted through that momentous day, and most of the night that followed. A vigorous and perhaps fateful step had been taken. The cheering crowds, the marching soldiers, the ringing bells that filled that exciting day were not applauding signatures to a document. They were celebrating LIBERTY, for which generations of the forebears of these now united peoples had struggled. Not a few of those that took part in this and in other like celebrations in the other colonies would soon lose homes, wealth, security, or even life itself. But Liberty and Freedom have their price, both in gaining and in maintaining them.

In the name of the officers and delegates to the Continental Congress the thirteen American colonies had declared themselves free and independent. Now they must achieve that independence through more than five years of heartbreak. The die had been cast; but the game was still to be won. The *Revolution* was now on in real earnest.

The War Years

S THE SHOUTING died down, the staggering task ahead was brought home to both the people and, in particular, its leaders. Washington had forced Lord Howe to evacuate Boston in March. A British attempt on Charleston, South Carolina, in June had been of no effect. But a ringing blow would soon be struck. The British with perhaps four hundred transports filled with men and supplies, convoyed by a fleet of ships of the line and armed auxiliaries, descended upon New York in late August. They pinned great hopes on holding control of the Hudson Valley.

Howe and his corps of generals had as many as twenty-five thousand men and were prepared to contest for control of both New York and New Jersey. Against these trained soldiers, Washington could count on no more than twelve thousand not very effective militiamen. Four encounters between then and mid-November went in favor of the British. They occupied New York and forced the Americans across the Hudson. It was not until the year's end that Washington, in two quick, skilful actions at Trenton, and then at Princeton, forced the British out of New Jersey.

The Congress had long recognized that outside assistance might be necessary, and as early as 1775 had set up a committee on foreign correspondence. Its purpose was to present the American position and the hopes and aspirations of the colonies to influential persons on the European continent.

Then, in March, 1776, Silas Deane of Connecticut was chosen to be our first ambassador and was sent to Paris. Although the British were attempting a blockade of the coast, American ships seem to have been slipping through. In the fall, after independence had been declared, Franklin and Jefferson were chosen to join Deane in France. But Jefferson had left the Congress on September 2 and returned to his home at Monticello, feeling that his duty at the moment was to aid in perfecting and liberalizing the new government of his native state.

In his stead, another Virginian, Arthur Lee, was selected to be the third member of this diplomatic mission. Somewhat later on, John Adams would be sent to Holland, and John Jay to Spain. Other agents, too, would go to Italy, Austria, Germany, and even to Russia. The new nation did all that it could to line up sentiment in the continental governments against Great Britain.

LAFAYETTE AND DE KALB ARRIVE TO OFFER THEIR SERVICES

By the end of this fateful year of 1776, several things became apparent. It would not be a short war, as the British had expected, and perhaps the Americans had hoped. For the former it was a sizable task. From New Hampshire to Georgia was near a thousand miles by a ruler on a map, but the shore line was even longer. And the scattered towns, villages, and few cities did not furnish a land from which their armies could live by forage or pillage. Supplies had to come from great distances, since it was as much as three thousand miles to British ports.

On leaving the coast and the shelter provided by heavily armed men-of-war, there was the risk of being drawn into a wilderness in which these rebels poured murderous fire, Indian fashion, from behind every tree, rock, or house corner. Further than that, the peo-ple in the back country were pretty much self-sustaining. They were not as dependent upon towns and cities as were Europeans. Thus there was staying power which wrecked every British attempt to move into the interior, and which became more apparent to them as the war dragged on.

This would be a long series of scattered engagements, rather than a campaign of a few decisive battles. Time would be on the side of the American forces, but there would be periods when it seemed a costly way to victory.

A huge task was laid upon Washington. The realization of how great it might prove was no doubt behind his deep concern when his appointment as commander-in-chief was bestowed. He had been so overcome by the confidence lodged in him, and by the grave question of his ability to prove worthy of it, that he had at first refused. But with his high sense of honor, he very much consecrated his life and energies to the service of his country.

AMERICAN ABILITY, AND FRIENDLY AID FROM EUROPE

Few of those Americans who served with him had extensive military experience. It was sixteen years since he had returned home from the French and Indian War to become a planter. This was largely true of both officers and men. But for the most part they were able and courageous and put whatever natural ability they had to excellent account. Among the leaders were such solid Patriots as: Nathanael Greene, the Rhode Island blacksmith and farmer; Dan Morgan, teamster and rifleman; John Sullivan, the New Hampshire lawyer; Israel Putnam, hero of the French and Indian War; Francis Marion, the Carolina planter; Mad Anthony Wayne, the former surveyor; and many others. Not the least in dash and ability was merchant and shipowner Benedict Arnold, finally to end as a contemptible traitor.

The American cause, however, made a strong appeal as well to men in other lands. Among those who volunteered their services were a number of experienced soldiers. One of the first to arrive was the young French Marquis de Lafayette, barely twenty years old. Not only was he of great service throughout the war, but he brought a number of companions with him who served most effectively. Among them was the much older Baron de Kalb, who became a major general and died of a wound received in the battle of Camden in 1780.

There were the two famous Poles, Kosciusko [kos-ih-US-koh] and Pulaski [pew-LAS-kee], both seasoned warriors. The latter, forced to flee from revolts in his homeland, became a cavalry leader and was mortally wounded at Savannah in 1779.

But surely one of the great contributions at a most critical time was that of the Baron von Steuben. A soldier at fourteen, he rose to become a staff officer in the German army of Frederick the Great. He reached here in 1778 and joined Washington in the darkest days at Valley Forge. He was at once made inspector general and set to work to reorganize the army, train it, and whip it into shape. This he did with true German thoroughness, even to acting as drill master on the snow-covered fields, slowly changing raw volunteers into competent soldiers.

OUR FIGHTING STRENGTH

Free men are never particularly willing soldiers. There was little military experience and no military caste in this country. American armies in major wars have always had to be built from raw materials. Also this was an enlisted army, and the newly formed states were most unwilling to provide troops for a long period of service. Thus the numbers under arms varied widely from time to time, and to Washington it often seemed to be on a day-to-day basis. At critical moments they appeared to fade away during the night. At no time did he ever have more than 40,000 effectuals, and more frequently their numbers were not over four or five thousand. Beyond that, they were usually scattered, first in the North, then later in the South.

The country could even in those days have drafted perhaps 300,000 or more men suitable for service; but that was totally impossible under the Continental Congress. Its weakness as a governing body rather than as a group of resolute men, of which it was surely composed, heavily restricted the war effort. Food, clothing, and equipment were always in short supply, and sometimes totally lacking, due principally to want of proper authority. But this latter condition had no bearing upon the slights almost to the point of insult and the unwarranted interference which Washington was forced to endure at its hands.

However, there were many problems involved in fighting this war. The British fleet had pretty well succeeded in shutting off commerce with other countries, which meant that whatever was needed must be produced at home. Although the colonies had been self-sustaining in the matter of food, excepting some luxuries, there was now a demand for tools, implements, weapons, and metal goods which in recent years had been restricted as to manufacture here by British laws. Thus iron working had to be greatly expanded. Mining was increased, furnaces

and small smelters built, and mechanics trained to man them and to aid in manufacturing. Some of this work was even forced upon war prisoners.

Textiles were especially in demand, and their increased use reached back to the raising of sheep, and the planting of flax and cotton. In fact, the scarcity of linen and wool gave a great impetus to the raising and use of cotton, and gave birth to a problem to be faced and overcome years later. The bulk of the spinning and weaving fell upon the women in the homes, to whom work was contracted out. Raw materials were supplied and the cloth collected for further finishing.

This manufacturing impulse was to stand the new country in good stead, nonetheless, for industrial development thus begun would mount rapidly in the years ahead.

The British driven from Boston had fastened their clutches firmly upon New

WASHINGTON PRAYS DURING DARK DAYS AT VALLEY FORGE

165

York. Their hold on the port at the mouth of the Hudson would remain unshaken for the rest of the war. If they could get control of the whole important river valley and the lakes lying to the north, they could cut off troublesome New England from the remainder of the colonies. Perhaps those to the south would prove less rebellious.

THE BRITISH FAIL TO
GAIN THE HUDSON VALLEY

In an attempt to get possession of these waterways, the British started a force south from Canada early in 1777. Burgoyne [bur-GOIN], who led it, issued rather boastful proclamations of his intents, possibly thinking to frighten the forces along his line of march. But the results were quite the contrary. Even Lord Howe was deceived and went on with his plans to capture Philadelphia.

The British succeeded in taking Fort Ticonderoga with their superior forces and artillery. This was a serious blow, which fell on July 6. The next battle came at Oriskany a month later. This time the victory went to the Americans, as it did on four more occasions. The last meeting, on October 7 at Bemis Heights, pitted 8,000 Americans against Burgoyne's forces, now whittled down to 5,000.

Here Burgoyne surrendered, the American soldiers gained control of the Hudson Valley, and the British were pushed out of New York State and New England. The Indians that had been allied to the forces of Burgoyne and his assistant St. Ledger continued to harry the settlers. But England's hopes of dividing the northern colonies were definitely stopped. This is often spoken of as the turning point in the war, despite bitter days ahead.

A grave error in the war ministry at home in England had kept Howe from going to the relief of Burgoyne. He had placed about 7,000 men on transports and set out to land his forces below Philadelphia and take it from the south. Washington had sent some of his men to aid in the battles up the Hudson. But with the remainder, perhaps just above 10,000, he marched overland to the vicinity of Wilmington, Delaware. Howe had effected his landing at Elk Creek at the northeast corner of Chesapeake Bay, and their forces met on the Brandywine near Chadds Ford on September 11. A blunder by one of the American generals lost them this battle and some 1,200 men. Washington fell back to Skippack Creek beyond Germantown, to the north of Philadelphia.

Terror swept that city. The Congress hastily voted the commander-in-chief great discretionary powers, and even more hastily moved the capital to Lancaster, seventy miles to the west. A little later it was pushed farther on and across the Susquehanna River to York.

PHILADELPHIA TAKEN

Howe encamped near Germantown and awaited the next move. It came about three weeks later on the foggy morning of October 4. Washington's forces had been able during the night to slip down some fourteen miles without detection. But the poor visibility turned the battle against them. They retreated a few miles to the west to Valley Forge, there to spend a shivering, starving winter.

The British took Philadelphia and spent the winter there in high revelry. With gold coin to back up their purchases, they began to buy up produce, and army contractors to the American troops turned supplies over to the enemy and became rich. Washington was finally forced to threaten local farmers with confiscation of their grain. And they demonstrated the depths to which their patriotism had fallen by burning it when seizure was at hand. This was indeed the low point of the war, and close at hand the cause may well have seemed lost.

Distances were great, however, and transmittal of news often took weeks in place of hours or even minutes today. But let us see how that condition sometimes worked to advantage. You will remember that a diplomatic mission had been sent the previous year to France. Franklin, then seventy and racked with gout, had risen to the occasion. He was a remarkable character, self-made into perhaps the most versatile American of his age. Writer, scientist, politician, he had also become the accomplished diplomat. And although he had not been formally received by the French monarch, he was the pride and toast of the French people, not excepting the king's confidants; and even the queen, Marie Antoinette, called him "our dear republican."

A MOST HELPFUL VICTORY

Anxious, of course, to press a thorn into the side of England, the French government still hesitated. The American cause was not, by reports, going too well during 1777. New York had been lost, and Howe seemed to be taking command of the situation. Success of Burgoyne's enterprise was not greatly in doubt, and it seemed prudent to wait further developments.

The most welcome news of Burgoyne's surrender came to the Americans at the French capital in December, 1777, two months after it occurred. And it was sufficiently heartening news so that Franklin

was able at a distance to make it truly the turning point of the struggle. Early in 1778 he had a treaty of alliance, and a promise of French aid. France recognized American independence and declared war upon King George. This led to Spanish intervention, in the hope of dislodging the British from Gibraltar, and later that of the Dutch, who wished to cripple England's might at sea.

FRENCH SHIPS, SOLDIERS, AND GOLD SENT TO AMERICA

French ships with soldiers, and especially supplies and gold, were dispatched across the ocean. The coming of these sinews of war had a salutary effect, although they did not mean a sudden ending of hostilities. Howe was forced to move out of Philadelphia in mid-June of 1778. On the 28th, Washington caught up with his retreating forces under Clinton at Monmouth, New Jersey. Through failure by one of his commanders, he was deprived of an overwhelming victory. The British managed to get their soldiers and supplies into New York and find some security. The war now turned to the western frontier.

Border incidents, principally Indian massacres, had continued to plague the settlers in the hill country in western New York and down into Pennsylvania since the previous summer. Under direction of prominent Tories, the savages, believing the settlers were a continuing threat, began to do their best to eliminate them. In a pitched battle in the Wyoming Valley along the Susquehanna in northern Pennsylvania on July 4, Zebulon Butler suffered defeat at the hands of a British and a Seneca Indian force led by his cousin John Butler. Thus were families divided in this struggle. On November 11 a force of Tories and Mohawks fell upon settlements in Cherry Valley in New York; and, despite the pleas for mercy by the Mohawk chief and British ally, Joseph Brant, it slew great numbers of defenseless people.

THE WAR IN THE WEST, AND NAVAL PREPAREDNESS

But at this same time George Rogers Clark was leading a small, hard-hitting force down the Ohio River. Here, with the aid of the French settlers now living under British rule, he was able to take the towns of Kaskaskia, Cahokia, and Vincennes, the last in February of 1779. By this maneuver, he established claim to possession of the Northwest Territory for the new nation in the making.

Daniel Boone, as the war was breaking out in 1776, had blazed a trail through the Cumberland Gap into the region of Kentucky. Six years earlier, James Robertson of North Carolina had pushed through the Smokies into Tennessee. Still farther south others were penetrating the country just east of the Mississippi. There were clashes with the Indians, but colonists moved in slowly to open up this area and make it secure for American claims.

Although Congress had recognized, as early as 1775, the need of carrying the war to the British fleet attempting to blockade the coast, little was accomplished that year, except perhaps the organization of one of the most famous of American fighting forces, the Marine Corps. Their authorization was by a resolution of the Congress dated November 10. Four months later they made their first amphibious landing for the capture of enemy munitions in the Bahamas. This was but the forerunner of many other ship-to-shore operations, including the single occasion during the Revolution when the Continentals set foot on English soil, as we shall soon see.

In 1776 a wealthy shipowner, John Barry, was commissioned to take command of the brig *Lexington;* and thus became the "father" of the United States Navy. His capture of the tender *Edward* was the first ship to be taken by an officer commissioned in that illustrious force.

By February, 1777, a 32-gun frigate had been made ready and stood out from Delaware Bay and began to seek out British shipping. It was but a few weeks later when she sailed into Charleston harbor herding six prizes. Fenced into that port until the early part of the next year, she sailed again with several local vessels, heading south. In March she started an encounter with a British ship with twice the armament, and was blown up. Her skipper, Captain Nicholas Biddle, and most of her more than three hundred seamen were lost.

JOHN PAUL JONES

Although he had been commissioned a lieutenant in 1776, it was not until November of the next year that the man whose name towers above all other naval commanders of the Revolution really saw action. Leaving Portsmouth, New Hampshire, in the tiny 18-gun *Ranger,* John Paul Jones began to prey upon British ships even to setting fire to vessels in the English harbor of Winterhaven on the Irish Sea. The Marines, too, began making landings upon foreign soil, of which there have been nearly three hundred through the years.

But great as some of these exploits were, which piled up the loss to their shipping at the hands of intrepid American captains and privateers, the British supremacy on the seas continued. It was not until French ships

THE TURNING POINT CAME AT KING'S MOUNTAIN

arrived in numbers that England's control of the American coast was really threatened.

In July, 1778, about a month after Howe withdrew his forces from that city, Congress returned to Philadelphia. Finances were in desperate straits. Paper money was easy to print, but its value depreciated so quickly that its purchasing power was limited. This condition was known to England, which now had hopes of quickly concluding the hostilities, despite the action of France.

Conditions in the South were very bad, too. There had been little of the real war in that area, but Tories were numerous, and in some sections virtual civil war smoldered and often broke out. This appeared to be the most likely point for the next campaign. Tory-led raids would be stepped up wherever possible; and plans were made to land sizable numbers of men at Charleston, to take advantage of such disturbance as could be achieved. As they came ashore, they were joined by Indians brought in from Florida and Alabama to assail the frontier. Others were promised from faraway Detroit, on the edge of the Northwest Territory.

Two battles were fought at Savannah, the first on December 28, 1778, and the next

the following October. Both were lost to the British, who thus reduced Georgia to submission. Finances had prevented sending greater help, and the year 1778 closed with opposing forces throughout the colonies in much the same position as at the end of 1776. The freeing of the South from Tory tyranny would have to wait two more years.

In July, 1779, a decisive victory for American forces at Stony Point gave the Americans undisputed control of the Hudson. At the end of August, a fair-sized expedition against the Indians in western New York greatly weakened the striking power of the tribes known as the *Six Nations*. Thus the pressure on the frontier was eased. The net result for the upper colonies was good, despite this being a relatively quiet year.

Exception could be taken to this in the South, however. Troops operating out of captured Georgia had made the situation in South Carolina rather critical. As a cruel winter settled down in the North, whose deep snows and intense cold killed both men and beasts, the British felt it an opportune time to turn their attention to the warmer area down the coast. There they counted on strong support from the many Tories.

A force sent by them from New York ran into storms and did not reach Charleston until late January. Between weather and American cruisers, this expedition was badly shaken. It was not until April, 1780, that that city could be put under siege. The situation within it was difficult, and became desperate when Lord Cornwallis arrived with three thousand fresh troops. By May 12 there was no other course but to surrender. This was a crushing blow, for five thousand Americans fell prisoner. North Carolina paid the heaviest price, for she lost all her regular soldiers and now seemed virtually defenseless.

CORNWALLIS' EARLY SUCCESS

This stinging defeat, however, had left at liberty the unassuming but very effective General Marion, now known for his military cunning as the "Swamp Fox." Also there were Colonels Sumter and Pickens and a number of other courageous leaders. By vigorous guerrilla warfare, they kept the interior unsafe for the British getting ready to press inland; and did much to offset such Tory activities as blazed up from time to time.

In August, Cornwallis met and defeated the Americans under Gates at Camden, South Carolina, about one hundred miles north of Charleston. His purpose was to sufficiently subdue the countryside so that allegiance to the British government might be exacted of the people, as it had been in the doomed city on the coast. The next objective would be Charlotte, up the Catawba River, and just over the line in North Carolina.

Realizing this, the governor of the "Old North State" made an appeal for help to the mountaineers and to the backwoodsmen of

Eastern Tennessee. Some nine hundred responded, including a force from the western tip of Virginia; and no braver group ever bore rifles or rode a horse. Under Shelby and Sevier, they met a slightly larger number of the enemy under command of a Colonel Ferguson on King's Mountain, about five miles over the border into South Carolina.

KING'S MOUNTAIN VICTORY A "TURNING OF THE TIDE"

Although Ferguson has picked a strong position, the mountain men were crack shots. The English commander fell in this savage engagement, as did three hundred of his men. The remainder had no choice but to surrender.

This heartening victory was sorely needed, and Jefferson spoke of it as the "joyful turning of the tide." It was in the best American tradition, equal in that respect to Lexington-Concord. It gave the depressed people new courage, as the other had given them common purpose, and brought a new aspect to the war. Morgan dealt the British another defeat at Cowpens in January of 1781. The next two engagements, at Guilford Court House in April, and at Hobkirk's Hill in May, went to the enemy. Finally at Eutaw Springs, in September that year, an American victory forced the British out and gave control of the South back to the Americans.

Nathanael Greene, the Rhode Islander who had taken over command in that area, was making it very uncomfortable for Cornwallis. So was the French fleet offshore, which cut off his supplies. The Britisher beat a hasty retreat toward Virginia, hoping to find relief at the hands of the British fleet in Chesapeake Bay. But although driving toward the coast, he was in reality setting a

CORNWALLIS SURRENDERS TO WASHINGTON

trap from which there was little hope of escape.

Washington at this time was at Dobbs Ferry planning to descend the Hudson, and, with French aid, dislodge the British from New York. When word came of the activities in the South, he abandoned this attempt, but managed to leave sufficient reasons lodged in the mind of Clinton, the British commander, that he was convinced the attempt would still be carried out. When American troops marched away, Clinton took it to be merely a feint in preparation for an attack.

By September 5, Washington's forces were camped at Chester, Pennsylvania. While the general made haste to Mt. Vernon for a two-day stay after an absence of six years, the Army continued south to join with Lafayette on the York Peninsula. On the 25th, the last of the Continental forces had arrived at Williamsburg. There were perhaps 20,000 effectives in all on the American side. Cornwallis, with not above 8,000, saw the trap about to be sprung.

He sent a frantic appeal to his superior, Lord Clinton, in New York. He must have aid, and at once, or expect to have most dismal news shortly.

But Admiral de Grasse and the French fleet had command of the entrance to Chesapeake Bay and had also succeeded in landing troops under Rochambeau [row-SHAM-bow].

On September 28 some 12,000 soldiers left Williamsburg for Yorktown, about twelve miles away near the mouth of the York River. British outposts were pressed back, and a horseshoe-shaped line thrown about the enemy army, with a space of two miles between the opposing men. After two

171

more days of squeezing, the Continental line reached to the river at both ends, and Cornwallis was surrounded on the land side. Assistance from British troops across the stream in Gloucester county was prevented, since they were held fast in their position there by the Virginia militia, aided by French soldiers and marines.

THE END IS IN SIGHT

As the pressure on him increased, Cornwallis made an attempt to cut a hole in the strangle-line of Americans and French by a spirited cavalry charge. But it was quickly routed, and the line drawn even tighter.

By the 9th of October, the American right flank had forced its way in close enough so that its artillery could be made effective. A cannonading now began. During the following night it was turned upon the British ships lying just offshore. Solid iron cannon balls were heated until white-hot in charcoal fires and popped into the muzzles of the guns just before they were fired. Several of these hot shots found their mark, and a number of the vessels were set afire.

As the line about them became slowly tighter, an epidemic broke out among the British, striking down about one-quarter of the men. Supplies also had run so low that the cavalry horses had had to be killed and thrown into the nearby river. This desperate situation forced an equally desperate decision upon Cornwallis. He would abandon his sick and his heavier baggage, try to slip across the river by night, and attempt to fight his way through the lighter forces gathered there. But a storm ruined his plans, and further resistance promised eventual annihilation.

He at once opened negotiations, and the terms of his surrender were signed on the 18th. Then, on that memorable afternoon of October 19 in the year 1781, the British troops marched out of Yorktown. Their colors were cased, and the tune they marched to was *"The World Turned Upside Down."* The last British army left on American soil had been whipped by what, according to European standards, was "a rabble bearing arms."

A New Era was born that day. But what had the victory cost? And was this young America strong enough to stand alone; or destined to become a pawn of nations across the sea, bent upon curbing proud Britain?

This British capitulation, at the hands of Lord Charles Cornwallis, virtually ended the war. But the peace still had to be made. And, more important still, the future had to be made secure.

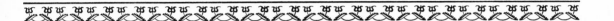

Not Worth a Continental

HE defeat at Yorktown had come in October of 1781. But two months later King George stoutly maintained that under no circumstances would he recognize American independence. By the following February, however, Parliament was ready to concede that the cause was lost, and the king was forced to yield.

In April of 1782 secret word came to Franklin in Paris that the British were now willing to begin discussing a settlement. Yet it was not until the next year that the treaty was signed. But it was worth waiting for, since it proved a complete victory for America.

Spain and France were also involved in drawing it. The former held Florida and also Louisiana, which had been ceded to Spain by France in 1763. The French, however, gained no territory on the North American continent at this time. England retained Canada, Newfoundland, and certain of the West Indies Islands. To the United States then fell undisputed possession of the territory reaching from the Great Lakes and upper St. Lawrence Valley to the Gulf; and from the Atlantic to the Mississippi.

The colonies' individual struggles for self-determination and then their combined effort toward independence had made a considerable impact upon European thought. Many of the state constitutions, with their guarantees of liberty and civil rights, had been printed and circulated abroad. Men were reading, thinking about, and, in France at least, preparing to demand some of the *rights* these documents promised. Said the Spanish ambassador at the peace conference, in a letter to his king: "This federal republic is born a pigmy, but the day will come when it will be a giant to be reckoned with."

By contrast, a British army officer said a few years later: "As to the future of America, and its being a rising empire . . . it is one of the idlest nations ever conceived. They have no center of union, and no common interest. They can never be united under any government whatever; a disunited people to the end of time, distrustful of each other, they will be divided and subdivided into little commonwealths."

And there was some reason to believe, even among thinking men in the colonies, that this might well prove true. A common danger and a common purpose had welded them together after a fashion through the war years. Now selfish local interests threatened to make thirteen little countries of them, subject to their being turned against one another.

TYPICAL LOCAL CONDITIONS

But let us see what was happening at the grass roots. We have already visited in the village of Farmington in the Connecticut colony. Now let us go back there and see how its people reacted to happenings. While the treaty at Versailles had been signed on January 20, 1783, it was March 27 before a chance letter from overseas brought the information to this village and to nearby Hartford.

In the latter place, there was rather a rousing celebration, with the ringing of church bells, the firing of cannon, and an evening illumination, which included fireworks. But if there was any special recognition of the momentous news in Farmington, then the larger of the two towns, it is not mentioned in town records. The people there seem to have been straining to right themselves from the prostrating conditions left by the war years.

From the stimulus given by the war effort, the new country had spiraled down rapidly to a low point. Banks were without cash. The farmers, still the large bulk of the population, were without credit. And the merchants were without goods. A scant twenty miles to the north of this village was the Massachusetts state line. Goods passing over it into Connecticut were forced to pay a duty to the latter state. New York, to the west, and Rhode Island, to the east, both taxed imports from Connecticut. Even the state boundaries themselves were not too well established and brought about tensions which threatened to flare into open warfare.

Money affairs which placed restrictions upon Farmington people were similarly a burden elsewhere. There was only a very limited amount of metal coinage. The colonies, now become *states,* had printed great quantities of paper currency. So had the Congress itself. These notes, known as *continentals,* rapidly sank in value until they were worth no more than from one to a few cents on the dollar of their face value. Rooms were papered with them. Men who had served in the armed forces and were paid off in these worthless notes paraded about with them sewed to their clothing. The utmost phrase of contempt of that time was *"not worth a continental."* And this phrase began to color the people's thinking in regard to the Congress established under the Articles of Confederation. It was powerless to deal with these questions and disputes between states and sections.

ARTICLES OF CONFEDERATION

When these Articles of Confederation had been proposed, a town meeting had been called in Farmington at some time in 1778, to instruct the town's representatives in the state legislature in regard to the attitude they should take in voting. There seemed to be much of promise in certain of the steps which these Articles proposed. But it was "with the utmost pain" that the town fathers thought they discovered certain proposals which would be very detrimental to New England, and to Connecticut in particular.

Playing for sectional advantage was widespread throughout the then but imperfectly *united* States; and attack or defense of the various aspects of these Articles of Confederation was the political sport of the times.

(*Continued on page 177*)

an American Creed

I believe in the united states of america as a government of the people, by the people, for the people, whose just powers are derived from the consent of the governed; a democracy in a republic, a sovereign nation of many sovereign states; a perfect union, one and inseparable, established upon the principles of freedom, equality, justice, and humanity for which american patriots sacrificed their lives and fortunes. I therefore believe it my duty to my country to love it, to support its constitution, to obey its laws, to respect its flag; and to defend it against all enemies.

William Tyler Page

the children's declaration

we, the children of the united states of america, born of farmers, storekeepers, clerks, iron workers, artists—on the plains, in the mountains, in the villages and in the cities, do hereby pledge our faith in the future. we have this faith because we are the future.

we are of all colors, creeds, and races. we have studied our country's historic documents, and we know that these are more than paper and parchment and words, and that we, the future, must keep their truths close to our hearts and make them live. we stand on the threshold of destiny in a world where ideas good and evil engulf us, to be boldly accepted or rejected. we are children, but unlike those of 1776, we can see and hear in our homes the actual sounds and visions of history at the moment it is made.

we know well the meaning of the sacrifices made by our fathers, brothers, and neighbors on the battlefields. we are not afraid of things to come. we believe that the god of our great, great grandfathers is just as near today; and we subscribe to this declaration, knowing that it is as real as our resolve to be free.

R. E. Beauchamp

Money matters were perhaps the greatest bone of contention in the postwar years, and its scarcity forced various methods of paying debts. In Virginia tobacco certificates were issued. In New England there were rye, hemp, and even pork certificates. Such *hard* money, or metal coinage, as there was still in circulation varied widely as to its value. The English shilling had in Colonial times been in common use. But in North Carolina after the war eight were reckoned a dollar; while in Massachusetts nine equaled a dollar and a half. One could either gain, or lose, about one-third of the value of such coins as he carried from one of these states into the other. Similarly, Spanish "pieces of eight" had widely different values in the various states. The result was financial confusion bordering on chaos.

FARM INTERESTS HOLD THE BALANCE OF POWER

The largest political block was, of course, the farmers. Many had served during the war, only to return home to neglected farms heavily loaded with debt and faced by sky-high taxes. Their insistent demands on state legislatures were either ignored or brought little relief. And as early as 1780 the farmers of New Hampshire took up arms and marched on their state legislature. This open rebellion was terminated peaceably, but with some difficulty.

Six years later, in 1786–87, there was a serious uprising in western Massachusetts, headed by an ex-officer named Daniel Shay. It was a protest against increasing burdens in such things as court fees, lawsuits, and especially imprisonment for debt. State governments, as well as the Confederation, were weak and unable to find means of providing men with ways in which they could work out their common problems without undue hardships.

OPEN REBELLION

Although the Shay forces of about 1,100 men attempted to capture the Springfield Arsenal and its war stores, the authorities did not dare deal harshly with them when they were repulsed. Word of this open rebellion threatened to touch off similar movements elsewhere; and word of it made a profound impression upon George Washington. He is reported to have said, "It was but the other day that we were shedding our blood to obtain the constitutions under which we now live. Now we are unsheathing our sword to overthrow them."

A civil war truly seemed to be in the making, and there were even ugly rumors of a dictatorship or the formation of a monarchy. Never before in all the world had so great a number of people, scattered over so immense a territory, attempted to govern themselves. Was this noble experiment doomed so soon to fail?

The hope was that common men could under freedom, liberty, and law properly manage their own affairs. Each was to have equal power, so that he would be free to struggle for his own self-interest and arrive at some satisfactory balance in his relations with other men. But he was not accomplishing these things at the level of the individual. Neither did the various state legislatures seem to be able to cut through selfish and class interests.

At the higher level, he was a citizen of a very loose confederation of states which occupied but a portion of this New World. Why, even his very freedom, for which he had just fought, could be endangered by Britain, France, or Spain, all of which still had a considerable stake in this Western Hemisphere.

He had learned to fear *authority* of the old pagan type, as represented in the persons of kings and monarchs who ruled by "divine right." He had done his share in keeping anything similar to such concentration of power out of the state constitutions and the Articles of Confederation. But he suddenly found himself powerless to cope with many of his most pressing personal problems. Something must be done, but what?

CONCENTRATION OF POWER

The common man, so close to his own immediate affairs that they loomed largest, tended to be a little biased in his thinking. He feared any concentration of power. But when he could bring himself to look abroad a little, he realized he probably did need a much stronger central government. It was not to rule him, but it did need to be strong enough to hold its own against the great world powers. And also it needed to be fully capable of pulling people together for common accomplishments, as in the war years. There was distinct need for great co-operation among the nearly three million people who now were citizens of these thirteen United States.

As soldiers in the Revolution, many of the men had served in various localities far beyond their own homes. With their brothers from other colonies, they had campaigned together, come to know one another better, and had laid down the foundation for inter-sectional understanding. Under pressure of necessity, they had probably found much common ground. But with the termination of hostilities, and a return to their homes and to hard times, this intermingling of considerable numbers largely ceased.

There had been considerable interchange of peoples between some of the colonies during the years of settlement before the war. But those that were now in transit were moving principally into new areas, and thereby tending to complicate problems. In the twenty years following the signing of the peace, no less than 147 families, perhaps as many as 750 people in all, left the village of Farmington. Many of them headed into Vermont, then opening up; or struck out for western New York State and on into the Northwest Territory.

For a number of years they had had to stand united. Now the common danger had been removed, at least temporarily, and their differences tended to come to the fore. While they still had one common concern, it worked to thrust them apart, rather than bind them together. They, and their fathers before them, had had bitter experiences with royal governors and other appointees exercising authority laid down at a distance, and without knowledge of local conditions. They wanted nothing faintly resembling this in any joint activities now undertaken.

LOCAL INTERESTS

Even in their various localities there were still vestiges of authority wielded "for the good of all," but which made independent thinking and action highly restricted. Such restrictions would begin to taper off rapidly in the years just ahead; but at the moment they dampened attempts at better understanding of common needs.

Education, too, was for the majority limited to little more than a bare smattering of the three "R's"—reading, writing, and arithmetic. An untutored man does not co-operate easily and successfully in large undertakings. Communication was very poor. Letters

SHAY'S FOLLOWERS SEIZE THE
ARSENAL AT SPRINGFIELD

were most infrequent, and the press was principally the mouthpiece of self-seeking individuals or controlled by powerful local groups. Its news-gathering facilities were limited; and at the close of the Revolution there were but forty-three newspapers throughout the colonies, all of them weeklies.

Thus the average man knew little about actual conditions beyond his daily round of activities. With his limited contacts, particularly outside his town, he was dependent upon those more fortunate in this respect or upon a biased press. With times becoming

more and more jumbled, he had to look to leaders for guidance and for a way out of difficulties which were slowly reaching down through to every last person. But even in his own locality, or surely in his state, there were wide differences of opinion to the point where acknowledged leaders were openly and roundly criticized and vilified. In private correspondence of the time no less a figure than "the father of his country" came in for his full share of abuse.

But it was this same George Washington, however, who began to make the constructive moves that were to bring order out of the grave confusion into which the new country was slipping with frightening speed. His personal contacts throughout the colonies were probably greater than those of any other person. But there were leaders, too,

179

like John Adams of Massachusetts, Alexander Hamilton in New York, Ben Franklin in Pennsylvania, Madison of Virginia, and the Pinckneys and John Rutledge of South Carolina, who had great numbers of acquaintances beyond their immediate areas with whom they kept in touch. Here was a nucleus about which something beneficial to all might be accomplished.

GRAVE COMMON PROBLEMS

A dispute had arisen over the use of the Potomac River sufficient to threaten grave trouble. To forestall it, Washington made a personal appeal for a meeting at Mount Vernon of representatives of the several states involved. And it was perhaps here that the seeds were first sown. There had been a widespread newspaper campaign, beginning as early as 1780, for revision of the *Articles,* and the time was ripening. In the hospitable atmosphere of the great home in Virginia, those gathered were probably impressed with the need for something positive being done to better the over-all picture.

The Virginia legislature soon afterward called upon the several states to send repre-

sentatives to a conference for that purpose. When it finally met in Annapolis in 1786, it was most disappointing to find that delegates from but five states had answered the call. But these delegates were enthused sufficiently so they went home and pressed the Congress of the United States to issue invitations for a second meeting, this one to be convened in Philadelphia. The call for it, which went out in February of 1787, was most urgent, and the firm promise was made that its purpose was limited to *revision* of the Articles of Confederation.

It would seem that, although the achievements under the Articles had, in many respects, been such that they were *not worth a continental,* there was still much fear of what might happen through any meddling. Ugly rumors of a dictatorship and of a monarchy had persisted. There were groups seeking special privilege at work throughout the states; and most men were on guard lest any of them were attempting to grasp further power.

It was somewhat consoling, then, when the delegates did assemble at Philadelphia in May of that same year, to find that every state, except Rhode Island, was represented.

We the People

NCE again Independence Hall was to be the meeting place of a group of patriots who would produce one of the most important documents in the history of the world. There were seventy-three delegates appointed, but no more than fifty-five of them appear on the rolls of the sessions. The average attendance was between thirty and thirty-five on meeting days which spread through the weeks from the organization of the Convention on May 25 to its adjournment on September 17.

We should perhaps give no special emphasis to Rhode Island's reluctance to be represented. Among individuals, no less a patriot than Patrick Henry of Virginia refused to appear. There were some other similarly prominent men who absented themselves, because they, too, were afraid that a national government, which might well develop from these sessions, would drain all power away from the individual states.

But some of the ablest men of the land were there, nearly all of them students of government and widely experienced in public affairs. And they were practical-minded men, rather than theorists. They had been heavily involved in the fight for freedom, and they were determined to protect civil rights and, above all, individual liberties. Although they did not know it at the time, there were among their numbers two future Presidents, and one Vice-President, as well as five Justices of the Supreme Court, two of whom were to become Chief Justices. Three had sat in the Stamp Act Congress in 1765, eight had signed the Declaration of Independence, all but twelve had served in the Congress, and no less than eighteen of them were still members of that body. Seven had been state governors, and at least four high officers in the Continental Army.

Here was an array of America's ablest talent. None of them wanted a strong central government. But they knew they must either have a stronger government or plunge into an anarchy in which their very freedom was at stake. James Madison, one of the truly great names in this Convention, keynoted what lay before them. Said he, "Our work will decide forever the fate of republican government."

The purpose for which they had been called was the possible alteration of the Articles; but it was quickly apparent that the needs led far beyond this limited approach. But it is said that in the hundred-odd years previous to this historic meeting, more than one hundred constitutions had been written, and many of them discarded, here on this continent. Many of these delegates had had a part in drawing some of these documents and were more or less familiar with the others. So another constitution would not be a journey into an unexplored area for them.

SECRET SESSIONS ONLY

At the risk of being thoroughly misunderstood, it was decided at the outset that the meetings should be completely secret. What they did there was to be secret not only for the duration of the Convention, but for the life of all its delegates as well. Even that grand old gentleman, Ben Franklin, who in his older years tended to talk perhaps too freely, was accompanied in public during the sessions by some discreet younger man to prevent him from giving away the subject matter being debated. Other equally extreme measures were adopted to stop possible leaks. And it is well that such precautions were taken, for open sessions or knowledge of what did transpire might well have brought these efforts to a speedy termination.

Another fortunate move was the choice of Washington as the presiding officer. Perhaps no one else could have held the delegates together or to their task. To further aid in maintaining order, very strict rules of procedure were put in force. But perfect secrecy was the watchword. When on one occasion a member carelessly dropped his copy of matters under discussion within the State House itself and the paper was recovered and laid on the presiding officer's desk, Washington sternly rebuked him before the gathering.

Only those motions put to a vote and the tally of the members' votes upon them were entered in the official record. This document

was very brief, told but little, and was not published until 1818, when Congress so ordered.

But James Madison kept very complete notes of the whole proceedings, including the speeches and debates. Other members at a later time aided him in revising and amplifying what he had recorded of the parts they had played. This was the only detailed record which was kept. And as though Fate decreed it, Madison was the last of the delegates to die. He had carefully guarded these secrets through the lifetime of them all. After his own death his notes were published, and from them and a few very fragmentary items left by others, comes our only knowledge of what actually took place.

DIVERSITY OF INTERESTS

The delegates gathered were from seaboard areas which stretched out for well over one thousand miles, a very considerable distance in those days. They were from widely differing backgrounds, and, being for the most part well-to-do, they tended, through their own interests, to accent the sectional differences and strong biases.

While similar conditions had prevailed some years before when the Continental Congress had first met, the common danger then had been so immediate and so clearcut that the compulsion to find quick solutions had been much greater. There was no Lord Howe with a sizable British force holding Boston. Neither was the English navy as yet patrolling the coast and ravaging shipping. There seemed more time in which to play for sectional advantage. But there was the highly disturbing feeling that something constructive must be done. And perhaps before their eyes was one of the early flags of the Revolution, bearing the motto, "United we stand; divided we fall," as a goad to accomplishments. Still the adjustments which must be made before there could be anything like a meeting of minds were huge, and many times seemed sufficient to send those gathered home with empty hands.

The first great clash came over whether they were merely to revise and amend the loose Confederation, or plunge ahead and form a new and more effective type of government. After much exertion, the bolder among them swung the majority over to the latter enterprise.

BY LAW, OR BY MEN?

Then they were confronted with the question of whether what they sought was to be a government by *law,* or by *men*. The choice was clear, it would be by law. But government by law was then a most daring experiment. It had never been tried before; and, less than two centuries old, is still something of an experiment, as yet not finally proven permanent and abiding. Such proof lies in our hands today, and in those of our children throughout the tomorrows ahead.

Next they must decide whether it was to be a government by states, or by the people. At this point the delegates from the smaller states immediately were on their guard against encroachments by the larger states. Also democracy—*the rule of the mob*—was highly feared. In fact the term *democracy* was not used in connection with the government of the United States until very recent years. When Edmund Randolph put forward the Virginia Plan, calling for a Congress of two houses, with members allotted among the states on a basis of wealth or of white population, turmoil broke loose.

The deadlock over this so-called tyrannical plan nearly broke up the Convention.

States as far removed as Massachusetts and South Carolina joined in opposition to any considerable voice by the common people. Pinckney of the latter state even went to the extreme at one point of demanding a guarantee that no man should be President unless he was worth at least $100,000, and federal judges and members of Congress must be large landholders. Something approaching rule by an *aristocracy* was often very much in evidence. By contrast, Franklin and James Wilson of Pennsylvania held out for popular elections.

Madison declared that at least one house should rest upon the people and thus win their loyalty. This pointed the way to an eventual compromise. The House of Representatives would be elected by direct vote. The Senate would give the states of various sizes more equal balance by having two members from each, to be selected by their legislatures. They, by the way, were not at first to represent the citizens, but were primarily to represent a state in its relation to other states. The President would be voted for, although by indirect means. Federal judges would not be elected, but would be appointed by the President and the Senate. This solution was reached over a rough path, with fighting every step of the way and with much opposition still remaining in many minds.

WHO SHOULD VOTE?

Then came another stiff hurdle—*who* should vote? "Landowners only," cried one group. "Was it not the landowning farmers who elected the state legislatures that have brought us to this confusion?" asked others. This was too thorny a question; and was finally by-passed by making suffrage the responsibility of the several states.

183

There was another sharp line of cleavage already forming which was one day to play a large part in the War between the States. The South was still and would long continue to be dependent upon agriculture. The North, on the other hand, was even then shifting over more and more toward industry and trade. The balance of population and of wealth lay in this latter section. Popular voting might well tend to impose a heavy burden upon the South in several ways. It could come through taxation, or be felt because of duties on imports, laid to protect northern manufacturers. Tobacco, rice, and other southern crops were shipped principally to England and to Europe, and manufactured goods taken from there in return.

QUESTION OF SLAVERY

Thus the South wanted no restrictions on this two-way commerce; while the North believed some regulation, and especially a "protective" tax on imports to be necessary. Power in the proposed Congress thus became a thorny issue, and to help settle it another compromise was pressed through. It revolved in large measure about those unfortunates held as slaves. They were not to be valued at full number, but three-fifths only should be reckoned in the apportionment of representatives between the states, or when direct taxes were imposed.

This tended to bring the whole question of slavery up for consideration. There was some debate over it as a moral and social problem. But the real point at issue was the Congress's control over interstate commerce. There was defense of the institution of slavery from both the North and the southern states. But there was opposition, too, and from northern delegates as well as from some from the upper South.

Thus another threatening issue had to be disposed of—but not permanently settled—by a compromise. No regulation prohibiting import of slaves from abroad could be put in force for at least twenty years. There could be no import duty higher than ten dollars per head. And ratification of any treaty with a foreign power required a two-thirds favorable vote by the Senate. Since such a treaty might well be needed to shut off the slave trade, the deep South felt it could always muster the votes needed to defeat any attempts in that direction. Still another concession granted was the demand to return runaway slaves. But since there were still many indentured servants in the North, it was readily acceded to.

June and July had passed by now, with tempers kept at high heat by continual debate and by Philadelphia summer weather. By the end of this second month, however, enough agreement had been reached so that a committee of five, headed by John Rutledge, war-time governor of South Carolina, was chosen to make a written draft of what was thus far acceptable. During ten days, while the Convention recessed, these men labored at their task.

Then began five more weeks of sessions, in which the delegates worked over what had been set down. It would seem that this first draft had been somewhat undistinguished. Jefferson, author of the beloved Declaration, was absent from the country, ambassador at the French court. Another document, destined to be similarly immortal, although the delegates again did not perhaps then recognize the fact, was in the making. It had need, however, to be clearly and forcefully worded. And once more a facile pen was ready for the task.

It was that of Gouverneur Morris of New York, one of the most colorful characters in

GOUVERNEUR MORRIS DRAFTING THE CONSTITUTION

Unlike the Declaration, the Constitution was debated first then put into words. While Morris'
work was outstanding, it was not the original contribution that Jefferson had made.

this country during the Revolution and until his death in the early 1800's. His eloquent pen had done much to build morale during the dark days of the war. Now it was enlisted to bring about greater common purpose. It began by a much better approach to such purpose in the very preamble itself.

This had first been drafted to read, "We the people of New Hampshire, of Massachusetts, etc., etc., etc.," naming the states represented, "do ordain, declare and establish the following Constitution . . ." Why continue to emphasize sectionalism? Why not set up something about which men could rally and toward which they could direct less biased thinking? With greater directness, Morris redrafted it, "We the people of the United States." What was their true purpose, just to have a Constitution? Far from it. So

he stated the purpose boldly, "in order to form a more perfect Union."

And with this effective objective before them, the delegates forged ahead, Morris catching their final decisions with crisp, direct words. The lawmaking body, the *Congress,* was authorized. To balance it and carry out its decisions, there would be an executive branch, the *Presidency.* Then to hold all decisions and acts to strict legality, within the scope of the powers laid down, there would be the judiciary, the *Federal Courts.* Checks and balances between these three branches were set up.

New powers over taxation, commerce, and money were vested in Congress. There was provision made for national defense. It could raise and employ armies and build and sail a navy, both in the interest of *all* citizens.

185

SAID DR. FRANKLIN, "I HAVE THE HAPPINESS TO
KNOW IT IS A RISING, AND NOT A SETTING, SUN."

Rather broad powers were conferred upon this new government, and certain restrictions laid upon the states.

And knowing, as the September days began to pass, that its work had involved much compromise, and was thus perhaps far from perfection, it made provision for changes in times ahead by means of *amendments*. Two-thirds of the states might appeal for a change, or the amendment might originate in a two-thirds vote within the Congress. But ratification must be by a three-fourths favorable vote by all the States. Thus change was possible, but not subject to headlong and ill-considered action, or the whims or fancies of any sectional group.

AGREEMENT IS REACHED

By Saturday, September 15, Madison was able to enter this item among his notes: "On the question to agree to the Constitution, all the states say 'aye.' " On the following Monday, the delegates met again briefly to listen to a speech from their presiding officer, who had been their unanimous choice. As the moment for adjournment pressed close, and while thirty-nine of the delegates who had continued to the end affixed their signatures to the document which they had wrought, Franklin asked permission to speak.

FRANKLIN'S APT COMMENT

His legs may still have been badly plagued by gout, but his mind was still quick, and his humor as ready as ever. Here was a man who had come up from most humble beginnings, and who, by his own native wit and his life-long study, had made himself a world-renowned figure. He relished, too, just such a moment as he had now chosen. Looking over the expectant faces turned toward him, he drew their eyes, with his own, to Washington in the high-backed chair on the raised platform at the end of the hall. Then, said he, with his customary oblique approach, "Painters have found it difficult to distinguish in their art a rising from a setting sun. I have often, in the course of a session, looked at the one behind the President without being able to tell whether it was rising or setting. But now at length I have the happiness to know that it is a rising, and not a setting, sun." It was a most admirable parting thought.

The necessary signatures were finally obtained. Sometimes angry but always alert and earnest men had produced a document destined to become the supreme law of the land. They had, perhaps, wrought better than they realized.

The Convention was then adjourned, and many of the delegates started for their homes, some of them a full two weeks' travel away. There, almost without exception, they would

be called upon to staunchly defend the actions taken.

Morris had wisely chosen to begin with the now memorable words, "We the people of the United States . . ." It was out of their needs that their chosen representatives had decided upon this course. In place of patching up a weak confederacy, they had hewn out the framework for a new and untried form of government—a republic.

What would the people's reaction be? In what manner would they accept or reject the results of so many weeks of laborious effort by so many highly dedicated men?

Launching the Ship of State

 T THE close of the Convention, the signed copy of the proposed Constitution was handed to Congress. On September 28, eleven days later, that body directed that it be "transmitted to the several legislatures in order to be submitted to a convention of delegates chosen in each state by the people thereof." Thus adoption or rejection would not be by direct popular vote, but by the action of groups chosen in each state after the manner of the selection of presidential electors today.

The first state to ratify was Delaware, by a convention which met on December 7. Within ten days Pennsylvania had followed her lead. On the second day of 1788 Georgia gave it unanimous assent, as had Delaware and New Jersey. In all other states the votes would be divided, and in some cases too close for comfort.

Then there was approval in Connecticut, in Massachusetts (by a vote of 187 to 168), in Maryland, and in South Carolina. Favorable action by this last state developed a critical moment, for the Constitution did not become law until nine states had given their consent.

Finally, on June 21, New Hampshire gave its approval. Virginia, which had hesitated because no provision was incorporated prohibiting the slave trade, finally ratified four days later. Then there was a pause of a month, and on July 26 New York became the last state to sanction the new government in the year 1788. But these sanctions had in many cases been given with the understanding that there would be certain amendments made to patch up what were considered to be weaknesses.

North Carolina rejected the Constitution, and Rhode Island refused to even vote on the issue. Thus these two states did not join the Union until after the new government was in operation.

The fourteen months from the first session of the Convention through to ratification by New York had been a perilous period. James Madison, then but thirty-six years old, is fully deserving of being known as "the father of the Constitution." He and the slightly younger Alexander Hamilton had played a most conspicuous place in the secret sessions which had brought this great frame of government into being. Along with them might be mentioned the canny Scot, James Wilson of Pennsylvania, and the shrewd Yankee, Roger Sherman of Connecticut. It should perhaps be noted again that Thomas Jefferson had no part in the drafting or acceptance of the Constitution, since he was then outside the country as ambassador to France.

OUTSTANDING CONTRIBUTION OF MADISON AND HAMILTON

Although many who had attended the Convention lent their aid to turning the mass of the people in favor of this new form of government, the brunt of the effort fell upon Hamilton, and especially Madison. In the series of eighty-five articles or essays written for newspaper publication, and later collected and titled *The Federalist,* Madison had been the author of fifty-one of them. This is one of the world's great texts upon government and did much to win popular approval.

There are a few mistaken ideas in connection with this historic document which may well be pointed out before we see how it was put into force. First let us consider the attitude of its framers.

As in the case of the Declaration, it is doubtful if its signers considered it either a perfect or a very long-lived document. Even Washington is claimed to have said he did not expect it to be in existence for more than twenty years. Still it now has the distinction of being the oldest frame of government in use in the world today.

To those who have not read it, even in part, since school days, it seems perhaps a very ponderous and wordy document. But actually Morris made it remarkable in its field for brevity, clarity, and exactness of language. Gladstone, prime minister of England at a later time, praised it as being "the most wonderful work ever struck off at a

given time by the brain and purpose of man."

Many think that the Constitution *gives* us our rights and liberties. This is not true. Our forefathers and we of today have them as our natural right. Its purpose is to *secure* them to us, and to our children after us. That is why this Constitution of ours is one of our great heritages, and one which we must guard if we wish to keep our freedoms. It is the protective instrument of "We the People"; and it says, and must continue to say to Congress, the President, and to the states, "This far can you go, but not one step beyond."

ELEVEN STATES RATIFY

Although there had been considerable bitter opposition, eleven states had approved, and now came the task of forming and putting the new government into operation. During the fall and winter of 1788–89 elections were held in these states now in the Union, and the choice for President was Washington and for Vice-President John Adams. State legislatures chose two Senators each, and congressional districts were set up and selected representatives in the lower chamber.

It was all so new that there were many delays, and it was April, 1789, before quorums of both houses of the new Congress had reached New York, which was to be the capital at first. There it counted the electoral votes delivered to it by the state conventions, and the choice of President was clear. The installation of this officer was to be an impressive affair.

At the risk of offending the great city of today, highly organized and cleaner than most cities, there were a few items which had to be taken care of before the ceremony could take place. It was necessary to clear the oxcarts from along the edges of Broadway and to corral the wandering hogs, the scavengers of that day, and get them securely into sties so they would not detract from the dignity of the occasion. Although it is well that we take something of a sentimental approach toward incidents in the early days, let us, too, realize that in some respects life was still fairly primitive by today's standards.

WASHINGTON INAUGURATED

With the city, then confined to the lower end of Manhattan Island, decked in flags and its people in the best holiday mood, Washington took the oath of office on April 30 at Federal Hall, on Wall Street. When the stately hero of the Revolution, and the father of his country, now fifty-seven, stooped and kissed the Bible, a mighty shout rang out from the assembled crowd, "Long live George Washington, *President of the United States.*" A new Ship of State had indeed been launched. But there were rough seas ahead.

It was but natural that men favorable to the new government should be chosen to fill the posts which must be manned. There was still much opposition scattered through even the states which had ratified. The three larger, Massachusetts, New York, and Virginia, had come in only by narrow majorities; and there were many demands for amendments already proposed by state conventions.

Madison, now leader in the House of Representatives, advocated that Congress adopt certain of these proposals. These demands by the states might be considered as "the final price of ratification." So ten propositions were framed and duly ratified by the states, and went into force in 1791. This group of amendments, not too accurately called the *Bill of Rights,* deserves careful

consideration. But first let us review what had been set up.

The United States was a *republic,* which means rule *for* the people, where a limit is set to the political power to be exercised. It recognizes there are *public* affairs, which are its province. But it also must recognize that there are *private* affairs over which it is not, and cannot be, concerned. It is, as in the case of any government by necessity, a smaller group of men in power over many men who have released certain limited authority to this group.

This governing body was divided into three sections, with balances between them to prevent the concentration of too much power in one group, or even among all three branches. There was the Congress to *think* things out, *express* the hopes of those it represented, and *decide* upon the course to be taken. Next there was the chief executive officer—the President—whose duty was to *get things done.* Then there was the judiciary, topped by a Supreme Court, with the task of acting as *referee* and of *judging* whether actions taken were in accordance with the will of "We the People."

NOT A DEMOCRACY!

This was thus not a *democracy,* which actually means a rule *by* the masses and can become mob rule, without thought of the rights and private affairs of the minority. Madison had pointed out in the *Federalist Papers:* "Democracies have ever been found incompatible with personal security or the rights of property; and have, in general, been as short in their lives as they have been violent in their deaths." There could be no individual freedom unless the individual was protected against pressure groups. Thus it was the purpose of these first ten amend-

WASHINGTON TAKES THE OATH OF OFFICE IN NEW YORK

ments to set forth clearly, and especially to *secure,* certain inherent rights and freedoms.

They included freedom of speech, the freedom of press, of religion, and the right to trial by jury. Public officials were prevented from seizing or searching a person or his possessions or papers, except under definite provisions written into the law.

Of particular importance was the provision that private property could not be taken over for public use except by duly constituted legal processes and just compensation. This was probably the first time in history that the right to own and enjoy the use of property had been given complete legal recognition and extended to the most humble citizen.

The foregoing were thus not rights *granted,* for those rights were a part of the freedom which belonged to every American. Rather they were *prohibitions,* preventing the government from carelessly or callously interfering with an individual's life, liberty, and property rights.

In addition, there was a guarantee that any powers not specifically granted to the federal government were to remain in the hands of the people, or be held by their local governments in the states.

These amendments to the Constitution, as it had been first drawn and ratified, were very essential. They greatly strengthened it as a means by which liberties could be secured. They testified to the fact that there was no intent that the government should ever become an aristocracy on the one hand, or degenerate into mob rule on the other.

It was, however, a complete break with old pagan ideas of authority vested in one person or a small group, either by accident of birth and inheritance or by seized power.

(*Continued on page 198*)

191

BATTLE OF LAKE ERIE

Ambroise Louis Garneray
CHICAGO HISTORICAL SOCIETY

From the signing of the peace in 1783, Great Britain's policy toward American shipping had occasioned much friction between the two countries. This finally resulted in the War of 1812, which dragged on until the close of 1814. Our navy performed brilliantly on the sea in contrast to rather serious reverses ashore. Canada afforded an effective point from which to launch operations over the long border, and across the lakes. In 1813 Capt. Oliver Perry was ordered to Erie, Penna., where he built a fleet with which he won a brilliant victory over the enemy's vessels. After the *Lawrence* was disabled, he made the *Niagara* his flagship; and it was from the deck of this latter craft that he sent out his famous message, "We have met the enemy and they are ours." It was his younger brother, Matthew, who would some years later open up Japan to foreign commerce.

OPENING OF THE ERIE CANAL

Anthony Imbert
MUSEUM OF THE CITY OF NEW YORK

Transportation was one of the great factors in the development and growth of our country. A huge forward step in the opening up of the West came in the completion of the Erie Canal in 1825. The ocean, via the Hudson River, was joined to the Great Lakes. Its success was so startling that it touched off an era of canal building up and down the eastern seaboard and inland during the next twenty years. Many miles of these ambitious projects were soon abandoned, however, because of the rapid development of the railroad during the 1840's. The Erie continued to pay its way, however, and in more recent years was developed into the modern State Barge Canal system.

The artist here shows the ships drawn up in New York harbor to receive the *Seneca Chief,* first ship to make its way from Buffalo to New York by way of Albany, leading a fleet of canal boats. They were roundly welcomed at every point along the way.

THE FALL OF THE ALAMO

Joseph Boggs Beale
IN THE COLLECTION OF MODERN ENTERPRISES

Although the Spanish had a long start in the colonization of the New World, they made but indifferent progress due in no small measure to an inert and overpowering bureaucracy which tried to administer affairs from across the sea. By the time their American possessions had fallen to Mexico, the young nation to the north was growing to great size and power, and looking longingly at the great stretches of country west of the Louisiana Purchase lying largely undeveloped. A contest for the possession and use of this vast territory was inevitable. It came first in Texas, where American colonists had been induced to settle. There, in and about a mission building in San Antonio, 183 men and women laid down their lives during thirteen spring days in 1836. But they did not die in vain, for later that same year, at the battle of San Jacinto, Texas became an independent nation, which it remained until annexation to the United States in 1845.

ABOVE, **FALL OF THE ALAMO,** J. B. Beale, Modern Enterprises

PAGE ONE, TOP
BATTLE OF LAKE ERIE
A. L. Garneray, Chicago Hist. Soc.

PAGE THREE, TOP
A SPANISH MISSION
Nicholas Comito, Private Collection

PAGE FOUR, TOP
MINING FOR GOLD
W. F. Chadwick, C. J. Ryan Collection

PAGE ONE, BELOW
OPENING OF THE ERIE CANAL
Anthony Imbert, Museum City of New York

PAGE THREE, BELOW
SAN FRANCISCO, 1849
Henry Firks, Newport Hist. Soc.

PAGE FOUR, BELOW
NEW HOME IN THE WES
J. B. Beale, Modern Enterprises

A SPANISH MISSION

Nicholas Comito
PRIVATE COLLECTION

Although this painting is of Concepcion Mission, one of the five still standing today along the San Antonio River in Texas, it is typical of the long necklace of mission churches strung from the Rio Grande Valley to San Francisco. It was a part of the Spanish plan of conquest of the New World to convert the native peoples to Christianity. Priests were members of the earliest expeditions. Perhaps one of the first to see any considerable portion of what later became our country was Father Juan de Padilla, who in 1541 was with Coronado, who spent twenty-five days in the grass-hut villages of the Quiviran Indians in what today is Rice County, Kansas. The following year the brave *padre* returned alone to minister to these people. Here he was later slain by the Indians; and thus this Franciscan friar became the first Christian martyr in what is now the United States.

MINING FOR GOLD

W. F. Chadwick
CLENDENIN J. RYAN COLLECTION

The haunting call of *gold* found responsive hearers in virtually every city and town in the eastern portion of our country, and drew thousands from across the sea. In many places *companies* were formed, and a group went in a body either overland, by ship around Cape Horn, or by ship to Panama, then across the isthmus, and then by a second vessel up the coast. Thus the men shown in our picture may be old friends from some eastern community; or they can very likely be from as many different communities as there are hopeful miners in this group. They are working a rocker, to the bottom of which the heavy colors of gold make their way as the gravel is agitated in water. It is noteworthy that Col. John Sutter, on whose huge ranch gold was discovered, was ruined by the *rush* that ensued, and lies buried in a modest grave in a small town in Pennsylvania.

A NEW HOME IN THE WEST

Joseph Boggs Beale
IN THE COLLECTION OF MODERN ENTERPRISES

The log cabin, unknown to most of the earliest settlers on these shores, was brought by the Swedes to the Delaware Valley in the middle 1600's. One which they reputedly built on Darby Creek in Pennsylvania is still in use today as a Girl Scout rendezvous. It rapidly became popular as homes were pushed back from the seacoast, and before the Revolution had become the standard first habitation of the pioneers moving into the back country. Lack of logs for a cabin and their branches for firewood may account in part for the settlers' first avoidance of open prairie country. After plows equal to breaking the heavy sod were available, these treeless areas were homesteaded, the houses often being of sod, and fuel for cooking and heating was chiefly braided or twisted grass. It was in a Kentucky cabin, no more pretentious than that pictured, that Abraham Lincoln was born.

197

The century of the common man was even then dawning, and within twenty years it would be in full swing. This first group of amendments merely caught the deep ground swell of what Americans wished to have so fully and prominently stated in their basic law as respects their inherent rights that they need never again be contested. They wanted it fully understood that their government was indeed their servant. They wanted no doubt of the fact that men who accepted public office received *permission* to govern; and were not to attempt—no, they were not even to think they had any power—to hand out rights which were neither theirs nor even the government's.

It is the duty of every red-blooded American to get this distinction firmly in mind. And it is the responsibility of each to see that greedy officeholders or seekers after political power do not forget it either.

These things had been pushed up into the forefront of the thinking of the more than three million white people in this country, as disclosed by the first national census taken in 1790. It had required a long, hard, costly war to bring some of the conditions which they might again have to endure firmly into their consciousness. They were on their guard; and they watched the new federal organization with hawklike gaze. As a consequence, it moved with prudence and caution.

FINANCIAL PROBLEMS

Money troubles plagued it at the beginning. Revenue was raised, first by taxes, which of course brought resentment, and later by a mild protective tariff, which aroused much opposition in the South. Arrangements were made to pay off the national debt, and the federal government also assumed certain of the state debts incurred in connection with the Revolutionary War.

Something of the spirit of compromise used during the Constitutional Convention had to be employed in settling sectional differences in national affairs. This was evident in choosing a site for the national capital, which was really part of a deal involving methods of handling the national debt.

VOTE TRADING

Southern votes for assumption of the debt were given in return for northern votes in favor of locating a new capital at some point on the Potomac River. But to appease the Pennsylvanians, there had to be a "gentlemen's agreement" to locate the capital in Philadelphia for at least ten years. Horse trading, rather than a meeting of minds, has accounted for many of our national moves from the very beginning.

A currency and banking system was established, the latter in the hands of the rather short-lived United States Bank fostered by Hamilton. The federal courts were created, and an army and navy provided for and brought into being.

Although there was no provision for it, Washington had created a Cabinet, made up of the heads of government departments. Thomas Jefferson, home from France, was Secretary of State. Hamilton became Secretary of the Treasury. General Henry Knox, Revolutionary artillery commander, headed the War Department; and Edmund Randolph, of Virginia, was Attorney General.

Hamilton and Washington were ardent *Federalists,* favoring a strong central government. Jefferson took an opposing view and rapidly became head of what, at the time, was known as the Republican, or strict Construction party. This latter name meant that it proposed to abide by a literal interpretation of the Constitution's wording. Soon he and Hamilton were flailing each other in newspaper columns. Washington did his best to keep peace between them, but to no avail, and Jefferson finally withdrew from the Cabinet in 1793. Edmund Randolph shifted over to take his place, but was himself soon in trouble. Thus the presidential office has been a trying post for the thirty-odd men who have occupied it.

FRENCH MONARCHY FALLS

The fall of the French monarchy in 1789, and the establishment of a republic in that country, gave the new American government some embarrassment. This led finally to a European war in 1793 and further complications on this side of the ocean. English naval discipline was so harsh in those days that desertions were very extensive. Now engaged in the struggle with France, and needing every seaman, British armed vessels began stopping American ships on the high seas and even in shore waters, searching them for deserters and what the commanders considered to be British subjects. This breach of international law continued intermittently and finally brought on a second war between America and Great Britain in 1812.

The French also began to interfere with our shipping; and these international incidents were sufficient, for a time during Adams' administration, to bring the strong opposition forces in the new country together.

Washington had retired at the end of his second term. To find former friends actively arrayed against him convinced the man that eight years in the presidency were quite enough. He had read his great Farewell Address upon the eve of the elections in 1796,

and then returned to the peace of Mount Vernon.

But party strife was soon renewed under his successor. The Federalists resolved to make the fullest use of their superior voting power in Congress, possibly with the ultimate hope of making this a one-party system. And to accomplish their purposes they pushed four rather obnoxious laws through the Congress in 1798. Those are known as the Alien and Sedition Acts.

The first raised the residence period for becoming a naturalized citizen from five to fourteen years. The second authorized the President to order out of the country any aliens he might deem to be dangerous. These two were attempts to keep refugees from France from bringing any of the extravagant ideas being tested there to our shores. Then, too, there was danger of war with European countries not too partial to the American Experiment. Thus a third act extending this power of expulsion to citizens of any country with which the United States might be at war was also passed.

The fourth—the Sedition Act—provided fines and imprisonment for combining to oppose governmental measures and for false, scandalous, or malicious writing against the government or its officials.

STATES' RIGHTS

At once the lid was off again, and the states began the assertion of what is termed the *doctrine of states' rights*. First Virginia, in 1798, and then the next year Kentucky (admitted as a state in 1792), passed resolutions protesting the federal Alien and Sedition Acts. Virginia asserted the right of a state to *interpose* when the central government exercised dangerous power. Kentucky's resolve went much farther and declared the

199

doctrine of *nullification*. This meant that a state, so disposed, did not need to recognize or respect a federal act which seemed to it to be harmful. It would take a bitter civil war to finally stamp out this pattern of nullification.

The power grab hidden in the Alien and Sedition Acts reacted heavily upon the Federalists. Republican forces swept Jefferson in as President in the elections of 1800, with Aaron Burr as Vice-President. But the balloting for these two offices was not clear and had to be settled in the Congress. The two men had received the same number of electoral votes, and it took thirty-six ballots in the House of Representatives before Jefferson was declared the winner.

The final decision was no doubt helped along by the fact that Hamilton, Jefferson's bitter enemy, came out in his behalf, or, at least proclaimed him the less dangerous of the two. This brought on a political quarrel between Burr and Hamilton, which finally resulted in a duel between them. Hamilton was fatally wounded and died as a result on July 12, 1804.

It was in this year that the Twelfth Amendment to the Constitution was adopted, changing slightly the method of electing the President. There would now be a period of sixty-one years before another change by amendment would be ratified.

We have watched the building of the Ship of State behind closed doors in the Declaration Chamber of Independence Hall. We saw it declared seaworthy on the first Wednesday in March, 1789, after ratification by eleven of the states. We were there, too, as it actually took the waves when Washington was inaugurated on the balcony of Federal Hall in New York.

Its trial runs under the guidance of two Presidents showed some basic weakness and the need for a small amount of correction. Now, as it sets its prow confidently into the waves of the turbulent nineteenth century, let us turn to the land and its people; and with the poet Longfellow, chant the lines:

> Sail on, O Ship of State!
> Sail on, O Union, strong and great!
> Humanity with all its fears,
> With all the hopes of future years,
> Is hanging breathless in thy fate.

"Westward the Course of Empire Takes Its Way"

HE Irishman, George Berkeley, who later became Bishop of Cloyne and a famous idealist philosopher, visited in the colonies briefly in the early 1700's. His famous line, which is the title of this section, would one day win the distinction of having Berkeley, California, named for him. The empire which he saw coursing its way to the west was that of Great Britain. But his words were to be truly prophetic of accomplishments by free men who had but lately won that freedom from the British Empire's arduous laws.

There had been an increase of nearly one and a half million in the population in the ten years between 1790 and 1800, or about 35 per cent. In the next ten, it would increase by nearly two million more. The seaboard areas had long since been settled up with homesteads; and even in the early years of the Revolution the thrust deep inland had definitely begun.

Before the turn of the century three more states were added to the original thirteen, as well as the District of Columbia (1791). They were Vermont (1791), Kentucky (1792), and Tennessee (1796).

The treaty signed at Versailles in 1783 had given this country firm title to the area lying east of the Mississippi and north to the Great Lakes. A group of New England veterans had organized the Ohio Company and desired to buy a large tract from the Congress, with the intent of settling there. But they insisted on having an organized government which they could take with them into what was still largely a wilderness. They petitioned the federal lawmakers to this end, and on July 13, 1787, even as the Constitutional Convention was in session, Congress enacted one of the most commendable pieces of legislation ever framed in this country. Its title is, "An Ordinance for the Government of the Territory of the United States, North-West of the River Ohio."

Its author was Nathan Dane of Massachusetts, and it falls into two parts. The first outlines the government to be founded and intrusted to a governor and three judges. These were to be appointed by the Congress until the population totaled 5,000 adult whites. Then a two-house, elected legislature might be formed, to continue until there were 60,000 inhabitants, when a state constitution would be drawn up and the new state taken into the Union.

The second part consisted of six articles or statements of basic civil rights, many passages from which might well have been in the

Declaration and in the Constitution. But perhaps one of its finest provisions was to set aside one section in each township laid out for the support of public schools. This same example would be followed in a number of states which held land that had not been settled. More than one hundred years later, Theodore Roosevelt pronounced it one of the foremost of American state papers; and the pattern which it set did much to make possible the rapid western surge of people and our expansion to forty-eight states.

The seaboard colonies, particularly Massachusetts, Connecticut, and Virginia, had, by their colonial charters, claims upon this area. But they had been ceded under the Confederation. And with the Territory Act, these lands filled in, and three more states were soon born: Ohio (1803), Indiana (1816), and Illinois (1818).

In the deep South, Alabama had well over 100,000 population on admittance in 1819, while Mississippi had come into the Union two years before with some 75,000. Maine, far to the north, had had nearly 300,000 when accepted in 1812.

Hardly had Jefferson taken office in 1800, however, when protests began to roll in from the settlers who had pushed beyond the Appalachians. It would be more simple for them to ferry their goods down the rivers to New Orleans, for shipment to Europe, than to try to haul them back over the mountains to the eastern seaboard. Spain, then in control of the great city at the mouth of the Mississippi, had permitted American shipments through that port since Washington's second term. Then suddenly in 1801 the port was closed. Spain, so it was later learned, had ceded the *Louisiana Territory* back to France.

Jefferson, with many friends in Paris, selected his Virginia neighbor, James Monroe, and sent him to join Livingston, our ambassador there. But before Monroe's arrival, he had already convinced Napoleon to sell this area to the United States, rather than risk its loss to the British, with whom the then "first consul" was at war.

JEFFERSON ARRANGES
THE LOUISIANA PURCHASE

Although the Constitution gave him no such powers, and he would have been the first to condemn their use by another, Jefferson arranged for the purchase of this vast, little known, and unmapped area. The price was in all about fifteen million dollars. Some of the states immediately threatened to secede from the Union. But it was a master stroke, doubling the land area of the new country. All, or at least parts, of some twelve states would eventually be carved from it. Our flag was raised at New Orleans in December, 1803.

Early the next spring two able frontiersmen, Lewis and Clark, were sent up the long Missouri and over the Great Divide to take possession of the Oregon Territory. This they did in 1806. When their journal of the expedition was published shortly afterward, pioneers in great numbers pushed across the wide Mississippi and into the Great Plains country beyond.

But unfortunately the Napoleonic Wars began to have their effect in this country. France and England both began serious interference with American shipping. Jefferson had let the Navy deteriorate and was unprepared to contest with Britain or France in this matter. An Embargo Act was passed, forbidding American vessels from trading with Europe. But it only managed to spread hardship throughout the states, particularly in New England.

BRITISH IMPRESSMENT OF AMERICAN SAILORS

Madison took over from Jefferson on March 4, 1809. He had been Secretary of State for the previous eight years, and thus was well informed on conditions at home and abroad. He, like his predecessor, would have preferred to maintain peace. But he was confronted by a group in Congress, known as the *war hawks*, bent upon avenging the nation's honor. Their leader was Henry Clay, then Speaker of the House.

England's atrocious treatment of our seamen continued, and Madison was finally forced to ask Congress in June of 1812 for a declaration of war against Great Britain. This pitiful struggle dragged on for nearly two and a half years, without evident advantage to either side. Some of the northern states threatened to secede, the national capital was invaded and some of the public

buildings fired, and men and ships had been lost.

But on the opposite side of the ledger were other entries to be considered. America had, unwittingly perhaps, completed her independence. Gallant action by such commanders as Perry and MacDonough had prevented the loss of territory. The willingness to fight at all had made a lasting impression upon Europe. Dangerous Indian groups were broken up during the action that had taken place, easing pressure along the frontier. But greater still was the progress in self-sufficiency.

During the years when commerce had been harried by England, American enterprise had leaped ahead in the industrial revolution then under way. New manufacturing here gave more freedom from dependence upon Europe and a chance to build riches in the New World, with less and less reliance upon the Old World.

HENRY CLAY ADVOCATES THE AMERICAN SYSTEM

As the country caught its breath after the war, there seemed to be a period of better feeling. This brought about greater unity of purpose. The army and navy were strengthened. The Second National Bank was created. Roads were improved. Steamboats began to appear on the rivers. Land was cheap in the West, and prosperity flowed behind the *American System*, fostered by Henry Clay.

By this latter scheme, the South would furnish cotton to northern mills, which were to find markets for their products in both the South and the expanding West. The West, in turn, would exchange its grain and wool with other sections. A tariff wall would keep out foreign goods and let this circular motion of raw materials and manufactured products increase within our own boundaries.

To round out our possessions in the East, and excusing the move as one of protection against the Indians, the President dispatched General Jackson to Florida. By the spring of 1818 the control of the peninsula was in his hands, and the Spanish king had little choice but to cede his province to the United States. To save face, he was allowed to cancel about five million dollars in claims against his government then in the hands of American citizens.

Spain, once the foremost power in Europe, had long since come upon evil days. While Napoleon kept that continent busy with his wars, the Spanish colonies in South and Central America began to wrest their freedom from the mother country, using the United States as their example.

These audacious moves greatly worried the crowned heads on the European continent. These upstart republics were a thorn in their flesh, since they might foster revolutions in their own lands. When it looked as though some of these European nations might take a hand in American affairs, England very guardedly let it be known to our United States minister that she did not favor such moves. There was even a proposal for joint action.

THE MONROE DOCTRINE

This, however, Monroe, now president, disregarded. But he did send a message to Congress on December 2, 1823, which has come to be known as the *Monroe Doctrine*. It plainly stated that any interference by European countries in the Western Hemisphere would be regarded as an act hostile to this country. America was for Americans, and the United States was prepared to defend such a position. It can perhaps be said that in this action our nation came of age.

But the unity under which many of these things were accomplished could not last. There was a division between the two principal sections—the North and the South—which was deeper than any surface conditions and dropped down to fundamentals. This cleavage had come to the fore during Washington's first term, and found its earliest spokesmen in Hamilton and in Jefferson.

The former stood for business enterprise and in a form which was somewhat different in concept than we know it today. He not only advocated a strong central government, but he wished to keep governmental power in a few chosen hands. He had once con-

FRANCIS SCOTT KEY WRITES OUR NATIONAL ANTHEM

Temporarily detained aboard one of the several British ships attacking Fort McHenry at Baltimore, the sight of our flag still flying above the ramparts following a night of heavy shelling induced him to put his elated feelings into words—The Star Spangled Banner.

demned any tendency toward democracy by crying, "Your people is a beast!" He very much represented the moneyed interests, the new and growing crop of manufacturers, and the well-established commercial groups.

By contrast, Jefferson saw greatness and stability best assured in an agricultural economy of small independent landholders, willing to cherish their freedom and protect their God-given rights. His thinking along these lines perhaps stemmed from familiarity with the history of the later years of the Roman Republic. He did not wish to see here a repetition of its sorry days, with its sad story of dispossessed free farmers becom-

ing labor gangs on the great estates, or of those thus made poor being herded into city establishments as laborers in factories. Something of this very thing had been taking place in England toward the close of the 1600's. Many colonists here had come out of such pathetic conditions. He believed the best security against similar occurrences in America was a nation of free families, principally farmers, owning the soil they tilled.

These basic differences were primarily economic, although their social consequences would be considerable in the years ahead. They immediately took on political form as well, for the country's voters soon

205

lined up behind these competing philosophies; and they would some years later lead the nation into a heartbreaking war. While slavery loomed large in this division between whole sections, it was but one of the vexing problems brought into strong focus by these two very different schemes of life.

It did raise its ugly head and lunge to the front very suddenly, as the land beyond the Mississippi began to fill in with settlers.

East of that river, the area considered *free,* as distinguished from that in which slaves were held, was well understood. The two English surveyors, Charles Mason and Jeremiah Dixon, had fixed the boundary between Pennsylvania and Maryland in 1767. And this famous border—the Mason-Dixon Line—together with the Ohio River, had come to be regarded as the boundary between free and slave states.

The French had planted small settlements along the Ohio and Mississippi rivers in the early 1700's. Some few of them had been lively towns when Jefferson was still a boy. St. Genevieve had been settled in what was to become Missouri as early as 1735, and there was a trading post at St. Louis from 1765. While there was still elbowroom west of the river when the great Louisiana area came into the United States in 1804, some of this river country was by no means a trackless wilderness.

With the rapid influx of people, the towns began to boom. A newspaper had been established at St. Louis by 1808, and steamboats began to touch there in 1815. In no more than five years there would be enough people on hand within the limits of the Missouri territory to justify its admittance as a state. But that would pose a ticklish problem. Was it to be slave or free?

It required a pretty liberal view of the powers granted Congress by the Constitution to find a solution for this vexatious question. The southern bloc took the attitude that Congress had no constitutional authority to prohibit the ownership of slaves in the territories. This seemed to be clearly contrary to provisions in the Northwest Territory Ordinance of 1787. But the southerners were under considerable pressure. Maine was also due for statehood and would join the Union with four times as many inhabitants as would Missouri. The population advantage was still running strongly in favor of the North in the lower house of Congress. How many nonslave states might be carved out of these huge new western lands, to one day far outshadow the voting power of the "solid South"?

Trading was again resorted to, and a deal finally arranged. Under it Maine came in free, while Missouri would be a slave state. Its southern boundary, however, drawn on the line of 36° 30' north latitude, would then be the northern boundary of slavery in the remainder of the Louisiana Purchase. This was the famous *Missouri Compromise,* by which a broad interpretation of the Constitution was written into a law later to bring trouble and bloodshed.

But let us leave the trying political jumbles of the time and move among the peoples themselves. For something very worthwhile was happening to them, both here and in Europe as well, which was destined to make America a very great nation.

Freedom Stimulates Material Advances

ET us go back for a moment to those more than 7,000 hand-wrought nails in the stock of Mr. Saml. Gridley, the smith, when he first set himself up as a merchant in Farmington late in the 1600's. That may seem a rather odd point at which to begin to discuss the age in which the common man first began to come into his own. Yet it can be a very logical one.

Hand-wrought iron nails were by no means new. Was it not by their prints left in His hands that the risen Saviour had shown the doubting Thomas that He was indeed the Lord? They had been laboriously hammered out by hand down through the ages. It was said that in the time in which Mr. Gridley built up this modest stock, it took about as long to forge the necessary nails as it did to construct the house in which they were used. Legend has it that houses were sometimes burned down, and the ashes carefully sifted to recover the nails. And it is reported that Thomas Jefferson kept no fewer than eight slaves constantly busy forming nails to keep abreast of the extensive building at Monticello.

Nails were thus rather precious, while a man's time was much less valuable. That was an age-old attitude, due for overhauling and change. Mrs. Gridley gathered firewood and cooked over an open fire just as women had since the dawn of history. She carded wool and flax, spun out yarn and thread, and wove it into cloth with tools little better than those known and used a thousand years before Abraham was born. She boiled her own soap and dipped her own candles, while her husband carried on his farm work in ways and with crude tools older than written history.

Life was hard work, always had been, and always would be by the Old World conception of things. Its power was human power. Everything depended pretty much upon human muscles, with a little animal muscle added when it could be, or a little harnessing of wind or water where convenient. Men for the most part were drudges, burden-bearers. The Roman Empire had been built upon man power, cheap and degraded, much of it slave labor. This same attitude toward man in the mass had carried over into European affairs in the Dark Ages. Human beings were wanted only as human beings. There were plenty of them, and as long as they were kept subject to a reasonable amount of authority the work of the world would get done. If there were times of famine, and some of them starved, Nature would soon replace their ranks.

FORWARD THINKING

Then this sort of thinking started to change. As men began to gain more freedoms, their attitude toward life began to alter. For it is only as men are free that they begin to place a value upon their time. Then as their time comes to have greater value, there begins to be incentive to preserve human life. When the principal business of life is peaceful progress, rather than war and carnage, the value of both time and of human life increases greatly.

The colonists began to throw off the shackles of Old World tyranny and backward thinking about as fast as they stepped ashore in this New World. The outburst of human energy which the breathing of free air released, was terrific. But, even so, freedom was not too well rounded until the Revolutionary War had been won. Then, with a continent to be tamed and the freedom to do it, men began to look for time-saving means by which their efforts could be made to count for more, and with release from so much out-and-out drudgery. Inventiveness began to be appreciated, was encouraged, and the benefits it brought were rewarded by being accepted and put to use. Previously, progressive ideas were usually set aside because they disturbed the established order of things.

Let us not be misled, however, by feeling that all such progress originated in America. England, which had known a greater amount of freedom down through the ranks of its people than any other European country, had already started the ball rolling by the development of material knowledge. The earlier Italians, and to some extent the French and the Germans, had added to this knowledge. But its application to practical uses was probably greatest in this country; and the stimulus which was given set men to work here in real earnest.

William Lee had perfected a rather crude knitting machine in England as early as 1589, but its use seems to have been very limited. It was in 1767, the year after the repeal of the hated Stamp Act, that James Hargreaves, also in England, built the first spinning jenny. But such equipment would not come into its own until after the American, Eli Whitney, had perfected the cotton gin. This jumped the production of cotton from five to fifty million pounds in our own country in the ten years following 1793.

MACHINERY VS. HAND PRODUCTION

But how about Mr. Gridley's nails? Here is what happened in that respect. Even tacks had to be formed by hand, one at a time. Necessarily that made them pretty expensive. Suddenly Jeremiah Wilkinson, over in one of the Rhode Island towns, began to turn out several thousand a day in his little plant. How did he do it? He discovered that if you locked several bits of wire shank in a vise at one time, you could beat out heads on all of them by using a broad-face hammer. The year was 1776. By 1795 Jacob Perkins had a machine that would produce 60,000 each week; and twenty years later they were being popped out of machines at the rate of thousands an hour.

It was but ten years, however, after Wilkinson began to mass-produce tacks, that Ezekiel Reed had perfected a machine that would cut nails from iron sheets. Thus, from 1786 on, blacksmiths were wasting their time and skill less and less on beating out the ever-increasing number of nails needed for the houses to shelter a population increasing at the rate of one-third every ten years.

These houses would continue to be largely of wood, which had meant hours of toil patiently whipsawing the necessary lumber. In 1777 another Englishman, Samuel Miller, perfected the circular wood saw. With abundant water power to drive it, this tool was bound to find wide use in this new country. Also, quite by chance, it was to point the way to another huge development.

AT FIRST
PRAIRIE LAND WAS AVOIDED

As they were opened up to settlement, the great prairie areas in the West were at first considered of doubtful value. The feeling was that land which did not produce trees would hardly produce crops. Another handicap was the very heavy sod that covered these treeless stretches. When it was dry, the crude early plows could not break it up. When it was wet, it merely clung to them in great chunks and threw the plow clear of the earth.

Thomas Jefferson had designed the perfect curve for a moldboard for a plow. Then Jethro Wood began to cast them in iron. But they were heavy and clumsy and they did not "scour," or free themselves from the earth they broke up. Worse still, there was a widespread belief that metal "poisoned" the ground. Thus it looked for a time as though the great plains might be left as buffalo pastures.

A Yankee blacksmith from Vermont, John Deere, who had migrated to the Mississippi Valley, soon came to grips with this dilemma. He was willing to admit that the cast-iron plow was not the answer, but the belief that metal had any effect upon crops was just silly. The answer that occurred to him was a smooth steel share. So he found a discarded circular "buzz" saw, and went to work.

JOHN DEERE'S PLOW

Forging it to the proper shape, he bolted it to a light, strong frame. He tried it out, and found it worked. Then he went in search of customers. Being a powerful man and wanting to overcome the mistaken idea of excessive weight, he threw it across his shoulders and strode off over the plains country.

Tradition breaks down more easily in lands where men are free, and it was not many seasons before his newfangled plow was in wide demand. It wore a pathway to a whole new series of farming tools. By 1831 Cyrus McCormick had invented his reaping machine, and the prairies began to be broken up and to contribute their part to America's greatness.

You may recall the fact having been emphasized that there was but one clock and one watch in the thriving village of Farmington in the early 1700's. The pendulum clock was then fairly new, the principle of it having been developed by the Hollander, Huygens, about 1657. Until the time of the Revolution it was still a rarity. The very finest had works laboriously worked out in metal by hand. But mostly they were of wood, which was easier to make into the necessary parts. Soon they would be produced in quantity; but the impulse to that production came in a strange way, through gun manufacture.

Eli Whitney, originally from Massachusetts and a graduate of Yale, was living on a plantation in Georgia and reading law, when he perfected the cotton gin. Although he re-

209 ತಿ

ceived no money for this huge contribution, it did turn him from the law to mechanics. In 1798 he set himself up in a tiny manufacturing business at the edge of New Haven in Connecticut.

EARLY MASS PRODUCTION

Guns were then made as single items. The gunsmith beat out the flat bars which he welded into a long spiral to form the barrel. He worked out the butt with a drawshave from a walnut block. Then he forged the hammer, trigger, and parts of the flintlock, and by tedious filing and fitting at long last had a completed gun. But this gun was a gun distinct from every other gun, no matter how much they looked alike. Parts from one gun would not fit another; and if anything about it broke, a new part, just fitted to that gun, had to be made.

During the Revolution there had been a gun factory on Zack's Brook, over in the northwest corner of Farmington township. Here guns were turned out at the rate of about four hundred a year. Each gun was the complete product of one man, from muzzle to butt-plate. And it was just as much of an individual as the smith who made it differed from the man working at the next bench. Eli Whitney set out to change all this.

He took a contract to build ten thousand guns for the government during a two-year period. The number was considerable, but that was not the remarkable feature of the undertaking. They were to be made so like each other in every respect that their parts could be interchanged right on the battle-field, and without the services of a professional gunsmith.

Whitney nearly lost the contract because it took him so long to get the tools ready to go into production. But produce the guns he did, and with standard parts, as he had promised. Such mass production had been advocated long before; but it took an American to really put it to work. Out of this accomplishment came the long line of Winchester rifles that were so much a part of the American scene in the winning of the West. Also it may have helped inspire Sam Colt of Hartford, whose "six guns" became a companion of the plainsmen, and without which the contemporary western motion picture would hardly be possible.

TEN-DOLLAR CLOCKS!

What Witney did with guns set fire to the imagination of another Eli—Eli Terry. He was a clocksmith in the little hill town of Plymouth, just beyond the western border of the original Farmington grant. For a number of years he had been making high-priced clocks and selling them about the neighboring countryside. He had to charge enough for them so that they were sold mostly on the instalment basis. Why not a clock with interchangeable wooden parts, to sell, not at twenty-five dollars, the going price of individually made clocks, but at ten dollars?

He determined to try five hundred as a starter. The idea caught on, the clocks sold out of hand, and in three years he and his partner, Seth Thomas, had disposed of no fewer than five thousand. Soon neighboring towns broke out in a rash of clock factories. Deft-fingered young women began to find employment assembling the works, painting the faces, and ornamenting the cases.

Enterprising young men, who liked to travel and enjoyed meeting people, were in demand to sell clocks throughout the land. A large stock was shipped by boat from nearby Hartford to, say, Norfolk. There the salesman who went along with them bought a

THE MANY NEW PRODUCTS WERE SOLD HOME TO HOME

horse and wagon, and set off through tide-water Virginia, disposing of his clocks from home to home. The itinerant clock salesman had taken his place beside the direct sales-man of books, whom we will also soon meet.

From Mr. Gridley's nails, a trail leads out in another direction, to a smaller item of similar shape, the common pin. In Colonial times they were large, cruder, and by no means common. They were then handmade. A bit of wire was pointed at one end, and a head brazed onto it at the other. The result was a cherished item, a most appreciated gift, and worth, in Revolutionary times, about twenty cents each, or one-fifth of the day's wages paid a skilled man. They so often took the place of small coins in trans-actions that we still have the term *pin money*.

L. W. Wright had a machine turning them out in quantities by 1824; and a few years later they were being sold "by the paper," as they are to this day, a machine

even fitting them into place in this novel container.

This, and wire nails and tacks, had been dependent upon progress in drawing wire. But sufficient advancement had been made so that the first wire suspension bridge had been erected in 1816 in Philadelphia.

It was in this same field, and also in the casting and working of large pieces of metal, that two advances were made which were indispensable to the future of America. Without them, what is now the United States could very probably have been several smaller, separate nations. Distance and lack of prompt means of communication made much of the difficulty in properly uniting widely separated states.

After his defeat at the hands of the Rus-sians in 1812, Napoleon fled back to Paris to raise new armies to face a combination of all Europe against him. Speed was very urgent, and everything was done to make the trip with the utmost dispatch, using carriages. The distance from Vilna, in Poland, to Paris was just an even 1,400 miles. The elapsed time for the trip was 312 hours. The hard-pressed emperor was just under two weeks en route, and thus averaged *less* than five miles per hour. And there were better roads over which to travel than would have been found at that time in much of America.

SPEEDING UP TRAVEL

The distance was about the same as between New York and New Orleans or Kansas City. The capital, located in Washington because it was then a central point, would, in but a few years, be about 1,400 miles from Austin, Texas; and more than twice as far from San Francisco, Portland, or Seattle.

The steamboat helped in breaking down distances, in that it was not dependent upon favorable winds. But navigable waters were not always either direct or convenient. As early as 1786 John Fitch, who lived just north of Philadelphia, had first driven a vessel by means of a steam engine. While Washington was President, he had a steam packet plying daily between Philadelphia and Trenton. But lack of financial backing soon terminated his enterprise. Colonel John Stevens had launched his third boat before Fulton sailed the *Clermont* up the Hudson, with its engine imported from England.

Fulton had, through political connivance, obtained a monopoly of steam navigation in New York State waters. This forced Colonel Stevens to put to sea, and he started the water-run from Hoboken to Philadelphia. With this first successful *ocean* venture, courage mounted; and by 1818 the *Savannah* crossed the ocean to Cork, Ireland. But as helpful as vessels propelled by steam would be in river traffic, and later in reaching the West Coast, it was not the final answer in breaking down distance.

While a steam locomotive had operated in England as early as 1804, it would be twenty-five years before a fully successful one would be produced. However, the chartering of railroads began in America as early as 1826. The following year the Baltimore and Ohio received its charter, and its first rail was laid on July 4, 1828, by John Carroll, the only surviving signer of the Declaration. Its first locomotive went into operation in 1830.

Two years later construction began upon what became the New York Central System, with seventeen miles of track put in operation. Within twelve years it reached to Buffalo.

THE GRADUAL ELIMINATION OF DISTANCE

Other roads began to thrust out from other cities in the North and East, and in ten years no less than 2,818 miles of track had been laid. Here was an instrument that divided space first in two, then by five, and before long by ten, as respects traveling time. Here were sinews needed to tie the country together. They required but one addition, message transmission that was even faster.

Franklin, flying his kite in a thunderstorm in the fields near where the City Hall now stands in Philadelphia, may have cut an odd figure before the sober citizenry. But he started men thinking and contriving here and abroad. It would be forty-seven years before an Italian, Volta, would produce electricity from batteries. Then six years later another Italian would put it to work at electroplating. Great things would flow from the taming and use of this tremendous unseen power, electricity.

**FULTON'S CLERMONT
STEAMS UP THE HUDSON**

The man who would give it impulse in this country and provide that second sinew to bind the states more surely together was an American inventor. In 1835 S. F. B. Morse, already a well-known painter who had experimented with electricity on the side, hit upon a method of sending messages for long distances over wires. So essential did it seem in the better administration of government that in 1843 the Congress granted $30,000 to defray the cost of an experimental line of fifty miles. This was constructed between Baltimore and Washington, and on May 24, 1844, the project was crowned with success.

Railroad rails, paralleled by telegraph wires, began to bind the nation into a definite Union. These and other advances in material knowledge were to bring many benefits. John Deere's plows would break the sod of western prairies, and the grain would, of itself and as fodder for cattle and hogs, help to feed the industrial North and permit the South to go more and more into the raising of cotton.

Whitney's gin would pick linters from ever-greater quantities of inland short-staple varieties for processing in mills in England across the ocean, and also in New England, where new mill towns were growing up. The first complete cotton spinning mill was in operation early in the 1800's at Pawtucket, Rhode Island. And by 1814 the Lowell Mill at Waltham, Massachusetts, received raw cotton and processed it through to finished cloth under one roof.

Thus was the start made upon Henry Clay's *American System,* which would one day, but still long hence, make the United States the greatest market for goods the world has ever known.

Actually, however, America did not grow great because of nails, pins, plows, cotton gins, or eight-day clocks. It grew great because men were free, and made their freedom work for their greater advantage. The American Heritage is far more than politics or gadgets; and we will do well to look into some of its other aspects as well.

213

An American Civilization Develops

HE church and the clergy had been powerful factors during the Colonial period, and in many sections sought to continue their dominant role. They had succeeded in passing very rigorous laws in several of the New England colonies for the regulation of both religious and personal conduct. The Congregational was the official church in most of this area, and continued to collect taxes for its support in some instances well into the 1800's. This condition obtained in New Hampshire until 1817, in Connecticut until 1818, and in Massachusetts until as late as 1833. The following incident illustrates how seriously those of the church accepted responsibility as their *brother's keeper,* even thirty years after the Declaration of Independence.

Let us return to Farmington in the year 1770. The Ecclesiastical Society had voted the previous year to build a new church structure, and the plans and construction were to be in the capable hands of the local architect and master builder, Judah Woodruff. Because laws passed in 1710 in far-off England had set aside the best white, and other pine trees in much of New England for ships' masts in the Royal Navy, he had to

make the long and difficult journey to the woods in Maine to procure the necessary timber. This incident may have even that early in his career given him a *set* against arbitrary authority. In 1772, however, the handsome structure, still in regular use, was dedicated.

He had served as a first lieutenant in the French and Indian War, and then as a captain during the Revolution. He became prominent and respected in the community and continued active in his profession. But he was thoroughly independent and courageous in thought and action. Suddenly, in late 1795 or early the following year, he stopped attendance at church. This in a community where outward show of religious observance was virtually obligatory.

His neglect of the meetinghouse, which, by the way, he had built, occasioned much comment, until, on April 19, 1796, he was served with a summons to appear before the Church Society. But the seventy-four-year-old captain did not heed this demand.

A year passed, and again on April 19, another citation to present himself for "public admonition" was read in his presence. But the captain remained adamant. In earlier days pressure would have been exerted.

**THE CHURCH CAPTAIN JUDAH
BUILT AND THEN FORSOOK**

Four months later there was a third call upon this unrepentant brother. Still he did not respond, although he did send two pointed letters to the minister expressing his opinions and convictions of the church body. Patience was by then exhausted; he was excommunicated by a vote of the church that same December. Some years earlier he might even have been driven out of the community.

While this was an isolated case, it was in keeping with a new attitude toward the earlier intrenched position of religious authority. The growing tolerance had been expressed in the First Amendment to the Constitution in 1791. The *Blue Laws,* and dominance by any one church group, were on their way out. In 1833 the Methodist Society was also granted permission to erect

a meetinghouse on Farmington's public green. And Catholic and Episcopalian parishes would be established about midway through that century.

MANY RELIGIOUS CHANGES

The Church of England had had an official position in at least six states. But its privileged place was threatened during the Revolution. Then, in 1786, the state of Virginia passed its famous statute on religious freedom. By it no one in that state could be forced to attend any church, or to pay taxes for the support of any religious enterprise. Religious liberty continued to broaden, and tolerance increased.

In 1789 the Diocese of Baltimore was formed, and the Pope appointed the Most Reverend John Carroll the first Roman Catholic Bishop in the United States. There was a diocese established in New Orleans in 1793, and in 1808 four more were added in New York, Boston, Philadelphia, and Louisville.

Jews had begun to arrive in the colonies before 1650, fleeing Europe because of persecution. A considerable number who had first gone to Brazil appeared in New Amsterdam, and established the first congregation in North America there in 1656. The second was probably formed at Newport, Rhode Island, in 1658, for there was extreme tolerance in that colony from its outset. Their numbers were not considerable before 1800, and while they were deprived of a vote in many of the colonies, they were free to engage in trade. A stouthearted but little known patriot was Haym Salomon of Philadelphia. He supplied cash to members of the Congress and to some of the officers of the Continental Army, to the extent of a half-million dollars, most of which was not re-

215

paid. He and his people were to win religious equality, but slowly.

Newer faiths, some transplanted from England, but many founded here, were springing up and winning converts. The older order in religious affairs was shifting rapidly, and in many respects taking on greater vitality.

HUMANITARIAN INTERESTS

A missionary zeal began to appear following the War of 1812. This was in evidence in the *circuit riders,* who were common and very important figures on the frontier. Other chosen men, and some women, were dispatched to Africa, Asia, and especially the Hawaiian Islands, to spread the Gospel. To the end that the circuit rider might have the Word of God in his saddlebags, and the missionary in foreign lands might have access to Scripture portions in native tongues, the American Bible Society was launched in 1816.

Industrialization in the Northeast was bringing with it rather sordid conditions in the mill communities. This brought agitation for corrections as respects employed children in particular, and helped to stimulate the Sunday-school movement for their religious instruction.

Other humane endeavors won better treatment for the insane, through the establishment of asylums for their housing and care. Along with this went prison reform, with separate cells for each prisoner in the very progressive Eastern Penitentiary, built in Philadelphia in 1830. Also the poor debtor laws were modified during this same era. One of the prime movers in such work was a woman, Dorothea Dix.

Along lines of morality there was a wave of feeling against an old and vexing situa-tion. Drunkenness had been a prominent vice in Colonial times and through the early days of the republic. It was not uncommon for rather prominent men to be designated a "one-bottle man," or a "two-bottle man," dependent upon the quantity of wine he customarily disposed of on his own during an evening. Agitation began to shape up as temperance societies, the first of which was organized in Boston in 1824. By 1840 the movement had spread rather widely; and the first state-wide prohibition law was adopted in Maine in 1846.

Men were learning that freedom could be overdone, and that liberty can degenerate into unrestrained license.

INTEREST IN EDUCATION

At the time the Constitution was being framed, there was an appreciation on the part of leading men that one price of liberty was reasonable and widespread education. The Congress had recognized this fact with a provision for support of schools in the territories by its act of 1787. But the Constitution left such matters in the hands of the already established states.

There were many educational projects advanced in the next few years, even one favored by leading members of the new federal government for the creation of a national university. Washington even willed money for this purpose at his death. But education on a national scale was not to be attempted.

There was at first much apprehension in some quarters as to what might happen as a result of educating "the masses." Many of the colleges started for the education of clergymen, or at least the "better people," preferred to stick to their classical studies, and cared neither to throw open their gates

A COUNTRY SCHOOL OF THE EARLY 1800'S

to all comers nor to find themselves in competition with more utilitarian types of higher education. The taxpayers rebelled at taxes for "free" education; and the clergy were appalled by secular and public schools, which they were certain would wean children away from religion.

But the demand for broader-gauged schools was still there, and state universities began to come into being. Georgia chartered such an enterprise in 1784, but it was 1801 before the university was founded at Athens. North Carolina was next, granting a charter in 1789. But it was six years before sessions began, and then largely because of private gifts. Next to make the attempt was Tennessee. Largely through the personal enterprise of Jefferson, Virginia achieved her university, the charter being granted in 1819, and students were in residence before his death in 1826.

But the colleges were still relatively small. As late as 1815, Harvard graduated that year but 66; Yale, 69; Princeton, 40; Pennsylvania, 15; and the University of South Carolina, 37.

By 1820 the population had jumped to just under ten million. Then the founding of American colleges began in earnest. Many of them were started by the independent religious denominations. Where formerly the great bulk of the graduates had gone into the ministry or the law, from now on more and more went into commercial pursuits. Engineering, too, began to be recognized, and Rensselaer, founded at Troy in 1824, would soon be a full-fledged engineering school.

Higher education for women was also being discussed, and in 1837 Mary Lyon would establish her famous seminary at South Hadley, Massachusetts, which would

217

become Mount Holyoke College. Because of her pioneering and wide lecturing, many similar schools came into being.

But elementary education was still pretty much limited to the "little red schoolhouse." As it turned into the 1800's, the country was primarily rural. There were but eleven towns in all the states and territories that had above five thousand inhabitants. In Colonial times these "district schools" had been open to pupils from four to twenty-one. The younger children attended a summer session, the older ones went during the winter months when farm chores were lighter. The age limit was later lowered to fourteen years. In many sections they continued to be supported by, or were under the direction of, church authorities.

LIMITED SCHOOLING COMMON

While they seem to have been well established before the Revolution, they had a period of decay after the war, due both to weakened finances and shifting conditions. It is said that by 1800 the situation was so bad that the average citizen did not receive more than eighty-two days of schooling in his whole lifetime. Even in settled communities the conditions were chaotic. In the back country, facilities for the most part just did not exist.

It was well into the 1830's before the overall situation began to mend. Between 1835 and 1838 Massachusetts, Connecticut, and Ohio had set up state boards of education. These made provision for teacher training, and the grave situation began to remedy somewhat. But the sense of democracy and the rights of the common man had to spread and find acceptance before elementary education could be fully emancipated and look to tax money for support.

It would be 1852 before Massachusetts would become the first state to pass a compulsory educational law; and into the 1880's before such laws would be fully enforced. It would not be until after the War between the States that much of the South would have anything approaching a public-school system.

Even completely "free" elementary schools were not universal until fairly recent years. It was 1873 before the last of the northern states abandoned "rate bills," by which the pupils paid some part of the maintenance expense. Also public-school education long terminated at age fourteen, and high schools at public expense only began to come into being as child-labor laws and other influences brought the need for the lengthening of school life.

At least American schools had been from the outset "reading" schools, rather than the oral schools of Europe, where the pupils learned solely, or principally, by listening to the teacher. Thus Americans for the most part could read. And newspapers were considered something of a necessity.

NEWSPAPERS INCREASE

During Colonial days newspapers had been under restrictions at times, and this was not entirely remedied until the Revolution. Their freedom was guaranteed by the First Amendment; and that freedom would not be too seriously threatened until executive orders were issued during the War between the States. There was, however, an attempt to dampen criticisms made by them under the Sedition Act in 1798. There were other attacks on the press from time to time. But the number of newspapers increased from the 43 published in 1783, to more than 350 in 1813. About one out of each ten of these was now a daily. By the middle of the century there would be a total of 2,600 newspapers throughout the land.

MAGAZINES AND BOOKS BECOME GENERALLY POPULAR

Behind the newspapers was the more solid fare of magazines and books. The former had begun to appear before the Revolution and flowed in greater number after the war. They were mostly monthlies, with a few appearing weekly. Among the latter, still known to us today, is the *Saturday Evening Post,* started by Ben Franklin in 1728 as the *Pennsylvania Gazette.* It was a little magazine, too, *The Pennsylvanian,* that Thomas Paine was hired to edit at five dollars per month, and in the first edition of which he published in 1775 the gunpowder receipt. They had thus for some years been bringing their readers what was then available in the way of helpful information.

Those magazines dealt with popular interests of the day, from cooking, homemaking, husbandry and costuming through morals, art, and literature to the sciences. Addressed first to men, then to the family, there were finally women's magazines, evidence that the ladies were seeking and coming into their "rights."

Books were coming into their own, too. The strong taste for religious texts in Colonial times was broadening rapidly. A title to be considered a best seller in the decade in which the Revolution was fought would need to sell better than 20,000 copies. Among those which achieved this goal were such favorites as: Goldsmith's *The Vicar of Wakefield,* Sterne's *Tristam Shandy,* Defoe's *Robinson Crusoe,* Milton's *Paradise Lost,* Paine's *Common Sense,* and at least four others less well known. Seven of them were published in Philadelphia, then the printing center.

By 1800 the best-seller class called for a distribution of at least 50,000. It was in that year that Matthew Carey, a bright Irish lad, befriended as a refugee in Paris and helped into the publishing business in America by Franklin, issued his *Life of Washington.* It was by Mason L. ("Parson") Weems, who had sold books for Carey house-to-house up and down the Atlantic seaboard and far inland as well. It contained the pure fabrication of the Parson's fertile mind regarding the youthful Washington and the episode of the cherry tree, which has managed to put cherry pie on many a dinner table on February 22 since it first appeared.

In the twenty years that followed, Sir Walter Scott's novels, as well as the tales of two native authors, would be most popular reading. The two Americans were Washington Irving and James Fenimore Cooper. In the 1830's Victor Hugo and Charles Dickens would compete for honors with Nathaniel Hawthorne and Henry Wadsworth Longfellow. There would be two women on the best-seller list in this decade, too, the English Jane Austen and the American Hannah Lee.

DISSENSIONS WERE ACTIVELY EXPLOITED

Another woman, unhappily an American, would also squeeze into the list, and with an incredible and totally unjustified volume set at Catholic-baiting, titled *Awful Disclosures.* This was perhaps not the first time, and surely it would not be the last, that the reading public would be roundly duped and served sensational and malicious falsehood offered as sober fact. Her nefarious text must have sold more than 125,000 copies to have placed it in a list with the other quite acceptable books.

Painting, art, and architecture were also forging ahead. In these, as in literature, there was still some leaning upon Europe; but much of what was being produced had a new and distinct American flavor. There had been some attempt after the Constitution had been placed in force to rally art and literature to a common support and pro-motion of the new government. But the spirit of freedom was sufficient so that the arts were not dominated; and artists and writers went their own ways and did their share in developing a separate and unmistakable *American Civilization*.

It might be well, at this point, if we returned briefly to political considerations and looked at them as a concern of the individual man and woman.

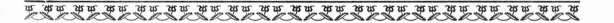

Who May Vote?

LTHOUGH many ticklish points in connection with the development of the Constitution had been settled by compromise, the question of who could vote had been too stormy a one to handle at the national level. It had been thrown back for each state to decide on the basis of conditions within its own area. This was perhaps not too fortunate a solution. The open question still continues as to whether the mere attainment to the age of twenty-one is sufficient in itself to justify the enjoyment of the franchise. Arrival at the traditional age of manhood, ability to read, and being a citizen are the chief requirements laid upon at least the white members of our society. Should there be more?

We must recall, however, that the delegates who framed this Constitution, almost to a man, were either wealthy or closely represented wealth. And throughout Colonial times the right to vote had depended principally upon *ownership of land*. Even then the land must be owned outright, and it must either total a certain amount in value or extent, or be subject to a specified amount of taxes.

It was in the nature of a concession, then, that three of the states, between 1776 and 1798, extended the ballot to *all* who paid taxes of any sort or amount. Other states continued to cling to the idea that only sizable ownership of land gave evidence of sufficient interest in community affairs to permit an expression in connection with them by a vote.

But even those who could vote did not have a free choice as to whom they might elect to fill public offices. A man to be elected governor of South Carolina in the early days had to be worth £10,000, or about $50,000, a very considerable amount. In Maryland it was one-half that sum, and in a number of others £1,000 was the minimum amount. State senators in New Jersey had to have land or property valued at at least £1,000; and there were similar fairly high requirements in many other states. There were also somewhat lower qualifications for election to the lower houses of the legislatures.

Restrictions on voting or officeholding based upon ownership of land or improved property debarred not only the very small landholders and the poorer classes generally, but many prominent people as well. As some of the towns grew into small cities, and a few into metropolises, merchants, doctors, lawyers, and other professional people

221 ʒ❧

were deprived of the vote and of the right to hold certain public offices.

ALL MEN CREATED EQUAL

It was hard indeed to make this condition agree with the high-sounding phrases which had been written into the Declaration of Independence. They read: "We hold these truths to be self-evident—that all men are created equal; that they are endowed by their Creator with certain inalienable rights; that among these are life, liberty, and the pursuit of happiness. That, to secure these rights, governments are instituted among men, deriving their just powers from the consent of the governed . . ." The question on more and more lips was, "How can we register our consent—or our dissent—except we be allowed to vote?"

This question must have had a rather bitter flavor on the lips of those in particular who were denied this right because of religious views. And there were states in which no one could vote who was anything but a *Protestant*. Others had a limitation against any not classed as *Christians*. One state required belief in the *Trinity* and in the divine inspiration of the Scriptures. Virginia and New York were the first to remove any and all such religious limitations upon either voting or officeholding.

Although the Federalists, who had favored the strong central government, had been very opposed to any but the wealthy and powerful participating in governmental affairs, they were by no means alone in this respect. Anything that smattered of democracy, or *rule by the many,* would have been just about as unthinkable to Jefferson, despite his emphasis some years before on "liberty and equality." There were many blunt expressions of fear of the great bulk of the people made in public utterances during more than thirty years after the Constitution went into effect. And many more of them appeared in private correspondence and exchanges.

This somewhat aristocratic attitude broke down slowly. But as men laid aside satin knee breeches and powdered wigs, their thinking began to be more liberal as well. Pressure to do away with voting restrictions came largely from two sections, the industrial Northeast and the territories now filling in rapidly. We have already discussed many of the things that were happening in these latter areas. And in the next section we will have to move West with some of the settlers and see how conditions they encountered began to react upon the older sections along the seaboard. But right now let us see what industry was doing along the upper Atlantic coast.

BUSINESS CHANGES

Out of such enterprises as Mr. Gridley's blacksmith shop, many small factories had developed in the early 1800's. For a time they were family affairs. Then, largely under demands set up by the Revolution, they began to expand. With freedom and the improvements and development which took place rapidly after the war, these plants began to grow into sizable operations.

Perhaps the greatest single impulse came from abundant cotton to be processed into cloth. Mills to handle this business sprang up, with a great demand for employees. About the mills were towns, made up for the most part of "company houses," rented to employees and large enough so that many "boarders" could be accommodated. In some instances there were dormitories for the unmarried.

A PAUL REVERE CLOCK

The great patriot built this clock sometime about the year 1795. It was operated by weights, which exerted their pull by means of cables fed through a tube beneath the sidewalk from the cellar of the owner's store, and then up the hollow post to the works. It kept time at its last location for near 100 years, until hit by a truck, and its cast iron base and case totally ruined.

Farms had been pretty well brought under cultivation, families were still large, and there were both sons and daughters who were becoming excess laborers on home places. The former could, and many of them did, push on westward, taking some of the latter as wives. But there was a goodly number who turned to these newly built mills for a livelihood. In some cases the mill-owners enlisted the clergy for miles around, and many sermons were preached calling upon the younger generation to enter such employment as a patriotic duty. Support from this angle tended to break down older attitudes about woman's place being in the home. The mills began to fill up, and since spinning called for deft fingers many of the new *hands* were women.

INCREASE OF INDUSTRY

But there were other developments beyond those in textiles. The patriot Paul Revere, at first a jeweler, silversmith, and clockmaker, began to branch out into heavier metal work. He and others began to roll copper, brass, and then iron sheets. With increased sheets and bar stock of the various metals thus available, metalworking plants came into being to fabricate these into hundreds of items, from fishhooks to suspension bridges. There was work for an ever-increasing number of men, women, and even young children.

Some very pitiful stories found their way into early 19th century literature, picturing the condition of children of that time thrust into factory work and the sordid life of the mill towns. But childhood was very different at best in those now far away days; and in this connection, a paragraph or two quoted from the story of the Revolutionary patriot, Ebenezer Fox, published in 1838, may be particularly pertinent and informing. He says:

> Nothing out of the ordinary course of human events occurred, of which I have any recollection, until I reached the age of seven. My father, who was a tailor, being poor, and having a large family, thought that my physical powers were adequate at this time of life to my own maintenance; and placed me under the care of a farmer named Pelham.
>
> With him I continued five years, performing such services in the house and upon the farm as were adapted to my age and strength. I imagined, however, that I suffered many privations and endured many hardships; which was undoubtedly true, were my situation compared with that of other boys of my age, at that time, or in this *more refined* period.
>
> I made frequent complaints of a grievous nature to my father, but he paid no attention to them, supposing that they arose merely from a spirit of discontent which would soon subside.

Fancy it, boys of seven were generally expected to be self-supporting by their own labor; either at home or when bound out. This was also true in that *more refined* period when the factories were building up and drawing their full quota of these tiny tots, often roundly beaten because they fell asleep on the job. The age at which children, and boys in particular, were ready to go on their own raised slowly. But in many sections it was still as low as nine years long after the Civil War.

Thus began the industrial growth which would one day be the wonder of the modern world. But in it there are chapters that are rather sordid. Industrialization was largely new to a world that had been primarily agricultural, and it brought many human problems to be solved.

Industrial developments were quite in contrast to Jefferson's ideas of a nation of small farmers. Also they added rapidly to a group without strong ties in a locality through ownership of property. Many of these millworkers had little beyond a few personal possessions, some craft tools, and a pay envelope. As immigration increased, and workers were brought over directly from Europe by the industrialists, these people in the urban areas from Massachusetts down to Pennsylvania began to demand what they considered their *rights*.

Jefferson's embargo on shipping had given a clear indication of how narrow their margin of safety really was. Other disturbances that closed the mills and plants in which they worked, and rather promptly threw them onto starvation rations, or even the poor rolls, further pointed up their plight. The business panics of 1819 and 1828 brought widespread suffering; labor began to find leaders, and trade unions appeared. There had been craft unions as early as the Revolution, or even before.

"THE STRIKE" AS A WEAPON

The *strike* is not a new weapon. There is the record of one among the printing craftsmen of Lyons, France, in April and May of 1539. Their grievances? The masters did not supply sufficient food, the wages had been reduced, and there were too many compulsory holidays. But beyond that, the work day began at two in the morning and lasted until eight or nine at night. When this strike spread to Paris, it had to be arbitrated. The work day was then cut to five in the morning until eight at night. It was then still a fifteen-hour day.

Such days were not uncommon in English mills in the early 1800's, nor were they by any means unknown in America. Twelve- and thirteen-hour days were very common, and longer when required. Overtime was an unheard-of term.

LABOR AGITATION

The earliest labor agitations here were for increased pay and shorter hours. Along with these demands went others of a political nature. Workers were being arrested and imprisoned for unionizing, and especially for causing work stoppages. Now they began to demand the right to vote. On their side were the dispossessed of other classes. And this bloc demanding a manhood suffrage that reached to every citizen began to strike fear among the groups, both North and South, hoping to limit the franchise and officeholding to the limited propertied group.

It should perhaps be observed at this point that when the vote was granted, it was *appreciated* by the people for many years, until they began to consider this right as inherent. Then, when there was no longer any question about this right, people began to be indifferent toward what they had once fought to gain. It is not uncommon today for even half the voters to fail to exercise their right to vote. In such indifference there is grave danger.

But democracy was then just beginning to raise its head and use its voice. The once roundly hated term began to be heard more and more frequently. The nation itself was a *republic,* and would long continue to be so termed officially. The leaders, too, had thought of themselves as *republicans.* And Jefferson, more liberal than some, had so called his followers. Then slowly, and not universally at first, these same followers altered this designation to Democratic-Republicans. This would have been after Jefferson was no longer active in national affairs. But before his death in 1826 the party which he had founded had pretty much narrowed the name down to Democratic.

People began to look in the direction of the Democratic party for relief in connection with a widening range of problems. They wanted a vote; they wanted the right to join together in unions to bargain collectively. There was some demand even for woman's suffrage. The less fortunate group wanted access to better education for their children. Three months' total schooling in a lifetime was not enough. Also they wanted that schooling to be paid for out of public funds. And they would like to have hard money—money that was not subject to violent fluctuations in what it would buy.

To these larger issues, there were many lesser demands, some advocated by crackpots and by members of the lunatic fringe that always edges any spreading movement for reform. The idea of socialism—the equal division of property—was in the minds of some of the European intellectuals and spilled over into this country. But among people who had the right to own property, in contrast to their European brothers, and who were striving to enjoy that right, such unsound doctrines made little impression.

However, there were sober questions to be considered. And when there are sizable numbers living in a land where they have some measure of freedom and a deep conviction they have wrongs which can be righted, there is usually a political figure who is willing to champion their cause. The growing legions of industrial workers, together with smaller numbers of other groups whose members saw eye to eye with them on some issues, were in need of such a champion for their cause.

225

"Far from the Old Folks at Home"

Y THE TIME Horace Greeley, editor of the powerful New York *Tribune,* would pronounce his famous dictum, "Go West, young man," that very act would have long since become a common practice. Daniel Boone had been one of its originators, and we have already looked at this westward thrust of peoples somewhat from a political angle. We will do well now to look at it further from the angle of the men, women, and children who pioneered the move. For the pioneer instinct in America, as applied to politics, to industrial development, and to land settlement, has been one of our finest impulses. May we never lose it. We have brought peace and plenty to a continent; and our destiny seems to be cast in helping the whole broad world to better achievements along these lines. May we now find similar strengths for this larger task.

It takes a bold, brave man to set his face against nature and find a footpath over mountains, through a primeval forest, and across trackless plains. But Washington, Jefferson's father, and other hardy Virginians had blazed the way for what became the most extensively used of four overland routes into the interior, and then to the Mississippi, and which at first was called Braddock's Road. With government aid at a later time it would run from western Maryland, through Pittsburgh, and finally on to Vandalia, Illinois, roughly paralleling the present motor route U.S. 40 over much of that distance. It would give access to the great inland traffic artery, the Ohio River, and would feed in settlers from Philadelphia, Baltimore, and Alexandria, Virginia.

To the north was the Genesee Road, a water-level route over much of its way from Albany to Buffalo and the chain of Great Lakes, handling traffic from New York and New England.

There was the more rugged road, or trail, from Alexandria through the mountains to Boonesboro in Kentucky, and thence to the trading post at St. Louis. Then there was the fourth, Boone's trail through the Cumberland Gap and into the Kentucky section of what was originally part of Virginia.

Conestoga Road, west through today's suburban Philadelphia was the first stretch of the trail taken by many a pioneer family. Most at first came from the older settlements. More and more in the early 1800's would come from Europe as immigrants.

CONESTOGA WAGONS ALONG THE NATIONAL ROAD

Canvas-covered wagons—Conestogas—cost about $50, and a stout team to haul one was $120 more. The price was higher for both in either Baltimore or Alexandria. Then, too, there must be provisions and tools, money to buy land and to pay tolls along the way. It thus took a bit of capital before one could get under way, and then get to his destination, acquire a piece of land, and bring in the first crops. And beyond capital it took backbreaking toil, and lots of it for every member of the party. The pioneer women had to be just as rugged as their menfolk—and they did their full share, and more, in winning the West.

By the time the delegates were writing the new Constitution in 1787, the flow to the West was on in earnest. Near a thousand flatboats floated down the Ohio and deposited some twenty thousand men, women, and children, and their wagons, creatures, and possessions, into new homes along its banks in that year alone. And that was traffic over the Braddock Road principally.

The other roads carried their full complement as well.

The French had opened up much of this territory years before, yet had made but indifferent progress in its colonization. Perhaps the following experiences of the first American to press beyond the Mississippi will show why.

He was a go-getting Connecticut Yankee, named Moses Austin. France had secretly ceded the great Louisiana area to Spain, and New Spain had granted this enterprising man nine square miles of rich mining land to develop. He had by 1789 made and lost two fortunes in land speculation east of the river, and was now starting in afresh in the Missouri area. He needed first of all a grist mill. But any and all improvements made had to be cleared with the then Spanish governor in faraway New Orleans. After a reasonable wait, he decided to go ahead with the mill; he set his foreman to work and went himself to St. Louis to pick up the per-

(Continued on page 234)

227

CALIFORNIA NEWS
William Sidney Mount
SUFFOLK MUSEUM, STONYBROOK, L.I.

There was more than gold to call men and women to California and other points in the West. With his phrase, "Go west, young man," Horace Greeley had given thousands the hope that there they might come to closer grips with Opportunity. Land speculators were just as anxious that they should go, and so help dispose of their holdings at a handsome profit. It was not until during the Civil War that free land became available, and by then the railroads were clamoring for traffic. Beginning with the earliest settlements and continuing through the 19th century great pressure was brought to induce people to migrate to these shores, and then to fill in the back country through to the Pacific Ocean. William Penn was a master at writing such promotional literature, which brought hordes of Palatinate Germans here. In our picture men in the East are enthusing about the "prospects" beyond the horizon; and one young emigrant has seemingly been able to build up considerable eagerness in his wife.

BOMBARDMENT OF FORT SUMTER
Albert Bierstadt
UNION LEAGUE, PHILADELPHIA

While not a single man was killed on either side during the two-day engagement pictured, it was still a costly affair; for by it the die was cast, and the war that followed pitted brother against brother, and took its bitter toll in lives and treasure. Sumter was a new fortification of brick masonry, built on a shoal in the narrowest part of the harbor of Charleston, South Carolina. When that state seceded from the Union on December 20, 1860, it was still incomplete. Guns were being mounted, but no troops had as yet been garrisoned there. Expecting it would be seized, Union soldiers were moved there from nearby Fort Moultrie on the day following Christmas.

The weeks then rolled on without particular incident. Finally on April 12, 1861, a bombardment began, the surrounding installations pouring shells onto the new fort which was so located that it could command this strategic harbor. By the 14th, their supplies totally exhausted, the less than one hundred soldiers who had manned the post had no choice but to evacuate it. Thus were the opening shots of a cruel war fired here.

It was unfortunate that there were in the South leaders willing to undertake war rather than remain in the Union. It was equally unfortunate that other leaders in the North were similarly willing to fight rather than permit a single state to leave the Union. There had been two or more generations of political maneuvering and ferocious debate over the problems involved, which had produced no lasting settlement. Tempers and restraint had worn thin. And on April 12th, as the shells began to scream across Charleston harbor, peaceful means were set aside, and the long contest was moved up to a settlement by conflict on the battlefield. It was a dark day indeed in our glorious history.

ABOVE, **ERIE CANAL,** W. R. Miller, New York Hist. Soc.

BELOW, **HOUSE OF REPRESENTATIVES,** S. F. B. Morse, Corcoran Gallery

PAGE ONE
CALIFORNIA NEWS
W. S. Mount, Suffolk Museum

PREVIOUS SPREAD, TOP
BOMBARDMENT OF FORT SUMTER
Albert Bierstadt, Union League, Phila.

PREVIOUS SPREAD, BELOW
CROSSING THE POTOMAC
D. G. Blythe, Hall of Fame, Cooperstown

DOUBLEDAY'S TROOPS CROSSING THE POTOMAC

David Gilmore Blythe

BASEBALL HALL OF FAME, COOPERSTOWN, N.Y.

The artist, who died in 1865, must have painted this interesting scene soon after it took place in September 1862. Gen. Doubleday was moving his division to take part in the battle of Antietam-Sharpsburg. In the foreground, marching in column of squads, an infantry brigade is crossing a bridge over the Chesapeake and Ohio Canal. Between them and another brigade negotiating the shallow ford in the river are two field pieces. Then further on beyond the Potomac we see the files following the dusty road up over the hill. At the lower right are the muzzles of two artillery pieces covering this crossing, and another battery seems to be stationed by the lone tree opposite the house half way up the hill beyond the river. The artillery officer leaning against the barrel of one of his guns assumes a bit of swagger to impress the spectators being held back by the heavily bearded guard at the lower left.

ERIE CANAL NEAR LITTLE FALLS

William R. Miller

NEW YORK HISTORICAL SOCIETY

Clinton's *big ditch* as it was called was one of the great achievements of the first quarter of the 19th century. When it had first been proposed, Jefferson had remarked, "Talk of making a canal 350 miles through a wilderness is little short of madness at this day." It did take eight years to complete, but it was a huge success. Grain, fruit, and cattle flowed east, settlers headed west. Many of the latter stopped off along the way, and towns and cities sprang up and grew rapidly. Life by its banks and on its boats was rough, tough, and colorful, and seemed to call for music and much singing. Songs and chanties without number soon came into being, some sung by passengers or crew, while others were bawled out by the lonely *hoggies* as they plodded behind their mules along the tow path. Travel was leisurely, but not without its moments of excitement and even danger; and Miller, who knew it well, has captured the spirit of the canal in his picture.

THE OLD HOUSE OF REPRESENTATIVES

Samuel Finley Breese Morse

CORCORAN GALLERY OF ART, WASHINGTON

This scene in the lower house of Congress would have been most familiar to Clay, Webster, Hayne, Calhoun and the other great names who in the forepart of the last century raised their voices to advocate or oppose various courses of action for the Republic.

The artist, too, should have known it well, for he pleaded long hours with men who sat within its walls in behalf of financial support for a great project of his own—the *electric telegraph*. He had experimented with electric impulses and their transmission since 1832. Then in 1835 he applied for a patent, and filed a caveat with the Congress asking $30,000 to build an experimental line. It was not until 1843 that funds were forthcoming; and on May 24 of the following year the first telegraph message was sent between Washington and Baltimore.

233

mit. It was there; and he returned to his claim, only to find the foreman had decided to delay the work until it was certain the necessary permit had arrived.

SPANISH METHODS

Austin, furious at time thus lost on completing this prime necessity in his venture, fired the foreman. Then to his great chagrin he found this was not possible until the discharge had the approval of the local alcalde. Although there were postponements, the action was finally approved and work under a new foreman was resumed. Hampering restrictions under Spanish government (the French authority had been equally dilatory and confining) had held back this whole area. It had taken a year or more to complete a badly needed facility which otherwise could have been in operation within three weeks or a month.

Now the Americans filling in east of the river, and soon to spread across it, were there in no small part to make their freedom more complete. They would abide no such restrictions upon them by the hands of any government they would sanction. And they made this spirit so apparent that it was a source of worry to the staid politicians manning the newly formed federal government back home.

In the northern sections, and even in Tennessee and upper Alabama and other portions of the southern reaches also rapidly filling in, these people became small farmers. The quarter section—160 acres—was the average homestead. There was a striking equality among them. Those they raised to office were rapidly rotated, so that power did not lodge for long in one set of hands, and so that as many as possible with the necessary *ability* had an opportunity to hold office. Ownership and wealth did not count with them. Hard work and straight thinking did.

When, as has been related, their access to markets through New Orleans was shut off, they stormed the government to do something, and to do it fast. For a time there were ugly rumors in Washington and the East that this Mississippi section planned to attach itself to Spain, and thus withdraw from the Union. It is even reported that General Wilkinson, commander of the United States forces on the frontier, had actually sold Kentucky to the Spanish governor at New Orleans, only to find that France had again reclaimed her great western territory.

TROUBLE IN THE WEST

There was a real peril in this situation. Even President Washington admitted its gravity. Later, when Aaron Burr, who had killed Hamilton in a duel because the Federalist had declared him to be a most dangerous man, began to conspire to found an empire in Spanish territory in the Southwest, the fat was in the fire. Fear that this new West might attempt to rule the East flamed throughout the latter section. And for a time the conservative groups tried to keep it as a territory and under close domination.

But, by and large, these new westerners had no intention of leaving, or necessarily of dominating, the Union. They did want a market for their crops and an easier way to get products and finished goods from the East. The planters who were moving their cotton plantations across the southern tier of states, exhausting great tracts of land as they went, kept communication over the waters of the Gulf of Mexico. The rivers could be used successfully downstream, but working against the current meant a slow progress of only about one mile an hour. Flatboats carried produce downriver to New Orleans. Then the crew walked home again overland. Until steamboats were developed, the most practical answer appeared to be better roads.

DEVELOPMENT OF ROAD AND RIVER TRANSPORTATION

Congress, which had avoided "internal improvements," began to appropriate funds for road betterment. Work began in 1806, and at the end of nine years stagecoaches ran from the national capital to the Ohio River at Wheeling, then at the northern tip of the state of Virginia. It would take an additional sixteen years to complete this road to middle Ohio. And it was early in the 1850's that it reached Vandalia, sixty miles east of St. Louis. By then first steamboats, and then the railroads, had taken over the bulk of heavy-duty, long-distance haulage. Road improvement would lie largely dormant for nearly a hundred years, until the advent of the automobile.

But there was another development, short-lived for the most part but highly important for a few years, the canals. Washington, the young surveyor, had realized the possibility of joining the Potomac and Ohio rivers, and in 1775 chartered a company by which to accomplish this, either by canal or road. The Revolution and then the presidency prevented him carrying through this project.

Gallatin, Secretary of the Treasury under both Jefferson and Madison, had advocated canals along with work on the national road described above. The promoter, Robert Fulton, widely preached their construction and use. Then came the war of 1812 to hold back any attempts in this direction. About 1820 the contest over slavery managed to

put an end for a time to such internal improvements at federal expense.

The need of contact between the Hudson and Lake Erie at Buffalo was sufficient, however, so that New York State took over construction of a canal to link the two. The completion of this *Erie Canal* in 1825 touched off a series of such projects. Pennsylvania sought to connect Philadelphia and Pittsburgh by water traffic, and accomplished the task in 1834. The Potomac and the Ohio were also joined by a canal; and the Ohio and Lake Erie tied together by a ditch dug across the eastern portion of Ohio.

THE FRANTIC ERA OF CANAL BUILDING

Even places like little Farmington had their canals. By 1822 nearby Hartford and the other Connecticut River towns began to enjoy regular steamboat service; but navigation on that river was not practical much above the Massachusetts line, except where artificial means were provided around rapids and falls. As early as 1802 Vermont had bypassed Bellows Falls, and no less than six canals were put in operation to improve and promote river trade.

To join with this enterprise, a canal was projected from New Haven north to Farmington, and from there to the Massachusetts line. Here it was to be met with another section to join it to the Connecticut. From the headwaters of this latter stream, a third section was to reach over the line into Canada to the St. Lawrence. It was an ambitious project, but still typical of many, many others throughout the states. The two lower sections were completed about 1828, and were in use until 1845. The extension in Canada was not attempted. For the railroad had arrived by 1848, and canal traffic

AN ERIE CANAL BOAT

dropped in many instances to almost nothing.

Chief exception was the great Erie Canal, now much enlarged and still in profitable operation. This most successful of all such enterprises was able at its opening to cut haulage cost from 32¢ to 1¢ per ton mile, a more than 97 per cent saving.

Around it grew up a great saga of exploits and incidents, many of which took the form of songs. The westerners were pretty generally a hearty folk, as some of the songs they sang clearly show. Stephen Foster's first recollections must have been of this great western flow of people through his native Pittsburgh, and he became their minstrel. Many of his 175 published songs were widely popular, and they give an enlightening picture of hopes, aspirations, and life of that time.

Except some of the planters in the extreme South, none of these people who had moved beyond the mountains and then across the Mississippi was very rich. Not too many, by the same token, were very poor. They had worked hard for what they had. They prized their freedom; but they had learned to share any excessive burdens when heaped upon their neighbors. They were individualists, but they had fully learned the benefits that flow from willing co-operation. They managed to give a new, strong, richer flavor to the *democracy* that was surely coming to the fore, although out of somewhat different circumstances back in the Northeast.

These democratically minded peoples in the various sections began to feel the need of a champion for the causes in which they had a lively interest. And the farmers in the West, planter interests in the South, and the industrial classes back East found their man in a fiery, intrepid soldier-jurist from Tennessee. His name was Andrew Jackson.

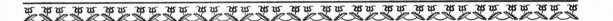

"To the Victors Belong the Spoils"

IX MEN had served as President. After Washington there had been John Adams; he was honest, fair-minded, and, though a Federalist, he had not been as extreme as Hamilton and his clique. He was followed by Jefferson, who served for two terms.

Jefferson was succeeded by James Madison, who had "fathered" the Constitution. His ability was more adapted to that task, for he lacked executive talent. Although re-elected in 1812, the war beginning with Britain in that year marred his second term. He was followed by James Monroe, a man of rather medium abilities, but who so balanced opposing forces that his eight years in office are spoken of as "the era of good feeling."

His Secretary of State had been John Quincy Adams, son of the second President. In that office this younger Adams had acquired Florida from Spain and aided Monroe in framing his famous *Doctrine* on America for Americans. In running for the presidency in 1824, he was opposed by Andrew Jackson. Since neither had a majority of electoral votes, the decision fell to the House of Representatives. Henry Clay

threw his support to Adams, and he was elected. He had many ambitious plans, but they were for the most part obstructed by Congress, and his was a rather uneventful administration.

The man who was to follow Adams was one of the most colorful who had yet occupied that highest office. He had been born in 1767 along the border between the Carolinas, where, as an orphan, he became a British war prisoner. Following the Revolution, he made his way into Tennessee, where he managed to study law, take part in Indian outbreaks, and serve in the state constitutional convention.

He was then elected to the federal lower house, and later to the Senate, resigning after a year in this latter body, to become a judge of the state Supreme Court. For several years Andrew Jackson lived the life of a judge and country gentleman at his beautiful home, the Hermitage, near Nashville.

In 1813 he had been given command of the Tennessee militia and sent against the warlike Creek Indians. He roundly defeated them a year later in the Battle of Horseshoe Bend. This action is often credited with breaking the power of the red men in this country. They would, as more and more of them were moved West into *reservations,* continue to make trouble up to the end of the century; but never again would they imperil any large area.

BATTLE OF NEW ORLEANS

Made a general in the United States Army, he defended New Orleans against the British attack on that important port on January 8, 1815. He had endeared himself to his troops by always sharing the rigors of campaigning on an equal basis with the lowliest soldier. And his successful defense of the key to the Mississippi Valley, even though peace had been signed in the meantime, gave him great and enduring popularity throughout the country.

Continuing his military career, he invaded Florida in 1818, took Pensacola, and created an international incident by hanging two Englishmen captured there.

Here was a "self-made" man, in contrast to the procession of men of wealth or of special talents who had been occupying the White House. He looked distinctly like their sort of man to the western farmers, and also to those in the industrial Northeast hoping for better representation of their trying problems. This hard-hitting, hard-bitten son of the soil, later dubbed *Old Hickory,* found himself as early as 1821 being boomed for the presidency. To further his chances, he managed to have himself returned to the Senate in 1823.

There were four candidates for President in 1824, Jackson, Adams, Clay, and William H. Crawford. There was a plurality of electoral votes for Jackson, although not a majority, and he received the popular vote as well. Clay and his friends turned their support to Adams; and Jackson was thrust aside, as was noted above.

Clay, however, to foster his *American System,* pushed a higher tariff through in 1828, looking toward internal improvements out of the increased revenues to garner votes in the forthcoming campaign. The purpose was to re-elect Adams. The South, nettled by these higher rates on its purchases from abroad, switched to Jackson. And when the electoral votes were counted after this second contest, Jackson had 178 to Adams' 83.

From the moment this tall, ramrod-straight, soldier-statesman from Tennessee took office early in 1829, the fur began to fly. Still bitterly resentful of his earlier defeat, he began a wholesale removal of federal officeholders. His doctrine when condemned in a Senate speech three years later was explained as, "to the victors belong the spoils." This would be the prevailing practice during more than fifty ensuing years, and until the establishment of civil-service reform.

THE KITCHEN CABINET

Very much of a martinet in office, Jackson had little use for his own appointees who made up his formal Cabinet, preferring to take counsel with a political group which came to be known as his "kitchen cabinet." His program at the outset was rather hazy. But he had been swept into the White House so decisively that he set out to expand both the power and prestige of the office.

The "old order" was due for change, and he soon set in motion a sweeping program of domestic reform. He pinched off the internal improvements started by his predecessor. Realizing the widespread interest in the unsettled money situation, then a subject of wide agitation, he began to close down on the reinstated United States Bank. When

YOUNG ANDY IS BEATEN BY A BRITISH OFFICER

During the Revolution Jackson, then a boy, was beaten for refusing to polish a British officer's boots. This violent incident left an indelible impression on his mind; and in old age he threw the weight of his influence against the British, then trying to keep Texas out of the Union.

its managers sought to renew its charter well in advance of its termination, he vetoed Congress's approval. His firm stand destroyed the Bank. Although this blow to the moneyed interests won great acclaim from his middle-class and frontier supporters, it was later to make grave trouble. Had he followed through, as finally had to be done, and placed money matters in the hands of the Treasury Department, his acts would have brought more lasting results.

Nonetheless, the immediate effects were an abundant prosperity. The national debt was wiped out, and there was every evidence a new era was opening up. The railroads were just beginning to run their earliest trains; and the first group of Indians, the Cherokees of Georgia, were removed to new lands assigned to them west of the Mississippi.

Jackson defeated Clay quite handily in 1832, but a different type of contest was already brewing. Another act had been passed upping the tariff, and South Carolina at once threatened to nullify the objectionable law by refusing to pay the duty imposed. If it became a necessity, this state would even withdraw from the Union. The President now had a fight on his hands, and involving no less a person than his Vice-President, John C. Calhoun of South Carolina. In a petulant moment Jackson threatened to have him arrested.

While a firm believer in *states' rights,* Old Hickory was an even more staunch advocate of the Union. Swearing the latter would be

239

preserved if he had to hang "as high as Haman" every man who raised a hand against it, he issued a proclamation. This denied the right of any state to secede or to declare inoperative any act of the Congress. It warned in no uncertain terms that the laws would be enforced, and by use of military power if need be. South Carolina's reply was a call for volunteer troops and the purchase of arms.

Jackson, an excellent judge of men, chose General Winfield Scott and sent him down to the scene of trouble. By tactful show of force, backed by rare good judgment and extreme courtesy, this able soldier forestalled the tolling of the alarm bell of Secession for another thirty years.

Taking an equally strong stand on debts owed by France, the President not only secured their payment, but he strengthened the position of this country in European opinion. When an American commercial vessel was set upon by natives in the far-off Dutch East Indies, he at once dispatched an armed frigate halfway around the world to redress the wrong. Closer at home, he finally managed to crush the power of the Seminole Indians in Florida. Both at home and abroad he was determined that the United States should be respected. He could handle a "big stick" as well as a later incumbent of the high office proved he could wield it.

But such a man was certain to attract enemies as well as friends. Thus it was that during his administration the first serious attempt on a President's life was made by a would-be assassin. This occurred at a public gathering, and the assailant attempted to fire two pistols at close range, only to have both of them miraculously misfire. Although the man was adjudged insane, there was evidence of the violent feelings which the office and its occupant can engender. There would

come a day when special guards would have as their chief duty the protection of the life of the President and the members of his family.

Arkansas was admitted to the Union in 1836; and early in the next year Michigan became the twenty-sixth state. The original thirteen had now doubled in number; and the population had increased five times to about fifteen million. Growth was now really getting well under way, with new moves into the West about to be launched.

In this connection, it is interesting to note that Jackson's last official act was in relation to rampant speculation in western lands. The new notes issued by state banks since the termination of the United States Bank were very insecure. They had been used in speculations in these western lands, and were of doubtful enough value so that all collectors of public revenue were now ordered to accept nothing in payments but silver and gold.

The reaction was swift and paralyzing. Early in 1837 the panic struck. Bank after bank went under, new western boom towns vanished, eastern mills closed down, and the country was virtually prostrate. Jackson had been able to have his favorite, Martin Van Buren, elected President in the 1836 election. But Van Buren's heritage from his predecessor was a most embarrassing one and tended to make his administration one of the least brilliant in our history.

Old Hickory had made the Jeffersonian party, the Democrats, a vital affair, however, and between 1829 and 1861 they would hold power in all except eight of these thirty-two years. Anticipating another Democratic President a hundred years later, he had sought out and played up the *forgotten man* and inaugurated a *new deal* in his behalf. He left his mark upon the land.

"From Sea to Shining Sea"

O YOU recall Moses Austin, who was having trouble with Spanish authorities over installing a grist mill in what later became Missouri? He had run up another fortune there, only to have it wiped out when one of the land booms burst like a pricked toy balloon. Without even a horse to bear him, the old man walked the 250 miles from St. Louis to Little Rock, only to find his son, Stephen, had just been defeated for a seat in the Arkansas legislature.

Picking up a mule and a slave as a bodyguard, old Moses pushed on some 750 miles farther to San Antonio. There he laid a plan of colonization before the Mexican authorities, and received a huge grant of free land. But the great exertion cost him his life, and his son had to carry on.

Stephen Austin had his father's ability and drive. In a few years he had brought so many people and so many advanced ideas and implements into this area, then known as *New Spain,* that the authorities were terror-stricken. There was friction, too, between colonists and those originally in the land. Even while in office, Jackson had sought to bring pressure upon Mexico to

cede the territory, claiming it to be a part of the Louisiana Purchase.

But by 1835 the Texans were numerous and strong enough to revolt. This they did, declaring Texas to be independent. Santa Anna, the Mexican president, at once invaded the territory, and the fall of the Alamo resulted. But shortly afterward in 1836 Sam Houston with a small force fell upon Santa Anna's army at San Jacinto and almost annihilated it, taking its leader prisoner. This badly frightened man, recalling his cruelty at the Alamo, where he had slaughtered the remnant that had surrendered, quickly signed a treaty granting independence.

This was repudiated later; but Texas became an independent republic, with Sam Houston as its first president. It asked to be admitted to the Union during Van Buren's term, but was refused by him, since such action seemed certain to bring war with Mexico.

Finally in 1843 the question came up again for debate in Congress. Admission pointed up the grave sectional difference still plaguing the Union, and become more acute. The South was in favor, since it would add a vast slave area, which might be broken up in quite a number of separate states. The

North was opposed for this same reason. The matter took two years to adjust, but Texas was finally admitted late in 1845. James K. Polk was then President. Florida had been brought in earlier that year, and Iowa would be admitted in 1846, with Wisconsin to follow in 1848.

OREGON TERRITORY

Since 1818 there had been a ticklish situation developing in the extreme Northwest. Following the Rogers and Clark expedition, some settlers had moved into the Oregon area, and this section had been jointly occupied under an agreement with Great Britain. The boundary question began to fester, and there were some mutterings of war. Then in 1846 agreement was reached that the line between United States and Canada should be along the 49th parallel. With this matter adjusted, the Oregon territory was established two years later, and the United States now reached through from the Atlantic to the Pacific. Its western coast line was soon to be extended hundreds of miles to the south.

Hardly had Polk been inaugurated than a break came with Mexico. The immediate cause was the western boundary of Texas, and the resulting war could probably have been settled in that area. But, partly for political purposes, it was extended to include a campaign against the Mexican capital. With the fall of that city, the Mexicans capitulated. In a peace arranged in February, 1848, we were yielded possession of California and northern portions of Arizona and New Mexico, a huge area. For this virtual "empire," Mexico received some fifteen million in cash, and the cancellation of substantial claims held by American citizens. In 1853 the boundary was adjusted by a further

treaty in which we received another 45,000 square miles in southern Arizona and New Mexico.

The United States had grown remarkably, and its continental limits were now established. Perhaps there were conservative thinkers then, as there had been when Jefferson bought the Louisiana Purchase, who wondered if it would ever be settled and brought into use.

But beyond this, we were, as a nation, following the intrepid New England ship captains into the Orient. By 1844 official relations had been established with the Chinese government at Peking. Soon Commander Perry would be knocking at the fast-closed door of Japan, and encouraging that then backward nation to open its ports to the commerce of the world. Before California would achieve statehood but a few years later, American ships were making scheduled trips between the West Coast, Hawaii, and Asian ports.

CALIFORNIA GOLD RUSH

Thus California was not unknown to Americans by the time it was acquired. They had already thrust into its northern portion, together with some Europeans who had been granted extensive privileges by its former owners. And while peace negotiations were under way, came news that set fire to millions of imaginations. *Gold had been discovered.*

Despite the fact that some attempts had been made to keep the news secret, it spread across three thousand miles to the Atlantic seaboard like wildfire, and on to the uttermost parts of the world. Then began an emigration such as had never been seen before. Men of all kinds and conditions threw up what they were doing, and set out for the

WOUNDED GEN. HOUSTON RECEIVES THE SURRENDER
OF WOUNDED GEN. SANTA ANNA AT SAN JACINTO

gold diggings. Some went overland by the long wagon trails. Others made the long water haul around Cape Horn at the tip of South America. Still others went by boat to Panama, crossed through the jungles where one day there would be a canal, and completed the journey by boat to the now booming port of San Francisco.

Although a half billion in gold would be recovered in the next dozen years from the rich gravels in the northern California hills, these riches were as nothing to the settlement which this golden horde brought about. Within two years there were enough people here to justify its admittance as a state. And, despite strong opposition in the South, it joined the list of free states in 1850.

We were now halfway through the 1800's; and this new nation—new particularly in kind—had become a young giant. When the first census was taken in 1790, it had occupied but 867,980 square miles. Now its domain had grown to 2,944,337 square miles. The number of inhabitants, at first just under four million, now totaled more than twenty-three million. Where there had once been but 4.5 people to each square mile, there were now, even with this much greater land area, as many as eight per mile. This meant that cities and towns were growing rapidly, too.

In place of the two thousand that had come from Europe and other lands each year at the beginning of the century, immi-

243

grants were now pouring in at the rate of 370,000 a year. Liberty and opportunity were magnets of such great power they could be felt across broad oceans. Democracy had given a new tone to life in these United States, of which there were now thirty-three.

With great strides in industry and the perfection of machinery, many startling developments were taking place. One of the most potent was the power printing press, which made possible penny newspapers. Magazines and books also multiplied rapidly. Public schools were being established in some of the states. Halls and meeting places permitted orators and agitators to address and sway ever-larger audiences. In many, many ways life was becoming increasingly democratic, fuller, richer, and lived more in common and at a livelier pace.

But the seeds of conflict, long since sown, had sprouted and were growing, too. A bloody harvest lay not too far ahead. The coming decade—1850–60—would be a most critical one.

"If a House Be Divided"

E HAVE already seen how the North, soon after the Revolution, began to turn strongly toward industry and commerce. By contrast, the South, and particularly the deep South, had continued to develop almost entirely along agricultural lines.

In this latter area, after the introduction of the power gin which had permitted planting of more and more short-staple varieties, cotton had become *king*. There had been some hope in Colonial times of success with other products, such as rice and indigo. Tobacco, the first large crop, continued. But the soaring demand for cotton soon made that the number-one consideration. To produce it profitably called for cheap land and cheap labor. Cotton planting became a highly specialized form of agriculture.

Just as success in manufacturing enterprise was measured principally by the size of the plant and number of employees, so cotton planting began to tend toward larger and larger land holdings, called *plantations,* and greater and greater numbers of hands, principally slave labor. In certain respects, the ambitions, outlook upon life, and the moral impulses of the large planters were not unlike those of the larger industrialists.

Let us not, however, be deceived in respect to *bigness*. There were then none of the huge corporate organizations employing people by the thousands. There were large industrial plants in the North and large plantations in the South. And in both instances their owners managed collectively to exert extensive political pressure upon lawmaking bodies, both in their respective states and at the federal level. But while there were some great plantations, only about one in fifty planters held fifty or more slaves. Thus the great bulk of them were moderate-sized operators. Still, irrespective of size, they faced very similar economic and labor conditions; and planters had to see eye to eye and stand together.

While northern manufacturers did sell in foreign markets, they were strongly in favor of Henry Clay's American System. This would permit them to build up a large domestic market. But to cultivate it, they felt they needed protection through a tariff to overcome the competition of European products produced by labor paid pitifully low wages.

The South, although not self-sufficient even in foodstuffs, could not take so wholeheartedly to the *American System*. It tended to limit its freedom of action and its eventual profits and wealth. Europe, and especially England, formed a very considerable market for raw cotton. Also it provided an excellent source of many of the manufactured products the South consumed. These could be taken conveniently in exchange for exported cotton, and usually at more favorable prices when not subject to the heavy duties said to be needed to protect northern enterprise.

While this sectional bias had not by then been nearly so acute, the compromise at the Constitutional Convention over the arrangements of the Senate and its powers had been made to preserve some balance between the states in the North and the South. This economic difference had persisted and strengthened, and came more and more to be pointed up in the question of the right to own slaves.

COTTON POSES MANY PROBLEMS

Within the cotton-planting South, certain cleavages also grew up. One was the fact that in early days, before fertilization was extensively employed, the demands of this crop rapidly exhausted the land. Small landholders, dependent upon their own and their family's efforts, could not compete with slave labor. Many of them lost their places and migrated out of cotton areas, while others lived as best they could at a bare subsistence level. Those that remained would one day become "share croppers." Slowly, too, the planters took over firm control of politics. And a close, well-organized control it was.

The slavery which continued in the South after it had been terminated in the North also had a strong influence upon immigration into this country. To Europeans, it was abhorrent as an institution; and they had no

wish, for the most part, either to live where it flourished or to be forced to compete with it. Thus the influx of peoples from abroad went principally into the North, and from there on into the upper tier of states where slavery did not occur. This tended, with other conditions, to make the North more populous, and to make the thrust toward the West more vigorous from that section.

THE PLANTERS
MOVE RAPIDLY TO THE WEST

However, depleted fields and cheap land pushed cotton planting westward also. It moved rapidly out through Alabama and Mississippi into Louisiana, and into Texas, turning north into Missouri and Arkansas. Demand in world markets was mounting rapidly, and production did its best to keep pace.

So much emphasis upon one crop had latent dangers, however. The expanding market must be maintained and seemed better assured in Europe. The planters thus focused their attention beyond the ocean. Also with this demand to "make cotton," and the resulting profits, the institution of slavery changed materially, and conditions for the slaves became much harsher. Planting had become pretty much industrialized, and the remainder of southern agriculture was forced to go along with the dominant planter group.

But whether it willed it that way or not, the North still was an important factor in affairs in Dixie. Goods from Europe flowed in through northern ports and merchants. Cotton was shipped on northern vessels, and land and slaves were often financed through northern capital. It was only natural that such conditions would prove irksome below the Mason-Dixon Line.

THE FUR TRAPPERS WHO PIONEERED THE WEST

Never has there been a more colorful group of men than the fur trappers who roamed far and wide in the early days of the 19th century. Sometimes they worked in *companies*, but quite as often alone. They were restless, fearless men, and always interested in what lay just around the next corner. Their knowledge was of invaluable aid in opening up the West to settlement.

Still in 1849 there were thirty states—fifteen of them free, and fifteen of them slave. But there was no further slave territory ready for admission. California was ready for admission in 1850, and when she lined up with the free states, there was an immediate contest and need for compromise. To offset California, Utah and New Mexico were organized as territories, with the privilege of determining which course they would take.

The basic dispute lingered on, soon to blaze up anew. There was even talk of annexing Cuba, which would, of course, be slave territory. But it was side-tracked by trouble in Nebraska and Kansas. By the Missouri Compromise, these territories were to have been free. A new theory of "squatter sovereignty," by which settlers would make the final choice, was now being advocated by Stephen A. Douglas of Illinois. Immigrants poured into the territory from both North and South. Rival governments were soon set up, and when elections were held, sympathizers were secretly brought in from Missouri. There were bitter clashes, and in the murder and near civil war that followed, some two hundred lost their lives. President Polk finally intervened, and on July 4, 1856, broke up the free state government there. This tension became a pattern for a larger contest looming ahead.

Adjusting this difficulty brought about a new alignment of political parties, with the names as known to us today—Republicans and Democrats. The latter, however, won the election in 1856, and James Buchanan became President. But overshadowing this was the political contest that ensued and brought on in 1858 the historic debate between Douglas and a new figure in national affairs, Abraham Lincoln, also of Illinois. Both were candidates for state senator in Illinois. Douglas won the seat, but Lincoln forced him into a declaration which cost him the support of the southern Democrats.

This debate was largely instrumental in bringing about Lincoln's candidacy for President in 1860.

A SHIFT IN SENTIMENT

Northern antislavery sentiment had been for the most part an intellectual pursuit. Professional agitators, some of the clergy, and some of the literary element fulminated against it. But the great majority of the people had been but little moved one way or the other. This agitation had started in the 1830's, about which time southern leaders had begun to protect and advocate the institution. At the political level it had resulted in a long series of compromises.

Oregon would be brought in as free territory in 1859. There would be opposition, some of it hidden. Such was the appeal of Daniel Webster, who maintained the territory was too far from Washington. Members of Congress from there would find it difficult to reach Washington for duty and still return home in time for the next election. A new state always disturbed political balance, and, with slavery a live issue, precipitated a fight over admittance.

The new "fugitive slave law" which went into action in 1850 had teeth in it. And as Negroes were hunted down in northern cities and towns, and men and women who had lived peacefully in communities for years were dragged away by federal officers, the whole attitude of that area changed quickly. It may have been a violent and prejudiced book, but *Uncle Tom's Cabin* found millions of willing readers. What had been fundamentally an economic difference now became an earnestly discussed social and moral question.

This volume, appearing in 1852, found an answer in the South, which threw its strength behind the repealing of the Missouri Compromise. The Kansas-Nebraska affair recounted above followed as a result. In 1856 the southern Democrats found Congressional strength enough to lower the tariff. And almost at once the country was in the grip of a panic about as violent as the one twenty years before. The political alignment now became more strongly sectional, Lincoln and Douglas drawing the lines of impending battle.

THE SELF-APPOINTED MARTYR FROM KANSAS

Although this debate was followed throughout the country very closely, the real straw in the wind was the grim affair at Harpers Ferry in what was then still Virginia. Backed by rather stupid northern sympathizers, John Brown, a Kansas zealot, attempted to seize a federal arsenal, start an uprising, and free the slaves. He was readily captured and summarily hung. A martyr in the North, an arch villain in the South, Lincoln struck middle opinion by calling this ill-conceived move of a misguided man *absurd*. Whatever its reasoning, *Abolition's* methods promised to become too radical for safety.

This abortive raid became highly embarrassing to the Republican group as sides were taken for the campaign of 1860. The country was seething with unrest, and what had once been no worse than heated debate broke out as a free-for-all in the House of Representatives. There was a split in the making in Democratic ranks; and so fundamental and final was it that the party convention had to be adjourned. A second session opened the breach still wider, and the southern group finally withdrew and nominated its own candidate. There were attempts at compromise. But the result was the election of Abraham Lincoln as the sixteenth President, although he received but a minority of the popular vote.

The day following his election, steps were taken in South Carolina to call a secession convention. There was still a Union. But how long before a badly divided house might fall was not certain. The call was for abundant patience, and for cool heads and sober thinking. The passions aroused, however, were bitter indeed.

"Our Federal Union: It Must Be Preserved"

N DECEMBER 20, 1860, a convention assembled in South Carolina declared by unanimous vote that that state was no longer a part of the Union. Nullification, and even secession, had been threatened before, both in the North and in the South; but at last the threat was about to be made good. A month later Mississippi, Florida, Alabama, Georgia, Louisiana, and Texas followed South Carolina's lead. Four other states considered, but hesitated.

During February delegates from six of the foregoing met and drew up a constitution for the Confederate States of America, electing Jefferson Davis President for one year. Immediately southerners who had held civil or military offices in the United States government resigned. This act was a particularly heavy blow to the Union Army and Navy, many of its ablest officers having come from the southern states.

Sentiment in the North was divided. So powerful a voice as that of Horace Greeley of the New York *Herald* favored recognizing the newly formed Confederacy. It was not until March 4, 1861, that Lincoln took office; and in his inaugural address he clearly set forth his views. He did not believe that slavery should be interfered with where it was already established. But he was determined to preserve the Union and expressed belief in the complete lack of wisdom of seceding. He had, previous to taking office, made efforts in the direction of a peaceful settlement, but had been rebuffed.

THE OPPOSING SIDES

The opposing sides lining up seemed most illy matched. The North had more than two and a half times the population and potential fighting men, for there would eventually be eleven states pitted against twenty-three. Also it had virtually all of the industrial plants which would be needed to supply the sinews of war.

But the South had the able military commanders and a sound plan of dominating the interior through control of the Ohio and Mississippi river valleys. Their cotton would, they hoped, continue to flow to Europe; and their needs would be supplied from there. In a burst of confidence they embarked upon war, believing it would be a relatively short one.

On April 12, 1861, southern forces let go a bombardment on recently completed

Fort Sumter, in Charleston Harbor. This was an act of war, and three days later Lincoln called for 75,000 volunteers. The die was cast; and North Carolina, Virginia, Tennessee, and Arkansas joined the Confederacy. Northern sentiment stiffened, and a swift victory was the prevailing opinion there.

THE CONTEST IS MISJUDGED

Both sides seriously misjudged the other and heavily underestimated what lay ahead. After the contest was joined, first bursts of patriotism tended to cool, and each side finally had to resort to conscription to keep armies up to strength. At the end, the South was on the point of arming the slaves, for it fell to its lot to suffer more heavily in the long, bitter, bloody contest ahead. It is said that as many as nine out of each ten of its able-bodied men saw service.

This was in considerable contrast to one out of two who served in the North. There the industrial plant could be converted to war purposes and had to be manned. There was better mechanical equipment on its farms, and the railroads linked the North and East with the agriculture of the West. Thus conditions tipped the scales strongly in favor of the Union side.

It is not essential to the intents of this volume to recount the details of this heroic but most unfortunate and unhappy struggle. It will serve our purposes more fully to consider only its broad aspects, and particularly its effects upon those condemned to endure this frightful war, whose children would be forced to reconstruct their lives and the mighty UNION which is our common heritage.

While the first appeal for recruits in the North was promptly met, the response had fallen so rapidly by the middle of 1862 that a draft of the militia was necessary. By the early part of 1863 this was extended to cover every able-bodied man between the ages of twenty and forty-five. Quotas were set community by community and filled by the drawing of lots. Such service could be avoided by the selectee "buying" a substitute, or by his paying the government a sum, not to exceed three hundred dollars. The bitterness occasioned by this undemocratic arrangement was most intense. Rioting broke out in some of the larger cities, such as New York, and made serious trouble and much hard feeling in other localities. Before the war ended these one-sided provisions had to be cleared away.

MIXED SENTIMENT OBTAINS

Nor was sympathy with the southern *cause* completely nonexistent in the North throughout the war. To curb it, rather drastic powers were necessary, and both free speech and a free press were heavily restricted. Even that most basic of rights—*habeas corpus*—by which a person cannot be restrained or imprisoned without prompt hearing and trial, was set aside by executive order of the President.

Both sides would naturally look across the ocean for aid, or at least encouragement. The South needed markets for its cotton piling up in all its ports in great quantities. Also it needed supplies, recognition, and financial aid. The emperor of France was willing to do what could be done and attempted to enlist English co-operation. Parliament was favorable, but the English people generally, and even cotton spinners thrown out of work, were not. As the war continued, however, both England and France were able to offer the South some aid. Northern representatives in the former

IT WAS A WAR OF BROTHER AGAINST BROTHER

country were not too successful on the diplomatic front, and the northern press was pretty vitriolic. Also a seizure of Confederate agents from a British ship caused much friction. Still both that country and France were rendered more ineffectual than might possibly have been expected.

Anything like a blockade of southern points at the very outset was impossible, for the ships at the disposal of the Union were too few in number. But with ample ship-building facilities, the blockading fleet was soon sufficient to ruin Confederate commerce. Within two years cotton exports were cut by ninety-eight per cent. Perhaps more than any one other means, this strangle hold upon shipping forecast the final decision.

Even after fighting began, Lincoln had opposed any measures dealing with the termination of slavery. As the war dragged on,

more and more pressure was brought to bear upon him to take drastic action. But he still stoutly resisted all such attempts. After the first year of struggle, however, slavery began to shape up as a means of bargaining.

On April 10, 1862, Congress drew a measure offering financial aid to any states that would adopt emancipation over a number of years. And as evidence of its good intents, it freed the slaves held in the District of Columbia. Two months later slavery was abolished in the territories. There had been the famous Dred Scott decision by the Supreme Court casting doubt upon the legality of such federal action. But this was the middle of a devastating war, in no small part brought on by this very institution.

The President took this bold step as a measure vitally necessary in a period of emergency. Such extensions of the executive

AND ON SOME OCCASIONS IT WAS INDEED TRUE

In many instances close kin and even blood brothers were pitted against one another in this civil conflict. The bloodiest battle fought on Kentucky soil occurred at Perryville, 75 miles south of Louisville, on October 8, 1862. Here Generals Buell and Bragg, brothers-in-law, faced each other at the head of opposing troops.

power would be questioned on constitutional grounds for a hundred years or more. But the framework put together in Philadelphia in 1787 was a job of master building, and would continue to stand the tests of time.

The major step was already shaped up in Lincoln's mind, and six weeks or so later he read the first draft of a suitable Proclamation at a Cabinet meeting. This was late in July, and, while approved, the time of issuance did not seem to be at hand. In September, northern fortunes were enough brightened so that on the 22nd the *Emancipation* document was released to the public.

By it the states which had seceded were either to have rejoined the Union by Janu-

ary 1, 1863, or the slaves within their borders were declared free. Slavery, wherever else it existed within the United States, was not affected. A final Emancipation Proclamation was issued on January 1, 1863. But it would be more than two years yet, and take the Thirteenth Amendment to abolish slavery finally and presumably for all time.

The South had a natural barrier as a shield, consisting of mountains and hills running westward from the Potomac to the Mississippi. This latter stream could be and was promptly strongly fortified at a number of points. Thus most of the first three years were consumed in the West in a struggle for this mighty artery and of such rail lines as ran east from it or south from Louisville.

The Confederate armies had attempted to invade the North, but had been turned back in the fall of 1862 and met another final repulse at Gettysburg early in July of 1863. By then control of the Mississippi and the blockade of Atlantic and Gulf ports were weakening resistance. And while the Confederate troops fought brilliantly, numbers and equipment were against them. The South was entered and pitilessly ravaged in the middle of 1864. By September of that year Richmond had fallen.

It would not be until April 9, 1865, however, that hostilities could be terminated. On that day a short, stocky, black-bearded man wearing a blue uniform sat with a taller, rather striking soldier in gray in a small house in Appomattox Court House, Virginia. The quiet little town lay seventy miles west of Richmond and about twice that distance southwest of Washington. The gray-clad officer had just signed his name to a document on the table before him. There was deep sorrow, even a touch of heart-break, in his face. It was a tense moment, and there was no trace of exultation in the features of the blue-clad officer who sat opposite.

Perhaps this latter had vividly in mind a conversation of a few evenings before. The victory that was now his had seemed certain, and he had said to his superior who had made a surprise call at his headquarters tent, "What shall we do about Lee, seize him, to be tried and shot as a traitor?"

And the very tall, gaunt man, his face seamed with the four years of bitterness in this struggle of brother against brother, had replied slowly, softly, "Shoot Lee! If they do, they better shoot Abe Lincoln as well!"

"Yes, Mr. President," had been the reply. Now as his eyes met those of the brave soldier opposite him across the table, they both rose, and, as though it were the most natural gesture, their hands met in a firm grasp. Up to the moment of the signing of peace arrangements but a few moments before, they had commanded bitterly opposed armies. In this symbolic joining of hands, they were again brothers.

Said the blue-clad man, "Take your horses home with you. They will be needed for the spring plowing."

But there was plowing of another sort ahead, too, of plowing under bitter animosities. The seeds of understanding, forgiveness, and forbearance had to be sown and tenderly cultivated. Generals now gave place to politicians.

"WITH MALICE TOWARD NONE"

Lincoln had already realized that the war must soon terminate and had been shaping up plans for a sound and sensible reconstruction. By his thinking, the seceding states were to be treated as though they had never stepped out of the Union. There must be real peace, constructive and mutually profitable. And he was heavily involved in putting such plans into shape five days later, when it was suddenly suggested to him that an excellent play was opening that evening at a Washington theater. It was a broad comedy, filled with laughs, and might help him to relax a bit from the tremendous strain under which he had been for so long. And so it was that he, his wife, and two friends found their place in a box reserved for him on this fatal evening of April 14.

It was a few minutes past ten o'clock when an assassin threw open the door of the box, fired at short range with a derringer, and snuffed out the one man most needed at that critical moment. By early the next morning,

PRESIDENT LINCOLN IS ASSASSINATED

Abraham Lincoln was dead. The fate of the South was at once in less skilful and understanding hands. The life of an American immortal had been torn from the national scene at the very point where his tact, diplomacy, and common touch could not well be spared. His philosophy in the matter now before all America had been summed up in his second inaugural address, given but a little over a month before, "With malice toward *none;* with charity for *all,* let us strive on to finish the work we are in; to bind up the Nation's wounds."

Such a generous approach would be bound to arouse growing opposition from the Republican radicals, the extreme right-wingers in the party. Nonetheless, Andrew Johnson, who now succeeded to the presidency, set himself to carry out Lincoln's enlightened thinking. But he most unfortunately lacked the fortitude and drive to stave off opposition; and the tact and skill needed to win over the people, exhausted by the war, to his support. The South was consequently in for some unnecessarily bitter days, which left an indelible impression.

The powers exercised by the President during the war and still available for use excited the jealousy of Congress. Despite Johnson's best endeavors, his efforts were completely ignored, and the legislative body continued to treat the secession states as rebels. A million lives had been lost, or ruined through disease or crippling wounds. French armies were trampling the Monroe Doctrine in the dust in Mexico, and a united nation was desperately needed to deal with many matters. But politics must run its weary course.

The secession states had been instructed in this same year of 1865 to hold state conventions, adopt new constitutions, elect gover-

255

nors and legislatures, and ratify the Thirteenth Amendment, which abolished slavery. Thus by the end of that year state governments had been reorganized. But many things were still left undone. There were local frictions, which were translated to Washington. Then came the passage in early 1866 of the Civil Rights Bill, giving the freed slaves the same rights as all other citizens. This sudden elevation to the privileges of voting and holding office was to bring untold mischief in southern legislatures for a number of years.

A TRAVESTY ON JUSTICE

Jefferson Davis, together with members of his party, had been captured by Union forces, and he became a convenient scapegoat for the whole Confederate cause. He was clapped into prison and was not brought to trial. Finally, largely because of northern protests, he was released upon bail for six months in 1867, Horace Greeley, the famous editor, being one of his bondsmen. At long last any thought of prosecution was finally dropped in 1869. What a travesty on justice this was; and it was not the sole such instance.

There was a brief period during which there was particular alarm that the hundreds of thousands of men going out of uniform would become lawless and start to plunder. But there were no grounds for such fears. It is not in the American way of life.

By May 29, 1865, there was a proclamation of general amnesty for people in the Confederate states. No less than sixteen classes of persons were set up, however, who were excluded from its benefits. Those who fell within these classes, General Lee included, had to apply for special pardons. The whole flavor of the document was such that many leading southerners refused to take the oath of allegiance, preferring to continue "unreconstructed."

Finally 50,000 seasoned troops had to be massed on the Rio Grande to convince Napoleon III of France that he had better withdraw his armies from Mexico. He was supporting a coup by an Austrian archduke, Maximilian, who sought to make himself emperor in the Mexican republic, which had been torn by internal troubles. This plot was broken up, and Maximilian disposed of by a firing squad.

Irish revolutionists in 1866 attempted to strike at Great Britain through Canada, using this country as a jumping-off spot. Three such efforts were uncovered and stamped out that year. There were thus many available excuses for Congress in letting reconstruction take its time.

IMPEACHMENT PROCEEDINGS

The President lacked control over the heavy Republican majority in both houses of the Congress. In a vain effort to offset the excesses of its radical leaders, he took his case to the people in a series of addresses across the country. But Congress continued to tie his hands, and he became more aggressive. Finally he dismissed his outspoken Secretary of War, Edwin M. Stanton, in August, 1867.

Congress then seized upon this act and attempted to impeach the President. It was March of the following year before the trial was conducted at the bar of the Senate, with the Chief Justice presiding. Hearings lasted through thirty-two days, when a vote was taken. Thirty-five Senators pronounced him guilty, but nineteen were for his acquittal. Since it required two-thirds to convict, the President escaped, but by a single vote.

Someone has said that it is in the market place that man's peaceful ways are best expressed. And so it was that, quite apart from the wrangling politicians, some measure of sound reconstruction was moving forward. Out of dire need, men in the North and South had buried their ill will, and capital began to flow down into southern states, to help to rebuild devastated areas and put men to work again.

THE FOURTEENTH AMENDMENT

It was not until July, 1868, that the Fourteenth Amendment was added to the Constitution, defining citizenship and its privileges and setting up the new apportionment of representatives and dealing with the public debt. On Christmas Day, 1868, the South would receive a very belated Christmas gift, at least three years late in arriving. A wholesale and complete amnesty was then proclaimed. It takes time to make peace, even between brothers, if there is not the will to follow Christian teachings. There seemed to be one further guarantee to be exacted, however. Before it was time to inaugurate a new President the following March, the Fifteenth Amendment was pushed through. This forbade any distinction in regard to the right to vote because of education, creed, property, nativity, color, or race. Its application, though, still lay for the most part in the hands of the states.

The divided house had not fallen, but the task of repairing its divisions was limping along slowly and rather painfully. Slavery had been outlawed, but it left grievous problems for succeeding generations to meet and overcome. Much of the rural South was in financial straits; and while free labor would now, presumably, compete with free labor, there would long be a distinction and a need for payrolls to build purchasing power.

The Congress and the presidency had contested, but still not decisively, over the respective power of the two branches of the federal government. There were still states' rights, but they did not include complete sovereignty, and there would still be contention over just where the limits were. But a lot of people who had never enjoyed the right before could now vote, which right had seemingly been theirs under the Declaration of Independence. Some progress was surely being made, even though it appeared at times somewhat confused.

ACQUISITION OF ALASKA

Still we should not leave this period without commenting upon two happenings which were of importance in the years ahead. One was the purchase from Russia in 1867 of the territory of Alaska. It was our first step beyond the continental limits of the United States; and there would be more and bolder ones to come.

The other was the successful completion the year previous of a transatlantic cable. The telegraph had helped to make this land of ours "one nation." The new cable and other means of rapid communication between nations still to come would tend to make them "one world."

West Virginia had been split off from the Old Dominion in the height of the war and brought in as a state in 1863. Nebraska, scene of the border fighting over now outlawed slavery, was admitted in 1867. The march toward the West was perking up again and would soon become almost a stampede. The cry this time was not so much "gold," as *free land*.

Rebuilding the Nation

A HOMESTEAD ACT had been passed in 1862. By it up to 160 acres of land out of the public domain would be given to the head of a family who would live on it for five years and improve it. This drew swarms of settlers westward, and within ten years some twenty-eight million acres had been homesteaded. Since provisions were liberalized so that anyone over twenty-one years of age who declared he would become a citizen was eligible, this brought great numbers of immigrants from Europe. Fully half of them for a number of years went directly into the West. New territories were blocked out, and some of them were made states with only a minimum number of inhabitants. Nevada was one of these, having been conveniently brought in in 1864 with only 30,000 people to swell the Republican ranks in Congress by three more votes.

This opening up of lands in Nevada, Idaho, Montana, and Utah called for transportation and communication. The stagecoach and pony express played their part. But the need for a railroad was finally met in 1869 when the Central and the Union Pacific tracks were joined at Ogden, Utah. This was indeed a meeting of East and West.

Although not as spectacular, another railroad event this same year still contributes to our comfort and safety. On an April morning in 1869, a train left the Panhandle station in Pittsburgh equipped with a new invention, air brakes, a contribution of a twenty-two-year-old genius, George Westinghouse. For fifty years he would continue to pour out further patents in the railroading and electrical fields. Freedom to employ one's talents, to invent, produce, and market one's goods and services has made this country the great nation it is. May we never lose such freedom, either from without or within.

Ulysses S. Grant, Union commander at the termination of the war, had become President in 1869. It was a difficult period, rife with politics in which he had had little experience. This put him at a disadvantage, for, despite his own integrity, he managed to be imposed upon and even used by some unscrupulous rascals.

Claims against the British government over commerce raiders, built to prey upon the vessels blockading southern ports during the war, were successfully adjusted. The President also did his part in encouraging a sound money policy. But he supported the "carpetbag" legislatures that infested the

BELL DEMONSTRATES THE TELEPHONE AT PHILADELPHIA

southern states, and which politicians in his party insisted were needed to keep the Republicans in full control. This situation stimulated the early undercover activities of such organizations as the Ku Klux Klan, and caused untold bitterness when he sent federal troops into the South to support these offensive carpetbag governments.

Speculators from New York tried to use the President in a scheme to corner "free" gold, by holding the Treasury's supply off the open market. The result was "Black Friday," and one of the most tumultuous days Wall Street ever experienced.

Public dishonesty was rife, involving the Democratic organization in New York City in the sordid "Tweed Ring" scandal. Similar stains appeared upon certain members of Congress in connection with the financing of the transcontinental railways. There was graft in the Post Office Department, in In-

dian affairs, and in tax collections. The latter seemingly involved even the President, although it appears to have been without clear understanding on his part of what was happening. Morality either found hard sledding or could have been taking a long recess in these postwar years.

Despite a serious attempt to replace him, Grant was re-elected in the elections in the fall of 1872. But the people were now aroused and began to demand reforms. The "back salary grab" legislation, which would have upped certain federal salaries, including the President's, and dated these increases from two years before, was violently attacked and soon repealed. The "spoils system," instituted by Jackson, was solidifying the Republican hold on offices, votes, and power. Agitation was begun for a civil service, under which many government employees could find shelter from political winds of fortune and win both positions and advancement by competitive examinations. It would still be a dozen years before such a reform would be politically acceptable.

Carpetbag rule still plagued the South, there being a fair contribution to this vicious situation by some unprincipled southerners, who came to be known as "scalawags." This brought on virtual civil war in Arkansas in 1874, where internal troubles continued into the spring of the following year. South Carolina suffered from a like malady at this same time. Fortunately, such misrule was by then on the way out; and southern intelligence was able again to take over the ordering of its affairs.

100 YEARS OF INDEPENDENCE IS WIDELY CELEBRATED

On the July 4, 1876, the Declaration of Independence would be one hundred years old. Since the perfection of this document had been one of the greatest achievements in the long history of mankind, a fitting celebration was called for. Thirty-three nations had been asked to participate in a great Centennial Exposition to be held in Philadelphia. On 285 acres within its huge Fairmount Park, more than 200 buildings were erected, and President Grant opened the celebration on May 10 in the presence of 100,000 people. During six months just under ten million people visited the exposition, including thousands from other lands. Perhaps no one thing could have given so profound an impression of what America already meant and could mean in the years ahead. In this great fair, the true spirit of the United States was captured, portrayed, and taken home by its visitors. It was to pave the way for the real rebuilding of the nation which now was definitely under way.

Many of the devices on exhibit had fascinated the visitors, but none of them perhaps more than a contraption being demonstrated by a Dr. Bell—Alexander Graham Bell. By means of it you talked over a wire to people at a distance, and their voices came back to you through a cuplike thing held to your ear. It was really exciting to think what it might do in speeding up communication. This was the first demonstration of the telephone. And with the impulse given it by this public showing, it caught on rapidly. By the next year, 1877, the first telephone directories were published in a number of cities. They contained names, but no call numbers, and most subscribers were business firms. A few listings, however, contained the designation "social," meaning they were residence phones.

Hardly was this exposition opened, however, when word was received of Indian trouble in the West. Mention has been made of corruption in Indian affairs in Washington. This "Indian Ring" had swindled the red men out of rights solemnly promised as they were moved from their ancestral lands to reservations. It was but natural that they should resent such broken promises and become restive.

INDIAN RESISTANCE

The five nations moved to the Indian Territory had amply shown what these "savages" were capable of in accepting and adopting civilization. But too often the white men thought of little but trampling upon Indian rights. This phase of the matter was largely overlooked when the too intrepid General Custer allowed himself to be drawn into battle against overwhelming odds, in which he and five companies of cavalry were wiped out to a man. Jackson may have broken the

CATTLE TAKE THE PLACE OF THE BUFFALO ON OUR WESTERN PLAINS

Indian power at Horseshoe Bend sixty-two years before, but there would be scattered actions with certain of the tribes for the remainder of the century. America's handling of Indian matters from the very start is not one of the proudest pages in its accomplishments.

While the exposition was still in progress, Colorado, the "Centennial State," and the thirty-eighth to join, would be admitted to the Union. Also the political conventions had been in session. The fall elections that followed were such as to threaten revolution. Tilden, the Democratic nominee, clearly carried most of the larger northern states, and with expected support in the South was certain of election. But the casting out of votes in many districts in this latter section threw them into Republican columns. His opponent, Hayes, had a majority of one in the electoral college.

The Democrats, positive they had been flagrantly defrauded, swore they would see that Hayes was never inaugurated. So grave and earnest was their threat that the military forces were strengthened about the national capital. Also there were some traces of civil disorder in cities, towns, and villages across the country.

Once again a compromise was struck; an Electoral Commission was set up and reviewed all findings. Hayes's lead of one electoral vote was sustained, and the nineteenth President was placed in office peaceably. Democrats as well as Republicans had sinned politically in this unfortunate matter; but this flare-up marked the end of carpetbag rule in the South.

By the summer of 1877 labor trouble began to develop into widespread strikes. This weapon was not new by any means, but with the development of the country it was becoming more effective. When carpenters, shoemakers, and printers had unionized in 1791 and asserted their right to act in *union*, even to stopping work, they had been hailed

261

into court and charged with "conspiracies to restraint of trade." An eight-year legal battle had then been waged, and such union action was finally judged lawful. However, it had been attacked and tested many times in the interim. Where it had formerly been used against one or a few concerns in one locality, it now could affect many areas across the country.

Such was the railroad strike that soon got under way. There had been a ten per cent reduction in wages, which set off trouble

THE RAILROAD SPELLED "DOOM" TO THE INDIANS

As the railroads came in, the buffalo went out; and this animal was the Indians' *department store*. From it he obtained food, clothing, parts for his tools and weapons, clothing, shelter, and pretty much his whole living. As this once plentiful creature rapidly disappeared, the savages were hard pressed. Naturally they turned upon the white men who had taken away their livelihood.

first in Pittsburgh. There a mob of twenty thousand rioters took command, routed the militia sent to keep order, burned the Union Depot, and destroyed much rolling stock.

Sympathy strikes were soon called in other sections, rail traffic was virtually at a standstill, and other rioting broke out. Regular army troops had to be dispatched to Maryland, West Virginia, and a number of areas in Pennsylvania. In this latter state alone, one hundred people were killed and easily ten million dollars' worth of property destroyed. Why must men always resort to violence where differences of opinion occurred?

Some of the violence in these labor disputes stemmed from the spirit of vengeance brought into this country by certain groups from Europe. Typical instances of this kind

played havoc in the Pennsylvania coal fields for more than twenty years. A secret society had been formed in Ireland in 1843 to intimidate law-enforcement officers, and had taken the name "Molly Maguires." An organization using this same designation appeared in western Pennsylvania in 1854. There it spread terror and death, until a resourceful detective, at the risk of his life during many months, gathered sufficient evidence against ringleaders to break up this nefarious undercover guerrilla band.

However, much unrest was entirely native and was a reaction against a somewhat irresponsible "big business" then definitely in the making. Earliest enterprise in this country had been in the hands of individuals. There had been the "master and servant"

(*Continued on page 270*)

263 ⤷

PERRY CARRYING THE GOSPEL TO THE HEATHEN

James G. Evans

CHICAGO HISTORICAL SOCIETY

Matthew Perry, younger brother of the hero of Lake Erie, was also an able naval officer. He supervised the construction of the first regular steamship for the United States Navy in 1833, and thus won himself the name of "father of the steam navy." In 1852 he was sent to Japan to persuade that country to open its ports to commerce with the West, a treaty to that end being signed two years later.

One feature regarding this enterprise which is little known is the groundwork laid for it beyond government auspices. Ronald MacDonal, the adventurous son of the Hudson Bay Company's factor at Fort Colville, in what later became the State of Washington, planned a shipwreck on the shores of Japan at a time when all intruders were put to death. But he was not executed; and not only remained in that country for seven years, teaching English and explaining the outside world, but endeared himself also to its people. History of his stay there gives evidence that it was in no small measure because of his activities that the Perry Expedition's efforts were crowned with success. We may continually take pride in the fact that our history is studded and buttressed by the exploits of unsung men and women through the years who have made great contributions to our heritage, but lie today in unmarked graves.

THE COUNTRY SCHOOL

Winslow Homer

CITY ART MUSEUM, ST. LOUIS

This great American artist achieved deserved fame through his ability to portray life as it was seen through the eyes of the common man. Perhaps it was his years as a war artist at the front from 1861 to 1865 that gave an especial touch of realism to his work. In this scene he portrays the typical rural schoolhouse of the mid-century. It is perhaps a spring day, for the scholars are all young, and at this time of year their older brothers and sisters would be needed at home to help with the planting. Women by then were becoming the teachers, almost entirely a male occupation in earlier days.

READING THE EMANCIPATION PROCLAMATION

Francis Bicknell Carpenter

UNITED STATES CAPITOL, WASHINGTON

This canvas, painted by one of the leading portrait artists of the middle 1800's, was exhibited extensively in the cities of the North and East during 1864–65. Immediately following the battle of Antietam, Lincoln had proclaimed that he would declare freedom for the slaves in the seceding States unless the latter returned to the Union by the first day of 1863. This pronouncement met only with ridicule. A formal Proclamation was then prepared to be issued as of January 1st. Here we see it being read to the cabinet for their suggestions and sanction previous to its being made public.

ABOVE, **PERRY HEADING FOR JAPAN**   BELOW, **THE COUNTRY SCHOOL**

ABOVE

READING THE EMANCIPATION PROCLAMATION

F. B. Carpenter, U.S. Capitol, Washington

FOLLOWING PAGE, TOP

MONITOR AND THE MERRIMAC

Wm. Jorgerson, Chicago Hist. Soc.

FOLLOWING PAGE, BELOW

SPLICING THE ATLANTIC CABLE

Robert Dudley, Smithsonian Institute

BATTLE OF THE *MONITOR* AND *MERRIMAC*

William Jorgerson

CHICAGO HISTORICAL SOCIETY

Although little is known about this artist, he did leave at least five paintings of Civil War incidents, all of them in the possession of the Chicago Historical Society. One of the others is a scene within the turret of the *Monitor,* one of the contenders in our picture. The action took place in Hampton Roads but a mile or two offshore, and was the first contest between ironclad vessels. The *Merrimac* had actually become rechristened the *Virginia;* and the previous day had destroyed the *Congress* and the *Cumberland,* two wooden ships of the Union navy.

Like them, the *Virginia* had originally been a wooden frigate; but its sides had been covered with a metal plating, and a heavy iron prow had been added for ramming other ships. So equipped, it was hoped she might soon break up the blockade of Southern ports.

The *Monitor,* by contrast, was an entirely new conception in fighting ships. As its deck was nearly awash, it offered little freeboard as a target, for all that rose above the plated deck was a small smokestack, and a twenty-foot revolving turret, from which a heavy eleven-inch shell could be fired.

Since there was nothing for the *Virginia* to hit or ram, she was soon bested, and the *Monitor* had proved the decided advantages of ironclads even before it had been officially accepted by the government.

SPLICING THE ATLANTIC CABLE OFF IRELAND

Robert Dudley

SMITHSONIAN INSTITUTE, WASHINGTON

One of the truly great enterprises of the 19th century was the providing for rapid communication between distant lands by means of undersea cables. First experiments across short stretches of water in Europe encouraged a transatlantic cable in 1858. This first attempt ceased to give satisfactory service after the first few weeks of operation, a stunning disappointment, entailing a huge loss. It later developed the cable had snapped in two.

Although the group in New York that had backed the ambitious project was naturally discouraged, Cyrus W. Field, leading spirit among them, persisted, and in 1866, some eight years after the first failure, a permanent cable went into operation. Its western ocean terminus was Heart's Content, on Newfoundland, while its eastern end was Valencia, Ireland. It was off the latter that the scene in our picture is laid. These two places were chosen not only because the least number of water miles lay between them, but also because soundings had determined that the bottom across the ocean at this point was soft and reasonably level. So great was the interest in this scheme at the time work on it was under way, that thousands of six-inch sections of the cable being laid were eagerly bought up as souvenirs, and still turn up today long tucked away and forgotten.

situation, but it had been an intimate relation, and usually subject to adjustment by fully peaceful means. Then expansion came as two or more formed partnerships. There were still fairly close relations between employers and employed.

But there had been the pattern of still larger enterprise in the king's chartered companies in Colonial times. Out of it a corporate form of organization, first for towns and cities, and later for private endeavors, developed. Before 1860 such corporations usually took a special act of a legislature. Later enabling acts were passed to encourage their easier formation. Since many could invest money in them without the same liabilities as in a partnership, they came into ever-wider use.

This type of organization had many advantages. But it was also subject to certain abuses. By 1860 fully one-sixth of the population was dependent on manufacturing, most of them as wage earners, and another one-sixth was in mechanical trades and other industrial pursuits. The corporations seemed to have inside tracks to legislative halls, and it was even said that at one time the railroad interests had virtual control of lawmaking bodies in the states in which they operated. Such power, concentrated in relatively few hands, made the growing number of laborers uneasy, then restless.

There had been craft unions, similar to the ancient guilds, since Colonial times. Carpenters' Hall in Philadelphia, where the Continental Congress had first met, was the headquarters of the master carpenters. Then in 1834, after the first flush of industrial development, there had been an attempt to bring local unions together on a national basis. But it was more than thirty years before increased activities during the war made such endeavors fruitful. By its end

several craft unions on a nationwide basis were functioning.

In 1866 the National Labor Union was organized for political action. It leaned toward socialistic experiment, however, and was terminated at the end of six years. About 1869 another labor group started as a secret order, ultimately hoping to weld all labor together in a single organization. This was the Knights of Labor. Within twenty years it had grown to 700,000 members. Reliance was placed upon education and political action, rather than upon collective bargaining. But internal strife and confusion over its true purpose finally drove it on the rocks.

Labor, however, was in a position throughout this time to make its demands known, and was progressing toward the point, too, where it would one day make them heard.

FILLING IN RAPIDLY, THE WEST IS NO LONGER "WILD"

The "West," which had long meant the great unfilled reaches beyond which the advancing white men had not yet settled, was by now rapidly disappearing. There were still long stretches of "wide-open spaces," but even the section lying beyond the Mississippi was moving rapidly from a frontier area to real productiveness. The place of the fur trapper was being taken by the miner, the lumberman, the rancher, the orchardist, and the businessman.

Cattlemen began to find their cattle were in better condition and brought a better price at the slaughtering centers when shipped in by rail than when driven over the older trails. The cowboy may have lost something in colorfulness in these changes, but better pasturing, better breeding, and better handling were needed to keep up with expanding markets. Barbed wire for fencing became big business indeed.

All agriculture was feeling a change. Where it had once revolved about a single household, and its self-sufficient needs, it began to specialize more and more. The greater share of the people still lived close to the land, but life on the farm or ranch was much changed.

Railroads were still growing, and some 40,000 miles would be built between 1870 and 1880, almost as much as had been in operation up to that time. It cost a kingdom in land, granted free in many instances, to open up these transportation facilities in new areas. But we must recall that in those ten years two and three-quarter million people immigrated into this country from abroad; and that our total increase in population was eleven and a half million. The people living here had increased more than twelve times during the ninety years since the first census in 1790.

As this decade drew to a close, conditions in Washington deserve a little of our attention. Rutherford B. Hayes, President by the narrow margin of one electoral vote, had taken office, as you will recall, under trying circumstances. He was sensible, hard-working, and extremely conscientious. And he was far, far above the rank and file of his party in the Congress as respects integrity. Bent upon improving government service, he was for civil-service reform and the clearing out of incompetence. But Congress, with patronage foremost in its mind, called him "Granny" Hayes, and said all he was doing was trying to feather his own nest. The crowning insult came possibly when he issued an order that funds were not to be collected from government employees for party use. Despite his orders, such collections were continued, and Congress then set out to defeat his every move for betterment. But his efforts registered with the people, and one day soon his reforms would be carried through by others by popular demand. The party "stalwarts," however, made certain he was not their choice for re-election in the fall of 1880.

He had done very well, though, despite an obstinate Congress. The last of the federal troops had been withdrawn from the South; and the Reconstruction Period, begun by Lincoln even before peace had been made, may now be said to have ended.

The Age of Great Wealth

HE spoils system was very much in vogue as James A. Garfield took office in 1881. At once there was a contest between the President and Congress. The latter body was even demanding the right to select appointees to the highest posts, and Washington swarmed with office-seekers. Two New York Senators were so provoked over one appointment in their state which the President made independently of them that they resigned just previous to adjournment in June.

The President, intending to enjoy a few days of the coming holiday with his invalid wife, spending the summer on the Jersey seacoast, went to the Baltimore and Ohio station in the capital on July 2 to take the train. As he stood in the waiting room with friends, a disappointed office-seeker, named Guiteau, stole up behind him and shot him in the back with a pistol. The mortally wounded man lingered for some seven weeks, but finally died on September 21, a victim of what had become a fully vicious political system.

The Vice-President, Chester A. Arthur, was immediately sworn in. He had been dismissed from a post in New York City by President Hayes because he could not seem to stamp out the malpractices of his subordinates. Now he was to come face to face with very similar situations for which he would have to answer. One of the most flagrant was the "Star Routes" operated by the Post Office Department, from which some were becoming wealthy in a matter of months. This scandal was dragged into the open, and, while finally cleared away, it left the unsettling question of how much real rectitude there was anywhere in high places.

But the whole atmosphere of the time was strongly materialistic. Reliable statistics indicate that church membership was then proportionately less than one-half what it is today. Money was the measure of success, and its possession often led to excesses. Washington Irving had coined the phrase the *Almighty Dollar* in one of his books as early as 1837. Now it began to be a watchword in earnest, particularly in the North and West.

While the planters in the South had represented great, if sometimes fleeting and uncertain, wealth before the war, they had been pretty much wiped out by that conflict. Most of the old plantations had been broken up and were now worked as small farms; or, if the land was still held together, they were cultivated by share croppers. But what had been largely an agricultural economy slowly began to change. There was less emphasis upon cotton, although it was still the principal crop; but the real relief came when industry began to move in.

INDUSTRY MOVES SOUTH

There was abundant water power along the edge of the eastern highlands, and coal and some iron were scattered through this area 'way down into Alabama. Cotton manufacture began to move first into Virginia, and then the Carolinas. One day there would be more spindles operating in Gaston County, North Carolina, than in any other similar area in the world.

Birmingham, Alabama, would become a thriving coal and iron center, and other minerals, such as copper and phosphate, would aid in Georgia and Tennessee. Pine forests would yield valuable lumber, and industry would slowly become the foundation for a new prosperity in place of cotton. Fortunes would be made there, but perhaps not so rapidly and spectacularly as elsewhere.

Asked a naïve young lady of an American aviator sent to Italy for training in the first World War, "What is your father *king* of?" By then Europe believed all Americans were rich and controlled some segment of business. Thirty-five years before big business leaders were being spoken of as at least *barons.* There were oil barons, copper barons, iron barons, and cattle *kings.* In the growing, bustling economy these prize positions went to the shrewd and audacious, to those who "looked out for themselves," and who had little or no thought of giving quarter to others. Newport, Saratoga Springs, and other resorts were *the* places

at which to be seen, or to have a home, or in which to parade one's riches.

Display of this new-found wealth ran to huge excesses. There had been a reasonable amount of wealth in some cases in Colonial times, which had expressed itself in such restrained but handsome mansions as Mount Vernon. But this newer crop of rich folk were flamboyant, gaudy, and overstuffed. Houses and buildings were loaded down with gingerbread ornamentation and useless geegaws. Life suddenly became bloated with *things,* with anything which helped to make a show and dazzle one's neighbors.

HOW WEALTH WAS EMPLOYED

To some of them, America became too primitive, too gross, too common. Decadent Europe was explored for everything from art works to penniless titled sons for marriageable daughters. Coats of arms and a family tree, even with some decayed branches and manufactured leaves, were much in demand. Suddenly great numbers found it necessary to be descendants of those who came over on the *Mayflower* or other early settlers. Where there were perhaps three or four whose wealth was as much as a million dollars at the outbreak of the War between the States, there were by the mid-1880's no less than fifteen hundred who claimed to have reached the coveted goal of being rated a *millionaire.* And some of them were on their way to being in the hundred-million class. This was the "Horatio Alger" age.

Not all of the wealthy were committed to show an inordinate display. While some lavished money openly upon charities, other conservative families did much good in a quiet, effective way, feeling some responsibility for the fortunes intrusted to them. Those who preferred to advertise their riches

273

gave the impression that America was a land of unbounded opportunity for all. This notion began to take firm hold of the masses in Europe.

INCREASED IMMIGRATION

Where immigration in the first half of the nineteenth century had been principally from Great Britain and northern Europe, it began to taper off for a time beginning about 1874. Then, as the eighties rolled around, the tide again mounted, this time principally from southern and eastern Europe. To keep wages low, an ever-greater number of laborers were needed. So employers searched them out and induced them to come here by every means they could devise. Come they did, nearly half a million in the year 1880 alone, and more than five million between then and 1890. Someone had termed this country the "Great Melting Pot," and so it was, in a rugged sort of way.

While the tide was definitely rolling in, it would not reach its crest until the early years of the present century. Not only was it much greater in volume, but it was different in kind than it had been before the War between the States. Free land was no longer so plentiful, and many of these immigrants had no more than enough to take them to some eastern port. Some had relatives to help them get started in a new land. Others were easy prey for sharpers of many kinds.

It was an unforgettable experience to stand by the ferry stage at Castle Garden at the south end of Manhattan Island near the turn of the century, and see the ferries from Ellis Island, where immigrants first had to land, disgorge their human cargoes. It was an even more enlightening experience to follow many of them into the teeming slum section that stretched up along the Bowery and the East River in those days, into which new thousands were being continually absorbed.

A further experience might have been a visit to the "sweatshops," where many of them had their first taste of American industry and American life. This was a harsh introduction to the "land of the free," and many social problems would be created that would take two or three generations to adjust and iron out.

UNRESTRICTED IMMIGRATION BRINGS SOCIAL PROBLEMS

There were opportunities here, no doubt of that, and many business leaders, many top names in the entertainment and other fields today, rather proudly trace their beginnings to the slum areas of New York and other cities. But for millions of immigrants it was a disillusioning experience. Language barriers tended to build "Little Italys," "Little Polands," "Little Slovakias," with tensions between groups. The next generation, now that public schools could accept them and give them a common tongue, and a better approach to American ways, began to break down such differences as at first were emphasized.

It is true that many came here out of deep misery and even starvation in their former homes. But, too, many of the first generation to arrive were condemned to poverty and many restrictions during their lives here. This mass immigration gave America needed man power, but it also posed problems sufficient one day to cause it to be shut down to a bare trickle.

Even in the late eighties, labor was coming in more rapidly than it could be absorbed. Thus it was in oversupply, and, while an ideal condition apparently for employers, it was one of the causes of the extensive labor unrest.

All immigration, however, was not into the East Coast. Chinese laborers had been brought in in great numbers for railroad construction in the West. It, too, was now in oversupply. Trouble arose in California, severe enough finally so that immigration from China was closed off in 1885.

Labor unions sought to stem the influx from Europe; but about all they could achieve was some screening of those who entered. Laws were drawn to stop the entry of convicts, paupers, the mentally deranged, and bearers of contagious disease.

This is not to say that immigration did not add to the nation's wealth, as it had to its man power. Quite the contrary, it did. Many of these people, or their sons and daughters, would rise to fame and fortune, as has been pointed out above. They would, in time, become the backbone of our industry; and their sons would one day shed their blood in the nation's defense as willingly as any in two World Wars that lay ahead. The sad commentary is the callousness of their coming and the fact that better facilities were not provided for their absorption into the stream of American life.

UTAH AND THE MORMONS

Early in President Arthur's administration, attention began to focus on Utah. It had been settled by the Mormons, driven in an excess of religious intolerance from settlements they had made in Illinois in 1847. Under an excellent organizer and leader, Brigham Young, they made the long trek to and opened up land near the Great Salt Lake. There they built a solid, substantial colony. Their numbers had multiplied, but their belief in and practice of polygamy, or

plural wives, had subjected them to being virtually outlawed by other groups. There had been much strife over this situation from time to time. In 1882 a federal act directed principally at this situation was passed, and in 1890 the Mormon church agreed to abandon polygamy as a belief. This paved the way for statehood.

THE BROOKLYN BRIDGE

Back in the East, much attention centered on the construction of the Brooklyn Bridge. This was a considerable engineering feat in its day and became a popular symbol of the greatness that was America. It showed how American enterprise could conquer Nature's handicaps by inventiveness and industry. But an even finer symbol of what America really stood for would soon be erected, and but a few miles away.

Alaska was explored by private rather than public auspices in 1883, in the hope of stimulating the growth of that territory. Centennial celebrations of two Revolutionary incidents, the evacuation of New York, and the surrender of Yorktown, were held to focus attention on the nation's earlier history. Then another expedition, this under the direction of the Army, was started in the far North, to check weather data and magnetic conditions. At long last the sage observation of Columbus, as he sailed west nearly three hundred years before and saw the compass needle sway from due north, was to be proven true. There was a North Pole and also a north magnetic pole.

The Republicans had now controlled the presidency and the Congress for some twenty-five years. There had been much political scandal during this period, and growing dissatisfaction among much the same groups as those that had placed Jackson in office more than fifty years before. While the dominant party made the tariff its main issue, the Democrats chose one with much wider appeal, civil-service reform. The time for a change had come, and the Democratic choice, Grover Cleveland, was elected in 1884.

BITTER POLITICAL STRUGGLES

However, the contest was close and managed to be a particularly bitter one. This condition was brought about largely by a chance slogan voiced in a political speech. It referred to the Democrats as the party of "Rum, Romanism, and Rebellion." This inept comment was energetically put to use, but it boomeranged badly; and the offense to the growing number of Roman Catholic voters did much to assure Cleveland's success.

A new broom is supposed to sweep clean, and Democratic politicians, long out of the victor's seat, had many favors to be paid off with choice jobs. They were somewhat stunned when the President chose to abide by the chief plank in the platform on which he had been elected. Civil service was about to be placed above political tinkering.

Such reform had long been advocated and paid lip service. During these years an office-seeking class of considerable size had developed. Its chief contention was that the opportunity for change at the discretion of the leaders of the party in power prevented an intrenched, overbearing *bureaucracy*. That argument, however, was offset by the fact that this same scheming group did its level best to control state and national politics, and perpetuate itself and its hangers-on in office. The evils of the system had been pointed up in the wanton assassination of President Garfield.

In 1883 the Federal Civil Service Act was passed. This brought some measure of order out of what had been chaos, and took a portion of government employment out of the realm of political advantage. The great rank and file of those so employed were to win their places by competitive examination and not be mere party workers. They were eligible on merit to promotion to better position, rather than by political pull. No employees were under obligation to assessment or contribution to party funds. But they had this obligation, nonetheless. They held their jobs only as long as they showed competence and during good behavior. As long as they lived up to these requirements, they could not be removed, no matter how urgent the political need to replace them.

BEGINNINGS OF CIVIL SERVICE

While this first law covered but a part of all federal offices at that time, it was a sound beginning, to be added to in later years. But politics gives up its advantages slowly, and seventy years later such reform was still not yet universal at the national level, and far from it at state, county, and city levels. The cry of *bureaucracy* is still much in use. But its dangers are more often from uses made of civil employees by elected officials who are actually directly responsible to the voters.

The ideal of civil service had been elevated sharply, however, and the quality of that service began to improve markedly where it was put under sound legal control. Once again the rule of *law* over that of *men* proved superior.

In 1874 France was for the third time about to become a republic. Interest in the United States was thus keen, and a subscription was started there to prepare a token of the regard of the French people for presen-

UNCLE DICK WOOTAN, COLORADO SCOUT, ACTS AS
INTERPRETER AT AN INDIAN PARLEY

tation to the people of America. It was to be a huge symbolic statue of *Liberty,* to commemorate the 100th anniversary of Independence. It was not until 1877, however, that Congress voted to accept the gift and set apart Bedloe's Island in New York harbor as its site.

Made of huge copper segments, it was set up first in Paris, where it was received for the people of the United States by our minister there, on July 4, 1884. A popular subscription here provided funds for the masonry pedestal and it was unveiled in October, 1886. Probably no other one object represents in so many minds the true spirit of our country, both at home and throughout all the world. May the Light of Liberty, represented in the torch borne by this heroic figure, never be dimmed.

There were certain of the Indian tribes on the western plains, though, that did not feel that the rays of Liberty's torch reached to them. Many, and their forefathers before them, had suffered the grossest of injustices at the hands of land-hungry people forcing them on and on, and finally into almost unlivable areas. In some cases they had been reasonably provided for. The wholesale slaughter of the buffalo had raised havoc with thousands and taken away their principal livelihood. Many were in desperate straits in the latter quarter of the century.

A board of commissioners had been set up to handle their affairs as early as 1869, and two years later most of the tribes still roaming the West were pressed onto reservations. But the commission had been a political enterprise, often swayed by greed and

277

subject to double-dealing. Certain of these reservations had been poorly selected, and the soil was either worthless, the water unusable, or the climate so cold and forbidding as to make them almost uninhabitable.

An attempt had been made to settle some individuals as farmers, but by the time this policy was in operation the troubles had blazed up and spread from Canada down to the Mexican border. There were no more Custer Massacres, but the Army was to have its hands full for several years subduing these unwilling wards of the government.

The earth along the Atlantic seaboard and far inland had been orderly and well disposed. This was in contrast to the restlessness along the Pacific coast, which had brought occasional tremors since the first white men had appeared there. Wild excitement thus seized much of the East on the evening of August 31, 1886, when a severe earthquake shook the area from Wilmington, Delaware, deep into the South. Felt as far away as St. Louis, Chicago, Memphis, and Albany, it did its greatest damage in Charleston, South Carolina. Thus it became known as the *Charleston Earthquake*. The earth trembled on occasions during the three following months. Then, relieved of tension, it became quiet again.

Somewhat earlier another type of violent disturbance had shaken Chicago. Labor agitation there had come under the sway of a group of anarchists, who believed that all forms of government were harmful. Playing upon labor unrest, fiery preaching set off a series of violent riots, ending in a dynamite bombing in which thirty police were either killed or badly maimed.

The next year attention was focused some five thousand miles farther west. Trouble was fermenting in Hawaii. In the blaze of missionary zeal many years before, the islands had been introduced to Christianity. The sons of these missionaries stayed on and slowly took over the islands, setting up huge plantations and gathering the business interests into their hands. In 1849 a treaty of commerce was made with the United States, which was extended to reciprocity, or mutual assistance, in 1875. This boomed the sugar interests, virtually all in the hands of foreigners. The native king began to resent the hold these "off-islanders" were obtaining. Trouble which ensued finally relieved him of power, and in connection with the disturbance the United States was ceded rights to the finest naval station in the Pacific at Pearl Harbor. In 1898 the islands would be annexed to this country.

CLEVELAND IS DEFEATED

The year 1888 would be an election year. And as evidence of the restless mood of the country there would be no less than eight political parties supporting candidates. In addition to the Republicans and Democrats, there would be a Prohibition ticket, three separate ones from the ranks of Labor, one favoring industrial reform, and another fighting for equal rights.

There was but insignificant support of the latter six. But the surprising news was that Benjamin Harrison, riding Republican strength in some of the larger states, displaced Cleveland. Although the latter won on the popular vote, Harrison had sufficient electoral votes to place him in office. Once again, what now began to seem like an outmoded device had deprived the voters of direct expression of their choice.

He had not been in the White House two months, when one of the worst disasters the country has ever experienced struck. Johnstown, a manufacturing city seventy-eight

THE LAND-HUNGRY STREAM INTO OKLAHOMA

miles east of Pittsburgh, lived uneasily in a deep valley and below a lake owned by a hunting and fishing club. The dam which restrained this huge reservoir was of somewhat dubious construction, and there had been many near panics during several years by reports that it was about to go out.

There had been abundant rains during May, and danger began to mount. Suddenly, in the early morning of May 31, 1889, the lake level rose sharply, the dam burst, Johnstown was largely destroyed, and some two thousand lost their lives. This disaster had a nationwide impact. American generosity rose to the occasion, relief flowed in from across the country, and the Red Cross Society, founded eight years before, was among the first on the scene with aid.

In April there had been something of another flood, but of a quite different sort again. The old Indian Territory had been opened up to white settlement. The demand for new land to settle was rather insistent, so the government had bought out the Indians' rights and were to throw open huge tracts as of noon on the 22d. Troops guarded the border to keep out the "come earlies," but in the days and hours just before the deadline, thousands, on horseback, in carriages, on bicycles, and afoot, lined up for the dash into this El Dorado. When the bugle blew at high noon, this horde flooded in. Homesteads were staked out, towns began to spring up; and Oklahoma, meaning "beautiful land," began to fill up rapidly.

By the end of this same year, 1889, four territories would be added to the Union as states, the greatest number in any one year. They included North and South Dakota, Montana, and Washington. And in 1890 they would be followed by two more, Idaho and Wyoming.

279

There had been a strike of the New York City horsecar drivers and conductors in January, 1889, followed by another of the feather-workers there in March. Local conditions, plus Old World enmities, were causing much foment. These latter struck sparks which set off an international incident in New Orleans. The *Maffia,* a ruthless Italian secret society, which carried out its purposes by murder if need be, appeared in that city, and in October, 1890, disposed of the chief of police. Nineteen were taken into custody, and nine of them placed on trial. When they were either acquitted or released, the public became highly incensed.

Foolishly, they took the law into their own hands. Breaking into the jail, they lynched several of the suspects still there. At once the Italian government became interested. Although the affair was finally adjusted satisfactorily, there was much embarrassment in the need to explain away the corruption which had caused a mistrial, and thereby brought on this tragedy and also the employment of *lynch law*.

The next year there would be another international complication. This time it would involve Chile, and for a few tense weeks threaten war. Insurgents during an uprising there had threatened our ambassador, who had permitted political refugees to take shelter in the American legation. One naval vessel was in Chilean waters, and a second was sent to join it. Members of the crew of this second ship on shore leave in Valparaiso were attacked, two were killed, and several others badly hurt.

When asked to explain the affair, the Chilean government took a most indifferent attitude. When it became evident that it was merely bent upon evading the issue entirely, a pointed ultimatum was drawn and delivered to its representatives. Facing possible war, an apology was forthcoming; and the United States Supreme Court was allowed to set the amounts of indemnity to be paid the families of the dead and those who had been wounded.

There would be many, many other South and Central American incidents in the years ahead, not all of which would be so peaceably adjusted. But this Chilean matter did point up one situation. The Spanish ambassador, writing to his king from the Peace Conference at Versailles in 1783, had anticipated it. He had said, "A day will come when [these United States] will be a giant; even a colossus formidable to these countries." Indeed we were on our way to respect in international affairs. Even the kings of Spain would realize it in a few short years.

But the fact was beginning to be realized, and relished a little, at home. We had great markets within our own land; but at that time it seemed that they could only be expanded to take care of the increasing productiveness by new markets beyond our own shores. England and the European countries had long been extending their trading areas by colonial possessions. That seemed like a practicable step for us to take. It was contrary to American policy, but perhaps the idea could be sold to the American people. In the White House, and in the State Department, *imperialism,* or the rule over colonies or other countries, was being considered. The shadows were beginning to lengthen in that direction; and there might be some experimenting with such a policy one of these days.

The Gay Nineties

HE Indians were very much on the warpath in the winter of 1890–91. An Indian Bureau, which seemed to be dishonest to the core, was stimulating violence which could readily have been avoided. The savages were not above turning the white man's offerings against him. There had been much missionary effort expended, aiming to Christianize the red men. Now some of the teachings were to be twisted about and handed back.

To whip up frenzy, the Indians resorted to the "Messiah Craze," which whirled across the country. By it a chosen warrior claimed he had had a revelation from the Messiah. He had once come to save the whites, but had been rejected and killed. Now, in the spring, He would come to save His red children. All who believed this prophecy were to wear certain distinguishing clothing and practice the stupefying Ghost Dance. It was an ingenious device for spreading rebellion.

This scheme was indeed potent warpaint; and trouble broke out in the powerful Sioux tribe. It took the life of Sitting Bull, its chief, and those of many other Indians and soldiers, before this flare-up was quelled.

Back in Washington, too, all was not harmonious. President Harrison had pleased neither the party stalwarts nor yet the reform element in the party. Although renominated, he was again a private citizen in March of 1893. And another private citizen, after a peaceable absence of four years, took up residence in the White House again. Grover Cleveland had been re-elected.

PANIC OF 1893

The immediate reaction was a business panic. Whether it was due to uncontrollable causes, or stimulated, is still subject to argument. This was a violent cyclone, however, wiping out business concerns both large and small, and causing tremendous unrest throughout the country. Unemployment was widespread, and one concern, the great Pullman Company, tried to make work to hold its employees together. But to do so it cut wages in half, and there was soon a bad strike, with much violence.

This spread rapidly to the railways throughout the central part of the country, and, of course, tied up the United States mail. Determined that it would be handled, an executive order was issued, sending federal troops into Chicago, where the trouble seemed to be centered. Eugene V. Debs, then head of the railway union that had precipitated the train of strikes, was clapped into jail.

RADICAL REMEDIES CALLED FOR

Men who had been on the sidelines, but were either unemployed or had lost businesses, dropped their conservatism and joined a *Populist* group now arising. Labor and the lower middle classes, feeling themselves in the clutch of something which was strangling them, began to call for rather radical remedies. The dissatisfaction raised by this business recession would start a trend away from unrestrained freedom, what economists called a policy of *laissez faire* [lay zay fair], or the absence of regulation and interference by government. That trend is still very much in evidence today.

A typical conservative reaction to much that was being voiced rather shrilly in those days came from the Supreme Court itself. In the midst of turmoil, the Congress passed an Income Tax Law, to pad out its depleted revenues, which had fallen off markedly. While it was declared unconstitutional the following year, it brought terror to the conservative moneyed class. As the act was being argued before the high court, one of the Associate Justices made this observation: "The present assault upon capital is but the beginning. It will be but the stepping-stone to others larger and more sweeping, till our political conditions will become a war of the poor against the rich."

But again, it was merely an opinion. And while the unrestrained power of wealth would be pared down, there would be no *war*. Out of latent liberties, and the ingenuity which such liberties set in motion, America would move into new eras in which more and more men would enjoy the good things of life, and the nation's over-all wealth would become the wonder of the rest of the world.

Among other demands out of Populist and similar groups was that heard long before at the end of the Revolution, *cheap* money. The debtors were many; they had huge debts to pay off, and preferred, if possible, to do it as easily as could be. However, the President sided with the advocates of *sound* money, and thus lost the support of the free-silver section of his party. By advocating a lower tariff, he lost the aid of the protectionists.

Congress, still jealous of its powers, sought to control the presidency as far as possible. While this continuing contest seems at times to obstruct progress, it is, over the longer period, no doubt one of the great safeguards in our form of government. Since both the Congress and the President are in office through the vote of the people, any prolonged attempts to go against the will of the people, by either branch, can be corrected at the polls.

THE PANIC PERSISTS

The business recession was still clouding the country in 1896. The nineties to this point had not seemed too gay, despite the rollicking Columbian Exposition in Chicago in 1893, followed by a lesser one in San Francisco the following year. Then in 1895 the Cotton States Exposition opened in Atlanta. But still business seemed to hesitate. Once again the feeling began to prevail that recovery was being held back by money and political interests.

Cleveland had served the allotted two terms, which tradition had held to be enough for any man. So when the 1896 conventions rolled around, the progressive element of the Democratic party pressed to the fore a silver-tongued orator, by whose persuasive words

DESPITE A DEPRESSION AND THEN A WAR
THERE WAS GAIETY IN THE 1890'S

victory seemed secure. He was introduced as the "great commoner," and William Jennings Bryan started to throw fear into huge audiences, warning them against being crucified on a "cross of gold."

But the Republicans managed to elect William McKinley, who was prepared to put the country on a *gold standard*. It had taken considerable money and some of the most astute political connivance; but troubles began to evaporate, confidence came back, and there would be ten years of real prosperity ahead.

Utah had been brought in as a state early in 1896. Power generated from the falling waters of mighty Niagara would begin to flow that same year, the first of many huge hydroelectric developments now to come. England would be arbitrating a boundary question with Venezuela, with the United States as umpire. But the proposed *arbitration* treaty, by which England and the United States would always pursue this peaceful means of settlement of differences, and presented to Congress as one of Cleveland's last official acts, had failed of passage.

Thus the business panic had not stopped all activity at home and abroad. And as our part in international affairs multiplied, the nation began to give attention to building up the Navy.

By mid-1897 business conditions were in fair state again, payrolls were being spent, and a new note of confidence began to ring. Peary was having a try at reaching the North Pole; and Henry Ford, the ex-power station attendant, was tinkering with his horseless carriage. Edison, who had developed the electric-light bulb in 1879, had now been busy for more than ten years turning out further wonders from his Orange, New Jersey, laboratory. And the Dingley Tariff was bringing in revenue and tending to cut down competition from abroad. Gold had been found in the Klondike, and gaiety was greater on all sides, when a new concern arose.

Covetous glances had already been cast at the island of Cuba, only about 160 miles south of Key West across the Florida Strait. It had seemed like logical slave territory. Grant had once been ready to seize it, but changed his mind. It now began to look like a possible ward, particularly with the stronger imperial flavor on the palate of those now coming into high places.

What is more, there was a lively revolt in progress down there as early as 1895. The Cubans had decided to cut loose from decadent Spain. To this, the ancient nation which had sent Columbus here four hundred-odd years before, did not take at all kindly. Neither did she appreciate the money, arms, and other aid flowing to the insurgents, and none too secretly, from groups in this country.

When she sent forces in strength to restore order, American businessmen became alarmed. They had at least fifty million invested in Cuba, and a hundred million a year in trade would probably be shut off. There was a demand that something be done. This much had happened before the change in administration.

But when President Cleveland had tried to intercede, the Spanish government had promptly told him to mind his own affairs. As he doffed his hat to his successor, just inaugurated, he is reported to have said, "Mr. President, I bequeath you a war with Spain."

Conditions on the island were hideous. Spain's hand upon it had been an iron one,

and very bloody. Such suffering found ready response in this country and a willingness to help. Then a letter written by the Spanish ambassador, roundly insulting, to President McKinley, came into the hands of the American press and was published. Feelings surged to fever pitch, as the Spanish minister hurriedly left the country. Then came a happening that blew the lid sky-high.

SINKING OF THE MAINE HASTENS WAR WITH SPAIN

Only six days after this situation had been aired, the battleship *Maine,* lying in Havana harbor, exploded, with a loss of 266 officers and men. Although it was never later proved that this was a wilful enemy act, the first reaction was, of course, that it had been treachery. The evening after this news broke bonfires blazed in towns and hamlets across this land, and the cry went up and became a common form of greeting, "Remember the *Maine!*"

There was an immediate popular demand for war; but the President held it in check until an inquiry could be made. Then, illy prepared as this peaceable country always is for conflict, war was declared April 19. Spain took up the challenge two days later. England, to keep the record straight, immediately announced its complete neutrality.

Shore batteries then being installed along our coast were still incomplete, and there were probably two rounds each on hand for guns already in position. The Spaniards had their fleet in three squadrons, one of which could have played havoc along our eastern seaboard. Our own ships were scattered from here to Hong Kong.

In fact, when the news broke, Commodore George Dewey had a squadron of four

"THE MESSAGE TO GARCIA" IS DELIVERED

cruisers and two gunboats lying in this treaty port on the China coast. English authorities had to ask him to stand out to sea to preserve that country's neutrality. So he weighed anchor and headed for the Philippines, then Spanish territory. There, at daybreak on Sunday, May 1, he rode in past Cavite and found Spain's Far Eastern navy grouped like a flock of sitting ducks. Turning to the captain of his flagship, the *Olympia,* the future admiral calmly remarked, "You may fire when ready, Gridley."

About midmorning he swung his ships off to the western edge of the bay to give the crews a spot of breakfast and to take on coal and ammunition from the three tenders that had sailed with him. Then, swinging back, and by skilful maneuvering to keep his opponent's gunners off their targets, he went back to work at his grim business. Before

sundown he had disposed of one complete Spanish fleet of eleven vessels.

Then came two grave concerns growing out of this action in the Pacific. Full control of the Hawaiian Islands was needed to give a basing point and supply center in time of hostilities. Also there was need of a short cut between the two oceans. Something could be done rather promptly about the first. The other might have to wait, even though at that very moment it was giving the Navy Department some trying days.

As the clouds of war were closing down, the battleship *Oregon,* then pride of the Navy, lay in San Francisco. She was frantically needed around on the Atlantic coast, particularly in the West Indies. Orders were telegraphed, and on March 19 she stood out through the Golden Gate, swung south, coaled in Peru, rounded Cape Horn, and touched at Rio on April 30 for supplies. It was May 24 when she hove into Jupiter Inlet, just north of Palm Beach in Florida.

She had made the run of 14,133 nautical miles in 68 days, large parts of that distance at the then very high speed of 13 knots. It was a prodigious performance for the time, and the whole country, along with the Department of the Navy, heaved a sigh of relief when she was safe again in United States waters. Children would hear the mighty deed read about and discussed in school. And twenty years later many servicemen crossing on the Coronado Ferry used to "man the rail," and salute the doughty old lady as they passed her anchored in San Diego Bay during World War I. But what a blessing it would have been to have had a canal through Nicaragua, or where the French had tried and abandoned the project, lower on the isthmus in Panama.

There was a well-answered call for volunteers at home to fill out the national guard and the regular forces. There were parades as these men headed for camp, or, finally trained, left for action. The North largely forgot it was the *North,* and the South did likewise in this united purpose and effort. New generations were blanking out the scars of old wounds.

A MESSAGE TO GARCIA

A youngish army lieutenant, named Rowan, would plunge into Cuban jungles in search of a rebel leader and become a symbol for go-getters in the early years of the next century for having carried "A Message to Garcia." A navy lieutenant would head a daring scheme and elect to take "Hobson's choice" in carrying it out. A destroyer knifed in two by an aircraft carrier in maneuver thirty-four years later would bear his name.

And a sickly boy, grown into a robust extrovert of a man, bubbling with vitality and flashing an infectious, toothy smile, would lead a group of his cowboy friends in a famous charge up a Cuban hillside. The *Rough Riders* and "Teddy" Roosevelt would become household names overnight.

AMERICA'S NEW INTERESTS

This war did something to America. It was most noticeable at home and quickly apparent abroad. Weary old Spain had indeed tangled with a giant, soon had to sue for peace, and gave up Cuba, Puerto Rico, Guam, and the Philippines, and an indemnity of $20,000,000.

Some Senators brought up on strict interpretation of the Constitution, and with the full sense of the Declaration indelibly in their minds, rebelled at taking the Philippines. It was contrary to our traditions to become a colonial power and rule others. But the taste for a touch of imperialism was becoming more pronounced, even in liberal tongues, and we garnered in our new possessions and with them a stern armful of responsibilities.

England took the results of the war in stride. But other European courts were amazed. These Americans might soon be sitting in on their own game of dividing up the "backward" areas of the world. Had she not, under cover of this war, already annexed the Hawaiian Islands, the key to the greatest of oceans, the Pacific?

When peace was made in August of 1898, few would question the fact that this country was now a world power, and one to be reckoned with. Despite a somber beginning, the new confidence and exhilaration in the air was closing out the decade of the nineties in a much gayer mood.

In the midst of the war excitement, South Dakota had taken an historical step. In an attempt to stamp out boss rule, through the ability of leading politicians to form their own slates of candidates, it enacted the Direct Primary giving the voters a better chance to select candidates. It was then considered very "advanced" legislation, but was rapidly accepted in other states.

The protectorate over Cuba was for the most part well carried out, due in no small part to the ministrations of able General Leonard Wood. In about four years the island had its own government.

A new type of territorial setup was made for Puerto Rico, and that island is still a prosperous possession. But the Philippines were an utterly different problem, a definite concern, and would continue to be far into the future. Within two years they had us mixed up in internal affairs in China, along with several European nations.

In 1899 we were invited to attend a Peace Conference at the Hague. Our innate *isolationism* would have withheld our participation some years earlier. But it was a changing world in which we had arrived; and more and more it would impress the hard fact on men throughout the earth that it was indeed *one world*. Our place in its destinies was becoming more certain, and there could be no drawing back from our expanding responsibilities. We took our place at the Conference, not realizing that one day we would find the winning of peace more difficult in some respects than the winning of wars.

A New Century Looms Ahead

INCE the figure 1900 could not be divided by 400, rather than by 4, that year would not be a leap year. But far more important, despite the reasoning of some who insisted the true date would come a year later, it would usher in a *New Century*. That was something that deserved recognition. So early in December, 1899, more than the usual number of invitations went out for New Year's Eve parties and watch-night services.

College athletes who would graduate in the coming year had long reveled in the big "double oughts" sewed to the fronts of their sweaters. To many there seemed to be something mystical about this year 1900, and the *twentieth century* it would bring into being. Its arrival was given a rousing celebration.

Even young children, left at home with grandparents or the "hired girl," were permitted to stay up to the unseemly hour of midnight. Then, bundled up in dressing gowns over their flannel nightclothes, or with a shawl thrown across their shoulders, they were led outdoors briefly to hear the din of shouting, ringing bells, pistol and cannon shots, and a few exploding fireworks.

But the youngsters, and perhaps a few elders, too, were somewhat amazed. There was no quivering earth beneath their feet, no triple rainbow in the starry sky. The clocks had not struck thirteen; but continued to tick on in their same unhurried fashion. As the shouting and tumult died down, it turned out to be no more than just another New Year's Day—and Monday to boot.

No brave new world had appeared, floating down out of the heavens. At least none was immediately apparent. But it was, however, a fuller, more interesting, and more crowded life than the year 1800 had witnessed. The tempo would begin to rise rapidly from here on; and, if they could have been fully foreseen on that night of celebration, the changes of the fifty years ahead would indeed have been breath-taking.

The contrasts with the beginning of the century just closed were considerable. For one thing, there were seventy million more people living in these United States than there had been then. The census to be taken later in the year would disclose a population of better than seventy-five million. Eighty-five per cent of them would be native born, in spite of heavy immigration. The center of population in 1800 was at a point about eighteen miles west of Baltimore. It had now moved out to the neighborhood of Bloomington, Indiana.

Also, there were now forty-five of these United States. Free land had become something out of the past; and the Indians were less a bother. McKinley had returned prosperity, and strikes and labor disturbances had quickly tapered off. There was politics as usual; but some of its crudities had been swept away, and still more would soon go.

AN EDUCATION FOR ALL

Public schools had spread, and there were more than 630,000 children being educated at public expense. Some two hundred million would be spent that year on this enterprise.

Far more than half the people still lived in rural areas and were dependent upon farming for their livelihood. By contrast, in New York and New England more than half lived in towns and cities. But there were near a quarter-million miles of railroad tracks tying farm homes to markets, which had once been limited to about a twenty-mile radius.

Mr. Edison's electricity was powering more and more *electric railways,* speeding up transportation in cities and towns, and also binding towns more closely together. People could live farther from their work, and the suburbs began to fill in like necklaces about the larger cities. Soon one could ride electric trolleys all the way from Portland, Maine, to Reading, Pennsylvania, or from New York City—with two short breaks in New York State—as far west as Chicago. Such journeys took a lot of transferring; but they give evidence of how rapidly these street railways were constructed about the turn of the century.

Maine still clung to state-wide prohibition; and Kansas had joined her in barring the sale of alcoholic beverages.

INVENTIONS MULTIPLY

Out of Cyrus McCormick's reaper and John Deere's plow had come a wide variety of farm tools, which stepped up production of food. Also they were making labor on the farms so plentiful that the exodus from them to the cities would now begin in earnest. Goodyear had learned to vulcanize rubber, and air-filled bicycle tires had brought that vehicle to the point of being a rage. They had also provided flexible tires for the automobiles that Ford, Olds, and other pioneers were turning out, some eight thousand of which were registered in 1900.

Morse with the telegraph, and then Bell with the telephone, had helped to banish distance and save huge amounts of time and effort. Another great development was also under way, which would convey ideas to greater numbers than any other medium perfected up to that time. Flickering motion pictures were then being exhibited as curiosities, and were still primitive enough so they were used to clear audiences from vaudeville houses between shows.

Hoe had made the printing press a high-speed tool for use in education and enlightenment. And who in that forward-looking year could not afford a "dollar watch," with an ornate fob to dangle from it when carried in the watch pocket, now a standard feature in gentlemen's trousers.

Howe had given a boost to the household arts. Much clothing was still being made—and remade—at home by the sewing machine. But this contrivance was more and more being used to mass-produce clothing in factories. Sholes and Remington had per-

289

fected another device which was taking young women out of homes and finding employment for them in business offices, working typewriters. The number of patents registered in the Patent Office had built up to more than 600,000. America catered to invention; and the trend now was toward labor-saving machinery. Such equipment was at first greatly feared by labor; but slowly proved that in reality it could make labor's lot easier and its earnings greater.

WAGES AND PRICES

And, speaking of wages, a bang-up good mechanic could earn $1.75 for a ten-hour day in Bridgeport, Connecticut, that year. At the market, his wife could pick up eggs at 35¢ a dozen; ham at 11¢ a pound; while fresh haddock was 4¢; cheese, 12¢; coffee, 14¢; and a ton of hard coal cost $5.75 in the bin in the cellar.

There had been the Rockefellers, Morgans, Armours, Swifts, Carnegies, and a host of others to make business big and to stimulate questions about its bigness. But there were advantages in such size that were slowly becoming apparent.

There had been a full complement of literary men and women to picture the expanding American scene, and to cheer on its strong points and emphasize its weaknesses. In that focal year of 1900, the top seller among books published would be Mary Johnston's *To Have and to Hold,* an historical novel.

Ah yes, the century just laid to rest had, all things considered, been a proud one. No greater heritage had ever been built before in so short a time and involving so many people. It provided confidence with which to face the future, and which a very few advanced thinkers were willing to claim would be the *American Century.* That could be. Some who looked at it in that light tended to exaggerate a trifle. Such was the extravagant pronouncement of a well-known historian who contended that, "By the end of this coming century this country will have expanded to include one hundred states, and a *billion* inhabitants." But, for the most part, our fathers and grandfathers were willing to settle for much less phenomenal progress.

The prosperity, which had rolled across the land after he first took office, was almost bound to return McKinley for a second term. But to make vote-getting even more certain, it seemed prudent to add Theodore Roosevelt to the ticket as Vice-President. This slate proved unbeatable, and was readily elected in the fall of 1900.

Monday, March 14, 1901, dawned mild and pleasant, only to turn into a downpour before the inaugural parade got under way. This sudden shift in weather was perhaps a bit prophetic; but the administration moved ahead with confidence.

THIRD ASSASSINATION

The summer went along smoothly. There was a Pan-American Exposition in progress at Buffalo; and the President made a strong appeal for inter-American co-operation there on September 5. The following afternoon, in the midst of a reception at the fair grounds, a bullet from behind laid him low with a mortal wound. In the early evening eight days later, fire and church bells across the land began to toll fifty-eight long strokes, the President's age. An assassin had done to death a third chief executive. Violence was still too often the method of settling differences.

Roosevelt had been vacationing not far away in the Adirondacks and had sped to

AUTOMOBILES BEGAN TO APPEAR ON THE ROADS

Buffalo. There in a private home, on September 14, he took the oath of office; and the most colorful character to occupy the presidency since Andrew Jackson began to dominate the American scene. The moment seemed to demand just such a man, and destiny provided him.

He was a natural leader, and thus capable of making fast friends and equally bitter enemies. He had been born to wealth in New York, had raised cattle in the Dakotas, served on the Civil Service Commission, been Police Commissioner of New York City, Assistant Secretary of the Navy, and then the colorful head of the *Rough Riders*. Following the war, he had been elected governor of New York State; and then tucked into the vice-presidency by the political powers thinking to sidetrack his considerable ambitions. Now he was in the nation's top spot; and promptly became *Mr. America*, the embodiment of progressive ideas then in the forefront of the thinking of a considerable majority.

He spoke and wrote in words that all could quickly grasp. He was the darling of the cartoonists, whether they were for or against him. He had a keen sense of news values, and often held back news until the Monday morning editions when he felt it had a better chance of making the first page in screaming headlines. In the face of such competition, it is little wonder that a man named Marconi, who in 1902 succeeded in flashing telegraph signals over the ocean from Newfoundland to Europe by "wireless," seemed much less exciting than this new President.

But it was not all furor and agitation. He dug out the Sherman Antitrust Act passed some years before, dusted it off, and handed it to the Justice Department with the strong hint that they would do well to put it to work. In his own words, he intended to "tread lightly, but carry a big stick." And in that fashion he descended upon the trusts and upon the unrestrained financial combinations. He managed to settle a crippling

291

coal strike; and then he began to look abroad.

Having been in the Navy Department, he knew its needs like the back of his own hand. Recalling the *Oregon* episode, and the need for a short water-link between the two oceans, he began to give attention to a canal. The French had tried one at Panama and failed, largely because of yellow fever and malaria. An American enterprise had been organized to try to push one across Nicaragua; but had abandoned the project. To some, that still seemed the more practical point. But yellow fever had been conquered by work done on that disease in Cuba; and also a revolution was helpfully brewing in Panama, still a part of Colombia.

Imperialism was well enough developed as a policy so that this unrest might be put to good use. Trouble finally broke out on November 2, 1903; and that same day United States Marines from one of our ships, conveniently offshore, landed, and the next day the Republic of Panama was proclaimed. The "big stick" had been wielded, outside the country this time, and we soon had a treaty to build a canal through Panama. Colombia received some twenty-five million for viewing the matter realistically.

PANAMA CANAL OPENED

There were a lot of problems, human and otherwise, that had to be licked. In the twisted wrist of land where the two great land masses grasped each other, a big ditch was slowly cut through. Ten years later ships, surprisingly enough sailing smack into the setting sun on part of the trip, could come from the western Pacific into the Atlantic on the eastern side in the matter of a few hours. With control over this facility, we became a dominant factor in the affairs of the two continents in the Western Hemisphere. This, too, helped the man in the White House to continue to make *news*.

FIRST AIRPLANE FLIGHT

Man had had a desire to fly long before there was written history. And one day toward the middle of December, in 1903, two bicycle mechanics from Dayton, Ohio, succeeded in a series of mechanical flights at Kill Devil Hill, near Kitty Hawk, on the coast of North Carolina. There was reasonable doubt that Orville and Wilbur Wright had actually achieved what a few others had already attempted. When the news came through, one unbelieving publisher wired back to the correspondent who had filed the report, "Cut out sending in wild-cat stuff." But flight by heavier than air equipment had been accomplished, and a new era in world affairs was born that day. The impact of the airplane upon human life would be far beyond anything then anticipated.

The South and Central American "republics" would now become a distinct concern. Venezuela was the first. It had had a rapid succession of "presidents," a polite term for "strong men" in use in countries below the Rio Grande River. They had borrowed money in England, Italy, and Germany, and these creditors were asking to be paid. Governments of the first two countries were willing to arbitrate; but the German emperor preferred to speak with battleships. When he ordered some of his naval vessels into Venezuelan waters, Roosevelt sent some of ours, just in case.

No shots were fired, and the matter was adjusted peaceably. But the big stick had been waved; and for years our motives would be strongly questioned, no matter how good our intentions in trying to maintain

THE WRIGHT BROTHERS' FIRST SUCCESSFUL FLIGHT

peace among our neighbors to the south. We would be accused of "dollar diplomacy," and often subject to even less polite terms.

Santo Domingo was next on the list. In this country we had to step in and run its finances for twenty-odd years. We seemed to be in a fair way of becoming a harried godparent to these unstable governments.

It was quite natural when 1904 rolled around that the dynamic Roosevelt would be re-elected on his own. The Democrats and Republicans had somehow changed roles, however. When Jackson had started the first of these two parties, it had been a reform organization. For many years through the middle of the last century, it had been the opposition party, protesting creeping conservatism. Now the Republicans, much against the wishes of a large segment of the party, were in reality the reform group, and the Democrats had to again con-

tent themselves with protest from the sidelines.

Japan, opened up to the outside world as late as 1854, had made tremendous strides. In a contest over rights on the Asian mainland, it had given the Russian Bear a rough going-over. The President had, largely by his own personal efforts, brought this war to a close and guided the resulting Peace Conference, held at Portsmouth, New Hampshire, in 1905. By it, the energetic Japanese managed to get a firm hold on Korea and lay the seeds for later troubles. For his efforts, however, the President was awarded the Nobel Peace Prize. In 1906 he managed to settle French difficulties in Morocco; and thus he quite naturally took great interest in the second Peace Conference held the following year at The Hague.

Still he was a decided realist, and quite conscious of Washington's remark, "To be

293

prepared for war is one of the most effectual means of preserving peace." The Navy had been built up until it was a formidable weapon. And just so there would be no doubt but that we were prepared to go to war to contend for peace if need be, he had the battle fleet painted a gleaming white, and sent it on a "good-will cruise" around the world in 1908. "Tread lightly, but carry a big stick." It was more than a slogan; it was his policy.

But interests at home were not forgotten. Our natural resources were being wasted, and in our rapidly growing country they would one day be needed badly. Plunging with his unbounded enthusiasm into this vital problem, he worked up a program of conservation, which was perhaps his outstanding contribution to the betterment of America.

Many would willingly have voted for him for another term. But he had felt the confinements of the office and decided against upsetting the tradition of no more than two terms in office for any man. He hand-picked his successor in William Howard Taft, who had been his Secretary of War. Then, after seeing him installed in the White House in 1909, the restless "Teddy" was off, in a matter of a few weeks, on a big-game hunting expedition in Africa.

But he would be back again one of these days, to do a little political big-game hunting here at home.

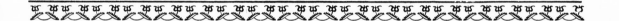

"No Sound Was Heard of Clashing Wars"

HERE had been a business recession in 1907. It was not as violent as that of 1893, but it had made the country a bit uneasy. Some said we were changing too rapidly, while others thought still more progressive ideas should be hurried through.

The new President had done an admirable job of bringing order out of chaos in the Philippines, and came into his new task with great promise. He sought to carry on many of his predecessor's policies, but he soon clashed with those in the more progressive wing of the party. This brought on a split in Republican ranks into two groups, the "Insurgents," and the "Stand-patters." The division was over reform, the former wishing to carry on further, while the latter wanted to call a halt. This divided attitude was felt strongly in the off-year elections in 1910. Many Democratic governors were voted into office; and the Republican majorities in Congress were reduced to the point where there was little co-operation between that branch and the presidency.

Insurgents within his own party now turned away from Taft and sought leadership in Roosevelt. They earnestly appealed to him to run in the 1912 elections. For a time he hesitated about becoming a candidate. Then with the characteristic challenge, "My hat is in the ring," he plunged into the campaign. The break with Taft was immediate. There would be another at the convention, when the *Insurgents* withdrew and organized the Progressive party. This division of Republican strength proved fatal; and the Democratic nominee, Woodrow Wilson, took office in 1913. There had been a Democratic sweep, in fact, for that party had a strong majority in both the House and Senate.

The new President's thinking was along much the same lines as Cleveland's and Theodore Roosevelt's. He believed the great majority were being injured by those who had controlled government and had amassed fortunes with little regard for the laborers, farmers, and small businessmen. What he visualized was a *new freedom,* in which these groups would receive a larger share of the national income.

One of his first acts was to approve the act of Congress which lowered the high protective tariff. Rates were cut to the lowest point since the War between the States. To offset the loss in revenue, a small tax was levied on incomes over four thousand dollars. This was another attempt at an income tax, made constitutional this time by the addition of the Sixteenth Amendment.

Banking was organized by the development of a Federal Reserve System. Then further controls over large corporations were put in force; and a Board created to adjust labor disputes without recourse to violence.

TROUBLE WITH MEXICO CAUSES EMBARRASSMENT

In international affairs, several treaties were arranged with other nations in a serious attempt to avoid wars. But one of our neighbors was then in the midst of a revolution which would bring some annoying and embarrassing moments. Mexico had been under the iron hand of a dictator, Porfirio Diaz [DEE-ath], for some thirty years. Because so heavy a hand could maintain order, considerable foreign capital had flowed into the country and gotten a firm grasp upon mining and oil properties.

But in 1912 the aging Diaz had been forced to flee the country, and a new dictator had tried to step into his place. His power was soon challenged, and still another strong man, Victoriano Huerta [WER-tah], seized the reins. Although twenty-six other nations recognized the shaky government he set up, President Wilson refused to do so. Soon our Navy had to go ashore at Tampico and take over the neighboring port of Vera Cruz.

Further incidents along the Mexican border forced the sending of our troops there. The Mexican affair became something of a farce, led to much criticism of the President, and was finally adjusted by that country without further intervention by the United States.

WORLD WAR I BEGINS

Then came a bombshell, the involvements of which would be more than any who had helped celebrate the entry of the new century but fourteen years before would have believed possible. Racial rivalries had been intense in eastern Europe. Plots and counterplots in the Balkans had created local disturbances and formed the basis for novels, stories, and plays. The area was a powder keg, but the explosion caused there on June 28, 1914, hardly seemed sufficient to start a world war. But that, indeed, was the result. Within six weeks England, France, Belgium, Germany, Austria-Hungary, and Russia had taken sides and were deep in the sorry business of carnage.

The President at once proclaimed neutrality, but sentiment here was bound to be divided. Our roots ran back into all these countries. From 1905 through 1914, immigration, the bulk of it from Europe, had been averaging just under one million people a year. Loyalties were thus bound to be split.

Also our trading rights were involved. First there was interference with our shipping by the British Navy. Then, early in 1915, the Germans began their submarine campaign. This latter menace came to a head with the sinking of the *Lusitania.* The President struggled to keep the peace, and this stand almost cost him re-election in 1916. Toward the end of that year peace feelers were put out by the opposing forces; but there seemed no points on which agreement could be reached.

By early 1917 the war was definitely deadlocked. The *Allies,* or those nations opposed to Germany and its associates, were heavily in debt to American bankers, businessmen, and investors. Unless the United States entered the war on their side, there could

THE MILITARY DRAFT WAS A NEW EXPERIENCE IN AMERICA

be huge losses or an indecisive peace, with continuing outbreaks of hostilities. Propaganda in favor of war began to pour out. But the final push came with the torpedoing of six merchant vessels by German submarines within a period of five weeks. On April 6, 1917, Congress declared war with Germany.

To clarify his stand, Wilson insisted that we had no selfish ends, were not seeking new territory, or dominion over other peoples. We wished only to preserve political liberties, and to "make the world safe for democracy."

This was a new type of war not limited to professional soldiers, but in the nations now locked in combat it involved pretty much the entire population and all usable resources. It was very much "total war"; and the United States was forced to enter it on that basis.

A universal draft was at once passed with a national army to be chosen from all ablebodied males from twenty-one to thirty-one years of age. Within three months these age limits were extended to eighteen to forty-five years. Enrolment was by lot; and women were accepted in some noncombatant services by enlistment.

There was a limited but insistent demand for a *conscription* of wealth to offset that of man power. But this was worked out on the basis of voluntary investment in a series of bond issues, called "Liberty Loans." The income tax, however, was stiffened and very much broadened. As a revenue-raising means it was here to stay, and eventually to reach into every man's pocket for an ever greater share of his earnings. For business, and particularly the larger concerns, there was an "excess profits" tax.

297

Industries were mobilized, and some of them, such as the railroads and telephone and telegraph lines, were actually taken over by the government. Others were regimented and closely controlled. Business was being looked upon in a very different light. It was not individual enterprise any longer, but something of a public trust. Labor, also, was asked to give its willing support to the war effort, and it did. There was a promise made that after the war had been won an international body would be created, so that labor in the various countries could interchange ideas for the common good.

The people were asked to make another contribution to safety and to the war effort. Grains badly needed to feed our people at home and our allies abroad were no longer to be made into alcoholic beverages. Also, it was felt that liquor would have a baneful effect upon both the men in training and the people who were being called upon to make greater effort in production. In almost record time the Eighteenth Amendment was added to the Constitution, prohibiting the manufacture and sale of intoxicating liquors.

EMERGENCY POWERS GREATER

Emergency measures enacted in this period were more far-reaching than the federal government had ever before attempted. By 1918 they even extended to food rationing, and sugar cards were issued. They provided a new pattern for what might be done at any time it could be claimed that an *emergency* existed and the exercise of such powers was needed for the public safety.

Since the Central Powers, grouped about Germany, had many operatives or spies in this country, working against the war efforts of the government, an antispying law, called the Espionage Act, was passed in

June, 1917. The following year, in May, this was extended by a Sedition Act, which gave very complete control over public opinion. This had not been attempted since a similar much-hated act in 1798. And while strongly resisted in the Congress itself, as conflicting with the inherent right to criticize governmental acts, it became a wartime measure.

TROOPS SENT TO FRANCE

While materials and equipment were being hurried through, men were being trained and transports readied to carry them to Europe. The Navy was to convoy them and was soon aiding in blockading the Central Powers. By June of 1917 General John J. Pershing arrived with the first contingent of the American Expeditionary Forces. The infantry was in the trenches by October and saw its first severe action in November.

It was about this time that a revolution within that country took Russia out of the war. There had long been internal strife there, and the revolutionary group, aided by the conditions brought about by the war, gave this *Bolshevik* clique an opportunity to seize power. The czar was deposed, the insurgents now changed their name to Communists; and in October, 1917, their leader, Nikolai Lenin, took over the government. This released German armies that had been tied to the eastern front for employment in the West.

Early in January the President in a message read to Congress set forth his famous "fourteen points," which gave the purposes for which we were fighting. Perhaps the most interesting to us today was the last, which proposed a *league,* or association, of nations, by which it was hoped relations between members might be adjusted without recourse to war.

"THE BIG FOUR" ATTEMPT TO BRING PEACE IN EUROPE

Although Germany was still hard-pressed, relief at the east gave it a chance to marshal its forces for one great attempt in the western sector in 1918. War in that area had become static because of the trench systems employed, and the Germans hoped for a break-through. But new American troops, some two million of which would be in France that summer, threw the advantage to the Allies. By early November the Germans were finished, and on November 11 an armistice was arranged and fighting ceased.

Short though our participation in actual fighting was, there had been more than 300,000 American casualties, and some 75,000 of these were soldiers and sailors who had given their lives. Now it would be necessary to find if the world had really been made safe for democracy.

The making of peace proved a difficult business, however. The President went to Europe, despite some grumbling at home, to join with representatives of England, France, and Italy, in drawing up peace terms. First there was the "Big Four." Then, when Italy withdrew, it was the "Big Three." The United States was now one among the giants.

Wilson, who could be a forceful and persuasive speaker, talked of his expectations to the common people in several European countries and gave them courage and temporary hope. The burden of his speeches was the formation of a league, and he won wide popular support for it abroad. When he returned home briefly to catch up on affairs here, the Old World politicians did their best to jettison his project. He defended it while at home; and then returned to attend the actual Peace Conference and did his best to build enthusiasm anew.

(*Continued on page 306*)

299

THE GETTYSBURG ADDRESS

Joseph Boggs Beale

In the Collection of Modern Enterprises

Probably no speech made in all American history will ever be more widely known than that delivered by Abraham Lincoln on November 19, 1863, at the dedication ceremonies at the National Cemetery set apart at Gettysburg, Pennsylvania. There are five known copies of the speech in the President's own handwriting, the original and a second draft being in the Library of Congress. The latter is thought to have been the *reading copy* held by him as he delivered the address. He had probably written it that morning at Judge Wills' home in Gettysburg, where he had spent the night; and in it some very slight changes had been made.

The principal speaker of the day, however, was Edward Everett, statesman, orator, and scholar of Massachusetts, who on that afternoon delivered the last of the great orations for which he had long been famous. He had thundered on and on for perhaps two hours, the crowd dwelling upon his words, and applauding noisily. At last he was finished; and when the tall, gaunt man that was to follow him rose, his plain, direct words simply spoken must have come as something of an anticlimax. There was a respectful hush as he began. But the speech was very short, and in a bit more than two minutes he was through.

The end had come unexpectedly, and there was but a faint and rather perfunctory ripple of applause. It is said that the President turned to Marshall Lamon beside him, and remarked a little wryly, "Lamon, that speech won't score. It is a flat failure."

This was one place in which posterity has not affirmed his judgment. Even Everett complimented him heartily, and told him his words would be remembered long after his own had been forgotten. Grateful for this praise, Lincoln made a handwritten copy for the great orator, whose judgment of the speech has been fully vindicated. Surely the number of schoolchildren who have learned it by heart in the past ninety or more years is beyond computation.

BATTLE OF GETTYSBURG

Paul Dommique Philippoteaux

Chicago Historical Society

This tremendous battle, which raged between July 1st and 3rd in 1863 involved about 165,000 men, their division favoring the Union side. It was Lee's second attempt to carry the war and its destruction into the North, disrupt its communications, and cut off its supplies from the West. He had been checked at Antietam the previous fall; but this time he had brought a much larger force for the task.

During the hot July days the battle ebbed and flowed, but superior numbers finally turned the tide, and the northern advance was stayed. While the decision stands as a Union victory, the Confederate forces escaped ruin. Whatever victory there was came less on the battlefield than in the area of international politics. The outcome at Vicksburg, and particularly at Gettysburg, in all probability withheld recognition of the Confederate cause by England and France.

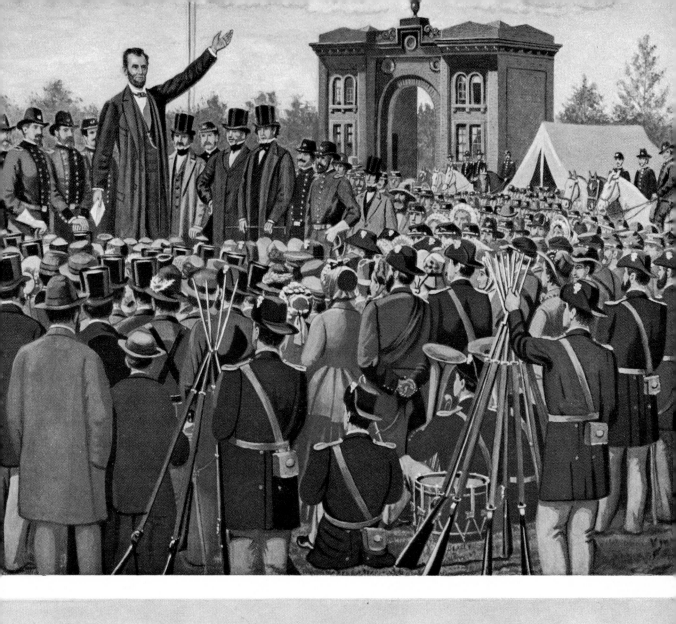

LET US HAVE PEACE

Jean Leon Gerome Ferris
Smithsonian Institute, Washington

Ferris, who did as many as fifty well-known paintings of American history, portrayed a great symbol in this scene. The occasion was worthy of it, for the spirit that prevailed during the brief meeting in the house in Appomattox Court House on that April day in 1865 was in the best American tradition. Grant had inquired of President Lincoln, who had paid a surprise visit to his tent a few nights previous, what action was to be taken as regards Gen. Lee. A hot head had demanded he be shot forthwith. But the grief-stricken Lincoln is reported to have replied, "Shoot Bob Lee! You might better shoot me than him."

Brother had fought brother, each thinking his cause to be right. The strife was now over, and they must return to brotherly regard once again. But a misguided killer struck down the great man who wished not only for peace, but for tolerance and complete understanding to reign. And with his untimely death ruthless and covetous men crowded upon the scene, and swept a *reconstruction period* into being which is a blot and an indelible stain upon our national honor.

ATTACK ON AN EMIGRANT TRAIN

Charles Wimar
Anheuser-Busch Collection, St. Louis

Although the artist who did this stirring scene died in 1862, it pictures the hazards encountered by several generations of pioneers moving into our West. With the opening up of government land to free homesteading in 1863, the migration which followed the close of the war between the states rose to a huge crescendo. It was perilous at best, and too great a risk to travel alone. So for protection's sake, the settlers formed themselves into great wagon trains. One then had aid if accidents occurred while on the trail, and the circle of wagons formed at night gave greater sense of security against attacks during the hours of darkness.

Even without the lurking savages, the trails were rough and difficult, and the distance seemingly endless. In the old days near Gardner in Johnson County, Kansas, there was a sign where the trails branched reading "Road to Oregon," and pointing to the north fork. There was no intimation that the destination was a good 2000 miles and probably one hundred or more days away. One trailhand is supposed to have observed, "That's a pretty short sign for so long a journey."

CUSTER'S LAST STAND

Cassily Adams
Anheuser-Busch Collection, St. Louis

One day in 1874, Custer on an expedition into the Black Hills country sent a scout galloping back to Ft. Laramie in eastern Wyoming with word of the recent local gold strike. This news, traveling like wildfire, set off an onrush of miners. Contrary to treaty provisions they invaded Sioux hunting grounds, and the enraged warriors went on a rampage. This Indian uprising was climaxed in the complete annihilation of the dashing Custer's inadequate forces.

Finally political forces over there yielded, and largely because of his personal efforts in its behalf the League of Nations was shaped up. When the President returned to press a treaty of peace through Congress, the League was a part of it. There was much in connection with peace terms to argue about. To some, the League looked like a mask behind which we would become deeply involved in the age-old animosities of Europe. Opposition, at first mild, began to solidify as the President sought to force the issue through the Senate.

He was so insistent that some of the Senators finally became adamant. There seemed to be no room for compromise. A spirit of isolationism was developing, and both the treaty and the League were rejected. What this action contributed to the unstable peace that followed and to the onset of the second World War is still subject to conflicting opinions.

But without benefit of our participation, the Assembly of the League of Nations convened at Geneva in Switzerland late in 1920.

Wilson, still hopeful, made the League an issue in the 1920 presidential campaign. At about this time long agitation by women's groups for the right of suffrage had resulted in the Nineteenth Amendment. In November the women of the nation would vote for a President for the first time.

The campaign was waxing hot, when, in September, the President suffered a collapse. He returned from a trip to the West an invalid, and carried on his duties during the closing months of his term from a wheel chair. The Democrats had to find a new standard-bearer.

Republicans had some difficulty in making a choice, and finally had to accept a "dark horse" candidate, Warren G. Harding of Ohio. He was teamed with a rock-ribbed New Englander, (John) Calvin Coolidge. But there was a landslide in their favor at the polls; and after eight years out of office the Republicans not only controlled the presidency, but Congress as well.

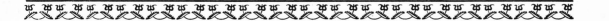

Boom and Bust

HE YEAR 1919 had been a restless one. The troops being moved home from Europe had probably been treated with greater consideration than any previous fighting men. But they were somewhat provoked to find how much better those who had managed to remain behind and work had fared financially. There was also enough slacking off in the business world so that jobs were not too easy to find either.

Labor at home had kept its promises about continuing at its jobs while the fighting lasted. Now with prices spiraling upward, and continuing employment highly uncertain, there was much unrest. There was an oil boom on in Texas; but elsewhere in the nation there was caution and misgivings. The letdown from the war tension tended to shift over into other types of tension here at home.

Thus Harding struck a popular note when he offered to lead the country back to "normalcy." It was a good word, but not too carefully defined. Perhaps it was good politics not to make any exact promises. Some of his Cabinet selections were excellent. There was Charles Evans Hughes for Secre-

tary of State, Herbert Hoover to head the expanding Commerce Department, and the shrewd "country banker," Andrew Mellon, as Secretary of the Treasury. Some of the remainder of his official family would provoke perhaps the greatest scandals ever connected with the Executive Branch of our government. Their moral impact on a morally indifferent age would be most unfortunate.

To offset the slackening in business, the old scheme of tariff protection was brought back, and a bill passed boosting duties to the highest point yet levied.

To somewhat pacify labor, and to give time for the assimilation of the huge number of immigrants that had entered the country in recent years, but principally to stop millions more anxious than ever to flee devastated Europe, immigration was sharply tapered off.

Europe was indeed in ferment, and happenings there created uncertainty and problems here. The German republic had by now been set on its unsteady course, and a direct peace treaty now had to be made with its people. Ireland had been created a free state in 1921. Egypt would be granted self-government in 1922, and that same year

Mussolini would become dictator of Italy, and Gandhi would start India on its march toward independent status. The old order, which had given considerable stability to world affairs while we were growing up as a nation, was now shaken to its foundations.

There was an arms conference involving the major nations held in Washington in 1922, but it accomplished little beyond impairing the strength of our Navy, and nothing in the way of lasting peace. Then the following year there were new threats of war in Europe and another shake-up in the government in Mexico. One world was growing progressively smaller, and troublesome incidents which once had very minor effects beyond the localities where they broke out, now began to disturb the whole world community. Even the League of Nations, with its limited powers, seemed unable to cope with these mighty ground swells. The common people all the way to the far corners of the earth were growing restless. The spirit of revolution appeared to be taking over, and the hoped-for "normal" conditions were indeed hard to come by.

HARDING'S SUDDEN DEATH

There was difficulty among the farmers in our own West, labor was embroiled in serious strikes, and returned veterans of the late war were clamoring for a *bonus*. Then in August, 1923, the President became seriously ill as he returned from a trip to Alaska and suddenly died. The Vice-President, on a visit to his boyhood home in Vermont, there received the sad news. By the light of a coal-oil lamp in the dead of night, his aged father administered the oath; and Calvin Coolidge became the twenty-ninth man to hold the highest office in the land.

Although he found himself at cross-purposes with Congress, this cautious, economical, rather glum man managed to secure a firm hold on the respect of the bulk of the people. There was still the futile hope of getting back to the "good old times," and he seemed ideally equipped as a guide in that direction. But how different the journey ahead was destined to be.

WASHINGTON SCANDALS

The impending scandals, centering in the Departments of Interior and of Justice, were soon uncovered. They would have broken the late President, had he lived; but no dishonor in connection with them attached to the man now in the White House. So great was the confidence in him that he turned wrath away from his party, too, and with it won election on his own quite handily in 1924.

Payment of the heavy penalties saddled on Germany by the peace settlement were revised by the "Dawes Plan." Immigration was further restricted, and the Soldiers' Bonus Bill passed over the President's veto. Our Marines were withdrawn from Nicaragua where they had been sent to quell another of the frequent revolutions. England was in the grip of a general strike; while hearts skipped a beat when Hindenburg, a famous wartime general, became president of Germany. Thus there were some still fairly light earth tremors in international affairs during the first two years of Coolidge's second period in office. The peace that had been made five years before was already proving an uncertain one.

At home, however, most lines of business had by now adjusted to postwar conditions, volume of production was high, and so was employment. Agriculture was still a soft spot

LINDBERGH FLIES
NONSTOP TO PARIS

in the economy, and coal mining and textiles could not seem to find the key to the new prosperity. American bankers were loaning money liberally in Europe and around the world, and goods were flowing out into markets which these funds opened up. But unfortunately we were being paid for our shipments into them primarily with our own money.

Several newer products together with changing conditions sparked this increased business tempo. It is said that World War I advanced the development of the airplane by as much as fifty years. While this may be an exaggeration, it did force its increased use and rapid improvement. From a curiosity, it became an important implement of war. And it then readily adapted itself to peaceful commercial uses. After Lindbergh's nonstop solo flight across the ocean to Paris, in 1927,

aviation received another tremendous forward thrust. Also, like some other enterprises at that time, commercial flying received some support and subsidy from government funds. In its case, such aid came through the then liberal payments made for carrying the mail.

The motor vehicle was another tremendous factor in the speed-up of business. There had been but eight thousand in use at the turn of the century. By 1919, the year after the close of the war, there were about six and three-quarter million passenger cars and an ever-increasing number of trucks. While this industry was not subsidized directly, it did receive the greatest possible assistance through the enormous postwar program of paved roads and highways. By 1929 there were over twenty-three million automobiles registered and in use, and this industry was by then taking near a quarter of the increasing steel production.

Shipping had had outright subsidies and was doing well; but it was in no measure the influence on the boom getting into high gear that the motion picture proved to be. This mass medium did much to carry the spirit of the times to every last village and hamlet; and also to build acceptance for the latest styles in mass-produced clothing and a long array of gaudy new gadgets for home and personal use. In this respect, it carried the American Story around the world, although not too accurately in all respects. With the addition of sound to motion, the "talking pictures" became a rage through the later years of the roaring twenties.

RADIO BROADCASTING

Also unsubsidized was another war development that the public began to take to its heart in this hectic period. Wireless telegraphy was well established before hostilities broke out. But by the end of the fighting in Europe, men were talking to each other over considerable distances by wireless telephones. The outcome was the radio. Broadcasting began in the early twenties; and Coolidge was the first President to have his voice heard nationwide, for the first coast-to-coast hookup was made to carry his inaugural address on March 4, 1925. Together with the movies, it was to become a powerful tool for the forming of mass opinion.

With a rapidly growing population, housing was in huge demand after the war and hit its peak in 1925 when near a million *non-farm* homes were built. With the situation on the farm still difficult, and many farmers being foreclosed and dispossessed, there was now a decided flow of people from rural areas into towns and cities. Also there was a startling boost in the number of "white-collar" workers, and an increase in the so-called "middle classes." This bred a demand for new and better homes, and their construction did much toward getting the business upswing under way. When the building boom tipped over sharply in 1926, a few hardy souls began to post warnings. This fact seemed to them to signal that there could be limits to which the boom could go. But such "kill-joys" received precious little attention.

INTERNATIONAL TRADE

America, which had been a *debtor* nation before the war, was now decidedly a *creditor* nation. The Department of Commerce was particularly busy seeking out new markets far and wide, and even to some extent helping to locate private capital to be rushed into them so American goods could follow close behind, in American ships, of course, to flood them.

In fact, new capital seemed to be endless. Business pushed through one merger after another, with liberal inclusions of "watered" stock, which the public always proved fully able to absorb. Local concerns began to sprawl out as *chains*. Big banks swallowed little banks; and even sports became big business and were thoroughly commercialized. Everything seemed to prosper but the farms, coal mining, and textiles. There were in all about two million unemployed, but the number did not cause particular concern.

But how about the man in the street? How was he reacting to all this furor? His job seemed most secure, and he was drawing down especially good wages. He had even bought a home of his own, heavily laden with a fairly large mortgage, of course, for prices were high. But many of the banks were heavily involved in financing the building and sale of such properties, and he was going along with the crowd. He even owned an automobile and a lot of new furniture and work-saving household gadgets. Here again, prices at least seemed high, but somehow he managed quite conveniently.

SEARCH FOR EASY MONEY

Also, he had been taught during the war to invest in *securities*. These had been war bonds backed by the government. Investment was pretty much a new experience for him. But Wall Street had always excited his interest, and even a little envy. So the shift over to purchase of stocks came fairly easily. Particularly was this so when many, many bankers were talking stocks. Large amounts of idle capital were flowing to Wall Street and to other points where it could be borrowed to buy stocks on *margin*. You paid down as little as ten or fifteen per cent in hard money, and a broker arranged for the difference on a loan. You were then an owner of securities, on paper at least; and brokers' men were beating the bushes 'way out into the small towns and countryside looking for new clients to join with them in "making some easy money." By 1928 there were some eighteen million individuals holding stock in this country, a greater proportion of the population than ever before. And of the people that patronized the brokerage houses in buying and selling stocks, one in each five was a woman. This was something quite new. More and more of the wealth and more and more of the purchasing was now in the hands of women.

And the man in the street noticed that things were different at home, too. With all these aids to easier housekeeping, many wives were holding onto jobs which they had taken during the war. They enjoyed the greater freedom and privileges which came with being self-sustaining; and the extra money came in handy for the mortgage on the home and other debts that seemed to be piling up.

Yes, the mother absent from home during working hours did leave the children alone and on their own resources more. They seemed so different, too, and so much more mature and independent. Surely they had much greater liberties of action and decision than this man and his wife had known at their age but a few short years before. Sometimes it seemed better this way. Then, again, there were sobering moments when much of what was going on all about was open to sober questioning.

A MORAL SETBACK

Morality surely appeared to have had a rude setback. Just the other day there had been the item in the paper telling of how rapidly the divorce rate was shooting up. And there was surely an appalling amount of crime, all up and down the scale, from highest to lowest. Could it be true that only about seven out of ten crimes resulted in an arrest? And that no more than five of those seven when taken into custody were eventually sentenced? That was really something to think about. But still when you mentioned such things in conversation, people more or less shrugged their shoulders. About the only thing most of them looked at in the newspapers anyway were the stock-market reports.

It was a robust, garish, irresponsible period, the "roaring twenties." There was greater abundance, more widely spread, than any nation had ever known before. But it was a time in which many of the older American virtues were frittered away. Per-

311

sonal discipline and self-control, and much of individual self-reliance, went by the board. The influences at work were mass influences, and the common man and woman were swept along in a stream of life so much bigger and all-embracing than what previous generations had experienced that they were washed away from old, familiar moorings, and were adrift in a restless torrent. It was a sort of wild joy ride, stirred up, kept in motion, and forced along, but without much in the way of sound guidance. There was bound to be a day of reckoning, but the present was so very much in evidence that the future seemed far away and remote.

A NOBLE ATTEMPT TO ACHIEVE WORLD PEACE

Abroad, where conditions were not nearly so fortunate, France suggested we draw a treaty with her agreeing never to resort to war in settling differences. Our Secretary of State, Mr. Kellogg, asked that this be made an international agreement. And in 1928, with much solemnity, the leading nations gathered in Paris and signed the Kellogg Peace Pact. For a few fleeting moments, conditions on the international front looked brighter.

Early that same year the question arose whether Coolidge would be a candidate and try for election on his own a second time. After much prodding by politicians and the press to arouse interest, he finally issued his cryptic statement, "I do not choose to run."

In the summer conventions the Republicans matched Herbert Hoover against the Democrats' "Al" Smith. Although there was much bitterness during the campaign, it apparently did not seem prudent to the majority to change horses in midstream in so rollicking a period of prosperity. Hoover won

hands down, and the "Hoover Boom" soared to new heights.

Perhaps no man since the time of Washington entered the White House so well and so favorably known. The new President had made an international reputation, first as an engineer, then by his aid in relief work in Belgium, and later among the destitute peoples of Europe. As head of the potent Commerce Department, he had for several years rendered constructive aid in business affairs at home and in the development of foreign markets. He stood at an advantageous place to view both the current American and the world scene. And as he took office, he said, "We in America are nearer the final triumph over poverty than ever before in the history of any land."

That much, on the surface at least, seemed to be substantially true. But then he added, "Given a chance to go forward with the policies of the last eight years, we shall soon, with the help of God, be in sight of the day when poverty will be banished from this nation."

It was an inspiring prospect, to which few groups, and notably the farmers, would at that moment take strong exception. Debt, falling prices, and oversupply of farm products had them mired in the mud of despondency. And they were so vocal in their protests that a special session of Congress was at once convened to try to improve their general condition.

But before much to relieve this sore spot could be accomplished, and with as little forewarning as customarily precedes a violent earthquake, the bottom dropped out of the stock market on October 29, 1929. Never was the end of an era more pointedly signaled.

Hoover, seven and a half months in office, would spend the remainder of his term in trying to stem the tides of misfortune. He had hoped to make good on his inaugural promises by a sound program of vigorous policies. But the economic hurricane would turn out to be a long and disastrous storm. He had been elected as something of a *miracle man*. But no man in his position could find an easy remedy for the mess brought on by moral and material excesses in which pretty much the whole nation had shared to some extent.

RECESSION UNDERESTIMATED

The first reactions were that this was a tornado, rather than a hurricane. Since the storm would soon blow itself out, leading men felt there was little purpose to be served in alarming the populace. The farmers, after long wrangling in Congress, had an Agricultural Marketing Act, backed by a half-billion dollars. Coolidge had vetoed a measure of this same type only a few years before; but the situation now demanded that something big be done, and quickly. The lawmakers then turned to the tariff and gave rates a stiff boost. Almost immediately twenty-five other nations countered by raising their tariff walls against American goods. America was not, it soon appeared, rolling alone down a one-way street. If we made it more difficult to sell goods here, they would make it more difficult for us to put our goods in their markets, which had become quite a feature in our distribution. International trade promptly began to dry up.

Many men and women of all degrees and stations were heavily in debt. Millions had been cleaned out of the stock market on the day prices broke. Buying sprees were over, and business began to shorten sail or go into bankruptcy. Unsound foundations on which the boom had been erected crumbled

rapidly, panic settled down, the worst in our history; and with world-wide effects as well. Within five months following the crash, unemployment had jumped to three million. For the next thirty long months it would grow progressively worse at an average increase of 400,000 a month. By October, 1932, a few weeks before the next presidential election, it would stand at the amazing total of twelve million.

There had been panics before, usually stemming from excesses of one sort or another. But disturbing as they were, they had never brought such acute suffering to such a preponderant fraction of all the people. Economic problems this time bore with them large and demanding social problems.

Lawlessness was, if anything, still on the increase. At least it loomed large; and the President appointed a commission to investigate it. One of the worst festering sores arose from the unpopular prohibition measures, which had bred "bootlegging," "speak-easies," and wholesale contempt for law. Recommendations made by this body came as somewhat of a surprise to many—prohibition should either be repealed or greatly modified.

MODERATE PUMP PRIMING

Public works were planned, and federal loans were made to banks and industries. But the President and his advisers were heartily opposed to direct grants from the federal government to the mounting ranks of the unemployed. Proper provision for the unfortunate was considered the task of local and state governments and organized charity. Washington seemed too far-removed from community needs to be able to deal with them wisely. There was strong precedent for such hands-off policy found in the attitudes of former Presidents, who believed that the federal government should not be come involved in local affairs.

Much editorial space in newspapers and magazines was given to exploring the probable causes of the economic disaster. And a similar amount of space began to fill with large-scale plans, usually involving the government, which it was hoped might iron out the broad fluctuations in conditions that resulted in boom and bust. Businessmen divided sharply on such proposals. Still every time they dared look over their shoulders, the ranks of the unemployed had increased. This meant less business volume and a continuation of the downward spiral. Was there no bottom to this recession, from which a start could be made in the other direction?

DISCOURAGEMENT INCREASES

It was disheartening to be out of a job, out of money, out of food. Some of the early settlers had experienced such times, no doubt, and had had to pull up their belts and ride out evil times as best they could. Perhaps some of them cursed the day they left an Old World where a master, or an overlord, could be looked to for assistance in such times of adversity. A few hardy souls who had been forced in from the farms decided to go back again, where at least one could raise one's food. But those who had been city dwellers through several generations had little to fall back on. Dispossessed of homes and without funds or the necessities of life, they began to demand direct assistance which, in many cases, the communities were unprepared to give to the extent to which it was needed.

The unemployed were able to point to the fact that the government had poured many millions into bailing out business and industry, or in subsidizing it by one means or another from a protective tariff to outright payments. It was a little difficult to give a sound reason why people who had been taxed in the past to provide such funds should not, in their time of adversity, look to the same source for aid and relief.

The politicians, always sensitive to any condition which would rebound to their advantage, were strongly in favor of direct aid, for it looked like a means of ready access to votes. Such is ever the danger of dependence upon political support—there is bound to be a day of reckoning and a payoff which can be embarrassing.

Also, first estimates of the extent and duration of this panic seemed to be all awry. Businesses which had weathered other storms were being engulfed by this one, which seemed to be more widespread than previous setbacks. Evidently the economy was being more closely knitted together. Even a few of the more determined of the business interests began to take a detailed

IT WAS DISHEARTENING TO BE OUT OF A JOB, OUT OF MONEY, OUT OF FOOD; BUT THERE WERE MILLIONS THAT WERE

look at some of the planning that was being proposed. Those about the President, however, still were certain that conditions would right themselves, given time and not too much interference by what they considered ill-advised schemes.

Thus there was strongly divided sentiment at home and a sullen and explosive world abroad. America's influence on international affairs had stepped up to the point where our difficulties were having a baneful influence over a wide area. It was reasoned that world conditions thrown out of adjustment by the war had never gotten properly righted, and such maladjustments could not be corrected in a day.

President Hoover's own confidence was not shaken, and he continued to believe and advocate that the principal needs were the keeping of order and a guarantee of the

soundness of money. If this was done, industry would begin to pick up confidence, labor would be employed, and the difficulties would be solved.

But he had been looked upon as something of a "miracle man" when he had taken office. And since he had worked no miracles; and unfortunately appeared to treat the whole situation with something akin to indifference, the rank and file lost faith in him. His public relations were perhaps to blame for this, but *the man in the street* was quite certain that he had little patience with his pressing problems. Maybe the core of Amer-

315 ᗡ

ican political and social thinking was sound. Maybe what was needed was greater individual initiative. But the man was hungry, there were holes in his shoes, and most of the plant gates were locked tight that morning as he had made the rounds searching for a job, *any* job. He and others like him quickly decided they needed a new champion.

The Democratic Convention managed to discover a man who might have wide appeal. He was the governor of New York, and his name was Franklin Delano Roosevelt. He had an aristocratic background and an accent that the man in the street couldn't quite place. But he talked slowly, let his words sink in, and they were picturesque words, too. What was that phrase he aimed right at all those who were looking for a new champion? Yes, that was it, the *forgotten man*. And he talked about a *new deal*. There had been a popular song the year before, "Brother, Can You Spare a Dime?" Not many could; but here was a candidate who looked as though he might be a willing touch. He even talked this forgotten man's language, after all.

And in November this distant cousin of the first Roosevelt won the election quite easily, and carried into office with him safe Democratic majorities in both Houses of Congress. He would dominate the American scene and much of the news of the world during the next fourteen years.

Testing Constitutional Government

HE depression was a full three years old by the time Franklin Roosevelt was elected in November, 1932. Month by month, conditions had worsened, the number of unemployed had mounted, and now the financial structure of the country seemed about to wither away.

Thomas Paine had written, back in the days of the Revolution, "These are the times that try men's souls." So, too, were the early weeks of 1933. Confidence, even in high places, could be bought at a heavy discount. The fixed stars were either clouded from view or seemed to be off their courses. And then banks began to close their doors. Those still fortunate enough to have such a luxury as a bank account hurried to withdraw it in cash and hide the banknotes beneath the cellar floor at home.

Oh, there were a few hardy souls in those days. Thrown on their own, they were trying every scheme they could think up to turn an honest penny. But pennies were scarce, and it took scheming and real effort to garner such as were still loose. There are always a few who never know when they are licked. Surprisingly, though, there were more than

you might at first have thought in those dark days. They had no intention of selling America *short,* and they worked their ingenuity overtime, determined to keep afloat by their own efforts. If jobs were to be had in no other way, they made them.

But a great many had much idle time on their hands and not too many facilities for employing it beyond soul-searching. They could see no error on their part. Their difficulties, they were confident, had been caused by conditions above and beyond their control, or so they reasoned. Something needed to be done to correct the situations apparently badly out of line. Things were evidently stacked against the great majority. At least that is the way they seemed to be. It was a pretty big problem, growing bigger by the year, too. There had been a lot of plans proposed to improve conditions. Maybe it would be a good idea to try some of them out. There wasn't much to be lost, and a lot, possibly, to be gained.

Now there was the subject of *money.* Everybody had to have it and use it. But money involved credit, loans, debts, mortgages, and also the price of things when they were bought and sold. It was indeed a big subject. But "someone" ought to have

317 &

"some" idea of what was needed in connection with this whole matter. Many would be quite willing to listen to any such person.

PUZZLING QUESTIONS

There was also this matter of *over-production*. The plants seemed to be turning out too many of some goods, while in a few cases there was not enough of others. But the farmers were raising too much of almost everything. Some of them were losing their farms, too, and coming into town to swell the ranks of unemployed job seekers. That didn't seem right. There was a need for "someone" to correct this situation, too.

And what had happened to all these proposals about *world* markets, and other fancy plans about paying higher wages, and so increasing the market for goods right here at home. How many potatoes should we plant? And how many bales of cotton? And why were farmers dumping milk in the creeks out in the West, when people in other sections were in dire need of it? As many a farmer, laborer, or small businessman, dipped into these problems, he felt himself a very little cog in a big, big wheel. But there must be "someone" that could solve these problems.

Such thinking made men conscious that year by year they were becoming more and more interdependent. It was an age of specialization; and when you begin to specialize, you are bound to be dependent upon others. It was a hard way to learn a fundamental truth, but it brought realization that town and country, farmer, laborer, storekeeper, and all others had definite need of each other. The better each of them managed, the better chances there were for all.

Foolishly, perhaps, many looked at this fact from the wrong direction. They didn't put quite enough emphasis on that first part —the better *each* of them managed by his individual efforts. That was truly the important part. The benefits flowed to all from the individual's willingness to be his own man. That was exactly what had made America great.

Actually the problems being wrestled with as the incoming administration took office in 1933 were anything but new. Some of them were as old as the nation itself. Others were the result of conditions which had had their beginning perhaps a hundred years before. But on all sides things were grinding to a standstill. There had been a three-year wait for conditions to right themselves. Patience had worn thin. There had been no "miracles" done by the man stepping out of the White House; and there was a burning hope that the age of miracles was not entirely past.

THE BANKS CLOSED

And with the bang of closing bank doors still in their ears, people gathered about their radios on that March 4 determined to pay closer attention to an inaugural address than had ever before been accorded one. The voice they heard had great assurance and a sincere note of confidence. It made a statement that cannot be questioned. A truly brave people " have nothing to fear but fear itself." That is a belief to be ever remembered and handed on to our children. The speech went on to promise action, which was quickly forthcoming.

Bank failures called for immediate attention to financial matters. So all banks were closed until it could be determined which were sound enough to reopen. Those that had been mismanaged, and some of them clearly had, pointed to the need for tighter control and supervision. It might be far better if the financial community could be trusted to police its own house. But confidence in financial matters was most imperative, and more authority over banking was lodged in the government.

When it developed that no less than twenty per cent of the national banks, and as many as thirty per cent of the state banks, were too shaky to reopen, it did indicate that a monitor was apparently needed where other people's money was being handled. A few asked the question, "Why can the government be trusted in money matters beyond those making up the industry itself?" But the need was urgent, there had to be a policeman from some source, and the task was handed to federal authorities.

SEARCH FOR A FORMULA FOR SOUND MONEY

The whole matter of money clamored for attention, for it seemed to be subject to control by a few who could use the power money exerts very much to their selfish benefit. As the subject was opened up for discussion, there were a number of groups who pressed forward and offered "foolproof" suggestions. But as these schemes were closely examined, they proved to work out to someone's particular advantage. Certain of the proposals were rather extreme; and an attempt was made to find a middle course that would yield *sound* money, without particular favoritism to any one section of the population.

The method finally employed took the currency off the gold standard. Coined gold and notes payable in gold were called in, and a new type of paper money backed by values other than gold was issued. This move did stimulate business somewhat. But within a year its influence had run its course; things

then sagged back, and "tampering" with money came in for strong condemnation.

Based on the reasoning that larger amounts of money in circulation would ease the excessive debt load and spark an upturn in industry, the government was made an even larger credit agency. Loans from the Treasury had flowed out during the war, and also in the Harding and Coolidge administrations. But they had gone principally to railways, banks, shipping, aviation, and some to the farmers. Under Hoover such loans had been extended to embrace small business and homeowners. Now the avenues of credit were greatly extended, and special attention was given to girding the security of the common man and to stabilizing family life on which the nation and its entire heritage were so much dependent.

While these enterprises were largely an extension of things which had been advocated and even tried in the past, they were now approaching a size and variety to class them as distinct steps away from what had been the traditional concept of government and its purpose. To those who had not lost sight of older attitudes, they looked very much like surrender of liberties for immediate and temporary benefits. However, there were other experiments to come which would go far beyond these acts and attempt utterly new uses of federal power.

OUTRIGHT RELIEF BEGINS

One of the earliest was an outright relief measure, aimed at employment of idle youth. A Civilian Conservation Corps was set up to do work on the protection and preservation of the nation's forests and watersheds. By this device, much-needed conservation work was accomplished, and employment was given to about a quarter-million young men, whose pay went in large part to families at home.

AGRICULTURE STIMULATED

Agriculture, long in the doldrums, now came in for thorough attention. The farmer, once pretty much self-sufficient, had slowly become a specialist, raising but one or a limited number of crops. Formerly any surpluses had gone into foreign markets, particularly during the war, when new land had been broken by the plow to the tune of millions of acres. But agricultural practices had improved in Europe, and to a startling degree in some of the more backward areas, especially India, Egypt, and South America, where wages and costs were very low.

Thus the farmer had had to depend for income on prices set in world markets. But he was forced to acquire land, ever scarcer, and buy his equipment, supplies, and needs at prices held at relatively high levels by protective tariffs and price-fixing agreements in operation in this country. He felt this inequity keenly, and demanded that something be done to give him greater *parity* between his income and outgo.

Since his foreign markets had fallen off and the depression had cut down his home market, farm products were strongly in oversupply. The harder he worked trying to raise enough to feed and clothe his family and meet the payments on his mortgages and loans, the less his products were worth.

In an attempt to relieve this vicious situation, and keep the farmer off relief rolls and on the farm where he would one day be needed, the Congress set up the Agricultural Adjustment Act in 1933. Many arguments were offered for making this a federal rather than a state endeavor. By it, the farmer would be paid for keeping a certain portion of his land and facilities out of production until demand caught up with supply. To him, some such arrangement seemed no more than his due and quite in line with the tariff which had been used to protect industry for at least a hundred years. But the great question was whether any such activities by government had been intended under the Constitution. It might take a little time, but an opinion would one day be handed down, and rather emphatically, too.

Industry, despite the controversial tariff, as well as virtually all lines of business were in differing degrees of difficulty. Idle plants swelled the ranks of the unemployed, while poor adjustment between supply or goods and the demand for them on the one hand, and between management and labor on the other, made the outlook dubious. The three great religious groups, too, had taken rather a strong stand against unrestrained competition and what was considered to be the "harsh struggles of the market place." Even some segments of business believed that a certain amount of enforced co-operation within and between industries would be beneficial. Since the industries seemed reluctant to police themselves, politicians were quite willing to press the use of the government's services.

REGIMENTATION TRIED

As a hopeful remedy, Congress, at the President's urging, passed the National Industrial Recovery Act, also in 1933. By it, various related industrial groups were called upon to draw up industry-wide regulations, known as *codes*. These were to specify what were generally considered *fair practices* by organizations involved. They dealt with maximum hours and conditions of employment, with price cutting, and similar com-

LARGE PUBLIC PROJECTS WERE LAUNCHED TO PROVIDE WORK AND TO STIMULATE BUSINESS

mon concerns. Then a code authority was set up under a separate act to enforce the agreed-upon regulations.

It was a huge endeavor, and, while probably some housecleaning would benefit the industries involved, as well as the public generally, it could and should have been done without governmental involvement. But if we will not pick up and undertake our individual and group responsibilities, we are from now on very liable to find a federal authority that will be more than willing to step in and try its not always practiced hand. This activity was a most distinct break with the past; and was so looked upon by most of those whom it involved.

Since the setups called for were made under great urgency, many imperfections found their way into the proposed codes.

There was a liberal amount of ballyhoo, including parades, brass bands, and many speeches, to launch this NRA program. But management was immediately irked by its restrictions, and labor soon showed its dissatisfaction by a series of strikes. Almost at once, too, it was headed for a series of court tests.

As the over-all program began to falter, special provisions were made for particularly hard-hit industries by the setting up of "little NRA's." Such as an example was the Guffey-Snyder Coal Act, passed in 1935.

Since corporations and financial organizations had been brought under firmer controls, some attention was now given to organized labor. After many court tests through more than a hundred years, the right to strike had finally been upheld beyond further question in 1914. However, since employers had been bargaining collectively in many instances, it was felt that similar rights should be secured to labor. So legislation to aid labor groups now commenced to flow.

GOVERNMENT MEDDLING WAS BY NO MEANS NEW

Many an individualist began to think of Moses Austin and his grist mill, and anticipated the stultifying effects which government meddling could and would continue to have on attempts to get the world's work done.

Conservation had been used to "make work" through the CCC. The dust storms which were by now beginning to blow from plowed lands in the West, little used since the end of World War I, pointed up erosion as another possible project. Since loose soil drained off from the farms during spring freshets and played havoc with the streams, this tied in with farming on the one hand, and with navigation, irrigation, flood control, and water power on the other. The Water Power Act in 1920, plus the harnessing of the Colorado River begun by Coolidge and continued under Hoover, gave a pattern for developments along similar lines.

The still uncompleted Wilson Dam and its accompanying but long idle Muscle Shoals nitrate plant in Alabama were taken in hand. They formed the beginning of a development program which finally embraced the whole Tennessee River Valley. Since several states were involved, it was done under federal auspices. Later there would be similar projects at Grand Coulee in the state of Washington, and at Bonneville on the Columbia River above Portland, Oregon.

Such moves quite naturally brought stiff resistance from the major utility companies. They were looked upon as distinct threats to private enterprise and to individual initiative, both of which had bulked large in the foundations on which the country had grown. But unfortunately certain of the utility combines were primarily holding companies and subject to some well-placed criticism as respects the public interest.

To break up those organizations which were not primarily in the business of producing and selling electrical current, the Holding Companies Act was passed in 1935. Stock issues and securities to float such combinations had not always been entirely above suspicion; and so the Securities and Exchange Commission was created to supervise the issuance and sale of all stocks and bonds.

OUR CLOSE KNIT ECONOMY

One thing seemed to lead to another in an economy bound ever closer and closer together. From power lines it was an easy step over into communication facilities furnished by telegraph, telephone, and radio. These enterprises were placed under control of a Federal Communications Commission. Then another step focused government attention on the increasing number of highway bus lines and the trucking fleets operating across state lines. The powers of the Interstate Commerce Commission, which had dealt with the railroads and pipelines, was extended to rule over the destinies of these other means of communication and haulage. Fuel for them, and for the greater number of industrial concerns swinging from coal to oil, suggested regulation of the whole petroleum industry.

The tent of government was becoming pretty big, indeed far too big in the thinking of many. For the amount of restrictive and regulatory legislation passed by the Congress during the years 1933 through 1935, much of it under direction from the President, was enormous and far-reaching. However, unemployment and poverty still persisted. The "corrective" legislation had not given sufficient confidence to business so it had taken up the slack and put people back to work. So "pump-priming" had to be resorted to.

Public works from local through national levels were stimulated. At first there had been an outright dole, camouflaged slightly in a few instances. But in 1935 Congress placed the gigantic sum of $4,880,000,000 pretty much in the President's hands to finance the Works Progress Administration.

Also an attack was made upon poverty and dependence among older people, and upon softening the blows of unemployment of those in the younger age brackets. For these purposes Congress passed the Social Security Act in that same year.

FOUNDING FATHERS SHOCKED

If the founding fathers of our nation could have been aware of what would be taking place during these years in the mid-thirties, they would have been frankly shocked. They would have been astonished, no doubt, by changes which had taken place in a little less than a century and a half. And they would have been perhaps a little dismayed by the problems which these changes had produced. But it is doubtful, indeed, if they would have sanctioned the federal government as the medium through which so many of them were to be adjusted. Champions of a strong central government, such as Hamilton or even Theodore Roosevelt, would certainly have paused long and earnestly before advocating some of the measures now being

pushed through Congress. Had men lost their tough fiber? Had they grown soft, that they were so ready to hand over their hard-won rights and privileges and knuckle down to regimentation by a central *authority?*

There were many who lived through those difficult and trying years of depression who asked themselves these very questions. They had wondered, too, about the Constitution. It was often called the *framework* of our laws. But was it intended to be sufficiently flexible so that it could be twisted, turned, and stretched to encompass every whim and fancy that could be thought up?

WHERE WILL IT ALL END?

What would be the ultimate effect of this wholesale gathering of power into the hands of federal authority? What would happen to state and local government? Were we to be governed solely by a group of bureaucratic "masterminds," far-removed from the real problems at stake? And were not the rights of citizens and groups of citizens being snatched away from them by big handfuls?

It would take the reasoned words of no less august a body than the Supreme Court to give a final answer. And its decisions on such controversial laws as the National Industrial Recovery Act, Agricultural Adjustment Act, Railway Pension Act, and the Guffey-Snyder Coal Act finally began to be handed down.

It had not been until 1803 that Chief Justice Marshall had made the ruling stick that the high court could pass on the constitutionality of legislation enacted by any statutory body. During the next 131 years only 64 acts of the federal Congress had been set aside. This was about an average of one every other year. But now, within a two-year period, no less than six major statutes

323

were voided. The social legislation of this administration began to crash down like a house of cards. The principal acts rejected had revolved largely about one moot point —whether or not it is proper for Congress to tax all the people to pay subsidies to a particular group.

THE CONSTITUTION DEBATED

The impact of these decisions was enormous. Attention was focused upon the Constitution as perhaps never before. What was this document that a group of earnest men had produced in 1787 behind locked doors, and largely by a long series of compromises? Was it an inflexible, unyielding core that made life static and tied it unchangeably to late eighteenth-century thought and conditions? Or was it an almost *inspired* document, and a perpetual guarantee that men's rights and freedoms would not be snatched away from them under pressure, or at the convenience of those thirsting for power? Out of the din and the shouting that ensued, the public pretty generally held to the latter view. They decided that progress could be made under the Constitution, and that it was perhaps wiser to make it under such auspices, even though it might come more slowly.

There might possibly be something amiss, too, with the laws in the form in which they had been passed. Or it could be that the Court might reverse itself in later decisions on some of the points covered. It had been known to do just that.

The administration shrewdly attacked the Court rather than the Constitution. There was even a plan for changing the membership of this supreme tribunal. Also there would be an election in the fall of that year, 1936; and the whole matter was made an issue in the campaign.

The "forgotten man," who believed that certain more fortunate groups had been favored by the government rather directly in the past, was still of the mind that something needed to be done for him. Consequently even the Republicans teamed up a very liberal slate, composed of Governor Alfred M. Landon of Kansas for President, and Frank Knox, a Chicago publisher, for Vice-President. They were backed up with a remarkably liberal platform; but the man already in the White House, and even whose initials, *F.D.R.*, seemed potent, outpromised them. He managed to carry every state but two, the greatest landslide since the election of Washington.

THE BEGINNING OF WELFARE LEGISLATION

This was interpreted as a *mandate* from the people to push ahead with such social legislation. Through deaths and resignations, the make-up of the Supreme Court altered markedly in a short time. Certain of the bills, such as the one to bring relief in agriculture and others to bolster the position of labor, were introduced in modified form, and this time were upheld by the high Court.

There had been dire prophecies of dictatorship by the ultraconservative elements. But the great majority, whether or not they were well advised in what they did, gave their support to much of the "welfare" legislation which was then pushed through. The Constitution had been sufficiently stretched by liberal interpretation so that there was no occasion for an attempt to take over power through any show of force.

But power and rights flowed unmistakably out of the hands of the people and into the grasp of those who formed the rapidly mounting bureaucracy in Washington.

Men's privacy now became a matter of public record. Protections afforded by the Bill of Rights were worn down paper-thin. Restrictions were clamped down on individual initiative, and an unbelievable amount of regimentation was heaped upon every man and woman.

Once again the Constitution had stood the test, and it had been proved that man can live by *law*. But it would take a generation, perhaps two, to prove whether personal freedoms offered by some on the altar of expediency, or torn away from many, by legal, if not completely moral, enactments had done permanent injury to the traditional *American Way of Life*.

The years ahead would not be an entirely fair trial of these things, since there would be the stimulation of war and continuing preparedness. The final answer would not come until such artificial stimulants were removed, and the economy had to carry through a period of inevitable adjustment on its own vitality. The question of individual initiative and direction versus government regimentation is still to be proved.

OUR FOREFATHERS FOUGHT OFF REGIMENTATION

This is the same father and his sons who had ceased from their reaping to glare at the king's forester when he appeared to blaze their best trees, and so appropriate them for the use of the king's navy. The act was but one among many such by which their rights and their liberties were wrested from them. Suddenly they realized that governments that take rights away seldom give them back without a struggle. Will the day ever come when we will have to bring pressure to regain the freedoms that are being torn away from us year by year?

"There Never Was a Good War"

THERE had been serious attempts made to outlaw war throughout the early years of the twentieth century. But when it came in 1914 it was a frightful business. More and more effective weapons and the involvement of greater numbers of men were making of it a ghastly affair. Surely there was a sincere hope behind President Wilson's words at the time of our entry into it that it might be a "war to end all wars." Then, having experienced it, he had great hopes for the League, in which for a time later on we did take a minor part.

But Europe had been crushed by its four terrible years of bloodshed and destruction. The *peace* settled upon the Central Powers had been a severe one, and the whole continent was badly depressed. Beyond that, revolutionary forces were at work across the world. There had been such periods of upheaval down through the ages; and people were learning that history is often more pleasant to read about than to live through.

Russia had fallen to the Communists in 1917, while in 1922 Italy had gone fascist; and in 1933 an insecure representative government in Germany had handed over that nation to the Nazi Hitler. On the other side

of the world, Japan had been building up military strength preparatory to taking over control of Asia.

All of these nations had paid loud lip service to the cause of peace. They had been members of the League of Nations, despite the absence of the United States. And, one by one, as restrictions were laid upon them and it suited their purposes, they dropped out of that body. Although there were a considerable number of Japanese now living along our Pacific coast, they were but few in comparison with the huge numbers who had streamed in as immigrants from the three unsettled European lands. Consequently, because of birthright or relatives still there, many of our people had a lively interest in the moves being made by these other nations. Also their political and military activities had a direct influence upon our commerce and our enterprises in foreign lands.

A little over two months after taking office in 1933, President Roosevelt called upon the leading nations of the world to subscribe to a nonaggression pact. It was barely three weeks after this invitation went out that England, France, Germany, and Italy did sign a solemn agreement to keep the peace for a ten-year period. But treaties had been in many cases looked upon as mere "scraps of paper" during World War I; and while this peace gesture appeared like progress on the surface, Germany was stirring up trouble in Austria before the year was out. Italy and Japan had shown unmistakable evidence that aggression had become a prime policy with them, and now Germany was pursuing the same course. The three countries were a most unsettling influence throughout 1934; and before that year had run out Italy was heavily involved in conquest in North Africa; and Manchuria, across the world in Asia, was in Japanese hands.

DICTATORS SEIZE POWER

Early in 1935 Italian troops had pushed into Ethiopia; Germany had claimed and taken over the rich Saar Valley; and Japan was sinking sharp claws deep into China. Later in that year we were close to trouble with Italy over her invasion of Ethiopia, because of oil rights hastily ceded to American interests by the emperor of that unhappy land. Although we were emerging slowly from the depression at home, dictators across the world were enough of a concern so that confidence was difficult to build.

The deep rumble of war on far horizons kept up throughout 1936. But when the army clique seized power in Japan in February, 1937, and Hitler marched troops into the Rhineland the following month, strife no longer seemed quite so remote. Then, to add further tinder, violent civil war broke out in Spain, and a few days later Greece fell into the hands of a dictator.

Together with social conditions at home, these international incidents, no doubt, lent considerable weight in bringing about the landslide which re-elected Roosevelt for a second term. Matters, fortunately, were fairly stable in this hemisphere. But with so many explosive forces at large, and some of them already ablaze, common defense prompted twenty-one American republics to sign a neutrality pact in December. Only five days earlier the world had been shocked by the abdication of the king of England. The question in many minds was whether there could be a deeper meaning in this move than that the man was determined to marry a commoner. The air was rife with suspicions and doubt, and international relations were at an extremely low ebb.

Russia had taken a lively part in League affairs for several years, but had been heavily involved within her own borders. Internal strife had divided her power, and the prevailing opinion was that this country was a huge sham, operating behind a curtain of propaganda. During 1937 a bloody purge finally concentrated control firmly in the hands of one group, and the Russians now seemed better prepared to look out upon and take a hand in the unsettled world conditions all about.

RULE BY MEN, NOT BY LAW

Italy and Germany agreed to aid the strong man trying to grasp power in Spain. Russia, having an interest in communist groups in that country, rose to the challenge and took sides in the fighting there. It was easy to see in these moves a sort of dress rehearsal for another world war. Peace still had its staunch advocates, especially our own President; but its probable chances grew slimmer, as one discouraging month followed hard on the heels of the one before.

There was further evidence of trouble in England. Stories began to leak out of the pacifist rallies among students, who protested they would not fight under any circumstances. Then the government fell, and in May, Chamberlain came into office. By fall the British cabinet was trying to dissuade Hitler from war by promising to cede colonies to Germany; and appeasement would be used to "buy" time in which to arm.

SEEMINGLY LITTLE HOPE FOR "PEACE IN OUR TIME"

In December the Japanese, now deep in China, bombed one of our gunboats, and a serious incident was avoided only by a prompt apology. The Land of the Rising Sun was not yet quite secure enough to risk a brush with Uncle Sam.

However, the President took this occasion to let the world know that we did not intend to bury our heads ostrich-like in the sands of isolation. We were definitely not interested in "peace at any price." And to add substance to his words, he asked Congress for two billion dollars to build up the Navy.

Italy and Japan had been busy carving out "a place in the sun"; and as 1938 began Hitler was now ready to put his growing military machine through a few practice marches. He seized personal control of the Army in February, and on March 12 swept into Austria. From then on the pace quickened.

The Austrian seizure was quickly accomplished; and in May the German dictator journeyed to Rome to join hands with Mussolini. Between them, they felt they were prepared to humble Europe and then give attention to a wider field. Internal trouble in France at about this same time seemed to indicate a soft spot to the west. Both because he needed all-out production, and for its propaganda value as well, the Nazi leader, now back at home, immediately put the entire German nation under forced labor.

But he still had situations which must be strengthened to the east. Shrieking out his demands for all the world to hear, he called for a slice of Czechoslovakia, basing his claim on the fact that the area was made up principally of German residents. With his demands went loud sword rattling, sufficient to bring a parley of France, Italy, Britain, and the Germans at Munich. From this historic session, Chamberlain flew home to cheering crowds in London with the spurious promise of "peace in our time."

Within a week Hitler had badgered England and France into agreeing to his taking an even greater slice of Czech territory than he had at first asked. The peace, such as it was, was being bought at an ever-stiffer price, and principally at the expense of the smaller powers.

TENSION MOUNTS AT HOME

Tension was mounting throughout the world, and here at home quite as much as in Europe and in Asia. Evidence of how extensive were its effects came in a Sunday evening radio broadcast which featured an "Attack from Mars" so dramatically that it caused a widespread panic up and down the Atlantic seaboard. As 1938 passed into history, a murky, cloudy twilight seemed to settle down over the hopes of peaceable men.

On the fourth of January, 1939, the President urgently asked Congress to vote an extensive defense program. The year ahead was unmistakably one of decision, and it began to shape up rapidly. By the end of March the Spanish civil war had burned out, and Hitler began to raise his shrill voice and extend his reach. Again facing to the east, his eye now seemed centered on Poland. Britain and France stiffened their re-

THE WORLD MARCHES THROUGH OUR LIVING ROOMS

First by radio and now by television the affairs of the whole earth are paraded past us as we sit in our own homes. We often see or hear news as it actually happens. Our world has become *one world*, whether for good, or for evil; and we are a distinct part of it, and thus have increased responsibilities we must fulfil. How expansive and complicated life has become in the years since our native land was founded!

sistance and promptly pledged aid to that country. Two weeks later Roosevelt promised to defend the "neighbors" of the United States with arms and financial aid. Sides were being taken, for appeasement was proving a dull weapon against the will of fanatical men in control in Rome and in Berlin.

The king and queen of England, on an official visit to Canada, dropped down for a call in Washington; and at a state dinner, the President gave them a strong pledge of friendship. As though to counter this gesture, and to throw the lineup off balance, Hitler suddenly signed a nonaggression pact with Russia on August 21. The immediate purpose of this move was clearly evident, and brought a plea from the White House for

avoidance of war between Germany and Poland. The latter country willingly agreed to keep the peace. The former was naturally noncommittal.

The handwriting was by now beginning to glow on the wall; and on August 25, the English Parliament voted war powers to the government. On the last day of that month Hitler received a curt note from the British refusing to coerce the Poles into giving up Danzig and other territory.

This act pulled the trigger, and the following day, September 1, in a broad path cut by a hail of aerial bombs, the German host swept into Poland. Two months short of twenty-one years after the termination of the first holocaust, World War II began.

329

The United States would, for the time being, be an uneasy spectator on the sidelines. In the minds of some, the three thousand miles of ocean to the east and a wider ocean to the west would insulate this nation from the war. We had become embroiled in the previous contest through our extensive shipment of arms and the granting of financial aid. Although *neutral* at the moment, there would again be a demand for assistance. And to meet it this time without entanglements, we would put all war shipments on a "cash and carry" basis. But by early November, Congress repealed the embargo; and at the turn of the year the President asked this body to grant him war powers.

Germany made an easy conquest in the East, and early in 1940 overran Denmark, Norway, Holland, Belgium, and then took Paris. Russia had seized little Finland; and the all-out pounding of England from the air was getting under way.

To the accompaniment of distant shellfire and exploding bombs, two unprecedented political steps were taken in this country. On June 19, the President named two unusually able Republicans to his official family, thus forming a *coalition* Cabinet. Henry M. Stimson became Secretary of War, and Frank Knox, the vice-presidential candidate in the last campaign, was made Secretary of the Navy.

About a month later, the Democratic Convention, meeting in Chicago, nominated Franklin Roosevelt to run for a *third* term. A tradition in regard to the highest office in the land which had carried forward from the time of Washington was about to be shattered. In the November elections Roosevelt won over the Republican candidate, Wendell Willkie. Sentiment had run high during the campaign; but the country was now definitely girding for war, and some sixteen and a half million men had already been registered for "selective service."

In 1941 the European conflict flowed down across the Mediterranean into North Africa, while the Germans broke their agreement with the Russians and began their drive deep into the communist land. German submarines harrying our shipping attacked one destroyer, and then sank a second in the Atlantic. Consequently our attention was strongly focused toward Europe.

PEARL HARBOR ATTACKED

But behind our backs, the Japanese were making stealthy moves in the Pacific. By mid-October there was a Cabinet shake-up in that country, and an army firebrand seized tight control. Within a month this fanatical new government dispatched a special envoy to Washington for a parley. But the demands laid before our government were utterly out of reason, and the talks broke down at the end of November.

Tension then mounted rapidly, particularly when Japan began moving troops into Indo-China. There was a British fleet at Singapore, and a clash in that area seemed inevitable. As the situation rocketed on toward war, President Roosevelt sent a message direct to the Japanese emperor on December 6 urging peace.

The reply came the very next morning. But rather than being delivered through diplomatic channels to Washington, it burst out of the sky over our naval base in the mid-Pacific. Pearl Harbor had been attacked. The date was December 7, 1941.

As of that Sunday morning, the country was somewhat divided on many internal questions. Also, despite selective service trainees in great numbers in camps and a portion of the national guard already called to active duty, there was absolutely no enthusiasm for war. As first reports began to blare in over loud-speakers, the immediate reaction was another "Men from Mars" stunt, a radio gag in rather bad taste.

Then, as the truth of the sobering news stabbed home, jaws clamped shut, fists clenched up, and before nightfall this country was united as one man, and to an extent which perhaps it had never known before. We, too, had our part in this grim "total" war. We had thrilled to the grit and resolve of Churchill as he had told the British, but eighteen months before, that their portion would be little but "blood, sweat, and tears." Now, and for the better part of the next four years, it would be our portion, too.

PEACE COMES AT LAST

The unconditional surrender in Europe would not terminate hostilities there until May 7, 1945. Then the humbled Japanese, finally crumbled into helplessness by two explosions of the most horrible and lethal weapon ever devised, finally laid down their arms on August 14. By the time of this final victory, President Roosevelt, but three months into his *fourth* term in office, would be dead of cerebral hemorrhage. And the United Nations, which had come into being as much by his instigation as by any other man's, would already be in session in San Francisco, trying to find sound ground on which to build a peace in what had become, without a trace of doubt, "One World."

Some lessons had been rather dearly learned from the war experience. Some had not been so firmly and fully grasped. Once again, as after the first World War, the hope

that peace would follow almost automatically caused an unsound decision to be made. And it was made, in no small part, at the breakfast tables across the land. The one idea was to get the "boys" home, wash away the stains and stresses of war, and get back to *normalcy* as rapidly as possible. Again we had forgotten that the world was peopled by some who were not exactly men of goodwill and who responded favorably only to force.

A FAULTY DECISION

Our armed forces were pared down to the lowest possible minimum. Our costly armor was either junked or put in "moth balls." We were thus placed in a precarious position in trying to maintain the peace in a world in large part dominated by those determined to live by bluff and by outmoded and fallacious pagan philosophies. The seeds of a second war had been sown in the devastation left by the first world-wide conflict. Could it be that the same thing was happening again?

It is, however, not within the scope of this work to relive those months of "blood, sweat, and tears" in the years from 1941 through 1945. Neither does it seem prudent to attempt a prophetic vision of what the years that spread ahead can or may hold.

However, we have come a long journey together in this, and in the companion first volume. They can, and should, have pointed up two mighty and priceless heritages which are our common possession. It may, therefore, be prudent in the concluding section which follows, to consider what our responsibilities in connection with them may be, so that our freedom in their enjoyment may be passed on unimpaired to our children.

The Hope of the Nation

T IS indeed a long time since that faraway day when an errant star swept past a young and still infirm earth, tore loose and dragged away a satellite that became our moon, and spread wide the land masses we call the continents. But what we are today is a summation of all that has happened since the earth was created.

Man has, so far as we are aware, left written records of what has befallen him during no more than the last six thousand years. It was at the beginning of that period that civilizations were growing up not far from the land bridge which is Palestine. Later these civilizing forces swept on to the West, first through Europe and then jumped across the ocean with the earliest settlers. Here in our own country, we have added our own contribution, the *American Way of Life,* perhaps the best expression in many ways of what God intended should be man's lot.

Surely human dignity has risen to greater heights for greater numbers in America than in any other country. In a little over three centuries man brought to finer fruition on these shores more real progress than the fifty-seven previous centuries had yielded anywhere else on earth. That is indeed a remarkable accomplishment and forms a proud heritage. To the American, the expression "My Country" can thus be a most comforting, a most securing thought.

Unfortunately there seems to have been a recent period in which "My Country" has been taken too casually and too much as a matter of course by too many people. There are situations developing in which it would appear that we, like Esau of old, tend to look upon what we have achieved as a mess of pottage, to be idly bartered for momentary advantages. Some serious-minded people begin to wonder if the expression "My Country" is now backed by the warmth and concern with which it was once buttressed, and with which it still must be, if our land is to continue the mighty heritage our fathers and grandfathers believed it to be.

Are we deceived into believing that the growth we have achieved and the accomplishments which have been made are unlimited? Are we falsely convinced that power built up in our past is so unlimited that any future demands can be met without earnest striving on our part? Is the structure that has been reared so tremendous that it is above both physical and moral laws, and capable of absorbing every demand which the misguided can thrust upon it? Are we too complacent and have we come to a point of apathy—of preferring to let matters take their course? Are we living in false security, prepared to see our freedoms and our liberties frittered away, while we attempt to make of life one long series of easy fleshpots?

These are stern questions, but they should lie squarely upon the heart of every red-blooded man and woman who does say with a touch of pride, "America is MY country."

In this volume we have seen little handfuls and small boatloads of men arrive on these shores, and by dint of extreme effort gain a foothold from unwilling Nature. It must have seemed to us almost as though a beneficent God had set apart this land so that a great experiment might here be carried through to successful fulfilment.

TWO FUNDAMENTALS WE MUST NEVER FORGET

What that experiment sought to prove was two very fundamental things. Both had been understood by few down through the long centuries. Many had striven to give them form and substance, while some had even sacrificed life itself in the hope that these truths might profit all men. But it was not until settlement began here that they became clear enough for men to fully understand them to the point where great numbers were willing to fight by every means at their command to make them come true for all.

The first was the fact that only the individual human being can generate human energy. Yes, he can be driven to it in a halfhearted way under the lash; but it was now shown, beyond all mistaking the truth, that such energy flows most abundantly when it is generated by the individual in his *self-interest*.

The companion truth was that this same individual *alone* can best control the energy he generates.

Here was a sharp break with the pagan past and the form of government and governmental authority which pagan philosophies had established and maintained, at least as long as man had recorded his experiences as written history.

By these two truths, man must be *Free,* so that he may better work out his own destiny. When he stands staunchly on his own two feet, is his own master, and employs his efforts under the drive of self-interest, he goes farther and faster, and with greater security to all concerned. There are bound to be points in such free competition where he may come into conflict with the rights of others. But where there is serious conflict of rights, his activities may approach a point where their further pursuit would no longer be in his self-interest. Self-interest will continue to rule in such situations; and he soon learns to join with others for common purposes beyond their capacity as individuals.

The colonists learned these deep truths quickly by first-hand experience. They proved to their complete satisfaction that they did best and made most certain progress when their efforts were untrammeled by man-made restrictions. They had shucked off the hampering restraints which they had known in the Old World at the hands of monarchial governments. And when these governments tried to transplant such handicaps into this country through royally appointed governors, the colonists were incensed; and in some cases resorted to arms to contest their rights.

Finally, there came a showdown in the matter of the right of the English Parliament to regiment them in the "public interest." The Revolutionary War was the result; and the Freedom thus bought was bound to be cherished and perpetuated. Their experience with government restrictions had been sufficient so that when they were forced to set up some common authority for the thirteen colonies, now states, it was at first so weak as to be well-nigh worthless. They preferred to err on the side of prudence.

ENERGETIC GOVERNMENT IS ALWAYS OPPRESSIVE

Even when the time came to strengthen this central government, so that there might be a "more perfect Union," Thomas Jefferson expressed the caution common to all, when he said, "I own I am not a friend of the energetic government. *It is always oppressive.*"

Thus it was the sincere hope of the framers of the Constitution that what they provided would be not only a government of law, rather than of men, but also that it would be so constituted that it would not become a heavy yoke about the necks of the governed.

The consequence was an authority most carefully thought out, and planned with the chief purpose of making freedom and liberty real and unalienable. And for many years it was the principal concern of electors, and of those whom they chose for office, to keep it so. The federal government—all government—was to be small in numbers and, by today's standards, in power. Still it was sufficient to adequately meet and overcome every situation with which it was confronted.

Actually it was not until well along toward the end of the last century that its original conception began to change, and then but slowly. Even during the early years of the present century our federal administrative body increased in numbers and in stature at a fairly moderate pace.

Then, in a moment of maladjustment, of uncertainty, and of doubt; and in no small measure with the support of a large proportion of its citizens, the whole philosophy of government was altered. Within twenty years our federal establishment has become probably the largest single human enterprise in the world. It has now more than two million employees, an increase in the nature of fourfold in the short space of twenty years. It currently deals with every possible phase of our national life from birth to death, and in such a manner that even the best intentioned person is bound to unwittingly run counter to its laws, edicts, and demands.

Its expenditures run into scores of billions of dollars, laying a burden—on the average —of more than one-quarter of the earning power of every employed man and woman in the land. This tax upon income is an ever-increasing and backbreaking *tithe*. Beyond that are a host of other "hidden" taxes which bulk large. But, worse still, its expenditures are so great that it dare not follow the pay-as-you-go method of meeting its outgo, and there is an accumulated debt that amounts to some $7,500 heaped upon every family in the United States.

THIS IS YOUR GOVERNMENT

This is *your* government, and under these conditions very definitely *your* deep concern. For there is no escaping the following brutal fact. Either you run your government, or it will surely run you. Either you put your shoulder to the wheel and get it back into the way it should be headed, or you may well find it bogged down in a morass, and your freedom and your fortunes with it.

Government is your business just as surely as the sun rises and sets day after day, year after year. And if you do not choose to make it your business, your liberties can go down with a setting sun at no distant time, and the night that ensues can be dark, long, and bleak.

Do not forget what the American Experiment carried out right here on this continent proved. You, and only you, can generate energy. And you, and only you, can expand that energy to the greatest possible benefit, not only of yourself but of all. In a moment of weakness and forgetfulness, we tended to lay these truths on the shelf. We let a new pattern creep into our thinking and into our scheme of government, and the trend is still dangerously in the false direction we chose to go—toward regimentation of our energy and of our lives.

KEEP THE RIGHT OF "CHOICE"

Certainly neither you nor your children would care to wake up some morning and find that you were no longer able to choose the job you would prefer. Or, quite frankly, would you rather have to obtain a work permit from some bureaucrat and then have him assign you to a job? Do not feel that such conditions cannot come about, for they lie ahead very certainly and down the pathway along which we are at present drifting. Government is not the only offender in this respect. There are others equally capable, and some of them seemingly quite anxious to put you under their control.

The criminal loses much of his individual identity when he becomes no more than a *number* on the records of a prison or penitentiary. By the same token, there is not much to guarantee individuality if one becomes no more than a number in a social-

**GOVERNMENT EXPRESSES
ITSELF AS POWER—
POLICE POWER**

security file, on an employee's identification button, or on a union dues card.

As we have seen, the early 1930's were a disturbing period. In some ways it was a "national emergency." So, too, were the years of the next decade, when revolutionary forces in search of freedom boiled over across the world. These forces are still seething, and times are unsettled. Thus the declaration of national emergency becomes a continuing pretext for the power-hungry to use. If it is employed enough times without serious opposition, the public comes to accept it as a

335

natural and to be expected condition. And therein lies a real threat.

RESIST REGIMENTATION

While we are willing to surrender certain liberties as a matter of self-interest in times of actual emergency, we are liable, if we do not contest every such demand, to find that we have been bluffed and cajoled into parting with our heritage. Further regimentation lies in back and just beyond every future seizure of rights by government. Our forefathers energetically resisted regimentation, and so should we.

Sometimes we rise to these occasions manfully, but in a way that is not always to our advantage in all respects. Such a decision was arrived at across the breakfast tables of this country in the summer of 1945, as was briefly mentioned in the previous section. It has caused us much harm since, in that we washed out our military power and jettisoned much of our armament before the world was ready for peace.

But parents wanted their sons and daughters home from the far corners of the world, and as soon as possible. The sons, particularly, had been irked by the forced equality, the lack of freedom of action, and the regimentation which the donning of a uniform always imposes. The war was over, the mass murder had ceased. So the natural urge was to help loved ones out of the stultifying conditions under which they had had to serve.

There was another consideration involved as well. The government had been forced to step in and break up families. And when it can control and direct the destinies of the family—the very basis of our national life—disaster stares us hard in the face. Each family wanted its sons and its daughters back. It preferred they live by self-control, rather

than by communal control. And so insistent was the demand that a somewhat reluctant government had no choice but to take heed.

Definitely we do not like to be equalized, to be leveled-off, to be reduced to common proportions. We are basically opposed to regimentation. Why then do we continue to tolerate it, yes, even to encourage it by partial support, or by indifference to the inroads being made? Are we actually courting our own undoing?

The foregoing brings up the fact that many of our excesses, particularly political ones, have been brought about by *anxieties*. Unfavorable conditions fill many with worry, uneasiness, dread, and misgiving. The tide of troubles cuts us adrift from former secure moorings; and we float with the current of uncertainty.

BEWARE OF PROMISES

The strong man, the dictator, or the clique seeking power either seize upon such states of mind when they are found ready-made, or they do their best to stimulate and expand such anxieties. Then, they fawningly offer leadership by any dubious methods they can make appear reasonable. People adrift, with little to believe in, will fall for anything. Craving "security," they willingly pawn their liberties for spurious promises.

It has been said that no dictatorship ever came into being without careful preparation for it; and there is one motive deep in human nature which it usually can work upon most successfully. The idea of *fatherhood* is, of course, universal. Consequently, those hoping to gain power over others do their best to have their dupes feel like *children*, and, in turn, have themselves accepted in the role of a *father*. We were joking about this situ-

(*Continued on page 369*)

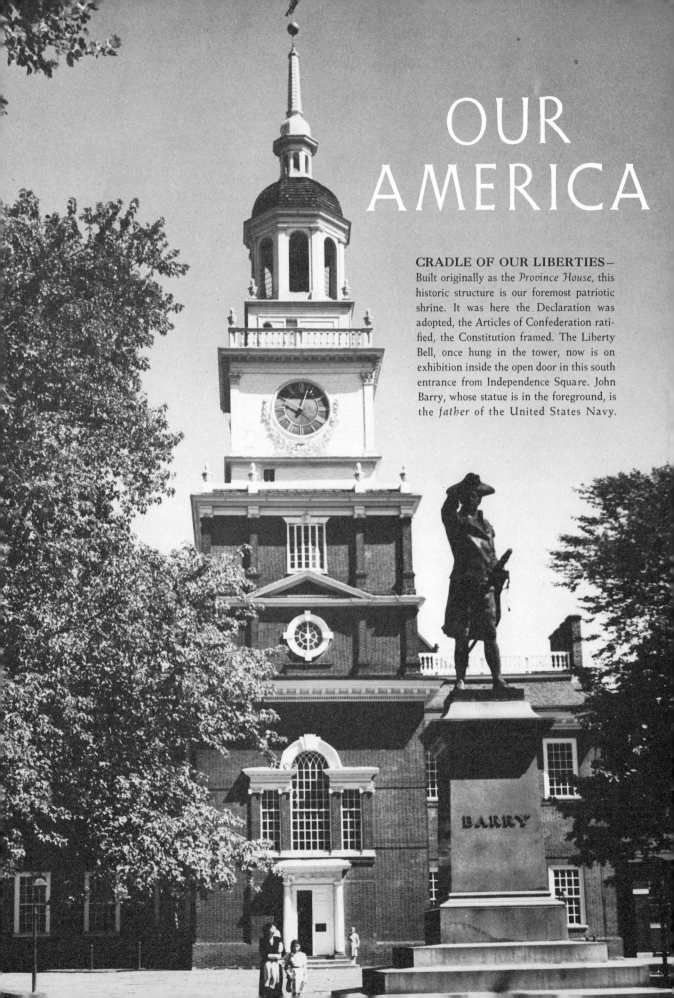

OUR AMERICA

CRADLE OF OUR LIBERTIES—
Built originally as the *Province House*, this
historic structure is our foremost patriotic
shrine. It was here the Declaration was
adopted, the Articles of Confederation ratified, the Constitution framed. The Liberty
Bell, once hung in the tower, now is on
exhibition inside the open door in this south
entrance from Independence Square. John
Barry, whose statue is in the foreground, is
the *father* of the United States Navy.

THE WHITE HOUSE—Official residence of the President, work on which was started in 1792, and first occupied by John Adams in 1800. Nothing now remains of the original but the outer shell, the entire interior having been built anew during the Truman administration, and reoccupied in 1952.

THE LINCOLN MEMORIAL—This very impressive structure, built of white Colorado marble in the form of a Greek temple, and which took 10 years to complete, houses the colossal seated figure of Lincoln, carved by Daniel Chester French the famous sculptor in Georgia marble.

JEFFERSON AND WASHINGTON MEMO-RIALS—The tall shaft of the Washington Monument, be-gun in 1848, but not completed until 1885, here shows far up the Mall from the more recently dedicated memorial to the author of the Declaration, who was our third president.

THE PENTAGON—The largest office building in the world, covering 29 acres, and the headquarters of the Department of National Defense. It is made up of five rings, five-sided, and five stories high. Bus lines land workers in the basement. Floors are joined by ramps, not by stairways.

MOUNT VERNON—The home of George and Martha Washington, on the west bank of the Potomac, 15 miles below the national capital. It was built by an elder brother in 1743, but added to after it passed into the hands of the *Father of His Country* in 1752. Now a most popular shrine.

GOVERNOR'S PALACE, WILLIAMSBURG, Va.—An exact restoration of the symbol of royal authority built in the colonial capital of Virginia in 1715. Here during 70 years lived the royal governors; and then Patrick Henry and Thomas Jefferson, governors under the United States.

OLD MAN OF THE MOUNTAINS – How this remarkable profile must have impressed the first white men who came upon it in Franconia Notch in New Hampshire. Of this, that state's most notable scenic feature, Daniel Webster once said, "Up in Franconia Mountains God Almighty has hung out a *Sign* to show that in New England He makes *men.*" The face is 48 feet from head to chin, and looks across Profile Lake lying some 1200 feet below.

TOMB OF THE UNKNOWN SOLDIER– Symbolic of all the graves, marked and unmarked, of those who have given their lives in the defense of our country. It stands in Arlington National Cemetery, 400 acres of landscaped woodland across the Potomac from Washington, and takes its name from *Arlington House,* once the home of Robert E. Lee. Beside this solemn shrine, visited by millions of Americans, ceremonies paying honor to the nation's heroes are held.

PORTLAND HEAD LIGHT, MAINE – As early as 1496, Sebastian Cabot sailed along the coast of what is now Maine. What an aid to the navigators of those early days such beacons as this famous light at the south edge of Casco Bay would have been. Of Maine's 16 counties, ten are on tidewater, and shipping has been most important in the state's development. Portland harbor, to which this light is a guide, is 116 miles nearer Europe than any other American port. First American ship was built nearby in 1607.

COOLIDGE HOME, PLYMOUTH, VERMONT–Several thousand people came to this home to confer with the newly elected Vice President as he vacationed here in 1920. Here, too, he was vacationing when word was brought from a neighboring home of the telephoned news of the death of President Harding. By the light of a coal oil lamp in its parlor, Calvin Coolidge repeated the oath read by his aged father, and in the early morning hours of August 2, 1923 became thirtieth president of the United States.

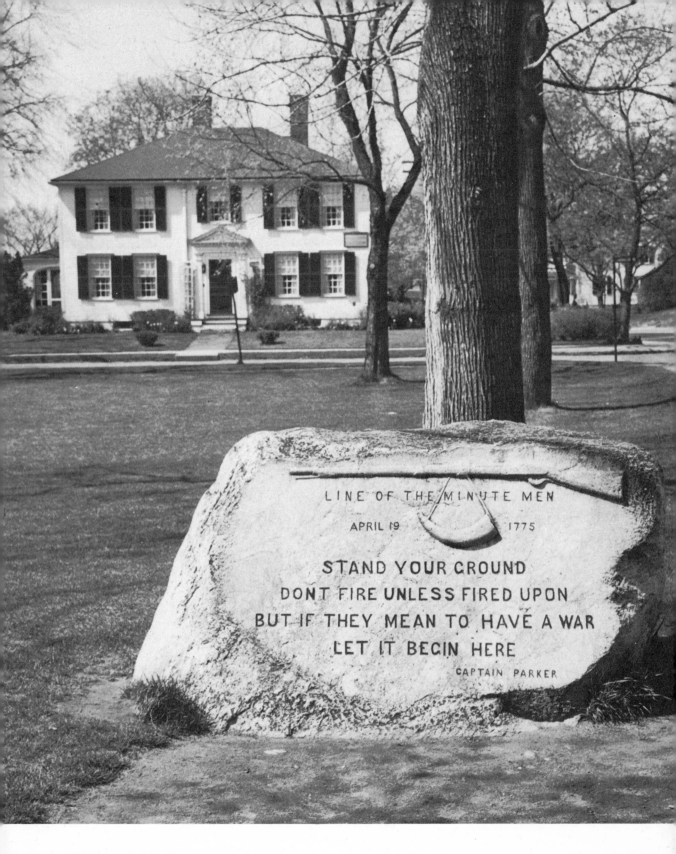

LINE OF THE MINUTE MEN

APRIL 19   1775

STAND YOUR GROUND
DON'T FIRE UNLESS FIRED UPON
BUT IF THEY MEAN TO HAVE A WAR
LET IT BEGIN HERE

CAPTAIN PARKER

LINE OF THE MINUTE MAN—Here on Lexington Common is probably the most historic spot in history-rich Massachusetts. It was near this monument that the *Shot Heard 'Round the World* was fired in the early morning of April 19, 1775, after Captain Parker had spoken the immortal words engraved upon this marker, showing the point where the *Minute Men* from surrounding towns had been drawn up to intercept the British force from Boston, against which Paul Revere had sounded the alarm during his famous ride. Which side fired this first shot has never been known, but patriots fell in the exchange that took place here. In the background is the home of one of them, Jonathan Harrington. Wounded in the early moments of the fray, he dragged himself to his front steps, and died at his wife's feet.

CONGREGATIONAL CHURCH, FARMINGTON—

One of the two Connecticut churches built on the *meeting house* plan still standing. The delicate lines of its Wren steeple are deceptive, for it has outlived hurricanes and gales since 1772; and many a surveyor working nearby has turned his transit upon it, only to find it setting as plum and true upon its six oak posts as it was the day that its master builder, Judah Woodruff, first erected his masterpiece. Two other churches preceded it.

OLD SLATER MILL, PAW-TUCKET, RHODE ISLAND

— Our smallest state is richly endowed with historic shrines; but few have greater significance than this mill for the power spinning of cotton, erected in 1790 by the textile pioneer, Samuel Slater, the first such plant in America. During the next 26 years he built other extensive cotton and woolen mills in this state and in Massachusetts, and may thus be considered the *father* of the highly important New England textile industry.

NIAGARA FALLS — Looking at the American and Canadian Falls from the center of Rainbow Bridge, which here spans the longest peaceful border in all the world. At the right, in troubled water stirred up by this mighty cataract, sails one of the most famous boats of all times, the *Maid of the Mist*, yet ever bent on peaceful missions. One of the great natural wonders of the world, the falls have long been the rendezvous of honeymoon couples. Spanning the border, as they do, makes these falls highly significant. The name is Indian, and of several possible derivations the most plausible is from a term meaning *thunder of water*, millions of tons of which drop 167 feet here every day.

FABULOUS NEW YORK CITY—At the left is a view of the midtown area showing the United Nations buildings in the foreground, and the *Empire State* and the *Chrysler* towers in the background, the two highest man-made structures. The glass-sided slab houses the *Secretariat* of the several nations, while the lower building with dome is the General Assembly Hall, international forum.

At the right, behind tiny Battery Park, are the spires of other tall buildings at the southern tip of Manhattan Island. Beyond stretches the whole of the island. How the early Dutch settlers would marvel at the use put to the land purchased so cheaply from its Indian owners in the year 1626.

Below is a corner of Central Park, whose 840 acres stretching 2½ miles along Fifth Avenue is the most valuable piece of undeveloped real estate in the world. This lake is a popular rendezvous of sailors on leave and usually covered with boats.

COURT HOUSE, NEW CAS-TLE, DELAWARE — New Castle was the first town laid out in Delaware, and the colonial capital until 1777. It was also the home of three signers of the Declaration. Ten years later the first ratification of the Constitution was made at the new State House, built in Dover.

BETSY ROSS HOUSE — In this typical pre-Revolutionary home, about two blocks from Independence Hall in Philadelphia, lived Mrs. John Ross, whose husband had signed the Declaration. Mrs. Ross is supposed to have made our first American flag in 1777, from a design just approved by the Congress.

GEORGE WASHINGTON BRIDGE — One of America's mighty traffic arteries, connecting upper New York City with New Jersey. Near its western end begins a Turnpike which each day permits huge numbers of trucks and autos to traverse New Jersey without encountering a single traffic light.

STATE HOUSE, ANNAPOLIS
— Many historic meetings have taken place in the fine old structure above. Near the center of population in Revolutionary times, it also lay midway between the newly formed states. The First Federal Constitutional Convention met here in 1786, paving the way for the successful session held in Philadelphia.

HISTORIC HARPERS FERRY
— Here on the extreme eastern edge of West Virginia, at the junction of the Potomac and Shenandoah Rivers, 55 miles northwest of Washington, the misguided Kansan, John Brown, attempted to seize the government arsenal in 1859, a nation-rocking incident at the time. The town is largely hidden at the right.

HIGHEST MOTOR ROAD IN THE EAST
—North Carolina's Great Smoky Mountains contain some of the most beautiful scenery in the world. Here we look from the Blue Ridge Parkway toward Mt. Mitchell, highest mountain in Eastern America. A motor road now runs to within a short distance of the top of this famous 6,684 foot peak.

CHURCH STREET, CHARLESTON, S.C.—Historic street in a gracious and historic city, filled with memories of its past, when it was the fourth city among those in the American colonies. The steeple is old St. Phillip's.

OLDEST HOUSE IN AMERICA—Built by the Spanish in St. Augustine, Florida, in 1565, it has flown four flags—Spanish, English, Confederate, and American. It is near the oldest fortress on our soil, now Fort Marion.

DETROIT FROM THE LAKE—Michigan's first city, and fourth in the nation, is the *motor capital* of the world. It was the territorial capital from 1805 to 1835; and was the state capital until 1847, when the state government moved to Lansing.

LINCOLN VILLAGE — An authentic reproduction at Rockport, Indiana, of the frontier settlement near and in which Abraham Lincoln spent 14 formative years. Here he went to school briefly, and here he was employed at farm work and as a store clerk. From its leading citizens he borrowed books, began to read law, and add to his limited schooling.

NEWCOM TAVERN, DAYTON, OHIO — The river from which this state, the *gateway to the west*, takes its name was the settlers' first means of entry to its rich lands. So great was their influx that many hostelries sprung up to care for these travelers. Many of them are still preserved today, proud reminders of this proud state's part in the westward thrust of our country. Their guest books would list many names famous in our history in early days of the 19th century.

OGLETHORPE STATUE, SAVANNAH — Erected in memory of the socially-minded soldier by whose determination the Georgia colony was founded in 1733, Savannah being its first settlement. The original site selected for this city was on a 40 foot bluff, 18 miles from the mouth of the Savannah River up stream.

OUR NATIONAL CAPITAL—Now the meeting place of the two houses of Congress, this handsome structure formerly housed the Supreme Court as well. It is 751 by 350 feet, and was built of Virginia sandstone painted white, while the extensions are of Massachusetts marble. The wings, added in 1811, were partially burned by the British in 1814. The central building with its then low dome was completed in 1827; but the present dome was not in place until 1865. During recent years the building has undergone extensive interior alterations, strengthening, and redecoration and modernization, but in keeping with its original design. *Freedom* tops the lantern above the dome.

ABRAHAM LINCOLN'S BIRTHPLACE – Of its many historic shrines, none is more popular than this humble cabin, housed in an imposing granite structure on the original Thomas Lincoln farm, three miles south of Hodgensville, Kentucky. At Knob Creek is the site of the first home Lincoln remembered; and many of the scenes associated with his boyhood in this area have been sought out and suitably marked.

THE HERMITAGE, HOME OF JACKSON – This is the stately entrance to the beautiful home built by *Old Hickory*, twelve miles from Nashville, Tennessee. It was here that he returned from the battle of New Orleans a conquering hero and the idol of the Nation; and from here he guided the destiny of the Republic during the *Jacksonian Era*. He, and his beloved wife, Rachel, are buried in a garden near the house.

VULCAN — This largest iron man in the world looks out over Birmingham, Ala., great southern iron producing center from the top of nearby Red Mountain. He is 53 feet tall, exceeded in size only by the Statue of Liberty, and was cast from pig iron smelted from ore in local blast furnaces.

RUNE STONE — A replica five times its original size of the *Kensington Stone*, believed to have been left by Norse explorers in 1362 near the present site of Alexandria, Minnesota. Its lakes, not too far from the Great Lakes, would have been the practical means of travel of these early voyagers.

SAUK COUNTY DAIRY FARM — On such finely equipped farms located in an area noted for its deep, rich soil, Wisconsin depends for its dominant position in the production of dairy products. Here, at the grass roots, is this and several other states' real and lasting wealth, its farms.

BEAUVOIR — The last home of Jefferson Davis, Confederate president, near Biloxi, Mississippi. While not as pretentious as many, it is characteristic of the plantation houses built by the well-to-do cotton planters in the period when this crop often brought great wealth during the early 1800's.

MICHIGAN AVENUE SKYLINE, CHICAGO
— Looking across Grant Park toward the so-called *Fabulous Mile*. The large structure just above the band shell is the Conrad Hilton Hotel, world's largest, probably host to more conventions than any other. View is from Shedd Aquarium.

IOWA CAPITOL, DES MOINES — This five-domed structure rises in a busy city that has the friendliness of a small town; and which is close in distance and spirit to the prairies which have made it the capital of a thriving state of ninety-nine counties. Agriculture reaches its zenith here.

CUTLER BRIDGE, MADISON COUNTY – Covered bridges, relics of an older time, are by no means limited to the seacoast states. This Iowa structure is one of some 2000 through the country, more than one quarter of them in the State of Ohio, which claims 562.

PONY EXPRESS RIDER – The jumping off place for the *Wild West* was old St. Jo in Missouri. Here, in bronze, one of the mail riders streaks out toward the Pacific Coast. They began riding a weekly schedule in April, 1860, kept it up until the telegraph's completion in '61.

CONTOUR FARMING – Such scientific handling of sloping land in a manner to stop erosion of the soil has been the salvation of many areas. This airplane view shows an excellent employment of this technique in the State of Iowa, where its use is actively encouraged.

INTERNATIONAL BOUNDARY LINE — Fully conscious of the great benefits of a peaceful boundary between neighbor nations, North Dakota and Canada jointly dedicated this International Peace Garden and the cairn marking the border, pledging that "as long as men shall live, we will not take up arms against each other." This 2,200 acre natural park, north of Dunseith, lies partly in Dakota, partly in Manitoba, in the Turtle Mountain area. Much of the state is flat, but hardly monotonous.

WHITE RIVER AT CALICO ROCKS — Scenic beauty and natural phenomena lend variety and the spice of adventure to the Arkansas countryside. Here the White River, famous for its fine bass fishing, swings placidly beside cliffs, in a wide range of colors, which it cut away in the far distant past. Long ago the mountaineers along this stream took up fishing from *floats*, by which they perfected the means of getting the maximum in fishing pleasure, with a bare minimum of effort and discomfort.

MT. RUSHMORE MEMORIAL
— South Dakota's *Emblem of Democracy* takes the form of the heads of four great Americans — Washington, Jefferson, Lincoln, and Theodore Roosevelt, carved on a mountain side. Work is now under way carving another mountain top into the form of a mounted Indian warrior.

STATE HOUSE, LINCOLN —
The present capitol of Nebraska is considered to be one of the most beautiful government buildings in the world. But one of the most remarkable things about it was its construction on a pay-as-you-go basis; thus it was fully paid for on its completion. Nebraskans dislike debt.

GEODETIC CENTER OF NORTH AMERICA — Kansas is at
the very center of things. This young lady points to the *primary station*, near Osborne, on which all surveys in North America are based. The geographic center of the United States lies only 42 miles north of here in Smith County.

OIL FIELDS AND STATE CAPITOL – Practical minded Oklahomans saw no good purpose being served by an ornate dome on their State Capitol. Neither did they see any reason why producing oil wells should not be located right on the capitol grounds. Such down-to-earth approach to life may in part help to explain this Aladdin-and-the-Lamp wonderland, third youngest of our states, and admitted in 1907.

FRENCH QUARTER, NEW ORLEANS – The *Vieux Carre* is a bit of old France built by her sons and daughters in the New World, when New Orleans was the key to French hopes in America. In all, ten flags have flown over Louisiana as province and state. Surprisingly much of the lovely iron work, as seen here, came down the river from Ohio.

THE ALAMO – This *Shrine of Texas Liberty* was the chapel of a Spanish mission, erected in 1718. Then on the morning of February 21, 1836 it suddenly became a fortress, when the Mexican drove the Texans to seek shelter in it. By March 3rd its defenders totalled 187 men. On the following day, the enemy fell upon this brave handful, the final assault coming at dawn on the 6th, and breaking through on the third try. Every Texan died fighting, but only after slaying 1500 Mexicans; and paving the way for Texas independence six weeks later. "Remember the Alamo" was their war cry.

INTERNATIONAL BOUND-ARY — Looking down the Rio Grande to the highway bridge connecting Laredo, Texas, with Nuevo Laredo in Mexico, the latter being at the right. Because of a treaty between the two countries, no boats are permitted upon this fine stream where it forms our border for about one half of its 2,000 mile course from Colorado down to the Gulf.

INDIAN CEREMONIAL DANCE, NEW MEXICO — There are still eighteen Indian pueblos in New Mexico in which the descendants of the early native population live in communal groups, perpetuating their age-old customs. There is a fair sprinkling of tourists among the audience gathered to watch the dancers stomp out intricate steps to the rhythm of drums and rattles.

SAN JACINTO BATTLE MONUMENT — This 567 foot shaft marks the spot where the Texans under Sam Houston defeated the Mexican army under Santa Anna in a furious half-hour battle that erased their loss of the Alamo, and won them their independence. Here Houston, himself wounded spared the life of the Mexican President, also very severely injured.

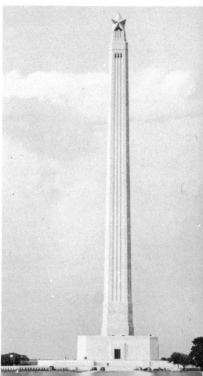

OLD FAITHFUL GEYSER—

As early as 1806 John Colter, a former member of the Lewis and Clark Expedition, explored the scenic area we know today as Yellowstone Park in northwestern Wyoming. But so unusual were many of the things seen there by this first white American in the territory, that traders and trappers for many years spoke of the section as *Colter's Hell*. This mighty geyser, with a prologue of rumbling and hissing, throws a huge stream of boiling water 120 feet into the air with clock-like regularity every hour.

LOGAN PASS, GLACIER NATL. PARK—

At the portal to a tunnel on *Going-to-the-Sun Highway* we look out toward Mt. Clements. This section of the Montana Rockies is a land of shimmering, breath-taking mountains, patched with snow fields and glaciers, that feed jade green lakes, often through tumbling streams and lacy waterfalls. This mountain wonderland, breaking across the line into Canada, is second to none in scenic grandeur, and has become one of the great vacation rendezvous in our American West, and a part of our glorious heritage.

PIKES PEAK — Looking across 100 million-year-old rocks of the Garden of the Gods to the snow covered mountain named for the intrepid soldier and explorer, Col. Zebulon Pike, who discovered this *Patriarch of the Rockies* in 1806. His visit opened up the Colorado area; and he was soon followed by such other famous pioneers as Freemont, Gunnison, Jim Bridger, Uncle Dick Wootton, Kit Carson, and others. The latter three, and other trappers and fur hunters, penetrated to the most secluded of the state's many mountain valleys in search of beaver pelts and excitement.

HARVESTING SALT

—William Sublette wintered in Cache Valley, Utah, in 1824-25. Young Jim Bridger was a member of this party, and to him came the distinction of discovering Great Salt Lake, whose waters average about one-fifth salt. Here we see the great *pans*, formed by throwing up low dikes, into which the lake water is pumped. Since the air is very *dry*, the water evaporates rapidly, leaving a thick layer of salt. This is then scraped up into vast piles, such as those shown, and is now ready for loading and shipment.

SALMON RIVER, IDAHO — Rugged Idaho, once a part of Oregon Territory, has for its motto the phrase *It Is Forever*. This view down the rocky gorge of Salmon River Canyon in the east central part of the state makes it appear as though great permanence was built into this area. In the northern panhandle it takes a road some 63 miles long to travel an air distance of 26 miles; while at another point the Snake River twists for 40 miles through Hells Canyon at an average elevation just under one mile high. Its Shoshone Falls are higher than far better-known Niagara.

GRAND CANYON OF THE COLORADO — The two light patches at the lower left are traces of the river which, through countless ages has carved this most magnificent spectacle. For more than 200 miles, chasms 4,000 to 6,000 feet deep, and 4 to 18 miles wide, line the Colorado.

MIGHTY MT. RAINIER — This third highest peak in the country dominates the Cascade range and the towns and cities in the Puget Sound area in the State of Washington. Its 14,408 foot summit, deep in perpetual snows, is one of the favorite objectives of mountain climbers and skiers.

HOOVER DAM—This mighty concrete plug, 727 feet high and 650 feet thick at the base, thrust between the sheer walls of Black Canyon, stores a huge lake of surplus water which brings life to millions of parched acres, and generates immense quantities of electric power, divided among three states.

GOLDEN GATE BRIDGE—Looking back from Marin County toward San Francisco, the aircraft carrier passing beneath gives some impression of the size of this longest single span in the world. The 746 foot towers are 4200 feet apart, and the shore approaches total some 2250 feet more.

SEQUOIA NATL. PARK — This grove of mighty trees, named for the brilliant Cherokee Indian, are the oldest living things in the world. The largest, the *General Sherman*, 36 feet at its greatest diameter and 3000-4000 years old, bears seed cones no bigger than good-sized English walnuts.

BONNEVILLE DAM — Spillway section of the great dual dam built by the Corps of Engineers, U.S.A., in the Columbia River. At the Washington end, in the foreground is a *fish ladder*, permitting the salmon to swim upstream. Its righthand end is anchored in Bradford Island. Further to the right, and not seen, is the great powerhouse, spanning the south channel between that island and the rugged Oregon shore.

SIGNAL HILL OIL FIELD — This maze of derricks is the field lying between Long Beach and Los Angeles. Other great fields lie to the north of the latter city in the Bakersfield area. Oil sands have long been exploited in the Santa Barbara region, where the deep holes are purposely *curved* as they are drilled, so they will reach far out under the ocean to tap off-shore pools.

DIAMOND HEAD, HAWAII — This lovely and spectacular headland thrusts south into the ocean from the island of Oahu, forming the eastern edge of the bay on which Honolulu stands, and from which Pearl Harbor, virtually land-locked, extends back deep into the island to the left.

LITTLE DIOMEDE VILLAGE, ALASKA — Looking westward across three miles of water into Russian territory. While some of the Aleutian Islands lie further west, this is the point where the United States and the U.S.S.R. come closest, the boundary passing between these islands.

ation in this country just a few years back; yet it is a condition to be watched carefully.

It is true that we wish our own children to respect us as parents during their formative years. Still our major task is to bring them to adult maturity, and then see that they stand squarely on their own two feet. To have conditioned them so that over their mature years they will turn to any *father* other than the Heavenly One, is to have done them a great disservice. Why hazard the risk of making them a prey to the overly ambitious who are ever with us.

DO NOT BE DECEIVED

Let us not be deceived either by the *strong man,* the would-be *dictator,* or the *big name,* who is very often merely the front for a clique or group. So-called "pressure groups" are nothing new in human affairs, and certainly not on our national scene. They were in action even when our Constitution was being drawn up; and threatened to ruin the effort. Their threat was so grave that George Washington had to sharply remind the assembly over which he presided, "If, to please the people, we offer what we ourselves disapprove, how can we afterwards defend our work? Let us raise a standard to which the wise and honest can repair. The event is in the hands of God." Keep those words ever by you as you consider proposals in connection with government.

But such groups have persisted; and today they bedevil government from all sides and at all levels. So serious is their pressure that honest attempts have been made by Congress to register all such *lobbyists,* and force their efforts out into the open where they can be evaluated by the public at large.

Whatever their *cause,* it is usually a seeking of their own good at the expense of others. The means employed are sometimes reasonable, but not infrequently morally foul. Such selfishness is, as has been pointed out, not new. But today it is more widespread and better organized. And the voices raised in special pleading are so shrill as to drown out much of the sincere efforts made toward achieving government of just proportions and purposes.

Certain of these pressure groups operate by a theme which is primarily hate—hate for anything which they regard as alien in the way of color, creed, or conduct. The more secretive they are, the more primitive their thinking and intents. Their plan is usually to substitute the rule of men for that of law, often by making local law enforcement, up through to state levels, subservient to their demands.

As un-American as are their purposes and activities, groups of this type have been all too common on the American scene in the past; and their traces are still too much in evidence.

RIGHT OF PROTEST

Pressures exerted by groups or segments of the population should always be examined critically. The right of protest is inherent in the *American Way of Life,* and nothing tending to bar it should be permitted. But before giving allegiance to any group whatsoever, it is the height of prudence to be certain that the purposes and methods employed are in keeping with what you believe to be the best for America, for you, and for your children.

Our form of government, then, is resolved from the influences brought to bear upon it. Thoughtlessly, we sometimes criticize it without realizing that we may well have contributed to what it is today, either through pressure we have helped to bring about, or by our indifference to pressure brought by others.

Also, we do well to keep before us a clear distinction between *government administration* and *politics*. There are thousands upon thousands of government employees trying to render constructive effort to our benefit within the framework of the laws now on the statute books, and by which they must work. They do—so far as they are permitted—attempt to serve the public good.

pediency is removed, and that government be trimmed to the size we deem essential.

The term *bureaucracy* is of recent vintage, but its form of ministration is not new, neither is it of American invention. You may remember how Moses Austin met with it in trying to erect his grist mill in the wilderness

PEOPLE OF THIS GENERATION HAVE MORE SKILFUL
PUBLICITY DIRECTED TO THEM THAN EVER BEFORE

By contrast, there are those in elective and in appointive offices whose one purpose is blindly to serve biased and narrow loyalties. Too often they are in a position to exert most unfortunate influence upon the activities of that greater number of responsible public servants, who, most unfortunately, are their subordinates in government service.

The difference between these two groups is a wide gulf. We do well to bear it indelibly in mind; and also to do all that we can by strong protest to the end that *political* ex-

that became Missouri. He suffered from it at the hands of Spain, which, with France, ruined its chances of empire in North America because of the throttling hand of bureaucratic rule over its colonies.

England palmed off much less of it upon the colonists than did these other two countries. Thus settlers in colonies under British authority managed to push such control aside and hurry on their way. When it did become overpowering, they fought it off, decisively and finally.

Bureaucracy began to grow up here during the War between the States, and from then on could not be dislodged. The thirst for places in it cost the lives of Presidents Garfield and McKinley. Still it did not come into its own in numbers and power until the first World War. Then it began its real growth, which was astonishingly rapid, as has been pointed out, during the 1930's and since. Such growth came at both national and at lower levels.

DANGER OF BUREAUCRACY

The immense danger is that bureaucracy can readily take the place of the aristocracy of older times. It has a tendency to look upon government as its own "vested interest." And with the huge numbers now involved, it is approaching the point where it can swing or control national elections. Thus, like the old man of the sea who sat upon the shoulders of Sinbad the Sailor, it can so dominate America that our freedoms will evaporate; and we can become bond servants of the bureaucratic government we have permitted to develop in our midst.

One of our chief contemporary weaknesses is complacency. No previous generation has had its passions so continuously exercised. Motion pictures, comic strips, television, radio, and other mediums play continually upon our emotions, until we are emotionally jaded. Few men today can become indignant with the fury that used to seize the members of the group ranged about the cracker barrel in the crossroads store of two generations ago. Where men used to raise their voices and pound their fists in the discussion of current affairs, today there is little more than a shrug of the shoulders. In such complacency there is great danger. It may be that we no longer value liberty of choice and action to the point where we are willing even to raise our voice in protest. Are we, unfortunately, being conditioned to a different outlook than were our parents?

This matter of conditioning is an important consideration. It applies to the individual and also to great segments of the population as well. Such English meddling as there was in colonial affairs during the 1700's was widespread enough so that the majority in the thirteen colonies were prepared to contest for their rights by so considerable an undertaking as the Revolution. There have been many instances of mass conditioning of the populace in years since its close; and many more attempts seem certain.

One notable example was the changed attitude brought about toward slavery through the enforcement at a federal level of the Fugitive Slave acts. With continuing improvements in communication and exchange of ideas by means of the press, radio, television, magazines, and a more mobile population, national thinking can now be influenced in the mass more effectively than ever before. Methods of changing the attitude of great numbers have been carefully thought out and have become highly perfected. And their use can be for our good, or for our complete undoing. We are today subjected to a constant barrage of propaganda and persuasion such as no generation of men before us ever had to withstand. No phase of our lives but is under pressure by some group through the spoken or written word. And the government has taken to itself many of the techniques made effective in the fields of advertising, promotion, and public relations.

By such means, different interpretations are being given to some of the older American attitudes from which we have drawn strength in the past. Belief in individual

371

initiative has been watered down. Self-reliance has been too extensively replaced by reliance upon others. And even our respect for age-old virtues and morality is being called in question.

Free schooling, fought for by the great bulk of the people during much of the last century, has become so much a matter of course that there is open question as to whether the schools are able to serve their purpose to the fullest. Now that education is not only free but compulsory, current generations treat school matters with startling indifference.

"EQUAL" IN WHAT RESPECT?

By fairly common consent, an interpretation has been put upon one clause in the Declaration that was never originally intended. In what respect are "all men created equal"? Equal in the sight and compassion of God the Father, surely. They were endowed with certain inalienable rights in the pursuit of Life, Liberty, and Happiness *according to their several abilities*. But it was surely not the intent of the author of that immortal document, or of those who subscribed to it by their signatures, to even intimate that we should attempt by devious legal means to *equalize* all men.

Even unschooled children have a fairly clear conception that no two persons are alike in respect to ability or ambition. Consequently, we cannot hope for equal results in accomplishments, and especially in material possessions. Free men and women would resist with every fiber of their beings outward attempts to make all people equal in physical, mental, and other characteristics. Still they seem ready to subscribe under persuasion to some measure of belief in what proves to be perhaps the most crafty

philosophy ever poured out for gullible mankind to swallow.

There was a self-appointed disciple of "downtrodden" peoples in the last century named Karl Marx. You may have heard of the doctrine he preached, known to us today as *communism*. The sugar-coated pill by which he hoped to cure the world's ills contained a sort of habit-forming drug. What he proposed was to *take* "from each according to his abilities," and then to *give* "to each according to his needs."

Read quickly and without thinking out all that it implies, this formula seemed almost inspired. Slyly arranged to lull people into unconsciousness like a powerful opiate, Marx was so certain of wide acceptance that he predicted that every nation in the world would make his malignant proposal the pattern of government. And unhappily he was right. The only difference between its application by the leading nations of today—our own included—is in the extent to which this nefarious principle is applied. In Russia it is frankly communism. In England it is socialism. While in this country, although we do not recognize from whom we have borrowed, it is sometimes reluctantly admitted to be the "welfare state."

GOVERNMENT DEFINED

By some sort of conditioning, we have come to think of government as being solely *for* the people. We do well to review Lincoln's Gettysburg Address, again and again, and learn that he outlined it as "government *of* the people," and then *"by* the people," since it is only in that way that it can be a government *"for* the people."

Mistaken emphasis on government being *for* you can be dangerous thinking. The ultimate in that direction would be for the gov-

GOVERNMENT IS OF AND BY THE PEOPLE, AS WELL AS BEING FOR THEM

One of the least things you can do so that your government will be *of* and *by* you is to vote in each and every election. It is regrettable to find that in many instances in the past less than one half the registered voters have gone to the polls and cast their votes.

ernment to take you over entirely; and then take *from* you all that you are able to produce according to your abilities, so that it might give the results of your labor to others according to their needs. Which party would benefit most is not hard to decide. It now does just this in part. And unless you wish it to go all the way in the direction in which government's social thinking is aimed, you had best do your bit to alter its course. Such a philosophy nearly wrecked Jamestown in 1607 and Plymouth in 1620. What reason is there to believe it will not have equally baneful results today?

Democracy, too, appears to have become a most flexible term. Even the Russians have appropriated it to their pagan form of control, perhaps hoping to add to the confusion. Primarily it means "rule by the people." Thus it can be rule by the majority. And by a majority vote, it would be possible to legislate another's money away, "due process of law" having been paid at least lip service. Such an act might be *legally* right, but its *moral* aspects are something else again. The vote provides the *might* by which it can be done; but does it truly, in the sight of God, give the moral *right* to do such things? For it is being done, and the morality involved appears to be of little concern today.

As the embarrassed Jefferson sat and heard the Declaration which he had drafted debated word by word by the Continental Congress, he no doubt subscribed readily to two changes which were made. They occur in the last and in the next to last sentences. In the latter instance, the assembly inserted the clause "appealing to the Supreme Judge of the world for the rectitude of our intentions." They went on record to show their willingness to submit their acts to the Father above to be judged.

In the last sentence they frankly sought His guidance and support, as indicated by the inclusion of "with firm reliance upon the protection of Divine Providence."

These early legislators wished their acts to be not only legally sound, but, more important still, morally honest as well. Such legislation, and such alone, is fit for American statute books. Our democracy should be on substantial moral foundations, so that we operate by *right*, rather than by mere *might*.

Security is another term the deep meaning of which has been lost in favor of dubious emphasis on but a part of what it should cover. And money is not the key, despite the fact that stocks and bonds have long been known as *securities*.

FINDING REAL SECURITY

Real, lasting, substantial security lies much, much deeper. The kind which makes life livable and enjoyable is mental and particularly spiritual. The material sort is fleeting and shallow. Our forefathers found it in abundance in the privilege which we formerly extended to each citizen of being responsible for his own welfare, and for that of those nominally dependent upon him.

The security that a resolute, free man really looks for in government is protection against restraint and against force employed by others. The *true* American Spirit can then come into full play; and people can build their own security according to their ability, their willingness, and their free choice.

The Bible does not say in so many words that "the Lord loves those who help themselves." But this truth is implied in countless places throughout the text. Security is an individual matter in most of life, and only by joint endeavor at those points where the situation is quite beyond individual ability.

STRAIGHT THINKING NEEDED

Unfortunate indeed was that day and hour in which great numbers of our people became conditioned to expect security from government auspices. Those who choose to look to government, rather than to their own abilities, have no moral right to expect it to make good on misfortunes brought about by their exercise of free choice. That would be too much like expecting the same source to make good on the debts of an unlucky gambler.

Also we seem to have been rather unfortunately conditioned in our thinking about money. By the standards of our forebears, a dollar could not be spent until it was in hand. Or, if a dollar was borrowed and spent, it *had* to be repaid. Such beliefs were based on moral laws straight out of the Ten Commandments.

But in an era of easy morality hard money has softened; and our attitude toward the sound use of it has wilted even more. With the widely prevailing feeling that the government can take care of *everybody,* we seldom ask ourselves where the inevitable dollars are coming from. Even when it is made crystal-clear that more and more of them are extracted directly from our own pockets— and no evading the issue—we are coming to

THE HOPE OF THE NATION LIES IN ITS HOMES, AND IN THE TYPE OF LIFE LIVED IN THEM

take this as something which has always happened and is to be expected from here on out. A tax load that would have brought our grandfathers into open rebellion is today accepted as inevitable. Few of us even pause to ask whether the benefits received are worth the sacrifice which we have, by our votes or by the lack of them, allowed to be levied upon us.

Some of our coins still bear the inscription, "In God We Trust." That was and should be the chief place to base our reliance. As more and more of it is misplaced in government, we can come to the point already achieved by the Russians, where government becomes the ruling deity. Surely it cannot be that those who call themselves *Americans* are willingly headed in such a direction.

Can it be that our anxiety today really stems not so much from economic conditions as from weakened and no more than lukewarm morality? The early Puritans perhaps erred slightly in the direction of religious excesses; but the moral basis they and other settlers gave to Colonial times, and which was carried over into a young nation, was something to build upon.

Every public servant required to take the oath of allegiance when entering office completes it with the words, "so help me God." Divine help was never more needed than in the slough of despond in which so many wallow today. Especially is such guidance needed in high places.

Very fortunately, most of our contacts as individuals are conducted in mutual goodwill and reasonably considerate understand-

375

ing. But when we gather into groups to work our will upon others, we often lose our sense of proportion and especially of moral values. Our tolerance and native respect for the inherent rights of others break down rapidly. We become aggressive and militant, a part of the herd. Morality, then, is often pressed into the remote background.

STABLE MORAL CODE

Although a Justice of the Supreme Court contended in a recent decision that there are no longer any "absolutes," can that possibly be the prevailing feeling? Have the Ten Commandments no longer any standing at the bar of public opinion? Are there situations today where stealing, murder, adultery, or unbridled greed are to be condoned? What have become of our standards? Or have we none, other than personal advantage—"what's in it for me?"

Our moral laws should be as fixed as the stars in the sky, as little subject to repeal as the laws of gravity. Otherwise the *American Way of Life* has been moved off its solid-rock foundation and onto a bed of quick-sand.

Those motivated by sound moral impulses can, however, be deceived as they look about them. What we see in many places, particularly in government, makes it appear that corruption is so widespread that we are poised on the brink of moral bankruptcy. Our first impulse is to believe that yesterday was all moral rectitude, and what we need is a return to the "good old days." This is not necessarily true, neither is it a sound procedure to walk facing backwards. And when the future can hope to be no better than the past, America's days are numbered.

We do well to face the fact that there have been periods in our past when corruption has clouded our national life, both within and without the government. As but one instance, it badly tarnished some phases of the latter during the War between the States. But it is equally unpleasant to realize that the use of drugs became altogether too prevalent among the people themselves at about this same time. In fact it is not too many years ago that a well-known mail-order catalog prominently displayed a "cure" for those who had become addicted to narcotics.

It would be rank fallacy for us to think that human nature had altered greatly, and for the worse, in recent years. Conditions about us change, but man continues to be swayed by much the same impulses with which he was beset more than 3,400 years ago when the Ten Commandments were written out for his guidance on tables of stone by the finger of God.

We should not feel that these impulses were less strident among the people of this country in the past. In certain respects, they were under more general control. But men had to fight against them then, as is so necessary today; and the struggle was evident on the surface and widely decried then. Conditions are not so much worse today that nothing can be done about them.

Neither is lack of rectitude limited only to the federal government. A now famous crime investigation showed conclusively that many local administrations are far from being simon-pure. For those who unwisely feel inadequate to cope with conditions at the national level, there is much of a corrective nature that needs to be done much closer to home.

And lest we waver in our resolve, it should be realized that we have made some substantial progress in numerous aspects of government since the turn of the century. Even more remarkable is the cleaner hands of large segments of business than was indicated by their practices of some years back. Where the prevailing philosophy had been "Let the buyer beware," it has been replaced with that of "The customer is always right." The consequence is that we eat purer foods, wear less shoddy clothing, and fill our needs from sources that operate on the basis of "one price" to all. Such a change has proven decidedly to the benefit of the self-interest of manufacturers and distributors. Would there might be a similar inducement that would apply in government circles.

AN EVER-BETTER AMERICA

Said the psalmist, "Unless the Lord build the house, they labor in vain that build it." It was true more than two thousand years ago when these words were penned; our forefathers knew it to be true, and it must be our guide today. Without increased morality, the pressure of the present may become too great to be successfully borne. But beside that, our hope is clearly for an ever-better America.

And together with false standards of morality, we need to beware of false prophets. They come as individuals and also as "pressure groups." Be chary of giving yourself to their support until you know the *cause* espoused, and whether intents and purposes line up with your own real best interests. Too often they align class against class, in what should instead be an atmosphere of tolerance and forebearance. United we stand; but divided along lines of class, creed, color, and other minor differences, we can fall into weakness that will make us easy prey for dictators from within or conquerors from without.

Beware of those who conjure up magic terms, *welfare social security,* and other entrancing but deceitful phrases, which appear to be pure gold but are completely counterfeit.

DON'T VOTE FREEDOM AWAY

And never forget that Freedom can be *voted away* just as surely as it can be torn from you by violence.

Keep prominently in mind, too, the heartening fact that political parties in our country want to keep you Free. But you must recollect that they need your active encouragement and support. Why? Because their leaders are under continual pressure from groups who, knowingly or perhaps blindly, are moving toward the elimination of your Freedom.

But those among them who promise you *something for nothing* should be shunned like the plague. Always ask yourself in regard to any such proposal: What will this cost me, and my children after me, in taxes? Will this add to or detract from my personal freedom and my opportunities to be self-reliant?

Keep ever before you the fact that a government produces *nothing*. When a government *gives* it must first *take* from someone— and that someone is pretty certain to be YOU.

One privilege that is still yours and largely unimpaired is your *right* to vote. But it is surely a strong condemnation of its appreciation when we find how indifferently many of us use our franchise. When thirty, forty, even fifty per cent of the citizens refuse to exercise their right to state their preference for a man, or for a cause, our American Heritage seems to be in serious jeopardy. With your right to vote goes the responsibility to cast that vote understandingly and without fail. If our government is not *of* and *by* us, can it long be *for* us?

377 ২৯

Our future is as certainly in our hands as it was in those of our forebears who founded and sustained this broad and fruitful land. It is a challenge to us, just as it was to them. They rose to accept it, and gave it their best. A similar obligation rests upon us. It will be by our individual efforts and continuing staunch support that America will ever be a "Sweet Land of Liberty." Let us set our minds and hearts to work.

For our aid we have placed on page 175 of this volume an *American Pledge*. To it each of us should willingly subscribe. It should be repeated understandingly—yes, even reverently, and often. Then we may strive to put its admonitions to work in all our thoughts and acts. These are most exacting times. But if this pledge can but come alive in our hearts, we may become the HOPE OF THE NATION indeed.

I PLEDGE ALLEGIANCE TO THE FLAG OF THE UNITED STATES OF AMERICA AND TO THE REPUBLIC FOR WHICH IT STANDS; ONE NATION, UNDER GOD, INDIVISIBLE, WITH LIBERTY AND JUSTICE FOR ALL.

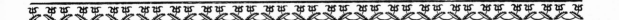

THREE GREAT
DOCUMENTS
IN OUR
AMERICAN
HERITAGE

The Constitution of the United States of America

The Declaration of Independence

The Gettysburg Address

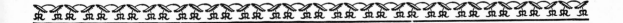

THE CONSTITUTION

OF THE UNITED STATES
OF AMERICA

WE THE PEOPLE of the United States, in Order to form a more perfect Union, establish Justice, insure domestic Tranquility, provide for the common Defence, promote the general Welfare, and secure the Blessings of Liberty to ourselves and our Posterity, do ordain and establish this CONSTITUTION for the United States of America.

ARTICLE I.

SECTION 1. All legislative Powers herein granted shall be vested in a Congress of the United States, which shall consist of a Senate and House of Representatives.

SECTION 2. The House of Representatives shall be composed of Members chosen every second Year by the People of the several States, and the Electors in each State shall have the Qualifications requisite for Electors of the most numerous Branch of the State Legislature.

No Person shall be a Representative who shall not have attained to the Age of twenty-five Years, and been seven Years a Citizen of the United States, and who shall not, when elected, be an Inhabitant of that State in which he shall be chosen.

[Representatives and direct Taxes shall be apportioned among the several States which may be included within this Union, according to their respective Numbers, which shall be determined by adding to the whole Number of free Persons, including those bound to Service for a Term of Years, and excluding Indians not taxed, three fifths of all other Persons.] The actual Enumeration shall be made within three Years after the first Meeting of the Congress of the United States, and within every subsequent Term of ten Years, in such Manner as they shall by Law direct. The Number of Representatives shall not exceed one for every thirty Thousand, but each State shall have at Least one Representative; and until such enumeration shall be made, the State of New Hampshire shall be entitled to chuse three, Massachusetts eight, Rhode-Island and Providence Plantations one, Connecticut five, New-York six, New Jersey four, Pennsylvania eight, Delaware one, Maryland six, Virginia ten, North Carolina five, South Carolina five, and Georgia three.

When vacancies happen in the Representation from any State, the Executive Authority thereof shall issue Writs of Election to fill such Vacancies.

The House of Representatives shall chuse their Speaker and other Officers; and shall have the sole Power of Impeachment.

SECTION 3. The Senate of the United States shall be composed of two Senators from each State, chosen by the Legislature thereof, for six Years; and each Senator shall have one Vote.

Immediately after they shall be assembled in Consequence of the first Election, they shall be divided as equally as may be into three Classes. The Seats of the Senators of the first Class shall be vacated at the Expiration of the second Year, of the second Class at the Expiration of the fourth Year, and of the third Class at the Expiration of the sixth Year, so that one-third may be chosen every second Year; and if Vacancies happen by Resignation, or otherwise, during the Recess of the Legislature of any State, the Executive thereof may make temporary Appointments until the next Meeting of the Legislature, which shall then fill such Vacancies.

No Person shall be a Senator who shall not have attained to the Age of thirty Years, and been nine Years a Citizen of the United States, and who shall not, when elected, be an Inhabitant of that State for which he shall be chosen.

The Vice President of the United States shall be President of the Senate, but shall have no Vote, unless they be equally divided.

The Senate shall chuse their other Officers, and also a President pro tempore, in the absence of the Vice President, or when he shall exercise the Office of President of the United States.

The Senate shall have the sole Power to try all Impeachments. When sitting for that Purpose, they shall be on Oath or Affirmation. When the President of the United States is tried, the Chief Justice shall preside: And no Person shall be convicted without the Concurrence of two thirds of the Members present.

Judgment in Cases of Impeachment shall not extend further than to removal from Office, and disqualification to hold and enjoy any Office of honor, Trust or Profit under the United States: but the Party convicted shall nevertheless be liable and subject to Indictment, Trial, Judgment and Punishment, according to Law.

SECTION 4. The Times, Places and Manner of holding Elections for Senators and Representatives, shall be prescribed in each State by the Legislature thereof; but the Congress may at any time by Law make or alter such Regulations, except as to the Place of Chusing Senators.

The Congress shall assemble at least once in every Year, and such Meeting shall be on the first Monday in December, unless they shall by Law appoint a different Day.

SECTION 5. Each House shall be the Judge of the Elections, Returns and Qualifications of its own Members, and a Majority of each shall constitute a Quorum to do Business; but a smaller number may adjourn from day to day, and may be authorized to compel the Attendance of absent Members, in such Manner, and under such Penalties as each House may provide.

Each House may determine the Rules of its Proceedings, punish its Members for disorderly Behavior, and, with the Concurrence of two thirds, expel a Member.

Each House shall keep a Journal of its Proceedings, and from time to time publish the same, excepting such Parts as may in their Judgment require Secrecy; and the Yeas and Nays of the Members of either House on any question shall, at the Desire of one fifth of those Present, be entered on the Journal.

Neither House, during the Session of Congress, shall, without the Consent of the other, adjourn for more than three days, nor to any other Place than that in which the two Houses shall be sitting.

SECTION 6. The Senators and Representatives shall receive a Compensation for their Services, to be ascertained by Law, and paid out of the Treasury of the United States. They shall in all Cases, except Treason, Felony and Breach of the Peace, be privileged from Arrest during their Attendance at the Session of their respective Houses, and in going to and returning from the same; and for any Speech or Debate in either House, they shall not be questioned in any other Place.

No Senator or Representative shall, during the Time for which he was elected, be appointed to any civil Office under the Authority of the United States, which shall have been created, or the Emoluments whereof shall have been encreased during such time; and no Person holding any Office under the United States, shall be a Member of either House during his Continuance in Office.

SECTION 7. All Bills for raising Revenue shall originate in the House of Representatives; but the Senate may propose or concur with Amendments as on other Bills.

Every Bill which shall have passed the House of Representatives and the Senate, shall, before it become a Law, be presented to the President of the United States; If he approve he shall sign it, but if not he shall return it, with his Objections to that House in which it shall have originated, who shall enter the Objections at large on their journal, and proceed to reconsider it. If after such Reconsideration two thirds of that House shall agree to pass the Bill, it shall be sent, together with the Objections, to the other House, by which it shall likewise be reconsidered, and if approved by two thirds of that House, it shall become a Law. But in all such Cases the Votes of both Houses shall be determined by Yeas and Nays, and the Names of the Persons voting for and against the Bill shall be entered on the Journal of each House respectively. If any Bill shall not be returned by the President within ten Days (Sundays excepted) after it shall have been presented to him, the Same shall be a Law, in like Manner as if he had signed it, unless the Congress by their Adjournment prevent its Return, in which Case it shall not be a Law.

Every Order, Resolution, or Vote to which the Concurrence of the Senate and House of Representatives may be necessary (except on a question of Adjournment) shall be presented to the President of the United States; and before the Same shall take Effect, shall be approved by him, or being disapproved by him, shall be repassed by two thirds of the Senate and House of Representatives, according to the Rules and Limitations prescribed in the Case of a Bill.

SECTION 8. The Congress shall have Power To lay and collect Taxes, Duties, Imposts and Excises, to pay the Debts and provide for the common Defence and general Welfare of the United States; but all Duties, Imposts and Excises shall be uniform throughout the United States;

To borrow money on the credit of the United States;

To regulate Commerce with foreign Nations, and among the several States, and with the Indian Tribes;

To establish an uniform Rule of Naturalization, and uniform Laws on the subject of Bankruptcies throughout the United States;

To coin Money, regulate the Value thereof, and of foreign Coin, and fix the Standard of Weights and Measures;

To provide for the Punishment of counterfeiting the Securities and current Coin of the United States;

To establish Post Offices and post Roads;

To promote the Progress of Science and useful Arts, by securing for limited Times to Authors and Inventors the exclusive Right to their respective Writings and Discoveries;

To constitute Tribunals inferior to the supreme Court;

To define and punish Piracies and Felonies committed on the high Seas, and Offenses against the Law of Nations;

To declare War, grant Letters of Marque and Reprisal, and make Rules concerning Captures on Land and Water;

To raise and support Armies, but no Appropriation of Money to that Use shall be for a longer Term than two Years;

To provide and maintain a Navy;

To make Rules for the Government and Regulation of the land and naval Forces;

To provide for calling forth the Militia to execute the Laws of the Union, suppress Insurrections and repel Invasions;

To provide for organizing, arming, and disciplining the Militia, and for governing such Part of them as may be employed in the Service of the United States, reserving to the States respectively, the Appointment of the Officers, and the Authority of training the Militia according to the discipline prescribed by Congress;

To exercise exclusive Legislation in all Cases whatsoever, over such District (not exceeding ten Miles square) as may, by Cession of particular States, and the acceptance of Congress, become the Seat of the Government of the United States, and to exercise like Authority over all Places purchased by the Consent of the Legislature of the State in which the Same shall be, for the Erection of Forts, Magazines, Arsenals, dock-Yards, and other needful Buildings;—And

To make all Laws which shall be necessary and proper for carrying into Execution the foregoing Powers, and all other Powers vested by this Constitution in the Government of the United States, or in any Department or Officer thereof.

SECTION 9. The Migration or Importation of such Persons as any of the States now existing shall think proper to admit, shall not be prohibited by the Congress prior to the Year one thousand eight hundred and eight, but a tax or duty may be imposed on such Imporation, not exceeding ten dollars for each Person.

The privilege of the Writ of Habeas Corpus shall not be suspended, unless when in Cases of Rebellion or Invasion the public Safety may require it.

No Bill of Attainder or ex post facto Law shall be passed.

No capitation, or other direct, Tax shall be laid, unless in Proportion to the Census or Enumeration herein before directed to be taken.

No Tax or Duty shall be laid on Articles exported from any State.

No Preference shall be given by any Regulation of Commerce or Revenue to the Ports of one State over those of another: nor shall Vessels bound to, or from, one State, be obliged to enter, clear, or pay Duties in another.

No Money shall be drawn from the Treasury, but in Consequence of Appropriations made by Law; and a regular Statement and Account of the Receipts and Expenditures of all public Money shall be published from time to time.

No Title of Nobility shall be granted by the United States: And no Person holding any Office of Profit or Trust under them, shall, without the Consent of the Congress, accept of any present, Emolument, Office, or Title, of any kind whatever, from any King, Prince, or foreign State.

SECTION 10. No State shall enter into any Treaty, Alliance, or Confederation; grant Letters of Marque and Reprisal; coin Money; emit Bills of Credit; make any Thing but gold and silver Coin a Tender in Payment of Debts; pass any Bill of Attainder, ex post facto Law, or Law impairing the Obligation of Contracts, or grant any Title of Nobility.

No State shall, without the Consent of the Congress, lay any Imposts or Duties on Imports or Exports, except what may be absolutely necessary for executing its inspection Laws: and the net Produce of all Duties and Imposts, laid by any

(Continued on page 390)

SHIPS OF THE PLAINS
Samuel Colman
COLLECTION OF HALL PARK McCULLOUGH, BROOKLYN MUSEUM, BROOKLYN, N.Y.

Without the covered wagon the winning of the west would have been delayed by several generations. In a previous picture we have seen them massed in a moment of peril. Here they are spread out along the trail, the patient oxen being hurried ahead to the next water hole. Oxen as draft animals were preferable, since they were more rugged, employed more simple harness, and if they broke a leg or had to be killed their flesh could be eaten.

THE LAST SPIKE
Thomas Hill
STATE HOUSE, SACRAMENTO

On the 10th of May in 1869, the two halves of a great continent were joined by a pair of rails. At Promontory Point in Utah the tracks of the Union Pacific and the Central Pacific met. Leland Stanford, president of the latter road, leaning on the handle of a sledge, is about to drive the golden spike that was a token of what had been accomplished. The colorful *Pony Express* had promptly disappeared eight years before on the completion of the transcontinental telegraph line. Now the days of the covered wagon were numbered. America was indeed coming of age, since nearly 50,000 miles of track were in use by 1870.

THE BELLE CREOLE
Unknown Artist
COLLECTION OF MRS. E. CRANE CHADBOURNE

The closing of the Mississippi at New Orleans by the Spanish almost throttled the first settlements west of the Appalachians. It took the Louisiana Purchase, and particularly the development of the steamboat, to open up a way to market for the settlers' products. During the last three-quarters of the 19th century river traffic handled great tonnages of goods; and, as more and more sumptuous vessels were built, they were often a preferred means of travel over the earlier railroads. Our literature is rich with river lore, and one of our greatest authors took his pen name from a river pilots' term, *Mark Twain,* meaning two fathoms of water.

THE GREAT EAST RIVER SUSPENSION BRIDGE
C. H. Parsons & Atwater
LIBRARY OF CONGRESS, WASHINGTON

With the development of steamboats upon navigable streams there was a demand for a bridge which could leap from bank to bank without blocking the channel. For centuries a bridge *suspended* on ropes or long trailing vines had been used, and as the drawing of wire became better perfected, its use for bridges was advocated. Early in the 1800's small spans of this type were successfully erected. In the 70's it was decided that this technique could be adapted to bridging the East River from New York to Brooklyn. The 7500 foot span and its approaches was opened in 1883, and it immediately became and continued for many years one of the most noted landmarks in our country.

UNVEILING THE STATUE OF LIBERTY, Edward Moran, Private Collection

PAGE ONE, TOP
SHIPS OF THE PLAINS
Samuel Colman, Brooklyn Museum

PAGE TWO, TOP
THE BELLE CREOLE
Unknown Artist, Private Collection

PAGE THREE, TOP
SAN JUAN HILL
Fred. Remington, Yale University

PAGE ONE, BELOW
THE LAST SPIKE
Thos. Hill, State House, Sacramento

PAGE TWO, BELOW
OPENING OF THE BROOKLYN BRIDGE
Parsons & Atwater, Library of Congress

PAGE THREE, BELOW
CASTLE GARDEN
C. F. Ulrich, Corcoran Gallery

SCREAM OF SHRAPNEL ON SAN JUAN HILL
Frederic Remington
YALE UNIVERSITY ART GALLERY

Where the present younger generation garners its ideals of cowboy life from one or more of several motion picture idols, a previous generation found theirs in the highly authentic paintings of Frederic Remington. He had been a *cowhand* and stockman on the plains in the years when the West was being *won*. Thus he knew his soldiers, too. When Theodore Roosevelt called together his *Rough Riders* for the Spanish-American War campaign in Cuba, he had collected many of the very type of men among whom Remington had lived and whom he had painted. He was by this time a distinguished magazine illustrator, and he turned readily to the picturing of Cuban scenes and incidents encountered by our fighting men there. The capture of San Juan Hill was probably the most colorful happening in an otherwise rather drab war.

IN THE LAND OF PROMISE, CASTLE GARDEN
Charles Frederick Ulrich
CORCORAN GALLERY OF ART, WASHINGTON

Up to the time of World War I large numbers of our population were recruited abroad. This movement in great numbers began in the late 1840's as a result of the famine in Ireland, and spiraled upward until in the early 1900's there were about a million coming to our shores each year. New York was long the chief point of entry, and until the facilities on Ellis Island were opened in 1891, the Immigrant Station was at *Castle Garden* at the southern tip of Manhattan Island. Through this point passed a steady stream of newcomers, detained only long enough to be certain their papers were in order, and that they met the very modest requirements of the then lenient restrictions.

The artist, born in New York in 1858, probably knew Castle Garden well, and very likely made studies for the picture on the spot. It gained him the Clark Prize at the National Academy of Design in 1884.

UNVEILING OF THE STATUE OF LIBERTY
Edward Moran
COLLECTION OF MRS. HENRY SETON

The three foremost American symbols are our *Flag,* the *Liberty Bell,* and the inspiring figure bearing a lighted torch standing on Bedloe's Island in New York harbor—the *Statue of Liberty*. It was a present from the people of France, its cost having been met by small donations from thousands of private citizens, collection of which began in 1874. It was on Washington's birthday in 1877 that the Congress voted to accept the gift, and set aside this small island for its site. The official presentation was made to our ambassador in Paris on July 4, 1884. The statue, made up of many smaller sections, was then sent to this country, where a pedestal to receive it had been erected from contributions made by American schoolchildren. Dedication ceremonies were held on October 28, 1886; and this mighty symbol of our priceless liberties immediately won and has held a high place in our affection.

389

State on Imports or Exports, shall be for the Use of the Treasury of the United States; and all such Laws shall be subject to the Revision and Control of the Congress.

No State shall, without the Consent of Congress, lay any duty of Tonnage, keep Troops, or Ships of War in time of Peace, enter into any Agreement or Compact with another State, or with a foreign Power, or engage in War, unless actually invaded, or in such imminent Danger as will not admit of delay.

ARTICLE II.

Section 1. The executive Power shall be vested in a President of the United States of America. He shall hold his Office during the Term of four Years, and, together with the Vice-President, chosen for the same Term, be elected, as follows

Each State shall appoint, in such Manner as the Legislature thereof may direct, a Number of Electors, equal to the whole Number of Senators and Representatives to which the State may be entitled in the Congress: but no Senator or Representative, or Person holding an Office of Trust or Profit under the United States, shall be appointed an Elector.

[The Electors shall meet in their respective States, and vote by Ballot for two persons, of whom one at least shall not be an Inhabitant of the same State with themselves. And they shall make a List of all the Persons voted for, and of the Number of Votes for each; which List they shall sign and certify, and transmit sealed to the Seat of the Government of the United States, directed to the President of the Senate. The President of the Senate shall, in the Presence of the Senate and House of Representatives, open all the Certificates, and the Votes shall then be counted. The Person having the greatest Number of Votes shall be the President, if such Number be a Majority of the whole Number of Electors appointed; and if there be more than one who have such Majority, and have an equal Number of Votes, then the House of Representatives shall immediately chuse by Ballot one of them for President; and if no Person have a Majority, then from the five highest on the List the said House shall in like Manner chuse the President. But in chusing the President, the Votes shall be taken by States, the Representation from each State having one Vote; A quorum for this Purpose shall consist of a Member or Members from two-thirds of the States, and a Majority of all the States shall be necessary to a Choice. In every Case, after the Choice of the President, the Person having the greatest Number of Votes of the Electors shall be the Vice Presi-

dent. But if there should remain two or more who have equal Votes, the Senate shall chuse from them by Ballot the Vice-President.]

The Congress may determine the Time of chusing the Electors, and the Day on which they shall give their Votes; which Day shall be the same throughout the United States.

No person except a natural born Citizen, or a Citizen of the United States, at the time of the Adoption of this Constitution, shall be eligible to the Office of President; neither shall any Person be eligible to that Office who shall not have attained to the Age of thirty-five Years, and been fourteen Years a Resident within the United States.

In Case of the Removal of the President from Office, or of his Death, Resignation, or Inability to discharge the Powers and Duties of the said Office, the same shall devolve on the Vice President, and the Congress may by Law provide for the Case of Removal, Death, Resignation or Inability, both of the President and Vice President, declaring what Officer shall then act as President, and such Officer shall act accordingly, until the Disability be removed, or a President shall be elected.

The President shall, at stated Times, receive for his Services, a Compensation, which shall neither be encreased nor diminished during the Period for which he shall have been elected, and he shall not receive within that Period any other Emolument from the United States, or any of them.

Before he enter on the Execution of his Office, he shall take the following Oath or Affirmation:— "I do solemnly swear (or affirm) that I will faithfully execute the Office of President of the United States, and will to the best of my Ability, preserve, protect and defend the Constitution of the United States."

Section 2. The President shall be Commander in Chief of the Army and Navy of the United States, and of the Militia of the several States, when called into the actual Service of the United States; he may require the Opinion in writing, of the principal Officer in each of the executive Departments, upon any subject relating to the Duties of their respective Offices, and he shall have Power to Grant Reprieves and Pardons for Offenses against the United States, except in Cases of Impeachment.

He shall have Power, by and with the Advice and Consent of the Senate, to make Treaties, provided two-thirds of the Senators present concur; and he shall nominate, and by and with the Advice and Consent of the Senate, shall appoint Ambassadors, other public Ministers and Consuls, Judges of the supreme Court, and all other Officers of the

United States, whose Appointments are not herein otherwise provided for, and which shall be established by Law: but the Congress may by Law vest the Appointment of such inferior Officers, as they think proper, in the President alone, in the Courts of Law, or in the Heads of Departments.

The President shall have Power to fill up all Vacancies that may happen during the Recess of the Senate, by granting Commissions which shall expire at the End of their next Session.

SECTION 3. He shall from time to time give to the Congress Information of the State of the Union, and recommend to their Consideration such Measures as he shall judge necessary and expedient; he may, on extraordinary Occasions, convene both Houses, or either of them, and in Case of Disagreement between them, with Respect to the Time of Adjournment, he may adjourn them to such Time as he shall think proper; he shall receive Ambassadors and other public Ministers; he shall take Care that the Laws be faithfully executed, and shall Commission all the Officers of the United States.

SECTION 4. The President, Vice President and all civil Officers of the United States, shall be removed from Office on Impeachment for, and Conviction of, Treason, Bribery, or other high Crimes and Misdemeanors.

ARTICLE III.

SECTION 1. The judicial Power of the United States, shall be vested in one supreme Court, and in such inferior Courts as the Congress may from time to time ordain and establish. The Judges, both of the supreme and inferior Courts, shall hold their Offices during good Behaviour, and shall, at stated Times, receive for their Services a Compensation which shall not be diminished during their Continuance in Office.

SECTION 2. The judicial Power shall extend to all Cases, in Law and Equity, arising under this Constitution, the Laws of the United States, and Treaties made, or which shall be made, under their Authority;—to all Cases affecting Ambassadors, other public Ministers and Consuls;—to all Cases of admiralty and maritime Jurisdiction;—to Controversies to which the United States shall be a Party;—to Controversies between two or more States;—between a State and Citizens of another State;—between Citizens of different States;—between Citizens of the same State claiming Lands under Grants of different States, and between a State, or the Citizens thereof, and foreign States, Citizens or Subjects.

In all Cases affecting Ambassadors, other public Ministers and Consuls, and those in which a State shall be Party, the supreme Court shall have original Jurisdiction. In all the other Cases before mentioned, the supreme Court shall have appellate Jurisdiction, both as to Law and Fact, with such Exceptions, and under such Regulations as the Congress shall make.

The trial of all Crimes, except in Cases of Impeachment, shall be by Jury; and such Trial shall be held in the State where the said Crimes shall have been committed; but when not committed within any State, the Trial shall be at such Place or Places as the Congress may by Law have directed.

SECTION 3. Treason against the United States, shall consist only in levying War against them, or in adhering to their Enemies, giving them Aid and Comfort. No Person shall be convicted of Treason unless on the Testimony of two Witnesses to the same overt Act, or on Confession in open Court.

The Congress shall have power to declare the Punishment of Treason, but no Attainder of Treason shall work Corruption of Blood, or Forfeiture except during the Life of the Person attainted.

ARTICLE IV.

SECTION 1. Full Faith and Credit shall be given in each State to the public Acts, Records, and judicial Proceedings of every other State. And the Congress may by general Laws prescribe the Manner in which such Acts, Records and Proceedings shall be proved, and the Effect thereof.

SECTION 2. The Citizens of each State shall be entitled to all Privileges and Immunities of Citizens in the several States.

A Person charged in any State with Treason, Felony, or other Crime, who shall flee from Justice, and be found in another State, shall on demand of the executive Authority of the State from which he fled, be delivered up, to be removed to the State having Jurisdiction of the Crime.

No Person held to Service or Labour in one State, under the Laws thereof, escaping into another, shall, in Consequence of any Law or Regulation therein, be discharged from such Service or Labour, but shall be delivered up on Claim of the Party to whom such Service or Labour may be due.

SECTION 3. New States may be admitted by the Congress into this Union; but no new State shall be formed or erected within the Jurisdiction of any other State; nor any State be formed by the Junction of two or more States, or parts of States, without the Consent of the Legislatures of the States concerned as well as of the Congress.

The Congress shall have Power to dispose of and make all needful Rules and Regulations respecting the Territory or other Property belonging to the United States; and nothing in this Constitution shall be so construed as to Prejudice any Claims of the United States, or of any particular State.

SECTION 4. The United States shall guarantee to every State in this Union a Republican Form of Government, and shall protect each of them against Invasion; and on Application of the Legislature, or of the Executive (when the Legislature cannot be convened) against domestic Violence.

ARTICLE V.

The Congress, whenever two-thirds of both Houses shall deem it necessary, shall propose Amendments to this Constitution, or, on the Application of the Legislatures of two-thirds of the several States, shall call a Convention for proposing Amendments, which, in either Case, shall be valid to all Intents and Purposes, as part of this Constitution, when ratified by the Legislatures of three-fourths of the several States, or by Conventions in three-fourths thereof, as the one or the other Mode of Ratification may be proposed by the Congress; Provided that no Amendment which may be made prior to the Year One thousand eight hundred and eight shall in any Manner affect the first and fourth Clauses in the Ninth Section of the first Article; and that no State, without its Consent, shall be deprived of its equal Suffrage in the Senate.

ARTICLE VI.

All Debts contracted and Engagements entered into, before the Adoption of this Constitution, shall be as valid against the United States under this Constitution, as under the Confederation.

This Constitution, and the Laws of the United States which shall be made in Pursuance thereof; and all Treaties made, or which shall be made, under the Authority of the United States, shall be the supreme Law of the Land; and the Judges in every State shall be bound thereby, any Thing in the Constitution or Laws of any State to the Contrary notwithstanding.

The Senators and Representatives before mentioned, and the Members of the several State Legislatures, and all executive and judicial Officers, both of the United States and of the several States, shall be bound by Oath or Affirmation, to support this Constitution; but no religious Test shall ever be required as a Qualification to any Office or public Trust under the United States.

ARTICLE VII.

The Ratification of the Conventions of nine States shall be sufficient for the Establishment of this Constitution between the States so ratifying the Same.

DONE in Convention by the Unanimous Consent of the States present the Seventeenth Day of September in the Year of our Lord one thousand seven hundred and Eighty seven and of the Independence of the United States of America the Twelfth. In Witness whereof We have hereunto subscribed our Names.

Go WASHINGTON
Presidt and deputy from Virginia

New Hampshire.

JOHN LANGDON
NICHOLAS GILMAN

Massachusetts.

NATHANIEL GORHAM
RUFUS KING

Connecticut.

WM SAML JOHNSON
ROGER SHERMAN

New York.

ALEXANDER HAMILTON

New Jersey.

WIL: LIVINGSTON
DAVID BREARLEY
WM PATTERSON
JONA: DAYTON

Pennsylvania.

B. FRANKLIN
ROBT. MORRIS

THOS. FITZSIMONS
JAMES WILSON
THOMAS MIFFLIN
GEO. CLYMER
JARED INGERSOLL
GOUV MORRIS

Delaware.

GEO: READ
JOHN DICKINSON
JACO: BROOM
GUNNING BEDFORD jun
RICHARD BASSETT

Maryland.

JAMES MCHENRY
DANL CARROLL
DAN: of ST THOS JENIFER

Virginia.

JOHN BLAIR—
JAMES MADISON Jr.

North Carolina.

WM BLOUNT
HU WILLIAMSON
RICHD DOBBS SPAIGHT

South Carolina.

J. RUTLEDGE
CHARLES PINCKNEY
CHARLES COTESWORTH PINCKNEY
PIERCE BUTLER

Georgia.

WILLIAM FEW
ABR BALDWIN
Attest:
WILLIAM JACKSON, *Secretary.*

ARTICLES IN ADDITION TO, AND AMENDMENT OF, THE CONSTITUTION OF THE UNITED STATES OF AMERICA, PROPOSED BY CONGRESS, AND RATIFIED BY THE LEGISLATURES OF THE SEVERAL STATES, PURSUANT TO THE FIFTH ARTICLE OF THE ORIGINAL CONSTITUTION.

[ARTICLE I.]

Congress shall make no law respecting an establishment of religion, or prohibiting the free exercise thereof; or abridging the freedom of speech, or of the press; or the right of the people peaceably to assemble, and to petition the Government for a redress of grievances.

[ARTICLE II.]

A well regulated Militia, being necessary to the security of a free State, the right of the people to keep and bear Arms, shall not be infringed.

[ARTICLE III.]

No soldier shall, in time of peace be quartered in any house, without the consent of the Owner, nor in time of war, but in a manner to be prescribed by law.

[ARTICLE IV.]

The right of the people to be secure in their persons, houses, papers, and effects, against unreasonable searches and seizures, shall not be violated, and no Warrants shall issue, but upon probable cause, supported by Oath or affirmation, and particularly describing the place to be searched, and the persons or things to be seized.

[ARTICLE V.]

No person shall be held to answer for a capital, or otherwise infamous crime, unless on a presentment or indictment of a Grand Jury, except in cases arising in the land or naval forces, or in the Militia, when in actual service in time of War or public danger; nor shall any person be subject for the same offence to be twice put in jeopardy of life or limb; nor shall be compelled in any criminal case to be a witness against himself, nor be deprived of life, liberty, or property, without due process of law; nor shall private property be taken for public use, without just compensation.

[ARTICLE VI.]

In all criminal prosecutions, the accused shall enjoy the right to a speedy and public trial, by an impartial jury of the State and district wherein the crime shall have been committed, which district shall have been previously ascertained by law, and

393 ⁊❧

to be informed of the nature and cause of the accusation; to be confronted with the witnesses against him; to have compulsory process for obtaining witnesses in his favor, and to have the Assistance of Counsel for his defence.

[ARTICLE VII.]

In suits at common law, where the value in controversy shall exceed twenty dollars, the right of trial by jury shall be preserved, and no fact tried by a jury, shall be otherwise re-examined in any Court of the United States, than according to the rules of the common law.

[ARTICLE VIII.]

Excessive bail shall not be required, nor excessive fines imposed, nor cruel and unusual punishments inflicted.

[ARTICLE IX.]

The enumeration in the Constitution, of certain rights, shall not be construed to deny or disparage others retained by the people.

[ARTICLE X.]

The powers not delegated to the United States by the Constitution, nor prohibited by it to the States, are reserved to the States respectively, or to the people.

ARTICLE XI.

The Judicial power of the United States shall not be construed to extend to any suit in law or equity, commenced or prosecuted against one of the United States by Citizens of another State, or by Citizens or Subjects of any Foreign State.

ARTICLE XII.

The Electors shall meet in their respective states and vote by ballot for President and Vice-President, one of whom, at least, shall not be an inhabitant of the same state with themselves; they shall name in their ballots the person voted for as President, and in distinct ballots the person voted for as Vice-President, and they shall make distinct lists of all persons voted for as President, and of all persons voted for as Vice-President, and of the number of votes for each, which lists they shall sign and certify, and transmit sealed to the seat of the government of the United States, directed to the President of the Senate;—The President of the Senate shall, in presence of the Senate and House of Representatives, open all the certificates and the votes shall then be counted;—The person having the greatest number of votes for President, shall be the President, if such number be a majority of the whole number of Electors appointed; and if no person have such majority, then from the persons having the highest numbers not exceeding three on the list of those voted for as President, the House of Representatives shall choose immediately, by ballot, the President. But in choosing the President, the votes shall be taken by states, the representation from each state having one vote; a quorum for this purpose shall consist of a member or members from two-thirds of the states, and a majority of all the states shall be necessary to a choice. And if the House of Representatives shall not choose a President whenever the right of choice shall devolve upon them, before the fourth day of March next following, then the Vice-President shall act as President, as in the case of the death or other constitutional disability of the President.—The person having the greatest number of votes as Vice-President, shall be the Vice-President, if such number be a majority of the whole number of Electors appointed, and if no person have a majority, then from the two highest numbers on the list, the Senate shall choose the Vice-President; a quorum for the purpose shall consist of two-thirds of the whole number of Senators, and a majority of the whole number shall be necessary to a choice. But no person constitutionally ineligible to the office of President shall be eligible to that of Vice-President of the United States.

ARTICLE XIII.

SECTION 1. Neither slavery nor involuntary servitude, except as a punishment for crime whereof the party shall have been duly convicted, shall exist within the United States, or any place subject to their jurisdiction.

SECTION 2. Congress shall have power to enforce this article by appropriate legislation.

ARTICLE XIV.

SECTION 1. All persons born or naturalized in the United States, and subject to the jurisdiction thereof, are citizens of the United States and of the State wherein they reside. No State shall make or enforce any law which shall abridge the privileges or immunities of citizens of the United States; nor shall any State deprive any person of life, liberty, or property, without due process of law; nor deny to any person within its jurisdiction the equal protection of the laws.

SECTION 2. Representatives shall be apportioned among the several States according to their respective numbers, counting the whole number of persons in each State, excluding Indians not taxed. But when the right to vote at any election for the choice of electors for President and Vice-President of the United States, Representatives in Congress, the Executive and Judicial officers of a State, or the members of the Legislature thereof, is denied to any of the male inhabitants of such State, being twenty-one years of age, and citizens of the United States, or in any way abridged, except for participation in rebellion, or other crime, the basis of representation therein shall be reduced in the proportion which the number of such male citizens shall bear to the whole number of male citizens twenty-one years of age in such State.

SECTION 3. No person shall be a Senator or Representative in Congress, or elector of President and Vice-President, or hold any office, civil or military, under the United States, or under any State, who, having previously taken an oath, as a member of Congress, or as an officer of the United States, or as a member of any State legislature, or as an executive or judicial officer of any State, to support the Constitution of the United States, shall have engaged in insurrection or rebellion against the same, or given aid or comfort to the enemies thereof. But Congress may by a vote of two-thirds of each House, remove such disability.

SECTION 4. The validity of the public debt of the United States, authorized by law, including debts incurred for payment of pensions and bounties for services in suppressing insurrection or rebellion, shall not be questioned. But neither the United States nor any State shall assume or pay any debt or obligation incurred in aid of insurrection or rebellion against the United States, or any claim for the loss or emancipation of any slave; but all such debts, obligations and claims shall be held illegal and void.

SECTION 5. The Congress shall have power to enforce, by appropriate legislation, the provisions of this article.

ARTICLE XV.

SECTION 1. The right of citizens of the United States to vote shall not be denied or abridged by the United States or by any State on account of race, color, or previous condition of servitude—

SECTION 2. The Congress shall have power to enforce this article by appropriate legislation.

ARTICLE XVI.

The Congress shall have power to lay and collect taxes on incomes, from whatever source derived, without apportionment among the several States, and without regard to any census or enumeration.

ARTICLE XVII.

The Senate of the United States shall be composed of two Senators from each State, elected by the people thereof, for six years; and each Senator shall have one vote. The electors in each State shall have the qualifications requisite for electors of the most numerous branch of the State legislatures.

When vacancies happen in the representation of any State in the Senate, the executive authority of such State shall issue writs of election to fill such vacancies: *Provided,* That the legislature of any State may empower the executive thereof to make temporary appointments until the people fill the vacancies by election as the legislature may direct.

This amendment shall not be so construed as to affect the election or term of any Senator chosen before it becomes valid as part of the Constitution.

ARTICLE XVIII.

SECTION 1. After one year from the ratification of this article the manufacture, sale, or transportation of intoxicating liquors within, the importation thereof into, or the exportation thereof from the United States and all territory subject to the jurisdiction thereof for beverage purposes is hereby prohibited.

SECTION 2. The Congress and the several States shall have concurrent power to enforce this article by appropriate legislation.

SECTION 3. This article shall be inoperative unless it shall have been ratified as an amendment to the Constitution by the legislatures of the several States, as provided in the Constitution, within seven years from the date of the submission hereof to the States by the Congress.

ARTICLE XIX.

The right of citizens of the United States to vote shall not be denied or abridged by the United States or by any State on account of sex.

Congress shall have power to enforce this article by appropriate legislation.

ARTICLE XX.

SECTION 1. The terms of the President and Vice President shall end at noon on the 20th day of January, and the terms of Senators and Representatives at noon on the 3d day of January, of the years in which such terms would have ended if this article had not been ratified; and the terms of their successors shall then begin.

SECTION 2. The Congress shall assemble at least once in every year, and such meeting shall begin at noon on the 3d day of January, unless they shall by law appoint a different day.

SECTION 3. If, at the time fixed for the beginning of the term of the President, the President elect shall have died, the Vice President elect shall become President. If a President shall not have been chosen before the time fixed for the beginning of his term, or if the President elect shall have failed to qualify, then the Vice President elect shall act as President until a President shall have qualified; and the Congress may by law provide for the case wherein neither a President elect nor a Vice President elect shall have qualified, declaring who shall then act as President, or the manner in which one who is to act shall be selected, and such person shall act accordingly until a President or Vice President shall have qualified.

SECTION 4. The Congress may by law provide for the case of the death of any of the persons from whom the House of Representatives may choose a President whenever the right of choice shall have devolved upon them, and for the case of the death of any of the persons from whom the Senate may choose a Vice President whenever the right of choice shall have devolved upon them.

SECTION 5. Sections 1 and 2 shall take effect on the 15th day of October following the ratification of this article.

SECTION 6. This article shall be inoperative unless it shall have been ratified as an amendment to the Constitution by the legislatures of three-fourths of the several States within seven years from the date of its submission.

ARTICLE XXI.

SECTION 1. The eighteenth article of amendment to the Constitution of the United States is hereby repealed.

SECTION 2. The transportation or importation into any State, Territory, or possession of the United States for delivery or use therein of intoxicating liquors, in violation of the laws thereof, is hereby prohibited.

SECTION 3. This article shall be inoperative unless it shall have been ratified as an amendment to the Constitution by conventions in the several States, as provided in the Constitution, within seven years from the date of the submission hereof to the States by the Congress.

ARTICLE XXII.

SECTION 1. No person shall be elected to the office of the President more than twice, and no person who has held the office of President, or acted as President, for more than two years of a term to which some other person was elected President shall be elected to the office of the President more than once. But this Article shall not apply to any person holding the office of President when this Article was proposed by the Congress, and shall not prevent any person who may be holding the office of President, or acting as President, during the term within which this Article becomes operative from holding the office of President or acting as President during the remainder of such term.

SECTION 2. This article shall be inoperative unless it shall have been ratified as an amendment to the Constitution by the legislatures of three-fourths of the several States within seven years from the date of its submission to the States by the Congress.

★ ★ ★ ★ ★ ★ ★ ★ ★ ★ ★ ★ ★

DECLARATION OF INDEPENDENCE
In Congress, July 4, 1776

The unanimous Declaration of the thirteen united States of America,

WHEN in the Course of human events, it becomes necessary for one people to dissolve the political bands which have connected them with another, and to assume among the Powers of the earth, the separate and equal station to which the Laws of Nature and of Nature's God entitle them, a decent respect to the opinions of mankind requires that they should declare the causes which impel them to the separation.

We hold these truths to be self-evident, that all men are created equal, that they are endowed by their Creator with certain unalienable Rights, that among these are Life, Liberty and the pursuit of Happiness. That to secure these rights, Governments are instituted among Men, deriving their just powers from the consent of the governed, That whenever any Form of Government becomes destructive of these ends, it is the Right of the People to alter or to abolish it, and to institute new Government, laying its foundation on such principles and organizing its powers in such form, as to them shall seem most likely to effect their Safety and Happiness. Prudence, indeed, will dictate that Governments long established should not be changed for light and transient causes; and accordingly all experience hath shown, that mankind are more disposed to suffer, while evils are sufferable, than to right themselves by abolishing the forms to which they are accustomed. But when a long train of abuses and usurpations, pursuing invariably the same Object evinces a design to reduce them under absolute Despotism, it is their right, it is their duty, to throw off such Government, and to provide new Guards for their future security.—Such has been the patient sufferance of these Colonies; and such is now the necessity which constrains them to alter their former Systems of Government. The history of the present King of Great Britain is a history of repeated injuries and usurpations, all having in direct object the establishment of an absolute Tyranny over these States. To prove this, let Facts be submitted to a candid world.

He has refused his Assent to Laws, the most wholesome and necessary for the public good.

He has forbidden his Governors to pass Laws of immediate and pressing importance, unless suspended in their operation till his Assent should be obtained; and when so suspended, he has utterly neglected to attend to them.

He has refused to pass other Laws for the accommodation of large districts of people, unless those people would relinquish the right of Representation in the Legislature, a right inestimable to them and formidable to tyrants only.

He has called together legislative bodies at places unusual, uncomfortable, and distant from the depository of their Public Records, for the sole purpose of fatiguing them into compliance with his measures.

He has dissolved Representative Houses repeatedly, for opposing with manly firmness his invasions on the rights of the people.

He has refused for a long time, after such dissolutions, to cause others to be elected; whereby the Legislative Powers, incapable of Annihilation, have returned to the People at large for their exercise; the State remaining in the mean time exposed to all the dangers of invasion from without, and convulsions within.

He has endeavoured to prevent the population of these States; for that purpose obstructing the Laws for Naturalization of Foreigners; refusing to pass others to encourage their migrations hither, and raising the conditions of new Appropriations of Lands.

He has obstructed the Administration of Justice, by refusing his Assent to Laws for establishing Judiciary Powers.

He has made Judges dependent on his Will alone, for the tenure of their offices, and the amount and payment of their salaries.

He has erected a multitude of New Offices, and sent hither swarms of Officers to harass our people, and eat out their substance.

He has kept among us, in times of peace, Standing Armies without the Consent of our legislatures.

He has affected to render the Military independent of and superior to the Civil Power.

He has combined with others to subject us to a jurisdiction foreign to our constitution, and unacknowledged by our laws; giving his Assent to their acts of pretended Legislation:

For quartering large bodies of armed troops among us:

For protecting them, by a mock Trial, from Punishment for any Murders which they should commit on the Inhabitants of these States:

For cutting off our Trade with all parts of the world:

For imposing taxes on us without our Consent:

For depriving us in many cases, of the benefits of Trial by Jury:

For transporting us beyond Seas to be tried for pretended offences:

For abolishing the free System of English Laws in a neighbouring Province, establishing therein an Arbitrary government, and enlarging its Boundaries so as to render it at once an example and fit instrument for introducing the same absolute rule into these Colonies:

For taking away our Charters, abolishing our most valuable Laws, and altering fundamentally the Forms of our Governments:

For suspending our own Legislatures, and declaring themselves invested with Power to legislate for us in all cases whatsoever.

He has abdicated Government here, by declaring us out of his Protection and waging War against us.

He has plundered our seas, ravaged our Coasts, burnt our towns, and destroyed the lives of our people.

He is at this time transporting large armies of foreign mercenaries to compleat the works of death, desolation and tyranny, already begun with circumstances of Cruelty & perfidy scarcely paralleled in the most barbarous ages, and totally unworthy the Head of a civilized nation.

He has constrained our fellow Citizens taken Captive on the high Seas to bear Arms against their Country, to become the executioners of their friends and Brethren, or to fall themselves by their Hands.

He has excited domestic insurrections amongst us, and has endeavoured to bring on the inhabitants of our frontiers, the merciless Indian Savages, whose known rule of warfare, is an undistinguished destruction of all ages, sexes and conditions.

In every stage of these Oppressions We have Petitioned for Redress in the most humble terms: Our repeated Petitions have been answered only by repeated injury. A Prince, whose character is thus marked by every act which may define a Tyrant, is unfit to be the ruler of a free people.

Nor have We been wanting in attentions to our British brethren. We have warned them from time to time of attempts by their legislature to extend an unwarrantable jurisdiction over us. We have reminded them of the circumstances of our emigration and settlement here. We have appealed to their native justice and magnanimity, and we have conjured them by the ties of our common kindred to disavow these usurpations which, would inevitably interrupt our connections and correspondence. They too have been deaf to the voice of justice and of consanguinity. We must, therefore, acquiesce in the necessity, which denounces our Separation, and hold them, as we hold the rest of mankind, Enemies in War, in Peace Friends.

We, therefore, the Representatives of the united States of America, in General Congress, Assembled, appealing to the Supreme Judge of the world for the rectitude of our intentions, do, in the Name, and by authority of the good People of these Colonies, solemnly publish and declare, That these United Colonies are, and of Right ought to be Free and Independent States; that they are Absolved from all Allegiance to the British Crown, and that all political connection between them and the State of Great Britain, is and ought to be totally dissolved; and that as Free and Independent States, they have full power to levy War, conclude Peace, contract Alliances, establish Commerce, and to do all other Acts and Things which Independent States may of right do. And for the support of this Declaration, with a firm reliance on the Protection of Divine Providence, we mutually pledge to each other our Lives, our Fortunes and our sacred Honor.

JOHN HANCOCK.

BUTTON GWINNETT.
LYMAN HALL.
GEO. WALTON.
WM. HOOPER.
JOSEPH HEWES.
JOHN PENN.
EDWARD RUTLEDGE.
THOS. HEYWARD, Junr.
THOMAS LYNCH, Junr.
ARTHUR MIDDLETON.
SAMUEL CHASE.
WM. PACA.
THOS. STONE.
CHARLES CARROLL
    OF CARROLLTON.
GEORGE WYTHE.
RICHARD HENRY LEE.
TH. JEFFERSON.
BENJ. HARRISON.

THOS. NELSON, Jr.
FRANCIS LIGHTFOOT LEE.
CARTER BRAXTON.
ROBT. MORRIS.
BENJAMIN RUSH.
BENJA. FRANKLIN.
JOHN MORTON.
GEO. CLYMER.
JAS. SMITH.
GEO. TAYLOR.
JAMES WILSON.
GEO. ROSS.
CÆSAR RODNEY.
GEO. READ.
THO. M'KEAN.
WM. FLOYD.
PHIL. LIVINGSTON.
FRANS. LEWIS.

LEWIS MORRIS.
RICHD. STOCKTON.
JNO. WITHERSPOON.
FRAS. HOPKINSON.
JOHN HART.
ABRA. CLARK.
JOSIAH BARTLETT.
WM. WHIPPLE.
SAML. ADAMS.
JOHN ADAMS.
ROBT. TREAT PAINE.
ELBRIDGE GERRY.
STEP. HOPKINS.
WILLIAM ELLERY.
ROGER SHERMAN.
SAM'EL. HUNTINGTON.
WM. WILLIAMS.
OLIVER WOLCOTT.
MATTHEW THORNTON.

★ ★ ★ ★ ★ ★ ★ ★ ★ ★ ★ ★ ★

THE GETTYSBURG ADDRESS

DELIVERED AT THE DEDICATION OF THE NATIONAL CEMETERY
NOVEMBER 19, 1863

Fourscore and seven years ago our fathers brought forth on this continent a new nation, conceived in liberty, and dedicated to the proposition that all men are created equal.

Now we are engaged in a great civil war, testing whether that nation, or any nation so conceived and so dedicated, can long endure. We are met on a great battle-field of that war. We have come to dedicate a portion of that field as a final resting-place for those who here gave their lives that the nation might live. It is altogether fitting and proper that we should do this.

But, in a larger sense, we cannot dedicate—we cannot consecrate—we cannot hallow—this ground. The brave men, living and dead, who struggled here, have consecrated it far above our poor power to add or detract. The world will little note nor long remember what we say here, but it can never forget what they did here. It is for us, the living, rather, to be dedicated here to the unfinished work which they who fought here have thus far so nobly advanced. It is rather for us to be here dedicated to the great task remaining before us—that from these honored dead we take increased devotion to that cause for which they gave the last full measure of devotion; that we here highly resolve that these dead shall not have died in vain; that this nation, under God, shall have a new birth of freedom; and that government of the people, by the people, for the people, shall not perish from the earth.

★ ★ ★ ★

✄✄ *Acknowledgements* ✄✄

THE AUTHORS AND THE PUBLISHER wish to express their thanks to the following individuals and organizations for their cooperation in locating and supplying illustrations and materials used in this volume, and also in many instances for the permission for such use:

Alexandria, Minnesota Chamber of Commerce

American Flag House & Betsy Ross Memorial, Philadelphia

Ancient & Honorable Artillery Co., of Boston, Massachusetts

Anheuser-Busch, Inc., St. Louis

Arkansas Resources Development Commission, Little Rock

Collection of Oscar T. Barck

Baseball Hall of Fame & Museum, Cooperstown, New York

Black Star, New York

Boatmen's National Bank of St. Louis

Camera Clix, New York

Collection of Mrs. E. Crane Chadbourne

Chicago Historical Society

City Art Museum, St. Louis

Colonial Williamsburg

Connecticut Historical Society, Hartford

The Corcoran Gallery of Art, Washington, D. C.

Dayton Art Institute

Delaware Historical Society, Wilmington

Essex Institute, Salem, Massachusetts

Ewing Galloway, New York

Fairchild Aerial Surveys, Inc.

Frederic Lewis, New York

Grand Central Art Gallery, New York

Greater North Dakota Association, Fargo

Collection of Mrs. Seton Henry

Idaho State Chamber of Commerce

Indiana Highway Commission

Iowa Development Commission

Kentucky Lincoln Memorial Shrine, Hodgenville

Library of Congress

Life Magazine, New York

Maryland Department of Information, Annapolis

Maryland Historical Society

Collection of Hall Park McCullough, Brooklyn Museum

Collection of Ward Melville, Suffolk Museum at Stonybrook, Long Island

Missouri Resources Division—Massie

Modern Enterprises, Los Angeles, California

Museum of Art, Rhode Island School of Design, Providence

Museum of the City of New York

National Geographic Society

Nebraska Division of Resources

Newport Historical Society

New York Historical Society

New York Public Library

North Carolina News Bureau, Raleigh

North Dakota Automobile Club, Fargo

Old Slater Mill Association, Pawtucket, Rhode Island

The Osborne Company, Clifton, New Jersey

Pennsylvania Academy of Fine Arts, Philadelphia

Pilgrim Society, Plymouth, Massachusetts

Rhode Island Historical Society

Collection of Clendenin J. Ryan

Dr. Ernest N. Ryder

Sacramento, California State House

Shostal Press

Mrs. Robert Simon

Sons of the Revolution, Hq. Fraunces Tavern, New York

Collection of Robert L. Stuart

Three Lions, New York

Toledo Museum of Art

Union League, Philadelphia

United Nations, New York

U.S. Army Corps of Engineers, Portland, Oregon

U.S. Naval Academy, Annapolis

Virginia Industrial & Publicity Commission

Wisconsin Historical Society

"THE CHILDREN'S DECLARATION," developed by Mr. R. E. Beauchamp, was used as a part of the Philadelphia *Bulletin's* annual Independence Day celebration, and was recited for the first time at the program in Independence Hall on July 4, 1952.